The Peasant And His Landlord

Knorring, Sofia Margareta
Zelow Friherrina von, 1797-1848

THE

PEASANT

AND

HIS LANDLORD.

BY THE BARONESS KNORRING.

TRANSLATED BY MARY HOWITT.

NEW YORK:
HARPER & BROTHERS, PUBLISHERS,
82 CLIFF STREET.
1848.

TRANSLATOR'S PREFACE.

It is with great pleasure that I introduce to the English public another new Northern Author, well worthy to take her place beside Fredrika Bremer and Hans Christian Andersen. In her own country the Baroness Knorring stands side by side with the Author of " The Home" and " The Neighbors ;" and I feel sure that the peculiar excellence and originality of her writings will be equally acknowledged in this, when once they are made known to our reading public.

Of the particular story which I have selected as the commencement of this series of translations, I must be allowed to say, that, treating as it does thus livingly and powerfully of the life of the people in a country which is in many respects kindred to our own, it affords a striking lesson, and a deep moral which must be obvious to all. It affords one more of the many demonstrations which we every day meet with, of the highest and purest natures being driven from their proper course, and oppressed, and perverted by the worst. It affords also a grand lesson on the subject of Temperance; and proves, that though one false step often leads to ruin, which is retrievable only by death, yet that uprightness and virtue, through suffering and through death, work out their own salvation.

M. H.

THE ELMS, CLAPTON,
Feb. 1st, 1848.

AUTHORESS'S DEDICATION.

THIS sketch of a peasant and his connections is inscribed respectfully, affectionately, and gratefully to three female friends, to whom I owe all those feelings, and have done so from my latest childhood and earliest youth; namely, to the nobly born lady, the Countess C. M. Sommerhjelm (born Lewenhaupt), who has always gone as a guiding star before me; who held out her hand to me many a time when my step faltered; who, on manifold occasions, cheered and gladdened me, in part by her beloved presence, in part by her animated letters; and lastly, who, by obtaining for me the acquaintance of an inestimable friend,* has acquired an eternal claim to my gratitude. To dedicate now to her, who reckoned among her friends the kings and queens of our former dynasty, this " peasant story," seems indeed to be unlikely enough; but if there be any truth and nature found in my narrative, then there is no one who can better see and distinguish these than precisely this—friend of kings.

These unpretending pages are also dedicated to the well-born lady of Colonel Silfverstolpe (born Montgomery), who, in the young mind of the girl of thirteen, kindled the first sparks of other thoughts than those of the child—than of the giddy, dancing, playful girl; to her, who through her

------

* Fredrika Bremer.

whole life has known how to support and strengthen that
admiration and devotion which were so justly her due; to
her, whose judgment on the productions of mind or of the
pen all ought to wish for who have the courage to hear
how the highest degree of justice—the finest and the most
cultivated taste, expresses itself.

And, lastly, these sketches are inscribed also to thee,
thou old, dear friend, who didst originally come from the
peasant's cottage, thou faithful and devoted Svenborg,*
who didst guide with thy hand the very first tottering footsteps of my childhood, and who, with a gentle and courteous hand, didst lead me out of my gay and sportive story-
world up to God and His angels; and who didst understand
how, many a time, to restrain and to keep within bounds the
restless, sportive, over-hill-and-dale-flying fancy of the child.
To thee, also, are these pictures inscribed—to thee, who,
perhaps, best of all canst form a correct judgment of them,
partly through that clear glance which Mother Nature
gave to thee, and partly because thou didst not alone come
from, but also in the beautiful evening of thy life didst again
enter under, the sod roof of the cottage, rich in years, experience, and knowledge of life, and, God be thanked! not
poor in any thing which can contribute to the happiness of
life and the comfort of death.

To you—all three—highly beloved and venerated friends,
is inscribed this sketch, with all submission, by

THE AUTHORESS.

* Mrs. Svenborg Dalin (born Böcker), an old and excellent servant, and
children's friend, who for about fifty years lived in the family of the author's
father and mother.   (Author's note.)

PREFACE.

Bulwer expresses somewhere his dissatisfaction with any book which comes before the public without preface or address; and he is perhaps right. A book without these forerunners is like a person who is introduced into a great company with the simple and single title of Mr. This or That.

It is true that there are *some persons* gifted with so fine a power of discrimination, that they can immediately see at the first glance whether a man belong to the educated, the much-educated, the accomplished, the pseudo-accomplished, the mis-educated, the over-educated, or the entirely uneducated. And there are also *those* who never require any preface, but who can determine by the first page of a book what the whole of it is; but as these will always constitute the minority, and many others remain who require both titles to persons and prefaces to books, that they may know, as it were, on what ground they stand, we will furnish our little book with such a little preface, as shall tell about *whom* and *why* it is come forth, and so on.

The authoress, born and brought up in the country, and also compelled by her domestic circumstances, as well in

the home of her ancestors as in her own, to be at all times
surrounded by a great number of servants, and have numerous dependants, and often to come into contact with
the country people—has had from her very youth, oppor-
tunities of becoming acquainted with this class.   From the
earliest years of her life she has mixed herself up with
their mode of thinking, talking, and acting; has become
acquainted with their manners and customs, their friends
and enemies, their faults and their virtues, their many beautiful and many unpleasing aspects; and lastly, with their
sufferings, their vices, and, to speak shortly, the causes of
these.

The authoress has, in later years, by the aid of the acquaintance she particularly possessed of the country people,
at least in her own province, studied this natural class of
human beings, and seen how many beautiful and glorious
revelations are made to those who have eyes to see them;
how much noble seed shoots up in silence, and bears at
length divine fruit, while much also of the same kind per-
ishes from want of looking after and nurture, or because it
is cast into an altogether unprofitable soil.   She has seen
Roman virtues, sacrifices, and renunciations, so much the
greater because it was never expected that they should be
observed, admired, or even known.   She has seen great
genius and unmistakable capabilities, which lay so buried
by ignorance, poverty, and the caring for daily wants, and
thereby so hedged in on all sides, that they never were
able to press, with their light wings, through those heavy,
hard coverings.   She has seen among this class unselfishness, love, friendship, childlike submission, parental devotion, to that sublime degree which may, perhaps, be sought
for in vain any where excepting in romances or plays, and

scarcely even there; for if a work of genius is to become popular, and to obtain sympathy, it must do homage to the virtues of the age, and wealth and selfishness are indeed the two most highly exalted on the Olympus of our times. She (the authoress) has met with, also, among these rude, uneducated men, much natural smartness, much real, pure humor, heard many caustic jests, and light, merry pleasantries, although adapted to their roughly-hewn and unpolished ideas, which, nevertheless, are ideas, large and profound enough sometimes. She has seen in those low, crowded cottages, so much pleasantness, happiness, and comfort; so much enjoyment, so much good will and good temper in poverty, as entirely to compensate for wealth. She has, in a word, seen so much good and so little evil among these children of Nature, that she has many a time thanked God for having placed her among them, and that her nearest connections, on which she, like all other women, always depended, loved and highly respected them; and that they, by reason of their justice, their benevolence, and popularity, caused themselves to be beloved in return by these amiable children of Nature, whose love and devotion, whose hatred and whose aversions, are always, at least, of the true kind, and are not the offspring of any representation or self-interest.

It is true that she has seen among the lower classes of the country people crimes and coarse vices, but these former were nearly always unpremeditated, and the latter for the most part occasioned by circumstances which might easily have been altered, as being those which come from *without*, and not from *within*. Imperfect education, want of instruction in Christianity and morality, frequent intercourse with vagabonds and rude criminals, and the wretched example set by the higher classes: these are, in her opinion, most frequently the origin of those vices and crimes, if people would only give themselves the trouble to search into them.   Brandy, also, has often been the under-demon which has assisted in perfecting that which the other causes had begun, giving, as it were, wind to the sails of that evil which leads directly to perdition and misery; for brandy is, like so many other things, not an evil in itself, but a means in the hand of evil.

With the knowledge we thus have acquired respecting the country people and their way of life, it has often annoyed us to see representations of them in which merely want and poverty are placed by the side of wealth and superfluity; rudeness and ignorance by accomplishments and knowledge; just as if this class had nothing else which appealed to the heart but this misery and subjection, which always stand forth in far brighter colors than they have in reality, when they are set in contrast with our luxury and refinement; as if pity and kindness were the only good feelings which these beings should awaken within us! If it were so, how low is the condition of this so-called lowest class, and how small and miserable are, then, the means of awakening our interest! because who may not perish of hunger and nakedness? For such representations there requires, of a truth, no merits, no natural endowments; and *art* ought to discard, by this rule, the use of any means of giving life to its picture, except those of contrast, and thus elevating the lower classes at the expense of the higher. It is an unworthy fashion in art to work in light and shade, merely for the sake of effect.

This is, however, done very often; for most frequently when we (the so-called educated) would talk about or describe the lower people, we begin with their poverty, their rude manners, their uncultivated speech, their astonishment at every thing which our refinement has made articles of every-day use to us; their vices, which so often lie open to the day: and we remember all these immediately, because they are the first things which strike our eyes, as well as those in which they differ most from ourselves. But if we observe them more nearly and more carefully, we shall find that these traits are merely accidental, and certainly do not constitute that which properly distinguishes and characterizes them; but that they think, feel, act, rejoice, suffer, exactly as we do, although under equally different forms; and if they were to give an account of their thoughts and feelings, it would be in words as different as every thing else appears to be different between us and them.

We have now made a little attempt to paint them as we have seen them entirely independent of us; as we believe them to be among one another, and without being placed in comparison with any other than themselves. We have endeavored to place ourselves in these people's position, and to express their genuine feelings, which are fine without being refined, and pure without having been purified; we have endeavored to place ourselves in a human mind which thinks and acts entirely upon its own account, without all the help, and also without all the bewilderment, which education, reading, worldly wisdom, and experience give; we have endeavored to feel with their feelings, speak with their tongue, see with their eyes, to conceive and afterward to represent, what they had conceived, just as they themselves would do.

We have *attempted* all this, but whether we have suc-

ceeded or not, we do not know, and, worst of all, our gentlemen critics are least likely to know, because they are
very much less in connection with the country people than
ourselves are, and might, we fear, be very little capable of
judging whether we had failed, or whether we had succeeded in representing these unpolished diamonds, or granite blocks, as they really are, in their primitive circumstances. On the contrary, we appeal to you who are in
moderate circumstances, but in habits of life, which are
continually bringing you into connection with the people,
who live whole years through in a remote country place,
where *the town*, the nearest little town, has no influence
on the peasantry, but is for them merely a place where
they can buy " herrings and salt, spices, and purchasable
wares," as well as where they can sell at the fair " the
cow which is too old, or the bullock which can not be
fed ;" and which is not a Sodom under the shape of an
Eldorado, toward which all are yearning, a flaming *ignis
fatuus*, which the poor country people can not see without
being attracted to, and where like the moths with the candle, they burn first their wings and then themselves ; which
often is the case in great cities and their environs; we turn
to you, ye *working* clergymen, of whom we have endeavored to give a faint outline—ye divines in country places,
who *actually* are shepherds of your flocks, who love them,
watch them, tend them yourselves, and not by hirelings,
and who do not respect them merely for their fleeces.
These are the persons to whom we turn ; and we ask you
whether this Gunnar, in whom we have attempted to describe all that knight-like quality (we must be pardoned
for the use of a word which is dear to us of old, and which
alone expresses what we mean), all that independent and

manly determination, all that passionate, yielding, and pliable character, which nature has often placed in the same human breast, and which may be developed either into great virtues or great faults; and at the same time without education, obtained either in the bustling life of the world, or beneath the roof of a cottage : to you we turn, and ask whether *he* is merely a fancy picture, or whether you have not likewise seen, as we have done, a fac-simile of him, not, indeed, frequently and every where, but yet far less unfrequently than the gentry of towns, who make steamboat-excursions to become acquainted with the country and country people, might imagine. We say precisely the same about Elin and Mother Ingrid. And as to what concerns the rest, we see every day and every hour their prototypes.

That some of them are wicked, coarse, and rude, and must be thus represented, both with regard to their actions and their speech, as well as to form a contrast with those who through nature and a religious education are good, profound in thought, and of an elevated and expansive turn of mind, remains as a matter of course, and can, of a truth, be only blamed by those who are in the habit of straining at a gnat and swallowing a camel, but not by any friend of art. And let us here take the liberty of offering an apology for some of Olle's expressions, as well as others of the like kind, at which over-nice and prudish dames may consider it proper to purse up their mouths. They may also cast down their eyes, blush, and assume all manner of bashfulness, at the very beginning of our peasant-story, (N.B. in case any of them venture to take up the book with the very tips of their fingers); but if their delicate nerves should be too much shattered by this beginning, then they

may just throw aside our book, and take one of Eugene
Sue's, Balzac's, Frederic Soulie's, or any of our usual
novels and periodicals, in which fine, unrestrained life in the
darkest passages of the great cities is painted *con amore,*
and the vices, at all events, wear the beautiful and convenient masks which we deny to them.   They can take
these, in order somewhat to calm themselves, after reading in print of a little casualty—very vexatious, as God
knows, but which, nevertheless, is of daily occurrence even
in their own houses (if they have any), or in those of their
neighbors, if they have only their eyes and their ears
open.

In conclusion, a word may be said upon the language.
Many people have imagined that they could represent the
peasantry and the common people merely by imitating
their peasant-speech, which varies in every province, and
which is always more or less murdered Swedish; but in
so doing there is neither art in the author nor interest for
the reader, because words are never any thing else but
words, and the *dissimilar ideas* constitute, indeed, properly
the difference between these uneducated people and ourselves.   We have therefore endeavored to give these ideas
as we required them, and that as little as possible in their
own self-made language, which, however has not any thing
particularly characteristic in it but its perpetual contrac-
tions, which we also have occasionally profited by, that, at
all times, it may be borne in mind what sort of people are
talking.   We will also make a remark for the benefit of
our city readers, namely, that the lower classes, as well as
the higher, have a holiday language as well as one for
every-day use; and also that the holiday language among
the peasantry is almost always that employed in the trans-

lation of the Bible and the accompanying hymn-book, which constitute their entire reading, and that this bears the stamp of every body's highest degree of cultivation.

With this we here close our preface, in the hope that it may be read through, and deliberated upon, and also that it may incline every reader to a mild and charitable judgment upon that which we have attempted.

THE PEASANT AND HIS LANDLORD.

CHAPTER I.

" Qu'un moment de vivacité
Peut causer de calamité !"—Vieux Chanson.

ALL the men-servants belonging to the rich Mr. P., proprietor of the large and beautiful estate of Grantorp, in West-
gothland, had not spent the whole of the short December day
in the great business of threshing and corn-measuring. Some
of them had stayed in the house, and chopped and carried in
the Christmas firewood; and Gunnar, the youngest of them,
had helped the maid-servants to mangle the linen of the great
Christmas wash. But now the day was ended, the mangling
done; and after Gunnar, who was silent and full of thought,
had helped the laughing and gossiping girls to carry in the
baskets of clothes, he went, in the same state of mind, down
into the men-servants' room, which was empty, cold, and desolate, because none of the other laborers had returned from
their day's work.

Gunnar seated himself upon a chest, gazed into the moonlight, and heaved a deep sigh, which, however, did not come
freely forth, but the heaviest part of which remained in the
heavily-laden youthful breast. But now he heard the cheerful
voice of his fellow-servant Bengt. Bengt was about the age of
Gunnar, and came in singing a merry song, with a great bundle
of fagots and branches in his arms. On his entrance into the
room, which took place with a great deal of activity, bustle, and
noise, he threw his bundle of wood carelessly down before the
hearth, slapped his body several times with his arms, as is the
custom with country people when they are cold, and then,
singing very loudly all the time the fragment of a song, he

began to arrange the sticks in the fireplace for kindling; nor
was it till he had gone to the shelf above the window to search
for the tinder-box, that he saw, in the dim light, Gunnar, who
was sitting silently and immovably on the chest.

"Who have we here?" exclaimed Bengt instantly; but when
he went forward and found that it was Gunnar, he said to him,
laughingly, "What the deuce! Is it you, you sluggard, who
are sitting at your ease and resting yourself, instead of cutting
wood and making a fire?* What are you musing about?
But I know what it is: you have been working all day with the
young girls, and so now you are as fine-fingered as they are.
But look now, we have had something to do—that have we. The
squire has been out with us *himself;* he was with us at the
threshing all the blessed day long, and, though we worked like
slaves, he kept saying, 'Now, lads, get on, else we shall not
have done before Christmas!' To be sure we had a good
quantity of liquor in the afternoon; but what better were we
for that?—one knew nothing about it an hour afterward. But
what is the use of talking about drink to you? I fancy you
have had plenty, you!—and have had breakfast, and luncheon,
and coffee, and apples, and God knows what more, among the
girls! And what deuced trumpery sort of work is this mangling to ours! I know you well, you rascals; mangle and go
on as long as the least glimpse remains of the old ma'msell,
but in the mean time you may romp with the girls. Ay, ay,
thou tall fellow," continued Bengt, laughing, while he blew up
the fire, and swore at the squire and the damp fuel which they
were obliged to use, and bragged a little at having stolen some
dry wood among it; "ay, ay, don't you think but that I saw
you set yourself forward this morning, when Overseer Anders
said that *one* of us must go and mangle with the girls; don't
you think but that I heard you say, 'Yes, I can go and do
that.'"

"Nay, that is a cursed lie!" said Gunnar, who now first
opened his mouth, and who moved for the first time. "I said
not one word, but stood stock still, till he said, 'Where is
Gunnar? Thou shalt go and mangle to-day.'"

---

* For the information of the reader, it may be mentioned that it was an
agreement among the farm-servants of Grantorp, that he who first returned
home from work on winter evenings should, when he saw that it was
dark in the servants' room, take in with him a bundle of fagots and make
a fire.

"What!" interrupted Bengt; "can you deny that Overseer Anders said, 'It is a good thing that the girls will have their good-tempered Gunnar with them, or else they would ride over me—even would tear out my eyes, or snap off my nose!' Can you deny that he said that?"

"Nay, that I neither can nor will deny," replied Gunnar; "but that *I* never said a word, I will stand to the death for!"

"Ay, on my word, that may very well be," returned Bengt; "but, by all the cats, all went, and you nevertheless stayed; and this I can answer for, not a word did you say against it; that I remember, whether you remember it or not."

"Ha! it is all one to me, whatever it was," replied Gunnar; and there was something so melancholy and dejected in his tone, that Bengt started up from the fire, where otherwise he was warming himself with great satisfaction, and approached Gunnar, throwing at the same time upon him the light of a blazing brand, which he took from the hearth.

"What is amiss with you, Gunnar?" asked he, in a sympathizing voice; "are you out of spirits, or are you ill?—but as to tired, that I never saw you!"

"I am out of spirits," said Gunnar, and pushed his fingers through his dark-brown hair.

"Oh, there is nothing worth being out of spirits about," replied Bengt, encouragingly; but just then the door opened, and all the other and older laboring-men thronged in with Overseer Anders at their head. They came in covered with snow, cold, and half frozen; and before long the conversation was carried on in a loud voice, partly about the day's work, partly about the squire, who had been through the day "a regular Turk;" partly about "the cold," partly about "Christmas," which was just at hand, and the games which they had last Christmas, and those they expected to have this, and how especially stupidly it fell out this year that there should be no Christmas moonlight, which ended on the thirteenth.

During this time Bengt continued to question Gunnar in a low whisper, but Gunnar made no reply.

"Come, Gunnar," said Bengt at length, seeing him unwilling to talk in the room; "shall we two go out and get something more to lay on the fire?" and mechanically Gunnar accompanied him.

When they were come out beneath the fine and lofty expanse

of God's blue heaven, from which the moon and stars in thousands looked down upon them, the long pent-up tears streamed from the eyes of the youthful Gunnar, and he said, while they went softly toward the great gloomy avenues, the trees of which were hung with hoar-frost:

"Yes, there is, do you know, Bengt, an end of all happiness for me! I would just as willingly go and drown myself now as live. There is for me no more merriment and laughter with you, Bengt, as I have had hitherto, ever since we were little lads together."

"Yes, that say I," replied Bengt, who was more occupied by the last part of Gunnar's sentence than by the first—"this I say of a truth, that never, no never would I have taken earnest-money from the squire, if it had not been for living in the same place with you; and if you leave, then I will leave also : that is as clear as daylight, and as true as God the Father. That is sure and certain—but what have you got now to fret yourself about? Have you had a quarrel with the old ma'msell? Fie! for shame! that is not a thing to vex one's self about! The old woman does get angry sometimes, but for all that she is a very good sort of body. But as to any quarrels with women-folk, they are not things to put one out of the way. That is not it, though; have you been falling out with any of the lasses? Tist! now I know what it is! now it comes into my head! Lena, who is always running after you, both by night and day, has been cross with you, and has quarreled with you; and though you swore and mocked when she wanted to kiss you, yet now you are crying because she is angry."

"And then I should be crying for nothing at all!" said Gunnar, wiping away his tears. "No, believe me, it is a deal worse than that! God grant that she were angry with me, then it would be a deal better."

"Nay, what is it, then?" asked Bengt, whose curiosity increased every minute.

After several other questions from Bengt, to which he gave evasive answers, Gunnar said—

"Ah, yes! I may as well tell you how it is. We have now been good friends ever since we were little lads, and therefore I shall now tell you the honest truth, and show you how badly it falls out for me. Yes, look you. You yourself know that the cursed Lena (God forgive my sin for saying so!) run after me the whole year, as if she were mad, and I scarcely ever—

nay, never would have any'thing to say to her. Last autumn, however, in statutes week,* when we all went out a pleasuring, she was worse than ever, for she never once left me; and Heaven knows how it was! but on Sunday evening, when we went to Aspas, there was a desperate deal of drinking, and both you and I, who otherwise never drink, and because of it have both of us such good characters, got drunk as pipers. I do not know how I could ever have made such a fool of myself; but certain it is, that, since this time, I have got to dislike that cursed Lena (God forgive me for saying so!) more than ever. And now, look you, she comes weeping and wailing, and saying that I have made a miserable woman of her, and that it is all through me, and Heaven knows what; that she shall lose her good name, and that it is all my fault; and that I ought to marry her, and that the squire and Ma'msell Sara said that they would compel me to it; and many other such stupid things she said."

"Stuff and nonsense!" said Bengt, with disgust, "stuff and nonsense! that's not a thing to vex yourself about. There is not one among us but knows well enough how that limb of Satan has run after you, and any body with any sense can understand why. She is certainly full four or five-and-thirty years old, the vulgar wretch! and you are hardly three-and-twenty. Don't think about it. No, that will never come to pass: no, you must point-blank deny it, and let it take its own course."

"Yes, yes, but it's the truth for all that," said Gunnar, slowly and gloomily; "and it's not right to deny the truth, either before God or man."

"Why, yes, it may be the truth," said Bengt, who was not quite so conscientious as Gunnar, "but, you see, she can not bring forward any witnesses, and it will be altogether for the best that you deny it through thick and thin. Look you, if the child lives, then you can do something for it. Nothing in all this world should ever make me have Lena, if I were you. Good gracious! it would be standing like a dog to be fastened

---

* *Minnerveckan* (equivalent to our statutes) is the name given to the week following the 24th of October, when the servants who are changing their places are either at liberty or at leisure, and even those who still remain in their situations have more time allowed for themselves than common, when games, dances, and amusements are enjoyed by those in the country. (Author's note.)

up in a kennel! No, let come what would, *I* never would have Lena."

Thus talked the two young laborers till it was late in the evening; and when, at length, the others went into the kitchen for their supper, Gunnar said he did not want any, and remained behind in the servants' room.

"Yes, yes, you rascal!" said some of the other servants, "we understand it well enough; you have been having such splendid fare to-day with Lena and the rest of the girls, that you will not put up with 'stir-about.'"

Gunnar made no reply to this, nor did Bengt either, who yet at the same time went and ate his porridge, and took occasion to call Lena, who was standing by, a nightmare, an old corn-screen, and a good-for-nothing piece of goods; and on her part she found occasion to call Bengt a dog's whelp and a gallows-bird; and in conclusion wrought herself up to such a pitch of anger as to give him a heavy box on the ear, after which she sprung into the parlor, where she knew she was safe in her capacity of housemaid.

The remaining days of the week were employed in hard labor; and Gunnar went about with a dejected air and downcast eyes the whole time. Bengt continually repeated his advice, that he should deny, and unceasingly deny, which was the very best means of getting out of this mess. When Sunday came, however, and the command was given to Gunnar that he must go up to the squire in his own room, as he "wished to speak with him," a cold shudder went through him, and it seemed as if a stab was sent to his heart.

With heavy and slow steps Gunnar betook himself to his master, for whom he had but little esteem; and as soon as the crafty squire saw how his color changed from white to red, and how in his agitation he thumbed his Sunday hat, he was perfectly aware that poor Gunnar anticipated what the questions were which would be put to him. And during all the reproaches which his master heaped upon him with gravity rather than in a spirit of reprimand, he never once looked up, nor replied by a single word; but when the squire wished him to confess, and sought also to obtain from him a promise to marry Lena, in which case he offered him a very good little farm, the tenant of which was about to leave the coming spring, Gunnar still remained silent, and could by no means be prevailed upon to confess. All the more steadfastly did he stand by his denial, when the squire changed his mode of attack, and began in the first place to grumble and command, and then afterward to threaten and insult.

After nearly an hour's painful examination, Gunnar went his way, and the squire began to have some doubts whether he should be able " to bring Gunnar to ;" and the first words which Bengt said to his friend on meeting him were these :

"Well, I know that you have denied through thick and thin ?"

"Oh, yes !" repied Gunnar, with a mournful and spiritless voice ; for however courageously he had stood up for himself before the squire, whom he disliked, his heart failed him when he again found himself alone with God and his own conscience.

He did not trouble himself about dinner on Sunday ; and in order that he might escape Lena and all the others, he went out and laid himself down in the stable, where he was so happy as to fall asleep, spite of all his by no means trifling anxieties and pangs of conscience. From this sleep he was suddenly awoke in the afternoon by the disagreeable voice of Lena, who, however, merely announced to him that he must immediately go up to Ma'msell Sara, because "she wished to speak with him."

"Oh, Lord !" sighed he, and scratched himself behind the ear; "what sorrow and misfortune can come merely from that devilish brandy, with which, from this day forth, I will have nothing to do !"

It was with steps still slower and heavier than on the former occasion that Gunnar went up to the well-beloved and worthy old ma'msell, the squire's elder sister, who now, since the death of her sister-in-law, took care of her brother's house, household, and children, and that in such an excellent manner as only these old, devoted, unmarried sisters can do.

"Oh, my God ! what a strait am I got into !" thought poor Gunnar, while he went up the stairs, and remained standing a long time at the door before he could summon resolution to open it. At length he compelled himself to put his hand on the latch, and then the moment afterward he stood before the dreaded mistress ; for fear of a person proceeds just as often from love and esteem as from dread.

The old ma'msell, who otherwise was accustomed to look so kindly upon the young, brisk, willing, and helpful Gunnar, whose beautiful, pure, and open countenance softened every glance, especially a woman's, now looked grave and solemn, like one of Fredrika Bremer's very worst minster churches. Gunnar now ventured still less to lift up his eyes than before her red-headed, crafty brother; and when the old ma'msell, in a few but solemn and impressive words represented to him, not only how he had broken the word of God, but human law, without attempting any longer a hardened denial, Gunnar burst into tears. And when, shortly afterward, the pastor walked into the room by a side-door—the pastor who was beloved and esteemed by all his flock, and from whom Gunnar, but a few years before, had learned his well-understood Christian duties, as well as had received from him the Lord's Supper for the first time—when he, with a soft and solemn step, entered the room, and added his voice to that of the beloved mistress, he no longer was able to withstand the imperative voice of conscience, but, forgetful of all Bengt's well-intentioned counsel, and his own half-indignant and half-pardonable excuses, immediately acknowledged his sin.

But now came another chapter. He was *willing* to acknowledge the child, and he would marry Lena, if it lay in his power, but . . . . under no circumstances whatever would he marry her.

The clergyman and the old ma'msell represented to him, in vain, that when a person does wrong he must make reparation in the way which God commands, and not in that which suits his own pleasure, because in that way he can neither atone to God nor to the injured party. The worthy pastor spoke earnestly and persuasively, and the youth seemed to feel again that time returned when he had stood as a catechumen before the beloved teacher, when he had knelt at the communion-table, and had received from the hand of him who now spoke to him of his broken, holy vows, the grace of God in the form of bread and wine. Memory and affection overcame him; he was again a child, and he spoke that unhappy word of consent which bound gyves upon his limbs and laid a stone upon his heart, and which at a future time pressed tears of repentance from the eyes of the minister as well as from those of the old ma'msell.

"Yes, now it is done!" said he, in a voice of stupid desperation, when, on going down to the men-servant's room, he encountered Bengt.

The two young men went out together into the dim moon-light, and walked down the hoar-frost covered avenue. But how miserable was every thing now! They both walked on in silence. The one had no heart to tell any thing; the other had nothing more to advise.

"Yes! here we went on Sunday evening," said Gunnar, at length, "and I fancied myself unhappy *then;* but, look you, it was a *nothing* in comparison with what I *now* feel. I remember that I then looked up to heaven, and thought upon God the Father, wondering whether it could be His will that I should have her; and then I thought with myself that, if I could see the least black cloud on all the vault of heaven, then I should believe that it was His will. But I did not find a single one! But now see! Now there goes a great, black cloud right before the moon; and, look now! now I know that I should have been damned if I had not taken her; so said the minister, of a certainty."

"Asch!" said Bengt, who had within himself a great inclination for controverting this opinion, but who still had an equally great diffidence in directly declaring that to be "a lie" which the minister had said, because he himself had been one of his catechumens, and he had accustomed himself to regard the words of the teacher as coming from God the Father himself. The two young men walked on in silence; they neither of them had any of the sophisms of education and society with which to console themselves. What was said was said; what was done was done; and Gunnar believed himself to have lost, with his freedom, not a *part* of his happiness, but *all*. Bengt, otherwise so loquacious, did not even make any inquiries about the circumstances of Gunnar's conversation with the pastor and the gentlefolks, and seemed to wish to know no more than that the banns were to be published on Christmas-eve, which was on Sunday, and that Gunnar, at spring, should become the tenant of Vika, a large, and both good and beautiful farm, which lay upon a great inland lake.

"Well, at all events, you will have a tremendously grand wedding, if you must marry the nightmare," said Bengt, after a long silence, but in his customary gay and cheerful voice; for the thoughts of the wedding had, for the moment, put out of his head the thoughts of his friend's sorrow.

"Oh, yes," replied Gunnar, with indifference, and yet with a sigh; "but it's time enough to think of that."

B

"When will it be ?" inquired Bengt.

"Oh, on Twelfth-day, or thereabout !" answered Gunnar, with embarrassment.

"Ho, ho !" said Bengt, consolingly; "perhaps, in the long run, it will not turn out so badly, however ill the beginning may seem; and, after all, Lena is a clever, high-spirited woman, who will make a good housekeeper, and sufficiently——"

"Ah, spare me the hearing of it !" interrupted Gunnar. "You do not know, and nobody ever can know, how little I can bear her."

When Bengt found that none of his grounds of comfort were available, he determined to go home and to bed. Gunnar mechanically did the same, but he did not find his accustomed sound, youthful sleep upon his bed of straw that night.

CHAPTER II.

In the mean time, the gentlefolks upstairs sat around the tea-table that same Sunday evening, and accidentally they came to speak of the afternoon's scene.

"I do not know how it was," said the minister, "but it has seldom happened that the fulfillment of my duty has been so difficult to me as it has been to-day. There was a something in that poor youth's appearance which indicated an inward despair, which he in vain endeavored to control, but which, of a truth, made me wish that I might not one day repent the authority which I exercised over him and his future fate."

The squire kept stirring his tea, and never looked up.

"I say almost the same as the pastor," remarked Ma'msell Sara. "It went shockingly against me to act according to your desire, my dear brother, who are otherwise generally so tolerant in such cases, to persuade the poor lad to this marriage, which, after all, is not a suitable one."

"My desire ! Bless me ! How can you say so ?" stammered the squire. "I never heard but that you wished to have as much to do in the management of the house as I, or a little more; and I see nothing so unsuitable in this marriage between peasants, especially when one helps to set them on their legs after——after they both have served so many years here. He was so stubborn and so inflexible, the clown! toward me," continued the squire, as the others remained silent, "that——that if I had done right, then——"

But the sentence was not concluded.

"Oh, yes," replied the pastor, slowly; "I can not exactly say that it is the difference in the age—*that* does not furnish any sufficient reason why this marriage should be unsuitable, because one sees so often, among the peasantry, that the wife is older than the husband, and the married couple are quite happy for all that. I know not how it is, but this Gunnar, ever since he was a little lad, and especially since he read his lessons to me, has taken a great hold on my heart, and it has always been a pleasure to me to look into his pure, open, cheerful countenance, which reflected a soul and a heart equally open, pure, and good. Had the youth studied, he would have become a great light; for a brighter understanding and a clearer head I seldom have met with among those who are so entirely uneducated; and I always thought, when I saw him, that, were he not so happy in his ignorance, one might of a truth grieve that the sciences had not found their way into such a head as his. I saw him, however, now looking so wholly miserable, and a passing thought struck me, that if he had chosen such a path, he would at least have escaped *this* cup of sorrow; for I can not get the thought out of my heart how he can, merely out of a sense of duty, bring himself to unite his fate with that of Lena, whom I—God forgive me for it!—never rightly could endure since she, several years ago, removed into this church communion, although I must confess that I know nothing bad of her."

"Ah, then, the pastor thinks entirely as I do," observed Ma'msell Sara. "She is a clever person for her work—that I willingly concede; but she has for me something so repugnant in her appearance that I never can accustom myself to that sharp countenance, but always, as it were, feel as if I would avoid it."

"Ah, such fancies!" said the squire, rising up and walking impatiently up and down the room; "but it is so like you old maids. You never can endure handsome girls, even if they were the very best of their kind."

"Ah, my most worthy pastor," said Ma'msell Sara, smiling, "how can it ever come to pass that we poor old maids *always* should be accused of harboring within us the foul fiend Jealousy toward other young and more attractive women ? Certainly it must be, because we ourselves excite so little jealousy, but much more a feeling of compassion, blended with a good deal of contempt."

"Yes, so it is," replied the pastor. "Human beings judge of these as blindly, crookedly, and unreasonably as they judge of all others, which principally arises from no one knowing any one besides himself, and that, for the most, badly enough, because if we knew ourselves perfectly we should certainly be much more gentle in our judgment of others."

"Ah, yes; all that may be just as it will, and as it may," said the squire, who never had any thoughts beyond those of his own affairs, and who now had his own particular reasons, which were only known to himself, for wishing to introduce some new subject of conversation ; "all that may be as it will ; but certain it is that old maids and handsome girls never do pull well together, and, therefore, pastor, you and I will have a game at backgammon."

Ma'msell Sara, who now saw perfectly well that she should not have a chance of any more intellectual conversation with the minister, replied laughingly, while she set out the chess-board, "Yes, yes, I should think I deserved many a hard imputation if I envied Lena her jet-black hair, her penciled eyebrows, her keen eyes, and fine complexion. No, believe me, if I should envy her any thing, it would much rather be the young Gunnar, because he has always been a great favorite of mine !"

"Yes, yes, that I can very well believe !" said the squire, jestingly, and struck a heavy blow on the backgammon-board, exclaiming, "Tre deuce !" and now nothing was spoken of between the two gentlemen but "aces and doublets," and "cinq deuce." Ma'msell Sara, therefore, went out into another room, in which the squire's children, two half-grown boys, and their tutor, sat and amused themselves. She took to them a basket of apples, and joked merrily with them, gayly and affectionately, as she always did.

Not a word was said in the family about what was going to happen. The squire was right glad to avoid both thinking and talking about Lena and Gunnar; Ma'msell Sara was somewhat unwilling to talk of it before the banns were published; the tutor and the little boys knew nothing about it; Lena had her own notions, and wished on the Sunday to enjoy the people's astonishment; Gunnar kept silent and worked, saying all the time not a single word which he could avoid; and Bengt found, quite contrary to his custom, that it was better to be silent concerning some things about which he could have given information.

CHAPTER III.

On the evening before St. Thomas's day, Gunnar requested to have a part of the wages which were due to him, together with permission to go home to his old mother, and afterward to the town, to buy "the ring and the gifts."* To this he was rigorously urged by Lena, as well as by his own wishes; "for," thought he to himself, "as I have taken the Evil One into the boat, I will e'en bring him creditably to land, and then let it go as it may."

In the evening, when Gunnar had finished his work, he went with a heavy and deliberate step to the wood where his mother dwelled, in a little cottage, in which he himself had spent the greater part of his life. In his childhood, his father, who had been a well-to-do farmer, had left him and an elder brother, together with a widow, in great poverty, owing to his passion for drinking. From this cause it was that Gunnar had a great abhorrence of brandy, and often would pass through his mind the words which his mother had said to him when, as a boy, he left her to live with the rich squire of Grantorp.

"Yes, yes," she said to him, "had not thy father (God give his soul peace and mercy!) thought so much about the wicked brandy, then thou mightst have been spared going out to service, and mightst have stayed at home with thy mother, and taken care both of her and the place. Have a care, therefore, thyself of that wicked stuff!" And, now, how well had Gunnar followed that well-meant advice!

The way was long, and it was late in the night when Gunnar knocked at his mother's door.

* Presents which the bridegroom gives to the bride after the banns are published. (Author's note.)

"Merciful Heaven!" said the old woman, who did not at all expect her son on the evening of a week-day. "Who is it that comes with such great strides, and knocks at my door so late at night?"

"Oh, it is no thief," replied Gunnar; "it is nobody but I. Get up now for me, dearest mother."

"Bless me! it is thou, Gunnar!" exclaimed the mother, full of gladness. "Dost thou know that I was so frightened that every drop of blood stood still in my old veins? But what can it be that has brought thee here to-day? I did not look for thee before Christmas-day, as usual."

"Ah, yes, I shall come then, too," replied Gunnar, who well knew why the good old woman was a little anxious that he should come on Christmas-day as usual. And with that he threw himself, spite of the day's work, and the long walk through wood and morass, and, more than all, of his heavy thoughts, upon an old wooden sofa, upon which, in his boyish years, he had been accustomed to lie. There he remained silent for some moments with closed lips and eyes, considering, in a chaotic state of mind, how he should begin his confession to his mother. At length his mother went up to him with a burning brand in her hand, and threw the light of it upon his face.

"What in all the world is amiss with thee, lad?" said she; "thou lookest to me quite ill. Thou art as pale as a sheet. Thou hast never been getting some of that cursed drink, that wicked stuff?"

"Ah, no; there are other devilish things on the earth; other owls in the bog," said Gunnar, and raised himself up slowly.

"Merciful Heaven!" exclaimed the old woman, anxiously. "What can it be? Surely thou art not turned off by the squire? Hast thou got a thrashing? Surely thou hast not—" but the old woman could not say any more, for Gunnar raised himself up to his full height, which was six feet two inches, and quickly answered,

"I turned off by the squire! I got a thrashing from *him!* No; I would not advise him to attempt it. Oh, no! dearest mother, it is indeed *another thing*," continued he, in a low and melancholy voice; "it is all bad for me. Do you know what? Your poor Gunnar is obliged to go and be married!"

"Obliged!" said the old woman, at first a little astonished, but added, after a moment's reflection—"Ay, indeed! I understand; yes, it is not exactly the thing one likes; but even that is a thing which may be got over."

The old woman did not find the affair either so bad or so desperate as Gunnar himself, or as he believed she would.

"Well, and with which of the girls at the Hall may it be, because I can't think but it must be one of them? It can not be that impudent Lena; however?" asked Mother Ingrid.

"Yes, it is precisely *she*," replied Gunnar, with a deep sigh; and then recounted to his mother, but with greater amplification than he had done to Bengt, how that "Satan's drop," at Aspas had brought about his ruin, as he called it. Beyond this he told her—for he believed it would comfort her a little—that he was to go to a good farm at Lady-day, to have a splendid wedding at the Hall, and perhaps have a little help from the gentry to begin the world with. When he had ended, the old woman began the following monologue, because we must acknowledge that Gunnar lay down with closed eyes, and heard only little of what his mother said. He in no wise either despised what she said or went to sleep; but he rather lay and compared all his former rosy dreams with the thistly and thorny realities; compared the future which he had imagined with the one which stood grinning before him; sighed and compared.

In the mean time the old woman went on talking.

"Yes, yes," sighed she, "even *here* that devilish brandy has something to do in the business! But it may go better than one thinks for. Yes, God the Father give thee happiness and joy in this thy marriage, as in every thing else, my dearest Gunnar!" The old woman pondered a little, and then went on.

"So, so; in the statutes, then. But what a piece of folly it was! A lad might be decoyed by a pretty girl, but not by an old woman. But perhaps thy memory deceives thee. Oh, yes; no doubt. And a farm thou art to have is a very good thing: and a wedding thou art to have—dost thou not say? at the Hall, and dancing money.* It ought to be splendid, however. And so at spring thou art to go to Vika—but for that, look you, there will be wanted a cow, and other outfit, but perhaps that will come out of the dancing-money; but Lena is sure to put the best foot foremost, as the saying is."

Again she paused, and then inquired, "Well, and do you think that I shall be asked to the wedding?"

* The money which the wedding guests give to the bride. (Author's note.)

This last question, which was asked in a high and somewhat firm voice, roused up Gunnar, and he said, "Yes, bless you, dear mother; of that you may be sure."

"Yes, that you'll do of a certainty," said Mother Ingrid; "ask Lena for a new bit of edging for my old 'lin,'* and for another ribbon for my white cap, otherwise I can not at all come among such a parcel of folks."

"Oh, no, dearest mother," returned Gunnar; "be sure of this, that I never will ask any thing of Lena; I would a thousand times rather buy them for you among the things to-morrow in the town."

"Oh, bless me! thou shalt not lay out of thy poor hard-earned money on that trifle; thou wilt want all thou hast, and more than that, for thyself."

"Oh, never mind; it will suffice to purchase more than I shall want to-morrow in the town; and, look you, I want some advice," replied Gunnar, in a tone of indifference.

"Let me see; what, shalt thou buy every thing to-morrow?" asked the old woman.

"Yes," answered Gunnar, with the most freezing indifference; "there must be bought a ring, and then a book, and then a pair of gloves, and then she will have a silk handkerchief."

"Hush!" said the old warm-hearted mother, and hastened out to an ancient jet-black chest. "Hush! a silk handkerchief thou shalt have from me, and that a fine one too! If thou wilt buy me a bit of edging and ribbon, and a morsel of snuff besides, then I can help thee with thy wedding presents, and thou shalt have a silk handkerchief in return."

With this the old woman went to the chimney, lighted again a brand, and then unfolding triumphantly something which she held in her hand, and upon which she threw the light of the stick, she advanced to Gunnar, who all this time lay upon the hard wooden sofa.

"See, thou best one!" said the kindly-intentioned old woman, holding the blazing stick in her mouth; and Gunnar actually saw a dark piece of stuff, not really worn out, but altogether the worse for wear, and in which one single color could not be distinguished from another, looking altogether of a gray-brown hue, which of itself testified of its great age.

* The piece of muslin which is placed under the cap, cut of the same shape, and *always* furnished with a lace border, either narrower or wider. (Author's note.)

Gunnar took the old handkerchief, held it a little way from him, and it looked so unsightly to him that he was compelled to say—

"Ah, no, dearest mother, keep your silk handkerchief yourself. It is handsome enough, one must confess; but Lena, you see, will have something which is showy: she must have one with red, and green, and yellow, and all colors in it."

"Oh!" said the mother, a little repiningly, because she had always set a high value on this silk handkerchief, which had been given to her among her "bride gifts" in former days. "I think she is showy enough herself, with her coal-black eyes, her red cheeks, and her black parted hair, that she should be satisfied with dark-colored clothes, now that she is going to be a peasant's wife. Yes, yes," sighed the old woman, while she again folded it up with the greatest care, and replaced her treasure, still with the burning stick in her mouth. "Ay, ay; haughty and full of vanity, that she is, my poor Gunnar!"

Gunnar sighed; but whether it was with thinking of the haughtiness and vanity of Lena, or that the expression, "My poor Gunnar," from his mother's lips, called forth the sighs from her son's breast, is not so easy to determine. When a person suffers, he sighs if he be pitied, he sighs if he be not pitied, he sighs for every thing.

Gunnar had eaten his supper before he left the Hall; and besides this, if he had not, his mother had really nothing to give him, except a few sour apples, which Gunnar accepted with thanks, but did not eat, because he laid himself down, and, thanks to youth and labor, old age and weariness, sleep, that angel of the night, descended into the humble cottage, and laid its beneficent finger upon the eyes of both mother and son.

CHAPTER IV.

EARLY the following morning, Gunnar was ready to go to the town. He took a hasty but cordial farewell of his mother, who blessed at once, both solemnly and earnestly, his "incoming and his outgoing;" promised to come of a certainty to see her again on Christmas-day, and to bring with him the edging, the ribbon, and the snuff, and something besides these, which he was always accustomed to carry with him on the Christmas-day.

On his arrival in the city, Gunnar went first of all to the gold-smith's, handled and examined his rings, but allowed the shop-keeper himself to select one suitable for the large pattern, which was wrapped in paper, and Gunnar then paid five-and-twenty per cent. more than it was worth, according to a stereotyped joke of the goldsmiths, who are accustomed to make an extra charge whenever a handsome young peasant comes to buy a wedding-ring. This was of silver gilt, and in three large wavy stripes, so that it almost seemed as if there were three rings. After that he went to the bookbinder's, and asked to look at a "handsome book in a cover;" as, however, the bookseller was a cross old fellow, he escaped the customary joke, and paid for it merely the two rix-dollars. After that he went on to shopkeeper Bäckrot's, in the market-place. A little young lady stood in the shop, whom Gunnar knew, because he had often been there on errands, for both the squire and Ma'msell Sara.

"Yes," said Gunnar, embarrassed, when she came forward to serve him at the counter; "now I should like to have gloves, and a handsome silk handkerchief, some edging, and a cap."

Ma'msell attended to these somewhat enigmatical desires politely, kindly, and with smiles, all the while replying to the incessant questions of other peasant men and women, who were asking "what was the price of fish this year," and "of treacle," and "Christmas spices," and "mould candles," be-cause "on St. Thomas's day is the fair in every town," as the proverb says, and as the truth is, and the peasants then provide for their small Christmas wants; that is to say, fish, spice, candles, snuff, and tobacco.

When Gunnar turned his steps homeward, he was con-tinually saluted by his acquaintance, who, some riding and some walking, overtook or were overtaken by him on the road, each one with an ugly, long, dry, curled fish, called *rokka*, and a candle fastened in their hat; and, for the rest, with faces more or less red, in part from the keen severity of the season, or from the brandy, which was every where to be met with.

"Bless me! what a long face he has!" said many of those who saw Gunnar on the way; but many a creditable person saw not alone *one* Gunnar, but often *two;* and if the sun had pleased to show himself on that December day, they had of a certainty seen double suns likewise; and after that none at all, for then their heavy eyelids would have closed.

As soon as Gunnar reached home, he went up into his loft, hung up his holyday clothes, put on his working-day suit, and, late as it was in the day, went out to work.

" Nay, you ?" said Bengt, inquiringly.

" Yes, you !" replied Gunnar; "now it is settled and done."

And with that the conversation ceased, for Gunnar had now as little inclination for talking and merriment as he formerly had pleasure in it.

Christmas-eve was a dreadful time for Gunnar. During the whole forenoon he was invisible; nobody knew where he was; and at noon it was hardly possible to get him into the kitchen, where, according to an ancient custom on Christmas-eve, they " dipped in the pot,"* although he had not tasted the least morsel for breakfast. The weather was cold, the air full of snow, dark and heavy, so that only a very few from the Hall were at church, but these few quite sufficient to trumpet it abroad when they came home, that the banns had been published between Gunnar and Lena.

Lena walked about as proudly as a turkey-cock, but Bengt was obliged to drag poor Gunnar into the kitchen; and when he was fairly come in there was an end of all their laughter and jokes; and, worst of all, they fancied they saw something about Lena which they had not seen before, and which Gunnar could least of all comprehend had he looked at her, but he did not do so, and took the idle talk of the others for the coarse raillery which was customary among peasants. Lena began to be in some measure less proud, and even seemed a little abashed, on account of all that was said; and as she actually loved the young and handsome Gunnar with all the passion and the unbridled impulses of a woman's heart, she began to endeavor, by good words and a friendly behavior, to overcome his extreme coldness. By assiduous fondness, and, at the same time, by caustic and bitter words, she had gained nothing, which she had thought very extraordinary; now, therefore, she desired to do every thing to let Gunnar

* They take off with bread the fat which floats on the top of the pot in which meat is boiling. (Author's note.)

see her kind disposition, and that the other servants should
not have to say, " Poor Gunnar was compelled to marry her."
In the evening, therefore, when the servants had ended the
singing of a psalm, she left the abundantly-supplied Christmas
table, and went out to Gunnar with a large bundle in her
hand, and said to him, in a friendly and almost bashful manner,

" Dear Gunnar, I pray you to go home to-morrow to your
mother, as is customary with you on Christmas-day. Greet
her kindly from me, and beg her to be so friendly as to take
in good part the present of my Christmas-store, because I
have no person nearer than her to give it to. My mother and
sister are a long way from here ; if the letter reaches them,
then my sister at least will come here to—to our wedding."

The cunning Lena knew that his mother was the apple of
Gunnar's eye, and that in this way she should be best able to
move his heart, besides which she should stand in a good
point of view before him, if she could make him believe that
she felt attached to his mother.

" Many thanks," said Gunnar, making an embarrassed
movement, and taking, both willingly and unwillingly, the
bundle which held the customary " Christmas hoard," or the
four loaves of the various kinds of bread which every one
receives, a quantity of Christmas candles, together with some
pastry, apples, and other small trifles, collected from the
evening's abundance.

CHAPTER V.

THE morning of Christmas-day was unusually bright, mild,
and beautiful, and therefore brought a thaw with it ; and as
Bengt had asked permission to accompany Gunnar, the two
young men set off early, long before daybreak. The waning
moon shone brightly with a pure light upon the new-fallen
snow, which had not come down in any quantity, but only
lightly and smoothly, as if to adorn the old dingy earth for
Christmas ; and as the road was very wild and untracked, but
at the same time one of unusual beauty, this morning's journey

was possessed of a certain poetical delight which was by no means unperceived by these uneducated beings, who, however, had never heard *the word* poetry, but in whose hearts *the thing* itself found all the more room.

"Bless me!" said Bengt, "such a beautiful and fine Christmas dawn I think I never saw before."

"You say truly," replied Gunnar, "nor I either; and, do you know, Bengt, I have for my part a great desire to go to Norrlanda church. The cross-roads are not so very far round, and I think that it would really be something glorious and soothing to go in this divinely-beautiful Christmas dawn to hear the word of God, and to see all the lights burn, and then to hear the organ, which is my delight always; and, do you know, they have such a one at Norrlanda as we can hardly match in our parish."

"Yes, above all things," replied Bengt; and the two young men began visibly to increase their speed; for although Gunnar had spoken about the cross-roads not being much longer, yet it was a good three or four miles out of the way, one thing taken with another.

"God be praised and thanked that you *wish* for something!" said Bengt, after they had walked rapidly on some time in silence. "Of a truth I was regularly afraid for you all this week. You went about like some one who seeks for an opportunity to put an end to himself. I thanked God, of a truth, every evening when you came in, and had seated yourself in the servants' room, for I always feared lest you should not come, but be found hanging by a rope, or lying in a marsh, or that you should have shot yourself."

Gunnar walked on in silence.

"Yes, yes, you did go and think about something bad; I was not mistaken about it," continued Bengt, who was strengthened in his dreadful surmise by the silence of Gunnar.

"Oh, no!" replied Gunnar, after some reflection, "I never had such wicked thoughts, although I many a time prayed for death, if such were but His will. No, suicide I shall never commit, seeing I did it not when father died, and my brother fell into misfortune, and all that we were possessed of was burned to the ground, and all that because of wicked brandy. For, you see, father had the bad habit of drinking, and he taught it to Jonas, and Jonas fell into all sort of crime and misery, and went out tramping about the country, we never

knew where.   One evening, however, he came home, and
looked wretched and forlorn ; we had not seen him then for
many months, and he looked about in every corner of the
room, as if he were afraid of something.   Mother offered him
something to eat, but he insisted on having nothing but brandy ;
and so the bottle was brought out, and they sat themselves
down to drink, both father and Jonas, and that lasted till late
in the night ; and so both mother and I, since we found it was
in vain to beg and pray of them to leave off, went and laid us
down.   At last father rolled under the table.   Then we awoke
(though mother had never slept at all), and it was with great
difficulty that mother and I got him to bed ; for, you see,
Jonas did not offer to help a bit.   And then mother prayed
him so exceedingly earnestly, and with such tender words, to
leave off drinking, and to go and lie down with me on the
sofa ; but he said absolutely, ' No' to it all ; for he was not so
excessively drunk, because he could bear such a deal of liquor ;
but when the brandy was all drank out, he swore a little about
it, but soon after lighted father's tobacco-pipe and went out.
We fancied he would soon come in again, so we lay down and
left the door unfastened for him ; but he did not ever come in
again, and we slept soundly.   But, merciful Heaven, what a
waking we had !   All the room was in a bright blaze—the
cow-shed and barn were already burned down !

"It was with the utmost difficulty that mother and I could
get father out, and little, if any thing, from the house.   We
took and laid father on the cold ground, for he slept like a
stone, and Jonas was not any where to be found.   But you
may fancy, dear Bengt, that, nevertheless, that was not the
worst ; the day after the fire father died, and that same day
they took up Jonas, who had escaped out of the house of cor-
rection.   That same day he was taken to the assizes to receive
his sentence, and that was the reason why he would not sleep
in the house, but went out and lay down in the hay-loft, to
which he set fire with his lighted pipe, for that the fire came
from the cow-shed was shown by the wind.   He had driven
out the cattle—that was the only thing he had thought about
before he made his escape ; but he never imagined that the fire
would extend to the dwelling-house—I never can believe him
bad enough for that.

"And now I can tell you that the day father was buried,
when mother had not any thing to put over her head, and

when they came home from the assizes, and told that Jonas, whom they had taken again, had been flogged, then I went out to a great deep well which we had, and there I stood a long time, and looked down into the well, for, you see, I was not then confirmed, and God forgive me the thoughts which I had, because they were not good! and if I *then* did not throw myself into the well, I shall not do it *now*, when I know better, but shall try to bear my lot, however dark it may seem to be."

"Bless me!" said Bengt, in astonishment; "and you have never spoken to me about all this business before! And yet I have heard that there was a fire, and that you had a scoundrel of a brother, who is since dead, but I never knew how all this had gone."

"Oh, no," replied Gunnar; "it was, believe me, nothing so agreeable to talk about, and I should not have talked about it now either if it had not been so long since, and if I had not wished to prove to you that I never shall make away with myself, when I did not do it *then*."

"Was it, then, really your intention to throw yourself head first into the well?" inquired Bengt, astonished.

"Yes, my actual intention."

"And how happened it that you did not?"

"Ay, that I will tell you also. It was no merit of mine, believe me, but it was a dog that I had, which was called Zemire, that came and licked my legs and fondled me, and seemed as if it saluted me from mother, of whom I was so excessively fond that it was almost to avoid seeing her suffering that I was about to put an end to myself; and then, when I saw the dog looking just as if it spoke to me from her, I began to weep for the first time, and I wept very much; and then Zemire went on and I followed, and she kept looking back at every step she took, to see that I came with her; and it was very affecting to see, for it seemed all the time as if mother had told her to do it. And in that way we went on, Zemire going first and I after her, till we reached a miserable brew-house or kiln which we had, and which had not been burned down; and there sat mother upon a little chest, which we had succeeded in dragging out of the flames when the house was burned. She was weeping violently; but when she saw me come she threw her arms around me, and thanked God so fervently because I was saved to her; and then was I thoroughly glad that I had not destroyed myself and had thus spared her that sorrow. But now we will not talk any longer about these melancholy times. God be praised that they are passed, which is best! and now if I could only see things clear before me, and could get all right with that Vika and with Lena, and could manage to take mother home to live with me, so that she need not live in the wood all lonesome and helpless, and if she, Lena, would behave kindly toward mother, and not lead her a dog's life, then, perhaps, in the long run, it might turn out well. What do you think about it, Bengt?"

"Ay, faith, that I do believe!" replied Bengt, who had an indescribable satisfaction in again seeing Gunnar gay and cheerful, and who had, besides this, long since accustomed himself to the thoughts of the marriage. In a general way, Bengt neither thought long nor much on any subject, nor troubled himself greatly about any thing. "At Vika," continued he, "you can live in a famously grand and gallant style; and thou must have a man-servant to do day labor on the farm; and as thou knowest me to be as good as any other, I shall give warning to leave in spring, and so go and live with thee in the autumn; and that will be prodigiously charming and pleasant, and we two, together, shall be able to keep Lena in order, so that she does not become unmanageable."

Gunnar was silent for some time, and then said, "No, Bengt; do you know, that would never answer. First of all, as to what you say about its being so charming and pleasant to live with me as a servant, look at it a little nearer, and it will not do at all. No, it would never turn out well in the end, for you to be man and me master. You know that we are good friends, and if I should *think* any thing, then I must either hold my tongue about it, or if I should speak my mind, then you might get angry, and that might make me angry, and so we should get to words, and then there would be a quarrel, and you would leave me, and with that there would be an end of our friendship and our joy. No; a man-servant I must have, but it shall not be my best friend, he whom I will have now and then as a guest, and entertain with every thing which the house contains. And, besides this, you must consider what little wages and poor living there will be at a poor cottager's in comparison with a gentleman's house. No; that would cause a dreadful difference, which would distress both you and me: things are best as they are."

When Gunnar said these last words, the remembrance of

Lena passed through his mind, whom it seemed impossible for him to learn to endure, and he sighed deeply and sorrowfully, but with that manly and subdued sorrow which will neither bewail itself, nor which seeks to be bewailed.

"Oh, bless me!" answered Bengt, a little vexed; "I thought it would be so capital, and that you would be so pleased with it; but perhaps you are right, after all. You are far wiser than I am; I often find that out, although you did let Lena draw you astray."

Gunnar made no answer: he could now no longer continue the conversation about his misfortunes; they were confirmed, and there was no advantage in talking about them. Gunnar was one of those rare beings, gifted with so clear an intellect, that he learned by instinct the value of words, and taught himself not to make use of the tinkling brass, unless some profit were to be derived from it.

The two young men, through snow, moorland, and morass, had found for themselves a path through the wood, and were approaching the church they had spoken of, the sound of whose organ already was heard in the calm and clear winter morning, which was now lighted only by the thousand starry lamps of night, which would shortly retire before the single magnificent star of day.

"Good heavens!" said Gunnar, half to himself and half to Bengt; "how beautiful it is, though, to come out from the dark wood, and then to see how bright it shines through the tall arched windows of the old chuurch; and to hear the psalms and the organ which sound from it! It makes me feel quite as if I must shed tears; and God knows what that evil must be, which would not in some sort yield before such a sight as this, and such singing and music!"

Bengt sighed with a feeling of devotion, and felt in degree something of that of which Gunnar spoke, but, of a truth, far less deeply and less fervently. Silently, and with their hats before their mouths, the two entered into the sacred building, and stood in the aisle just before the pulpit, which a young man, at that moment, softly and solemnly entered. He spoke powerful and fervent words to the assembled people; spoke about their serious and holy duties to God and man; and, when Gunnar came out of the church into the gray dawn of morning, it was with the full intention of enduring Lena, and endeavoring to love her. But how he succeeded in this we leave at this time; such resolutions as these are among the most difficult of all to act upon.

The sun had already ascended over the edge of the mountain when the two young men arrived at Gunnar's mother's, who was sitting alone close within the chimney, singing out of an old hymn-book, and every now and then, in the midst of it, blowing the embers on the hearth, that they might not go out.

"So there thou art really!" said the old woman, joyfully, as Gunnar and Bengt entered. "I did not believe thou wouldst have come to-day as thou wast here so lately."

"But I said that I really should come as usual," returned Gunnar, a little annoyed at the old woman's doubt.

"Oh, yes, you young fellows promise so much, and perform so little," said Mother Ingrid; and then at the same moment welcomed Bengt with a friendly "God's peace be with you, Bengt! How are you? Good Christmas, my child! What now shall old Ingrid feast you with this Christmas-day? Ah!" sighed she, "it is not now with us as in the days of our prosperity! Then I might have had *something*, now there is nothing, or little enough."

Gunnar sighed deeply, and even Bengt could not resist a tear which started to his eyes as he thought upon the downfall and the misfortunes of this poor household, of which he had heard from Gunnar only so lately.

Before long, however, a sort of cheerfulness, called forth by Bengt, returned to them; for Bengt's tears ever fell over a laughing mouth, and he now began to talk a deal of idle nonsense to Mother Ingrid, who, we must confess, willingly listened to the cheerful-hearted young man, to whom the world, with all its great and small troubles, was nevertheless "a merry little world," as he was accustomed to express himself when he was in his gay and lively humor. The two young men brought out their bundles, and, with the help of a little butter and a little boiled milk, they both of them made, spite of the walk, a very delicious meal. Gunnar obtained the most extraordinary praise from Mother Ingrid for the edging and the new cap, all which the old woman contemplated with all the light which the little room afforded, not forgetting the blaze of the burning coals.

In the twilight, before the young men set out to go home, they talked a little, but very little, about the wedding which was to take place on Twelfth-day, and it was agreed that Bengt should come and fetch the old woman, who could not by her-self find her way through the wood.

"Ay, truly," said Bengt; "on this subject it shall go like a dance, and Mother Ingrid shall climb like a goat in the clefts of the mountains, and I shall take care that she does not tumble down, that we may not bring a funeral feast into the middle of the wedding dinner, for that would be very dull and trouble-some; that it would!"

On their homeward way, Bengt said to Gunnar, "I think you might have comforted the dear old soul a little more, when she cried, and said that now you were going a deal farther off, and she should never get to see you, and such like. I think you then might have told her you would take her to live with you at Vika."

"Oh, no!" returned Gunnar; "it was better not. I will first of all see how Lena behaves herself; for never, no *never* could I bear that she should behave ill to mother without my calling her to account. No, I thank you; I will first see how every thing goes on before I remove the old woman."

CHAPTER VI.

CHRISTMAS passed as usual, but every one, as well as Lena, saw how manly and grave was Gunnar's demeanor, and how all at once a change had come over him, from his being the most light-hearted and the gayest of youths; so that she now al-most shrunk before his stern glances, and endeavored in all kind of ways to give him pleasure, till he even began to believe that Lena, after all, might be a good sort of person, though it was so horribly difficult to make himself tolerate her.

Gunnar was also in another difficult strait at this time, be-tween Christmas-day and Twelfth-day, but which he likewise overcame. To make this intelligible we must go back for some considerable time. He had, several years before, when the valet was away on military service, waited upon the tutor, a young and amiable man, with a pure heart, pure habits, and one who took a cheerful view of things. The tutor, who had taken degrees in the college, and was called the magister, took a great liking to, and attached himself to his new attendant. Some time after this, when he fell sick of the scarlet fever, the tutor was often with him, gave him books, and read to him.

He was now, therefore, inexpressibly angry that they should throw away his favorite upon " that infamous, ugly, and abominable piece of goods," as he called Lena—perhaps not so altogether without reason. The tutor, young, and loving liberty himself, thought that such a misfortune would be worse than any other. He represented this to the squire with great openness; but the squire turned a deaf ear, laughed—although the laughter was a poor affair—and said, " They were already asked in church; that there was no good in talking any more about it."

He represented to the old, honorable, and wise Ma'msell Sara, the absurdity and the incompatibility of this union; but she answered with a sigh—

" Ah, yes! what can one do? In a large house, with many servants, order and discipline must be maintained. This marriage is shockingly against my feelings, but they are now both satisfied, as it seems; and, besides, they are asked in church."

The tutor preached to Gunnar, and besought him, for God's sake, to get out of this affair while it was yet possible; but Gunnar answered firmly and determinedly:

" Yes, it often appears so dark to me, as if it might be the death of me; but I have said it. The pastor has received my promise, and God at the same time, and I will not flinch from it."

The young tutor, who was somewhat smitten by the epidemic of *Det gar an,** talked broad and wide about how, if one took a wife whom one did not love, for whom one had no *sympathies,* whose inward being was not in harmony with our inward being, and to which merely feelings of duty dragged us, and a deal more of the same—then one bound a millstone round one's neck for one's whole life. But the young peasant inquired calmly whether it were not still worse that perjury and injustice should bind a millstone upon the conscience? " which of a surety would, in the end, drag it downward." And he continued firm in his determination.

The *educated man* remonstrated, called a number of arguments to his assistance, which were neither weak nor false, and, above all things, of the highest importance, according to

* See Howitt's Journal, vol. ii., page 212.

his view of the business; but the *uneducated man* had an answer for them all, and his replies were so simple, so pure—
they were diamonds broken from the rock, pearls taken from
the mussel—which no one, not even the greatest sophist, could
have declared false; and Gunnar's last word was, "Would to
God that my conscience would allow me to listen to the word
of the tutor! but it shrinks back before the bare thought of
escaping from my promise, and I *must* stand by it."

CHAPTER VII.

WE said just now, that Christmas passed on as usual, but
these words must be recalled. Outwardly, Christmas was like
itself, with its rest from all kinds of work, its infinite abundance of meat, its long holydays, short days, and interminable,
often unemployed, evenings; but the soul of all imaginable
Christmas pleasures among the many domestics of Grantorp
was entirely deadened. Formerly, it was always Gunnar, assisted by Bengt, who devised all possible sorts of games and
frolics; and his violin it was, upon which he played with an
unusual degree of peasant-skill, which first set the dance in motion, which he then was the most zealous to continue. Gunnar
was gifted by nature with an excellent ear, and a strong and
clear voice, so that he could play and sing without end; and,
hitherto, he had always, in his hours of leisure, and in the twilight of Christmas, amused his companions by these means.
His violin was highly valued by himself, and by all the others,
as a *ne plus ultra* of violins; and as it hung on the wall of the
men-servants' room, close by the side of his loaded gun, nobody
dared to touch them, or hardly to look at them, because, if they
did, they all knew they should offend Gunnar, and have a strict
calling to account. "Let my violin alone!" or "Let my gun
alone!" were words so often repeated by Gunnar, that they became a proverb in the family, which was made use of whenever
any one would forbid another to touch or to look into any thing.
And a rare violin it was; for if there were sometimes a
string gone, as would happen to this violin as well as to all
others, then Gunnar would sing the melody with a clear voice,

and play a sort of impromptu accompaniment upon the three strings, and would say afterward, " It is, indeed, an extraordinary affair, this violin of mine !"

But now, both gun and violin hung silent and dusty upon the wall. Gunnar, who was possessed of a quick eye, and who was a lucky marksman, was accustomed to go out with his gun on the mornings of holydays, " to spring upon a springer," as he himself said ; and then would often come home from the deep woods in good time on Sundays, but weary and warm, and with a fine Sunday's roast for Ma'msell Sara, whereby he did not sink, but, on the contrary, rose, in her favor. But now there came no white hare, or dark-plumaged bird into the kitchen. Gunnar started no leaping creature in the wood, and his loaded gun remained hanging on the wall; he also played but a short and silent part in a Christmas drama, which was, nevertheless, within a hair's-breadth of becoming a tragedy.

But before we can give an account of this, we must introduce on the scene two new personages. In the first place, a red-haired, ill-favored, crafty, ill-tempered, and jealous servant in the distillery, called Olle, who, a considerable time ago, paid court to Lena, but without much success, from which cause he now could not bear her ; and also the tidy kitchen-maid, little Lisa, towards whom Olle had for some time been looking with kindly eyes, partly for the sake of her rosy, cheerful countenance and small delicate figure, and partly because every kitchen-maid always *can*, if she *will*, treat the one who finds favor in her eyes, with meat and good things ; and now Still-man Olle, as he was generally called, was not only particularly devoted to the abundant brandy which he himself helped to prepare in the great distillery, the smell of which reached Grantorp night and day, but was likewise a great lover of *la bonne chère* (a yet untranslated Gallicism).

But now, as " chance," and, one must allow, misfortune for Still-man Olle, would have it, Lisa, the little, tidy Lisa *always* laid the largest portion of bacon, the longest slice of sausage, the best pickled meat, and the choicest pudding, upon Gunnar's plate, and also laded up the most barley in his gruel, and the greatest quantity of little pieces of meat in his soup, and laid the thickest cake before him. Nobody—certainly not Gunnar himself, who did not occupy his thoughts with little Lisa—was so exact an observer of this as Still-man Olle ; and every time that such an instance of little Lisa's regard occurred, Olle's hatred and jealousy of Gunnar increased, because not in *one* instance, but in *all*, this man stood in his way.

Olle, with neither ear nor voice, fancied that he could play the violin; but as he was a drunkard, and had hardly clothes to his body, much less any personal effects, he of a certainty was not worth a violin. He often endeavored, either by insolent demands or by craft, to possess himself of Gunnar's; but he had now been so often defeated that he hardly dared to renew the attempt. Every thing which concerned Gunnar excited his anger and his envy; and now this approaching wedding, and the fact of Gunnar's receiving a little farm, assistance from the gentlefolks of the hall, etc., for all of which Gunnar would gladly have given half his life could he but have escaped from them, excited Olle no little.

When, therefore, the banns for Gunnar and Lena had been published for the third and last time, Bengt, when he came in from church, said, with tearful eyes, to his comrades in the men-servants' room, "Yes, now it is done! Now Gunnar is as good as a married man."

Gunnar sat by, silent as a wall, with his eyes fixed gloomily on a distant bench.

"Yes," continued Still-man Olle, maliciously, "it is so; now he is as good as a married fellow; and Lena, at all events, now gets *one* safe father for her child."

Gunnar looked up hastily, looked at Still-man Olle, but lightning flashed from his glance; and, rising up softly and solemnly, he walked up to his gun, and, laying his hand upon it, said in a tone of voice in which lay the superlative degree of gravity, "Do not say that word again, Olle!"

Olle rushed away into the chimney corner behind Bengt and an old press which stood there, and begged earnestly for pardon, declaring that it was nothing at all but a pure jest.

"Yes," replied Gunnar, shortly, "either I or my gun shall teach you to jest."

Gunnar had the best and the tenderest of hearts. He could not bear to see even a worm suffer, and by will or knowledge would never have caused pain to a living being; nevertheless, if people excited him—and his passions were hastily roused— he knew not for a moment what he did, and then of a certainty, it was the best to get out of his way, for at such a moment the life of man was as nothing to him; and against our own will, we must acknowledge to Gunnar's shame, that he already had been once compelled to pay a fine for man-slaughter, and this circumstance had given him a still greater abhorrence of brandy, upon which then, also, the blame was laid. Had Gunnar, however, known himself better, he would rather have complained of his shockingly violent temper, which would slumber calmly for so long a time, but which all at once woke up, raging horribly for a short period.

It was not long, however, before Gunnar and Olle were tolerably good friends again; because, although Gunnar was so easily irritated his anger was not of long duration; and as Still-man Olle was in the highest degree a man of false char-acter, he could often, when any advantage was to be gained by it, disguise himself and entirely conceal his malignant and envious disposition. It was thus he acted during the Christmas week, and as he saw Gunnar's disinclination for his violin and for every thing else, he begged leave to play "a little while, quite beautifully, upon Gunnar's violin;" and occasionally it was granted, and, what was still more, Gunnar stood not now, as formerly, when Still-man Olle enjoyed this favor, like a brooding hen by his side, to take care of his treasure. On the contrary, he now let him work away as best he could upon the violin, but going out most frequently himself, with his fingers in his impatient and keenly-sensitive ears, which instinctively suffered from the false notes, and saying as he went out, " Dear me! I cannot bear to hear how badly thou playest; it cuts like a sharp, or rather like a dull knife through my whole body, from the crown of my head to the soles of my feet."

And Bengt sighed; because, thought he to himself, "if he do not trouble himself about his violin, but lets Olle do with it what he will, then depend upon it, it is bad with him."

———◆———

CHAPTER VIII.

THE wedding-day advanced with hasty strides. It was, as we know, fixed for Twelfth-day, and was expected with great impatience by all except by the bridegroom.

The Squire certainly was not a good man, but not a very bad one, either; and whether it was from cunning, from cal-

culation, or from a little touch of goodness of heart, one can
not justly determine, but in certain cases he actually was what
is called good to his domestics and dependants, because, while
at the same time that he was an extremely severe and exacting
master, who required that every one should labor and endeavor
to his utmost ability, still he was tolerably just, and often quite
generous. Gunnar had now served him ever since his seven-
teenth year, thus for seven full years; first as stable boy, and
then as laboring man; besides which, he had in every case
perfectly fulfilled all the duties imposed upon him by his
master, and *therefore* he should now have a great and respectable wedding. Lena had served for three years at Grantorp,
and had a good character; therefore should she also, before
the world's eyes, receive honor, though in a less degree; but
as they *two* were to become *one*, the Squire had his reasons for
wishing that there should be no difference made, but merely
recommended to the proper executive power, Ma'msell Sara,
that nothing should be spared, but that it should be a respectable wedding. With this Ma'msell Sara was not dissatisfied;
for she was just to the utmost, and goodness and benevolence
filled her heart; and as she never could rightly charge upon
Lena any thing worse than her unpleasing appearance, as well
as now and then a little outbreak of malice against her companions, which might be attributed to her violent temper,
while, on the contrary, she always found her willing, regular,
exact, and clever in her service, as well as quick in every kind
of woman's occupation in a great house in the country; therefore Ma'msell Sara also wished that she should be rewarded
with a respectable wedding. As regarded Gunnar, she was
accustomed to say, "I know that it is doing wrong, when we
are trusted with a governing power, ever to have a favorite;
but when we find some one who keeps to the law in *every thing*,
then it is difficult to avoid it." And Gunnar was her favorite.
Quick, willing, regular, and never at a loss, was he at all times.
Besides which, he was sober and honest; and lastly, he was—
what all ladies in the country set a great value upon—a pretty
good carpenter. If any thing fell to pieces, a bed, a table,
a chair, or if there needed a little footstool, drawer, or shelf,
or if the troublesome loom got somewhat into disorder,
Gunnar was instantly summoned, and he always immediately
understood what the question was about, and, which pleased
Ma'msell Sara as much, always knew how to remedy it. In

C

his leisure hours he had made an arm chair and a dresser for his old mother, and Lena often used to tell her companions about all the household goods which she meant to *let* Gunnar make when they came to Vika. Lena was very vain, and would have every thing as excellent as possible, a fault which Ma'msell Sara saw plainly enough, and shook her head over; but, as this did not properly interfere with her usefulness in service, she looked upon it, taken in connection with Lena's quickness, cleverness, and ability, as not so dangerous a failing.

It may be said with regard to Ma'msell Sara, that what she prepared for this wedding was done from a sense of justice as regarded Lena, but both from a sense of justice and *con amore* as far as Gunnar was concerned; and great and extraordinary were these preparations.

CHAPTER IX.

On the morning of Twelfth-day, when Bengt, impelled by a peculiar uneasiness, rose up before dawn, and made a fire in the men-servants' room by four o'clock, he missed Gunnar. His first impulse, after a low exclamation of " Merciful God !" was to cast a glance at the gun. But it hung there peaceably beside its old acquaintance, the violin; and Bengt heaved a deep sigh, partly from the pleasure of this discovery, and partly from grief, because he must shortly not only lose from the wall these two old acquaintances, but Gunnar himself, which was worse. In the mean time he did not trouble himself greatly about the fire, but dressed in haste, and went out, in the first place, to clear up the question concerning Gunnar, and then to set out for his mother, whom he had promised to fetch.

When he got out into the pitch-black morning, he looked around him, a little doubtful in what direction he should steer his course; but, while he stood wondering which would be the best, the old ox-herd came up, who, whether on holydays or whatever day it might be, never forgot his beloved oxen or neglected his duties. He came out with a lantern in his hand, and as soon as he saw Bengt, he said—

"The bridegroom sends his compliments to you. He bade me tell you that he is gone after his mother himself; but he told me to say that you must go and meet him about ten o'clock."

"Ah! I think I shall hardly trouble myself about that," muttered Bengt, rather vexed, "if he could not trust me about such a thing. To be sure, it would be fine slipping and sliding after an old woman, through wood and snow and morass, but then I thought he might have trusted me for all that."

Bengt went in again, and laid himself down, but he could not sleep.

And why had Gunnar really gone himself this time, as he knew so well that Bengt could do this errand, and would not fail in any way; and, besides, when he must have been aware that this conduct would wound Bengt, whom he was so heartily attached to?

Yes! the tutor's words had, after all, taken root in Gunnar's soul; and Lena's good behavior of late had done the same, and from these two opposite causes had arisen a peculiar doubt, a hesitation and a disquiet in the young man's soul, which he resolved to confide to the maternal bosom. When Gunnar went out of the men-servants' room, he took with him mechanically all the money of which he was possessed; his watch and a couple of shirts under his arm; and when he passed through the door of the men-servants' room, he turned himself hastily round, walked to the dark corner which held Bengt's bed, and thought hastily, "Perhaps I may never see him more, and then —may God be with him! And, perhaps, I may never more enter this door, and then—may God be merciful to me!"

With that, he went, with long and rapid strides, notwithstanding the dismal darkness; but he had, during these seven years, gone this way so many times, that every step which he took, whether to the right hand or whether to the left, was known to him. At about six o'clock he was at Mother Ingrid's cottage, and he knocked immediately at the bolted door, because he saw that there was already a light through the little cracked window, And there was a light; because Mother Ingrid had already made a little fire on the hearth, and now stood before it washing her old face with a bit of soap, that she might be regularly fine, clean, and shining upon her Gunnar's wedding-day.

"What! are you here already, dear Bengt?" said she, and

opened the door, but stepped backward, when she saw Gunnar, pale, and, as the mother's heart and the mother's eyes could instantly perceive, with an unusual look, and a strange expression of countenance.

"What, in the Lord's name, is on foot, that *thou* art here to-day?" exclaimed the old woman, and almost staggered backward.

"Nothing, nothing at all, dearest mother!" said Gunnar, and threw himself, wearied with his hasty walk and the thoughts which drew him forward, upon the old sofa; pushed his hair, wet with sweat, from his brow, and looked strangely around him.

"Thou shouldst hardly say that to *me*," answered Mother Ingrid; "I am too old, and I know thee too well, not to see that something bad is afloat; but, look you, I can not say what it is, I confess!"

"Oh, no, mother; do not be so unreasonably frightened! Do not stand and tremble, and let thy teeth chatter; but come and sit here, and then I will quite candidly tell thee how it is; and it is because I want to talk a little with thee to-day that I come before Bengt."

"Talk with me! and that just to-day! Yes, yes, it must indeed be a wonderful piece of business that thou wilt talk about! Merciful Lord Jesus! what shall I now be doomed to hear again? Never hitherto hast *thou* given me a moment's sorrow, and I was now, notwithstanding all things, both glad and satisfied at thy marriage. But I see plainly that some dust comes into the milk, and that thou—"

"Ah!" interrupted Gunnar; "sometimes you see such a many specks in the bright day; but, look you, it is not to be wondered at when you have suffered so much trouble. But if I now tell you that it stands for nothing; that no one knows that I am come here; that all is exactly as it was; and that—"

"Nay, then, why didst thou come, and not Bengt, as was already fixed?" interrupted the mother.

"Ay, dearest mother, for this reason," replied Gunnar, and wiped away once more the sweat from his brow; "I know not how, but I have some scruples in my mind. I never know, *notwithstanding*, whether .... whether I shall marry Lena" (the mother made a movement of astonishment). "Nay, nay, do not say any thing before I have said my say. I know well

enough you will argue about the banns, and so on : but on this
score I should not trouble myself; there might, indeed, be a
little difficulty there, but that I do not ask about—the banns
are merely a something to let it be known that two persons
wish to be married. That is of small account. But . . . . . on
the contrary, unless the minister read God's words over us it
would go for nothing, *that* I know; and therefore I wish to
talk with you before it is too late; to talk with you, and to ask
you, dearest mother, for advice, for you never gave me any
other than good advice, which God knows, certainly."

"Lord Jesus!" said the mother, sorrowfully, but calmly;
" has Lena, then, been behaving disagreeably and badly toward
thee within these last few days?"

"No, that is just what she has not done," replied Gunnar,
immediately. "She has, on the contrary, been good and kind
in every way; and it is exactly for this reason that I have a
weight upon my conscience, because, *notwithstanding*—I can
not like her! And now, I am afraid that I shall be the cause of
all her unhappiness as well as of my own; for, once indissolubly
united [an evident reminiscence of the tutor's representations],
then we should only make a hell upon earth together, and
break asunder from one another [again, a reminiscence]; and
therefore it would be a great deal better to make an end of it
now; and then—in that case—I should merely go on my own
course; go out into the wide world, and seek my fortune, and
pay to the child all that I could gain; and—"

"Ah, nay, do not talk any more in that way," interrupted
the mother. "I get quite miserable to hear it. Never—no,
never did I hear you talk in such a strange way! And I am
very much mistaken if somebody has not put this into your
head, for what is bad never would come into your mind of
itself. You! that you should become a liar and perjurer! run
away, and leave wife and child! And that, because—I am
ashamed of saying it—she is good and pious! I never heard
the like! No, my dear lad! Thou shalt, as is seemly and
proper for a good fellow, thou shalt stand by thy word, and try
to get over the little dislike thou hast to Lena, when she is
good, and like other folks—and thou shalt go on thy future
course as God appoints it for thee, and not set up thy will
against His; for then, of a surety, it will go ill all thy time.
And what, in all the world, is it that thou talkest about the
minister not having read God's word over thee and her? Thou

talkest entirely as if God had nothing to do with the affair!
What stupid and foolish talk it is! Canst thou, or can any
body else, undertake any thing with which God has not had to
do? Dost thou not tell the people in the banns that thou art
in the mind to marry Lena? Nay, is it not, in other words,
declaring before the people that which thou hast promised to
God, to her, and to thyself, and for which reason the clergyman
gives his blessing from the pulpit to this holy matrimonial bond?
Dost thou not remember that? And if thou dost not remember
it, then I remember it, and will remind thee of it now while
time is before thee. Bless me," continued she, after a little
pause, and as Gunnar remained silent, "I never thought to
have heard such sentiments from thee—hesitation, scruples,
and fickleness—when thou hadst once resolved! See, it is like
Jonas, thy brother, the poor lost lad whom, day and night, I
pray God to forgive, and not like thee, whom I always trusted
so entirely."

"Ah, yes, dearest mother! trust me really, I assure you that
is what I desire," said Gunnar, and great tears pearled in his
eyes. "It was precisely because I did not rightly know
whether I should do well or ill by marrying Lena that I wished
to ask you. But now I know it, for now you have told it me,
and now I believe it; and now will go straight forward to my
fate, let it henceforth be what it may: I trust in God and
you."

"Yes, do so, my dear, good Gunnar," said the old woman,
and dried his eyes, and was glad, and satisfied that she had so
easily overcome her son's scruples. But ah! there came a
time afterward, and how differently did she think then! How
she grieved, for having, by her maternal power, overruled her
son! How then did her conscience haunt her, and say that
she had spoken a deal about good things, a deal for Gunnar's
well-being, but—there was a grain of selfishness also in it too,
because she very well understood that Gunnar would merely
try how Lena conducted herself before he took his beloved
mother under his own roof, but that it should be so nevertheless; and see there!—*there* was Mother Ingrid's Eldorado for
this world. But how many a time in after days—for Mother
Ingrid's life was not a short one—did she exclaim, with deep
sighs, and, thinking upon this morning of Twelfth-day, "Oh, I,
short-sighted, conceited, foolish creature, who could let him
dance after my pipe instead of his own! Oh, I, wicked sinner,

who had his life's thread in my hand, and yet should so entangle it !"

But now it was done, and Gunnar was satisfied, because his scruples were not taken up as excuses, but were the feelings of his really upright heart, which wished only to do that which was right, and that which his mother advised, alike indifferent to his own inclination and fancy, which had not taken any particular direction. Gunnar was one of those young men—there are such, and may be found among all classes—who had never felt the omnipotence of a real love ; for this reason, that the women finding them so agreeable, fairly fling themselves at their heads instead of letting them seek after and woo them ; and Gunnar, like all such, imagined in this way that he could guide his heart according to his own fancy.

There was rather too much of "night and morning" with this old mother and this young son ; for the first had already forgotten that people can not put the bit and the bridle upon their feelings, and the latter believed, in his young strength, that people could always do that which they really would, and he had now determined with himself to love Lena. It will soon be seen how he succeeded.

With such thoughts and but few words in connection with the foregoing, the mother and son walked forth in the gray day-break, from the little cottage, which was carefully bolted ; but they had not gone far before they heard the jingle of bells, and the quick sound of a horse's feet, and immediately afterward they heard also the cheerful voice of Bengt, who called out to them :

"Look what I come with ! Bless me ! I thought I should have reached the cottage before you left it, and therefore I have driven so fast. Was it not handsome of the squire ? He sent down Magnus this morning to say that I, or some one of the other men, should drive to Guppa in a sledge, and fetch the mother-in-law. Now seat yourself in it, Mother Ingrid, and Gunnar and I will stand in the middle, and then we will go like singing !"

The old woman was quite beside herself for joy at being made so much of, and being conveyed in so comfortable a manner to the hall ; and with a sincere heart she blessed Gunnar's master. Gunnar did the same for the sake of his mother, but believed, nevertheless, that which he did believe—namely, that the first impulse to this, like many another good thing, by which the squire allowed his servants to be benefited, properly came from Ma'msell Sara.

When they arrived at the hall, Gunnar went into the men-servants' room, and Mother Ingrid was conducted to that of the women-servants. For ourselves, we wish for one moment to take the reader under the arm, and lead him through the lofty and vaulted hall, and up the broad, princely staircase, into another suite of apartments in this grand, old, gray-stone house, which looked in reality much more like a castle than a private residence. We should like to do so, because we have now an opportunity, for the first time, of informing the reader how this property was one of those large old inheritances which the aristocrat of birth found himself compelled by circumstances to give up into the hands of the aristocrat of money, and which now stood like a mausoleum over its former inward and outward splendor, over the knightly spirit and the high-bred manners, which prevailed there in the former time. As the house was in tolerably good condition when the squire came into possession of the whole estate for a mere trifling sum, he did not trouble himself about any needless repair and modernizing, but laid by his money where it could grow up again and bring an abundant harvest—namely, in agriculture, and the management of the land which lay here in a state of great neglect, leaving all ornament and elegance to a future time, which, perhaps, might never come. The squire, although he had received a remarkably good education, had, on the contrary, very little sense of that beauty which seems to be in every thing and every where, and which is very different to the sense of order which again constituted one of his most distinguishing virtues.

From this cause the old walls, gray, and with many a print of the tooth of time upon them, outwardly as well as inwardly, now stood either naked and unadorned as of old, or else clothed with those old hangings, partly of gilt leather, partly of other such-like stuffs of ancient days, as defied time and age, not, to be sure, in their primeval condition, but which, for all that, were quite capable of telling of the taste and customs of former times. Upon these walls grinned here and there horribly staring figures, and with them shepherdesses and beautiful proud ladies, who formerly looked down from them, but who now had a gray and spectral appearance, like all human works upon which time has laid his hands. There was a great deal of damp to be seen in the old house; but, we believe, for our part, that the many tears which often ran down these naked walls, were wept by the former *lares* and *penates* of the old house, who now saw so very little of that which they had formerly seen; heard no longer the sound of the hunting-horn, and the shivering war-horse stamp and paw on the pavement of the court; or the singers who carried the drinking cup round the company; or beautiful damsels who tripped through the corridors, and bold, proud knights who gladly met them; and love, and merriment, and songs, and musical instruments which formerly sounded within these walls. No; it was all in vain that they now listened for sounds such as these, and wept perhaps many tears over the mischance which allows the sole memory of the grandeur of former days still to remain, and perseveringly stand and tell great lies over the door, namely, the stone shield, well carved with the arms of the Creutz and the Natt-och-Dag family, which the present inhabitants of the house passed daily with indifference, not regarding it otherwise than as a usual door ornament.

At one end of this large house was situated the squire's chamber. He now went there on this morning of Twelfth-day, in dressing-gown and embroidered slippers, smoking-cap, and a large meerschaum, out of which a cloud was circling, and which soon directed its course up to the high vaulted roof, where some horrible personages from the Old Testament laughed scornfully at him. A gloom lay upon the squire's brow, for even he had a sort of conscience, although in certain cases it was not larger than a pea. But a pea even can swell and grow, and break the earth around it, and even the pea-sized conscience of the squire felt itself to-day oppressed and troubled by something. At length, however, he blew forth a cloud of smoke greater than any of the foregoing, and said, or thought—

"Pah! what good can not one do with money, especially among such people."

And with that he went to his bureau, drew out his money drawer, took from it a very handsome sum for the purpose, as it was called formerly, of "laying in the bowl," or "to give on the cake" to the newly-married couple, but which now was to be presented in a most tasteless manner, that is, during the dance with the bride.

This done, the squire was just about to drink his coffee, which stood waiting for him, when by chance he cast a glance

c*

into the court below, just at the moment when young Gunnar arrived, and with a solemn and gloomy countenance conducted his aged mother to the house. The squire drew back hastily, and felt all at once a couple of great talons which were struck into the *little* conscience, heaved a deep sigh out of his chest, which yet did not bring with it any relief; was silent, and mused for a while, and then said, or thought thus to himself:

"Pah! I will give him some cattle at Lady-day, when he will receive or set up his farm."

And now he went up to the cooled coffee, which he drank, and said aloud with an oath. that it did not taste good that day.

CHAPTER X.

IN another end of the same old house dwelt the Squire's elder sister, the old, excellent, Ma'msell Sara. She had already, the day before, arranged every thing perfectly for the approaching great wedding; and therefore it was that she was now rather weary, and was taking a good rest upon this morning of Twelfth-day, in order that she might be all the better able to stand the boisterous solemnities of the day. At half-past eight she arose, however, and rang several times for her maid Lotta; but as she did not come, she did not trouble herself about it, recollecting that Lotta that day had to attend both upon her and Lena. She went, therefore, and busied herself with a number of small things which she had not been able to do the evening before, among which was the arrangement of the bride's chair in the great hall, which ever since the days of old had gone by the name of the "King's Hall," because some one of the former Charleses—people did not then know which—had eaten and been entertained there by the then proprietor.

This was a long piece of work for Ma'msell Sara; the chair was to be covered with rose-colored silk, to stand upon a mat, and upon the chair was to lie a cushion which corresponded to it. All this the old lady prepared upon her knees; but it was now finished, and, with some difficulty, she rose up from the floor, where she had been kneeling. She heaved a deep sigh and said, or thought, "God give them happiness, comfort, and all good things in mutual love and unity!"

There is something painful and depressing in the thought that the prayers of the good and the righteous can not affect Providence, but that it pursues its own undeviating course, and is called Justice.

When Ma'msell Sara had finished her business she rang again, but this time for Magnus, the servant, who, she thought, would have plenty of time to help her in putting candles into the great chandelier; for since he had struck one candle-glass into a thousand pieces, had cracked another, had broken one pair of candles and let another pair dance down upon the floor, Ma'msell Sara took upon herself this business, although she did not find it very pleasant to mount up, first upon a rickety table, and after that upon a fragile stool, because, while all the walls, windows, doors, and ceilings, spoke loudly and haughtily of the ancient time, so, on the contrary, did all the furniture prattle about a newer time, probably eighteen or twenty years ago, or of exactly that period which was the most tasteless of all for furniture.

The clock struck half-past ten when Ma'msell Sara had finished this and other such small matters; and then throwing her green shawl over her shoulders, and taking her key-basket on her arm, and in her hand a little bundle, in which was something round and bowl-shaped, she betook herself to the lower regions of the household, to see whether every thing was in its proper order, as well as to cast an eye over the wedding-table, and then upon the bride and her adorning. The first place that Ma'msell Sara went into was a large, low, but arched hall, which had been called from the days of old the "guest-room," which name, conformably to old tradition, originated at the time when the house was only one story high, with two low towers; and then this hall was the most elegant state apartment, where strangers were received and entertained, at a long substantial oak table, which was now removed, and placed in one of the highest garrets. Now, however, this room was used at all times; in spring and summer to weave in—weaving being a something in which Ma'msell Sara, like all West Gothland ladies, excelled; in autumn for apples and every kind of fruit and garden apparatus, as well as in winter for all sorts of lumber.

All such things had now been cleared out; the hall well

washed, from the arched ceiling to the stone floor. Twigs of
the spruce fir were scattered over all, and as a so-called master
bricklayer had "peeped at the chimney," in which fire had not
been lighted for this many a long year, they had piled on much
fuel, which seemed to produce more smoke than warmth; but
Ma'msell Sara consoled herself with the thought that every
guest would bring his own stove with him.   Here a large table,
in the form of a horse-shoe, was spread for sixty people, with
beautiful table-cloths, a plate, a knife and fork, and a spoon, for
each person; but nothing served.   Upon the table there were
also ready set every kind of salads for the roast meat; fruit-
plates and baskets; rice-cream in a great dish, with preserved
whortle-berries on the top, together with huge tarts covered
with snow-moss, and pickles, and great dishes with pastry—
some in the shape of pyramids, and others erected with artistic
hand, and resting in air.   Great baskets of cut bread of every
variety, and of white bread no lack by any means, stood upon
the table likewise, one at every few ells.   For the rest, room
was left for dishes of enormous size, which should contain meat,
pork, bacon, and ox and pig puddings, and roast veal, fish, and
cheescake scattered over with sugar and cinnamon.   Here and
there stood large pewter dishes, which were to hold substantial
cabbages and abundance of peas.   As to sugar-basins, wine-
bottles, glass, and all other such table finery, they found no
room, nor were they there.

There stood upon another table great trays heaped up with
ready-cut bread and butter, covered with grated cheese and
smoked sausage.   There stood also, by dozens, bottles of
brandy, with their accompanying glasses and silver bowls, and
many other corked and red-sealing-waxed bottles, together with
various silver goblets and cups which were to be used for ale.

When Ma'msell Sara had seen all this, and changed and ad-
justed several things, as well as shaken her head at others, she
went *in lineâ rectâ* to the kitchen.   But—incredible! there she
found not a single person, excepting an old char-woman, who
blew up the fire, and moved about among the many pots.

"What is the meaning of this?" said Ma'msell Sara, with
much amazement, and in rather an angry tone, as she entered
into the empty kitchen.   "Where are all the people gone?
Where is the cook?   Where is Ma'msell Hallonquist?   Why
have they not yet lighted the oven?" asked she.

"Why-a," answered the woman, who was stone deaf, and

for that reason not exactly a favorite with Ma'msell Sara, who had a weak voice.

Wrinkling her eyebrows, she cleared her throat, and then screamed out again,

"Where are all the people? Where is ma'msell? Why is not every one in their place in the kitchen?"

"They are not here!" replied the woman, and laughed foolishly.

"Yes, I see that well enough, cat!" exclaimed Ma'msell Sara; "but where *are* they?"

"They are out," returned she.

"Yes, but, good Heavens! *where* are they?" repeated Ma'msell Sara.

"Well, I don't know of a certainty," replied she, laughing all the time; and then adding, in a whispering and sharp tone, "But I fancy they are gone into the housekeeper's room, and are dressing the bride."

"Ah, such a piece of folly!" said Ma'msell Sara, half aloud, and betook herself to the housekeeper's room. When she was come into the very neighborhood of this room, there certainly was no occasion for her to inquire where all the servant-maids were assembled, because such a tremendous chattering was heard there as could scarcely be conceived. But the moment that Ma'msell Sara opened the door, and became visible, all were silent as if they had taken hot porridge into their mouths. All looked taken in, and Ma'msell Sara astonished in the highest degree. She went forward, with slow steps, to the bride, who sat, horribly bedizened, amid a crowd of all the assembled maid-servants, and some strangers into the bargain. Ma'msell Sara surveyed her with a long and severe glance from head to foot, and then said, in a grave and dignified tone—

"I did not expect this of thee, my dear Lena!"

Lena looked down, blushed deeply, but answered not a word.

The cause of Ma'msell Sara's astonishment and anger was the following: Lena had, without asking her advice, or without following the universally-adopted custom of abandoning the bride's-crown when she is known not to be worthy to wear it, allowed herself to be bedizened, not alone with garland and crown, but with the latter of dimensions as large as that which King Pharaoh wears when he, in Hübner's Biblical History, sits and hardens his heart. She had, at the same time, a heap of flowers, pinchbeck, and finery, on her head, and in her ears, as well as having her hair frizzed into a bunch of disordered curls, which already hung as straight as a nail. For the rest, she had on an old black silk gown, three ells wide, which sat as scantily as a calfskin upon her already very massive figure, and which was too short, both in the body and the skirt, with short old-fashioned puffed-out sleeves, and horribly low in the bosom, which thus remained entirely bare, and was hung about with an incredible number of old pearl necklaces, brass chains, and suchlike trash. A broad crimson riband was tied on for a sash, with huge bows and hanging ends, thus completing the horribly tasteless toilette; and Lena, who otherwise had a very agreeable exterior, looked now like an actual scarecrow.

When Ma'msell Sara saw all this, and with it observed the foolish good-nature of the housekeeper, who had assisted in it—for she had lent Lena the black silk gown, and bedizened her up in this way—it was all she could do to avoid laughter; she succeeded, however, in doing so, and then, turning to this same housekeeper, she addressed her in the following manner, according to the expression always used in Voss's Louise:

"If Ma'msell had not come here, for the first time only in autumn, after the decease of the late lady, and therefore could not know the customs and manners of this family, as well as mine and my brother's wishes in a variety of cases, this childish bedizenment, which, I presume, is ma'msell's work, would greatly anger and astonish me. Now, however, it passes for nothing, but is readily forgiven for the good intention's sake, with the command that ma'msell immediately goes and attends to her duties as kitchen-maid; the dairy-maids to theirs; the poultry-woman to look after her hens; and every one, in one word, to her business, except Lotta, who, perhaps, can help poor Lena out of all this borrowed finery, as well as into her own handsome new black bombazine dress, with which she will wear the new silk handkerchief which she received from her husband; can help her also properly and decently arrange her beautiful hair, and to put it up into a so-called 'chinjong' in the neck, and then to place *this* upon it:" and with that Ma'msell Sara took out of the little bundle which she held in her hand an uncommonly beautiful white silk cap, with its beautiful rose in the neck, as well as a fine and ornamental piece of lace, or a so-called "lin," all which now were greatly admired by the whole assembly, but especially by old Mother

Ingrid, who, frozen and silent, sat in the chimney, and sipped out of a coffee-cup.

"Welcome, my dear Mother Ingrid! I did not see you for all these people," said Ma'msell Sara, and clapped the old and universally-beloved woman kindly on the shoulder.

"Nay, God bless you, ma'msell!" replied Gunnar's mother, and returned the clapping, and then spake still farther:

"Yes," said she, "that is something of a becoming head-or-nament for my future daughter-in-law. Nobody can hinder her from wearing *that*, and she will have use out of it as long as it lasts, for, look you, I had this cap of mine when I went for the first time to the Lord's table, and, God be praised! I saved both it and this black camlet dress when the fire went over us, for both of them lay in a chest which Gunnar got out almost at the risk of burning his clothes off him. And see, that cap of Lena's is spin and span new, and so terribly handsome and well-made."

The bride said nothing, and nobody knew in reality what she thought; but certain it is, that when she stood thus dress-ed, with the handsome new cap upon her glossy black hair, and with her bright complexion and dark eyes, she looked un-commonly well, although a something sharp, a something bold, a certain want of sensibility, lay in her glance and in her whole demeanor. Every body praised the new costume, and every thing now was once more good and beautiful, and full of bridal merriment.

"Gunnar must certainly have made a mistake about the *time*," thought Mother Ingrid silently to herself, as she looked with observing eyes at Lena, and saw the bulky figure of this otherwise smart girl.

CHAPTER XI.

THE time advanced now toward noon. Many of the wed-ding-guests were already come; and now even the rector and a few other gentry from the neighborhood had arrived. Every body, including the bridegroom, went up to the great hall— every one, with the exception of the bride, who went up by a back staircase to Ma'msell Sara's room, through the door-chinks of which she was to see the bridegroom in passing, but without being seen by him—an old custom which is never omitted among our West Gothland peasantry, but the particular meaning of which is unknown to the authoress, because the explanations which have been given to her seem so absurd, that she neither comprehends them nor troubles herself to quote them.

Every thing was now ready. The rector stood with gown and book, the clerk had given out the 337th hymn ; all the men stood with their hats in their hands ; the women with a devotional aspect and heaved sighs. Gunnar, who looked pale, but whose demeanor was manly, stood in the middle of the room, dressed in his simple blue home-spun coat, which was new, smart, and clean, with his hair in the old Swedish fashion parted on the forehead, and falling down each side of his face to the length of half an ell. His was a beautiful head, worthy of the pencil of Södermark, or the crayon of the good Marie Röhl ; and the expression, and the feelings which gave that expression life!—they ought to have been painted, and not by me, the unworthy one, but by my beloved Fredrika Bremer.

Mother Ingrid's tears fell fast down her furrowed cheeks, and Ma'msell Sara felt also moisture in her eyes, when she saw the young man who stood there, a living image of a silent, but great and mighty self-sacrifice. But now the squire came leading in Lena, and conducted her to the bride's chair, and such as took the trouble closely to observe him might have very soon remarked that he was deathly pale and trembled. But Lena! she kept her countenance well, and answered her *yes* loudly and distinctly. Gunnar made his response in a deep voice, and that only after a short pause, during which Mother Ingrid began to tremble, because once in her youth—not she herself, but a friend of one of her friends, was present, when the bridegroom said bluntly No, just when he ought to have said Yes. Her son, however, did not do so ; the pure, holy angel of truth pronounced with him his audible *yes*, but wept assuredly, because close beside the white-winged one, stood the black demon of falsehood, and whispered his base, cowardly Yes into the other ear. There stood they—Gunnar and Lena—like bright day and dark night, and their poor life became twilight.

When the marriage ceremony was over, the clergyman made

a short address to the new wedded pair; and almost every one thought they remarked that he spoke indulgently to the young married man, but somewhat severely to Lena. She cast her eyes down; her countenance was gloomy, and so was the expression of her glance.

After this the wedded couple were conducted to the sofa, and a tremendous wishing of good luck commenced. The first who offered their congratulations were the Squire, Ma'm-sell Sara, and Mother Ingrid. The Squire seemed not to know what he should properly fix his eyes upon, when he wished the new-married pair happiness, and by chance he just hit upon a piece of the old tapestry, which represented Satan tempting a human being. Mother Ingrid burst into tears, and Ma'msell Sara looked solemnly thoughtful, then mild and cordial as she took Gunnar's hand, and again a little gloomy as she offered hers to Lena.

Gunnar's thoughts during this time were as if they were benumbed, but they seemed to be suddenly aroused into life; when next after the three first congratulations, a young, unknown girl stepped forward, well dressed as a peasant maiden, but in the highest degree neat and elegant, although not properly in the costume of that part of the country. There were in her two large, oval, clear, blue eyes, two large round tears, as she heartily embraced Lena, and at the same time bashfully extended her warm hand to Gunnar. The girl herself looked as warm and excited as if she had just been dancing; a bright and clear crimson colored the beautiful round cheeks, which contrasted strongly with every one that was near her, who looked red-nosed and blue with the cold, because although for many days there had been fires in the great "king's hall," yet it was impossible to produce more than from eight to ten degrees of heat. The *lares* and *penates* wept through the whole day floods of tears, which ran down from the walls or else in deep window-niches, because they had from their hidden corners seen so many weddings, but seldom or never so much guile and deceit; seldom any thing which was so adverse; any thing which was so contrary to the feelings as was this farce.

If the moment had not been so solemn, Gunnar would have inquired who the young girl was, but now he thought that he could not do it, and the girl soon vanished in the crowd, and Gunnar forgot her, or rather thought no more about her.

And now came the hour of dinner, so much desired by so

many; and all the wedding guests betook themselves down
into the "guest-room," from which the odor of eatables came
perfuming the whole way.   It took a long time before every
body found a place, and they who had to arrange the guests
bawled themselves hoarse with saying, "Be so good!—Be so
good and step forward!"   And things did not get at all in
order, until they began almost to drag some of the guests
forward by the arms, and gently to push some others in the
back.   At length they were all seated; the clergyman beside
the bride, and Mother Ingrid beside her son.   These four
were quite silent in the beginning; every body else both ate
and talked softly, yet for all that there was a terrible noise, with
the stamping upon the stone floor of the whole number of
servant-maids in the family, while some strangers likewise, who
were running about and making as much noise as possible,
obstructed the attendants.   At last the minister began to say a
friendly word to the bride, and the bride boldly and freely
struck up a conversation with the minister.   With that Mother
Ingrid took occasion softly to clap Gunnar upon the arm, saying,
    "How art thou, my little Gunnar; thou lookest so pale?"
    "Oh, yes," replied Gunnar, "I am very well, only a little
out of sorts in my head.   But, dearest mother, who is that
young strange lass who sits there opposite, and nods so kindly
to Lena, and casts down her eyes so prettily; I scarcely ever
saw the like?"
    "Bless me!" answered Mother Ingrid, "do you not know
her?   It is Lena's sister—your new sister-in-law.   She is
named Elin, and only got here a little while ago, long after the
bride was dressed and all.   The horse was knocked up by the
way, so that she had to walk the last seven miles, and therefore she looks so warm."
    Lena, who heard this, and who wished much to have some
talk with Gunnar, joined in the conversation, and said,
    "Oh, bless me! in all the days of my life! is it possible that
you did not know my sister Elin?   I remember now, that you
were just then away when she was here for a short time, two
years ago.   She has come quite punctually to the wedding day;
though at the very last minute.   Mother, who lives a long way
up, in Wassbo, has been poorly; so Elin could not find in her
heart to set off before yesterday morning, for now she is better;
but she does not think she ought to stop here longer than the
day after to-morrow.   Do you think her like me?"

"Oh no, Heaven forbid!—not in the least! She is so very much younger than you are; and, besides, so merry and kind, and—and it seems to me as if you were not sisters," said Gunnar; and in Gunnar's answer it may be plainly seen that he had not been into the school of the great world, but merely in that of truthfulness and integrity.

"Yes, look you; the reason for our being so unlike," returned Lena, "is in this way. I favor father, and am dark, and she favors mother, who was always fair, like her; for all that, many people say that I am like her."

And now the bride called to Elin across the table, and every body was silent, to listen when the bride spoke.

"Bless me, Elin! Gunnar did not know thee! I did not remember that," said Lena cheerfully. Elin, however, blushed, and looked quite abashed, and Gunnar did just the same. Besides this, Lena's remark was made to Elin at the very moment when she was trying to avoid laughing at a good peasant woman, who sat close beside her at the table, and who, having managed with some difficulty, to cut her meat upon the plate with her knife and fork, laid them down as soon as that was done, and ate with her fingers. Elin had learned from her mother, who was brought up in a gentleman's family, and who had served in it till her marriage, and who now lived in a large church-town, a little more of the habits of civilized life than is found among the rural peasantry; besides this, as she did nothing but sit in the house and spin, weave, wash and get up the neighbors' fine caps, by which means her mother maintained herself, she therefore escaped a deal of the customary peasant habits, without being contaminated in any way by the vices and follies of city maidens. In her, there was a something simple and agreeable, which could not be called by any other name than that of good nature; and that, without doubt, is the most glorious gift which a woman can receive from the great Father of all.

Gunnar, as we know, drank no longer brandy, excepting now and then, when he was seduced to do so. He had not taken any abstinent pledge, but adhered to this system of temperance from pure conviction, because brandy, and the temper that it occasioned, were not attractive to Gunnar.

In the mean time, Ma'msell Sara knew that on this day he would not taste a drop of it, and for that reason she caused the strong and fragrant ale to circulate so much the more in-

dustriously.   Some of the less costly sorts of wine, also, were
from time to time carried round; and when it came to the
drinking of healths, two large bowls of punch and bishop were
brought in.   One would not be answerable for the rum coming
from Batavia, or the red wine from Bordeaux; but the mixture of all the ingredients was most delicious to those whose
taste was not spoiled; and it became a stimulus which, for the
first time in many weeks, had the power of diverting, in some
degree, the heart of the young bridegroom; and when the
guests, after having sat for several hours at the table, rose up,
he was no longer the pale gloomy Gunnar, who was lost in
strange thought, but the young man of former times, the gay,
merry, life-enjoying Gunnar, with blooming cheeks and flashing
eyes.   But those eyes, the truest interpreters of the children of
nature, sought only for one single object, and when it was found,
they rested calmly and joyfully upon it, forgetting *every thing* else.

The whole of the wedding company were soon requested to
go up again into the large "king's hall," where now the chandelier and the old fashioned lamps were lighted; those old-
fashioned lamps, set in mirrors, almost the only pieces of mov-
able furniture which had not been taken away when the place
passed from hand to hand, and which were still attached, as in
former days, to those old walls which they had reflected so
many hundred years, though now darkly and gloomily, because
the glass and the silvering were rather black than white.

Here they drank coffee, and here began general gayety and
merriment, which soon became noisy enough; the peasant
women grew talkative and excited, and the young fellows so
ill-mannered toward every one, that Ma'msell Sara thought it
high time to let the violins play, that a vigorous polska and the
dancing might begin.   That was soon arranged.   All those
who found themselves unstable in the legs, and who were the
most noisy, betook themselves quietly down to the laboring
men's apartment, or to the servants' hall; and those, again,
who were somewhat more moderate in the use of the excellent punch, made up for their short-comings by an immoderate
dance; and now nothing was heard but "Hurrah!   Hurrah!
Go on better!   Hurrah!   Let it now go as long as things will
hold together," etc. etc.

And look at Bengt, the gay, lively Bengt! he was the first,
and he was the last in the polska; and—which looked well—
the bridegroom was not much behind him.

"My word! that was a glorious polska! I never in all my time went through a better one!" said Gunnar, after a vehement dance, wiping his brow with the huge "bridegroom's kerchief," a gift from Ma'msell Sara; and then setting down his partner in the middle of the floor, who was quite unconscious, where she was, did as our lieutenants, chamberlains, royal secretaries, and many more can do, were it even through eight or ten rooms—dragged her off again, and placed her in the very same spot where he had brought her from. And for all that, ye lieutenants, secretaries, and squires! how many among you dance with any of our finical, ornamented, accomplished, and laced-up young ladies of the higher or middle ranks, with any thing like the spirit and youthful joy with which Gunnar danced with his young sister-in-law, Elin?

Very soon after this dance, and after the ale and punch had again briskly circulated, and when Gunnar was in such a state of animation and excitement as he had never been before, yet without being in the least degree what might be called intoxicated, it so happened that Elin and some other of the young wedding guests found themselves in one of the large, deep recesses of the windows in the great hall. Elin and the young girls were sitting, and Bengt and several other young fellows were standing before them, while Gunnar, who was taller than all the rest, leaned upon Bengt's shoulder, and talked with the girls.

"Ah, what a merry scene this is!" said the stranger girl; "we are sitting altogether as if in a little room of our own. I never saw such a queer house as this! I am both frightened and pleased when I come into it."

"Yes," replied Gunnar, "it would not be easy to find its fellow; and I say as you do, Elin dear; there is *something* which one feels, both good and bad, when one goes about in all these lofty rooms, and staircases, and passages, and hiding-places. I feel so strange at times — there goes quite a sudden thrill through me; but, for all that, it is very pleasant!"

"Oh, that was a lie!" said Still-man Olle, who had just then joined the group. What little bit of sense Olle had he had drowned in pure, good brandy, and he now was going about to pick a quarrel, were it even with the bridegroom, toward whom, as we know, he had no very friendly feelings. "It was a downright lie, that you liked it," continued he, turning to Gunnar, "but you are one of Satan's cowards and dastards, and, therefore, you are afraid of both goblins and ghosts, and such-like stuff; but look at *me!* I, on the contrary—"

"Yes, that is very well for you to say," answered Bengt, laughing. "It is good for us folks at the Hall not to remember any thing when we have to go in an evening up to the squire's loft and the count's chamber, in the southern tower there."

"Ah, how was that?" asked Elin, whose curiosity was excited in the highest degree by this conversation.

"Oh, yes, I'll tell you about that," whispered Gunnar in her ear, "as soon as Olle goes his way; but it is not worth while to begin about it while he stays, for he is now so fuddled that he does not know at all what he says."

Gunnar did not answer Olle, but asked Elin whether she had been all over this old goblin-nest."

"No, Heaven defend me! certainly not!" replied Elin. "I never was here but once before, and then I was only in the women-servants' room, and in the kitchen."

"Ah, that is charming!" exclaimed Gunnar; "then I will some day go about every where with you, for nobody knows better than I do every secret place, hole, and corner! For, you see, I have so often had to go about every where with Ma'msell Sara, when she wanted things putting to rights—repaired, or so."

"But I am sorry to say," answered Elin, rather mournfully, "I have not, indeed, many days to spend here; for I must set off home again, at farthest, the day after to-morrow."

"Ah, that is a great pity!" exclaimed Gunnar, anew, and his young, handsome, and but the moment before, so gay and animated countenance looked now quite tragic.

"But one might really go and see it to-morrow," remarked Bengt.

"Ah, yes, that can be done very well, and we will do it too; or what say you, dear Elin?" asked Gunnar, kindly, but not gayly.

"Nay, nay, look ye; there is no joking in that, as there can't be when he troubles himself so about the sister-in-law setting off back again. Ha! ha! ha!" screamed and laughed Olle. "Nay, nay, Gunnar will, maybe, keep her all his life," continued he, stupidly impudent, and at the same time in loud and derisive tone. "Perhaps he will make an exchange! Ha! ha! ha! Exchange our old, black Lena for that beautiful

young thing that sits there in the corner. Ha! ha! ha!
Come here with thee, thou little lass, so that I may have a
good look at thee, and give thee a kiss!"

And with that Olle crushed himself into the midst of them,
who tried to keep him back, and succeeded in catching hold of
Elin by the arm.

"The devil take you!" said Gunnar, in a whisper in Olle's
ear, and at the same time so emphatically, that he sneaked out
of the circle, and went his way.

"That was an unmannerly fellow!" said Elin, and put in
order her delicate little shawl, which Olle's rude hand had disarranged.

"Ah, he is a regular wretch!" said another of the young
girls.

"Yes, a perfect monster!" added a third.

Gunnar merely looked after Olle, and exchanged a glance
with Bengt, as well as a few words, of which only these were
audible, "Ah, I think you need not trouble yourself about
him;" and these words were said by Bengt to Gunnar.

"No," said Elin, who, with the quickness of invention usual
to women, sought now to divert the storm from the mind of the
men. "Now I shall get to know all that story of the count's
chamber in the southern tower, and why it was called so. I
know nothing about it except the name only: 'The count's
chamber in the southern tower' sounds like something spectral.
I don't at all believe, however, that I should see any thing,
though I were alone in the dark, even at this Grantorp."

The others laughed.

"Yes, you will have to believe that there is nothing to make
fun of," said Bengt; "but now Gunner shall begin and tell us—
for he knows it best—about the legend of the 'count's chamber,' and the 'loft,' and after that the history of one particular
evening when Olle was in a pretty stew!"

"Ah, yes, dear Gunnar! tell us about that," said Elin and
the other girls.

"Ay," said Gunnar, and drew in a chair, upon which he
seated himself just before Elin, "ay, as to the count's chamber
in the southern tower, that has to do with the manners of ancient days! Many, many years ago, there lived a count here
who owned the whole demesne, and because of this count, perhaps, it is that it is called 'the count's demesne' by many old
people; and this count was a horribly wicked man, both to-

ward his people and his wife. He seldom went away from home, and governed them like a Turk; but the countess, on the contrary, was the regular image of an angel, so good and compassionate, and so wonderfully beautiful, and therefore the count was jealous of all the menfolk that were about, and even of his own squire. And now it so happened that the count had to set out on a journey which would keep him away for several days, but just as he was about to cross the courtyard, with his squire beside him, his horse made such a devilish plunge, that the squire was thrown to the ground, and his arm was broken; and in the morning I will show you, Elin dear, where it was, because the stone stands there yet against which he broke his arm, and it is called to this day 'the squire's stone.' It has never been taken away, and it never can be, for they say that it goes nearly through the whole earth, just exactly as a good or a bad conscience goes through a man. But look you, now! the wicked count did not believe that the squire had broken his arm, for there was nothing at all to be seen there. The count, however, made pretence that he believed it, and took another squire with him, and went on his journey, and kissed his young wife when he set off; and I will show you in the morning, Elin dear, where she stood, for it was upon a stone which is to this day called the 'countess's stone;' and all young ladies and women of rank were accustomed at that time to mount upon it when they rode out on horseback.

"But now it was true that the squire had really broken his arm, and broken it very badly, and there was no doctor at hand to be had; but in the evening, when the squire's pains were very great, the countess, who was the best woman in the world, went up to his loft—and that you will, perhaps, see in the morning, Elin dear—where he lay high up under the roof. When the countess came up, the youth lay upon his bed, and she knelt down beside it, that she might bind up his arm with spices, and other healing means. But just as she was doing so —but it is a dreadful history, you must know—she heard heavy footsteps coming up the stairs, and as she knew that she was doing no wrong, she still continued on her knees, as she was, when—the count came through the doorway! And then, my friends, then he would not allow himself any time to hear the truth, but, piff! paff! he shot his wife with the one pistol, and the squire with the other; and so they both lay, and swam in their blood, with their heads together, and as if they had kissed each other. And there, in the loft, one sees the marks of the shot and the blood, which stuck to the wall; and those spots are called ' the kiss of death.'

"But now, look you, here comes the most remarkable part; just in the same moment when the count shot his wife and his young squire, repentance came over him; and when he learned from all his household how innocent the young death-sufferer was, then his remorse grew day by day, and he had no rest; but he traveled, first of all, as far as Jerusalem, to the grave of the Redeemer, and there he lamented his sin. He then came back, and never again was wicked, or cruel, or passionate, but pious as a lamb; and never once went out, but fastened up all these grand rooms, and lived himself, both night and day, up in the count's chamber in the southern tower, and that is the reason why the room is so called; and one can see very well, on the floor, how he walked up and down, from one corner to another, in his great and terrible repentance."

When Gunnar had ended, all remained silent, petrified with horror.

"Ha! that is a dreadful story," said Elin, at length; "and he was a terribly wicked gentleman who could act in that way to a virtuous wife."

"True," said Gunnar, after a little silence. "But, do you know, Elin dear, I have often and often thought about the business, and tried to put myself in the count's place; and, do you know, my friends, that I for my part can not so entirely blame him, for, do you know what—if one loved one's wife as much as he seemed to do" (and with this Gunnar heaved a deep and undissembled sigh), "and if he then doubted her, and then afterward found her beside the squire's bed! Yes, God knows what a poor wretch might do! and God be thanked for every day when one is not so tempted of the devil!"

"Yes, indeed; but—" sighed Elin, "but," added she after a short silence, "as we thanked Gunnar for this pleasant story, let us now know all about that evening of which you spoke."

"Ay, that was masterly," said Bengt, laughing; "now tell us about it, Gunnar."

"Yes," began Gunnar, "and, first of all, you must know that many people believe that both the count, and the countess, and the squire, and perhaps many more, haunt this old owlet's nest; and—God knows best whether one should believe so! I myself have never exactly seen any thing, but still I would not swear

D

that there is nothing to be seen, for all that. But as to that, let it be as it may; every body, be they better or be they worse, takes good care neither to go up into the loft, nor into the count's chamber in the southern tower; and there has been many a one here at the hall, who, for many and many a year, never at any time have put their noses in there, because they are well barred and bolted, and Ma'msell Sara keeps the keys in her own hands. Thus, at least, was it with me, for I had been here five whole years without having ever done more than peep through the keyhole one Sunday when the gentlefolks were out. However, about two years ago, when there was such an unmanageable quantity of fruit on all the trees, I had to help the gardener to carry up the apples one Saturday after-noon. Ma'msell Sara and the lasses, they spread them out, and I carried them up. But then, when the guest-room (where we ate our dinner) was as full as it would hold, Ma'msell Sara got into a trouble to know where she should ever put the rest. But, my troth! what did I do then but stand to it, that they could very well put all the rest of the fruit up in the loft, or else in the count's chamber, for, look you, I was determined that *there* I would go. But you should have seen what eyes I had brought on myself!

" The lasses looked as if they were frightened out of their senses; and Ma'msell Sara stared at me just as if she had said, ' And would you dare to do so in an evening!' But, look you, I dared to do it! But the gardener, you see, he is old, and an old crock into the bargain," (added Gunnar, in a low voice, be-cause the gardener and his whole family were among the wed-ding guests), "he was determined that he would not go, and none of the girls would, and so there I had to go down into the men-servants' room to get some help, but I found nobody there but Olle. Look you, however, when he knew what business was going on, and *where* he should have to go, he said directly that he had got such a dreadful headache he could not move from the spot. I laughed at him to his face, but he stuck to it, and with that story I was forced to go back and to carry up all the fruit by myself, for nobody but Ma'msell Sara and I undertook the business; and Heaven knows I did not hurry myself at all up there, for I wished to look well about me every where, when I had once got in. At last Ma'msell Sara laughed. and said that I must make haste, for she was so cold. But I fancy,' added he, in a lower voice, "that our good ma'msel' was a *little* bit afraid, for it was almost pitch dark when we came down.

"In the evening, when I went into the men-servants' room, we fellows talked about it, and Bengt was quite mad that he had not been with us; but look you, Olle, who always gets out of the way of danger, began to insult me, and said that I now talked so courageously and boldly, but that he knew precisely that I had been as frightened as a hare, and trembled in every joint, and that I had held by Ma'msell Sara's skirts; and God knows what stupidity besides he did not utter. And at last, when I got angry and threatened him with a stick, he then was silent for a while; but when he saw that I was in good humor again, he began once more, and at last defied me, for a whole measure of brandy, late, and dark, and dismal as it was, to go up alone, either to the loft or to the count's chamber; and, only think! both Lars and Overseer Anders held with him. Now, however, I was no longer angry, but hurt; because I never was angry with Anders, for he is a devilish good and clever fellow, nor with Lars either, for he is as stupid as a sow; but I was hurt at them, and I now was determined to show them what I dared and what I dared not do, and that without a drop, much more a measure of brandy; so therefore I took all three, Anders, and Lars, and Olle, with me, and Bengt followed for company's sake, and we all of us went up to speak with Ma'msell Sara, and I prayed her as civilly as I could to give me the key, that I might sleep up there the whole night; and I assured her on my conscience that I would not eat a single pear or apple, nor touch any thing else. Bengt remembers what was her answer:

"'No, Gunnar,' said she, 'you shall not do that. That you have courage and spirit to go up there, is plain enough by your begging so earnestly for it, but I have reasons of my own which determine me *never* to let this key go out of my hands, let it be to whomever it may, and I will never go from my determination.'

"I cannot deny but that I became nervous, when she said so: indeed, such a wise and excellent person as she is has her sufficient reasons, although she may keep them concealed. After that, not one of the fellows said a word, except Olle, who said that I was very glad to have escaped! Did one ever hear such a thing?" continued Gunnar after a little silence.

His auditors were silent, dejected, and amazed.

But now Olle came staggering back to them, and exclaimed in a loud voice,

"What in all the world! You are sitting here yet, you Gunnar, and making a fuss with your sister-in-law! I shall go and tell that to your old Lena, ha! ha! ha! Yes, that I shall do on the spot! ha! ha! ha!"

"Ah, thou art one of the devil's lubbers, and shalt hold thy peace!" said Gunnar, half aloud, and ground his teeth. With that he rose from his seat and walked across the room, and went up to Lena, to whom he spoke some kind words—impelled by, God knows best what sort of feeling.

When he left Lena, his mother pulled him by the coat, and, kindly nodding to him, said,

"You are soon going away, dear lad! You must always love and respect your wife, for then it will at all times go well with you."

Gunnar, pleased by his mother's approbation, nodded to her in return, and all the *lares* and the *penates* smiled at the genuine affection which filled these hastily exchanged glances. They smiled for joy, we say, because the *lares* and the *penates* are certainly all of them good, and they rejoice at the virtues of the good.

But now the time was come when people were *to dance with the bride*, because all those who had taken a drop too much were now come to themselves again.

This dance is conducted thus : All and each of the wedding-guests dance a turn or two with the bride, press her hand significantly, and give with this pressure the so-called " dance-money," be it more or less, according to every one's various means and opportunity. The bride makes a short bow or nod of acknowledgment, and gives that which she has received to some one else, who places it upon a tray or plate held for the purpose.

The squire began the dance. There was a something dull and strange about it. He did not properly go round with her, but the letter which he placed in Lena's hand, and which little Elin afterward received upon a silver waiter, was large, and contained gold. Ma'msell Sara did not give very much ; these were her thoughts : " If they need any thing more in the time to come, I would rather give it to Gunnar."

The young gentlemen of the house had each received his ten-dollar bank-note from papa, but little Janne had already lost his, and cried dreadfully, and then he found it again; and all this he told to Lena during the dance, because Lena had waited upon the tutor and the boys, and was a tolerable favorite with the latter. Mother Ingrid gave a silver three-dollar piece, which she had kept ever since she was young. The tutor went out of the way to avoid dancing with Lena, but laid his mite at once upon the waiter which Elin held.

Olle nearly threw down the bride, that he might give her a dirty, tattered twelve-penny note, so unstable was he on his legs. But when Bengt came with his new twenty-five-penny piece, what a dance there was! He swung Lena round at such a rate, that in a moment she was three-quarters round the room; and when he swung her past Olle, who stood leaning against a wall, not far from Gunnar, Olle exclaimed,

"No, no, you Bengt! no, no; go moderately! Use the bride gingerly, else how is she to get through all the bridal business? ha, ha, ha! Look at old Lena! how she scampers and goes! ha, ha, ha!"

"Be silent, you dog! If you can not keep your mouth shut, trouble may come of it: that I promise you!" whispered Gunnar, and cast, at the same time, such a glance at him, as sent him off, crest-fallen and staggering, to another corner of the room, where there stood a wooden can of ale.

Just then Elin came up with her waiter, and as Lena was dancing she stood beside Gunnar.

"That is too heavy for you, dear Elin," said he, with a certain kind of peasant politeness.

"Oh, nonsense!" replied Elin; "it is hardly any weight. I should not care if the tray were ever so heavy; but, as for me, poor creature," added she, in an under voice, and cast down her eyes so beautifully, "I have nothing to put upon it for my own part; I have not as much money as I would willingly give to you, and nothing to offer if I danced with Lena, unless I should, some time hence, give you something that you may like."

"Oh, indeed!" replied Gunnar, with all that politeness which, with the child of nature, comes direct from the heart; "I think you would do enough, little Elin, if you would hem the fine bride's-handkerchief for Lena, and make me a nightcap; then I should forget all my lifetime that I must some day be wrapped in a shroud."

"Hush! how you are talking!" said Elin, and looked up into the dark-blue eyes of her new brother.

But at length this disagreeable offering-dance came to an
end, and the tidings arrived that supper was ready for the
whole bridal company. And now nobody must by any means
imagine to themselves that it was a *société comme il faut*, who
quietly betook themselves by two and two down the stairs to
the supper-room. No, heaven forbid! Here all, and each one
for himself, rushed shrieking, crowding, pushing, thrusting,
down the stone stairs; and the voice of Olle was heard unceasingly bawling one fragment of an old song after another;
and when he saw Elin going down the stairs by the side of
Gunnar, he shouted at the top of his voice,

"Yes, indeed, Gunnar! now you can sing the song you love
best—

> 'Elin is my sugar deary;
> Lena is my coal-black sow;
> Elin is my bell so cheery;
> Lena is my milking cow!'

Ha, ha, ha! Is not thy song in that way? I fancy I can remember something like that. Ha, ha, ha!"

"How willingly would I teach him to keep his mouth shut,
if I were only near enough!" said Gunnar between his teeth;
but Elin, who heard what he said, answered him gently.

"Oh, Gunnar," she said, "you should not vex yourself about
him; he is really quite drunk."

When the whole of this excited wedding-company had
reached the so-called guest-room, which again served for their
eating-hall, there was seen another essential difference between
this assembly and one of the same kind among educated people, because, instead of gentlemen who drew in each his chair,
each one with his lady, in the midst of incessant conversation
and courtesies, there occurred here, among this noisy and half-
drunken company, some minutes of perfect silence and tranquillity. Every one stood with folded arms and bowed head
—the grace before meat was said; they thanked God for the
food which they were about to receive, while we, "educated
people," scarcely allow ourselves time for thanks for that which
we have already received; probably because we seldom reflect
how difficult it is to get, and how impossible, unless God assist
us. "*Voilà la différence.*"

But now the wedding-day was ended. It is true that they
danced for an hour after supper; but the dance did not take
its proper circuit, or, rather, it was quite too circuitous; for,

as the heads of the dancing cavaliers were much heavier than usual with the good ale, punch, and brandy, and the feet of the ladies varied so much from the true course, with the good fare of which they had partaken, all were glad to make the best of their way home, and sink into the embrace of Morpheus.

It was late before Gunnar slept, and then he dreamed that he was conducting Elin up to the squire's loft, and that they two stood together and contemplated "the kiss of death" upon the wall. He awoke.

"Yes, that may become true!" exclaimed he, as he awoke, and lay and thought about how, on the coming morrow, he should go up and thank the gentlefolks for all the great trouble and expense they had been at, and, at the same time, beg so urgently from Ma'msell Sara that Elin might have a peep into the squire's loft and the count's chamber, just to gratify her, because she was only going to stay over the day—which, to the great delight of every one, was Sunday, so that Christmas seemed to be a little extended. Gunnar could not sleep, but lay awake, and thought upon Elin! And we, we happen just now to think, why is it that people so frequently see great and terrible crimes committed among persons of the lower and un-educated classes, and so very seldom in the higher—where, again, small failings, vices under a thousand dissimilar forms, in part reveal themselves, in part hide in darkness, under the mask of dissimulation? May not the cause of this difference be sought for, and found, in the self-knowledge, which is a consequence of all cultivation, all study, all intuitive observa-tion of the world, and all its manifestations? People learn to know other men and other relationships, and, at the same time, to know themselves, and those who belong to them. Hence it is that we are on the look-out and watch over ourselves; that we consider, in the first place, what may be; that we set up defenses, and the palisadoes of experience, against the strong and powerfully insinuating passions, which appear large and apparent, like the lions and leopards of the woods, while the lesser failings are allowed to steal in unawares, without any opposition, like guileful vipers thronging in upon us from all sides. We educated people are thus at all times prepared for every thing which may occur. Whatever happens to us we have read of beforehand, heard of, seen examples of, and we know already how we should, ought, *must* conduct ourselves.

The uneducated man, on the other side, who has never before-hand considered a similar case to his own, rushes on to meet it merely in the way in which passion and instinct prompt him, and never guards himself from approaching the abyss of crime, merely because he does not see it, unless it should lie like a pitfall before him.

Gunnar thought upon Elin, and did not believe that in so doing he did any thing wrong. He did not, indeed, think of her in order to obtain her as his own, but merely of how good she looked—how smart and neat was her figure in the dance—how beautifully she talked—how cordially she seemed attached to her sister Lena—how full of affection in speaking of her mother—how gentle and polite toward the other girls—and how painful it was that she must so soon return home. Gunnar did not believe that he did wrong by these thoughts. On the contrary, he regarded them as good, and agreeable to God, and assuredly felt no regret on their account. But ah! how would one of us have acted? I know how, but I can scarcely explain it. Among a hundred, one might, perhaps, have driven away the thought as dangerous, and the others have retained it, with a mingled enjoyment and a bitter regret, thinking on the difference between the two sisters, and not having clearly ascertained in what direction the heart was going, and precisely by that means being enabled to lay the reins upon it.

Gunnar, however, did neither; he merely thought on Elin, and luxuriated in these thoughts.

CHAPTER XII.

WHEN at length the morning came, both Gunnar and Lena went up-stairs to the gentlefolks and thanked them.

The squire said, but without looking up, "You are very welcome to all; it is nothing to return thanks for."

"Yes, to be sure," replied Lena, pertly, and taking the lead in the conversation.

Ma'msell Sara took the new-married couple by the hand, wished them much happiness, and then made a little appropriate speech to them, to which Gunnar listened, weighing deeply every word, but with an unchanging countenance. Lena, on the contrary, shed torrents of tears, which she wiped away with the corner of her neckerchief—but without hearing or thinking about a single word.

The Squire stole away during this address; and this allowed Gunnar to act upon his resolve of begging just to have a peep into the loft to gratify little Elin.

"Oh, yes, willingly, my child, replied Ma'msell Sara, with a little smile. "Your sister Elin," continued she, turning to Lena, "is, I think, such an agreeable and well-behaved girl, that I will gladly give my permission for this, if it will gratify her. Go, therefore, down, and ask her to come up now, that I may go with you; I have some little matters to arrange up there."

And with that she took her green woolen shawl, and sought out the great rusty keys, while Lena went down for Elin. Elin, however, made her appearance alone; and they could not help remarking that Lena remained below.

"So you are, then, curious about the squire's loft, and the count's chamber, dear child?" said Ma'msell Sara to Elin, in a kindly and jocular tone, while they three were going up the many and steep stairs.

"Ah, yes," said Elin, feeling really ashamed that the polite ma'msell should take such a deal of trouble on her account. "Ah, yes, it is Gunnar's fault, who set me all agog about that old loft and the chamber; for I never have seen such a one before."

They were now come up to the loft, the door of which Ma'msell Sara opened; but instead of entering herself, she went into a garret to look at the old fur covering of a sledge, to see whether it was moth-eaten or not. Gunnar and Elin went, therefore, alone into the so-called squire's loft. The winter morning was cloudy and gray, and the daylight came scantily in through a small window high up in the wall, the little panes of which rattled to the keen north wind in their crazy leaden fastening.

"Ha!" said Elin, and crept involuntarily to Gunnar's side.

"You are cold, Elin, dear," said Gunnar, and wrapped around her the skirt of his new blue homespun coat; but Elin drew herself aside, and said—

"Oh, no! I really am not cold, but it is so mysterious and dismal, just like the inside of a church."

D*

"Perhaps you would like to go away?" inquired Gunnar.

"Oh, no!" replied Elin; "I really must look at the horrible stains."

Gunnar conducted her, silently and softly, to a gloomy corner of the room, and when there, he said, taking hold of her by the arm—

"Look here, Elin, dear; here stood the bed; there lay the young squire, and there bent the countess upon her knee, and" —with this he pointed with Elin's hand—"there, upon the wall, do you see?—the kiss of death!"

Elin crept nearer to Gunnar, and they stood silently for a long time, with their eyes riveted upon the stains of blood, nearly obliterated by age, which tradition insisted upon were the united blood of the young squire and his lady.

"Do you know, Elin," said Gunnar, after a long silence, "do you know, I have seen this before without exactly thinking so much about it; but now! do you know what comes into my mind? Ay, perhaps it is an unchristian thought! Do you believe, Elin, that it could be possible that she, the countess, did, after all, love him, the squire? Do you believe it? Tell me, Elin, do you think that she could be so wicked—in heart, though, for nobody could observe it, or insist upon its being true? What do you think about the matter, dear Elin?"

"Oh, I do not know exactly what to believe," answered Elin, who had become quite sad. "I never would willingly believe evil of any body; and it would, indeed, be a horrible sin for any one to love another instead of their own married partner."

"Yes, certainly, it would be so," replied Gunnar, sighing deeply, and letting go Elin's arm, which he had hitherto held close to his heart.

But now came in Ma'msell Sara, who looked rather cloudy, like every thing else, this winter morning; for, although she had not found a single moth in the fur, she had found three or four rat-holes.

"Well, my child," said she, "you have studied perfectly the whole of the squire's loft, I hope!"

After, therefore, the most hasty glance into the count's chamber, they went down into the more inhabited portions of the house.

This day put an end to all the business of the wedding. Elin returned home. Gunnar sighed deeply when he saw the

last glimpse of her vehicle; thought incessantly upon her, and
again returned to his daily work.   Lena did the same; but she
no longer took as much pains as formerly with her toilet, nor
yet to conceal her situation, which every body remarked, excepting Gunnar, who seldom looked at Lena, and who saw as
little of her as he could, although he always was kind and
friendly toward her.

Time went on in this way to the third winter month, and
March came with long, light days, but cold and harsh, just like
people in good circumstances who are totally free from passion.

CHAPTER XIII.

"I should very much like to go to the fair to buy myself a
cow and a couple of oxen," said Gunnar to the squire, on one
of the first days in March.

"You need not do that," replied his master, without looking
him in the face, and pushing his stick desperately in the ground
at the same time, as if he wanted to see how far it would go;
"you—you shall have the cattle from me at your first setting
up; afterward you—but no need to talk about that."

Gunnar was really very glad of this gift.   He had no love for
Lena; he did not long for the time when he should pass his
days alone with her; but still he longed, like every one else
who has passed his twentieth year, to see the smoke ascend
from his own hearth, to sleep under his own roof, and to eat of
his own food; in a word, to settle himself, and to be, at least,
master within the bounds of his own home.   To make this
home as comfortable and as excellent as possible was Gunnar's
wish—as, indeed, it is the wish of every other person in his, or
in far better circumstances.   All the money which remained
after the purchase of the cattle just mentioned, the means for
which was the sum which came in at the wedding, and the
unpaid wages of Lena and Gunnar, was to be appropriated to
the purchase of plenishing for the house; and now Gunnar was
enabled to add the sum which the cattle would have cost to the
other, which would thus provide them with many more com-
forts than he had hoped for at the beginning.   This really filled

Gunnar's heart with a youthful gladness; and in the evening he said to his companions in the men-servants' room—

"The squire is, after all, upon the whole, a good and honorable gentleman, although I never before could get that notion into my head, nor even bear him."

"And I *never* shall bear him," replied Bengt; "for he is a false and cunning fellow; never looks folks rightly in the face; says one thing and means another; and, according to my opinion, never does any thing for nothing; and some fine day, as true as I am speaking, he'll have his payment for the cattle, and will get it out of you by hard dealings: that you'll come to see, if you only live long enough. But as to ma'msell, she is good."

"Yes, yes, I'd have you think whether I shan't tell the squire what you have been saying about him," said Olle, with a malicious and hateful laugh.

"Yes, I shall trust you for doing that," replied Bengt, "for you have a red head, like the squire himself; and, hark ye! I never trust any body upon whose head our Lord has put a fox-skin cap."

"Nay, ugly they are," said Gunnar, who was thinking about something else, but who, nevertheless, would not let an opportunity pass without expressing his dislike of Olle, whom he never could bring himself to endure, because, envious and malicious as he always showed himself to be, he was when sober false and bad, and when drunk obstinate and bad. He was at this moment quite tipsy, and just in the humor to irritate Gunnar all the more, as he felt in a position to defend himself from attack, because he now placed himself in the doorway, and could in a moment be down at his beloved distillery, where Gunnar never went.

"Ay, ay!" said he, jeeringly; "you get cattle and other things from the squire; perhaps he may make you a present of an eldest son as well. Ha! ha! ha!"

"Only come out with such a word as that again!" said Gunnar, and looked up to his gun, which was hanging on the wall; but Olle had not stayed to hear the first word of Gunnar's reply: he was already in his brandy sanctuary before Gunnar had spoken, and had swallowed many gulps of this desolating water before Gunnar's blood subsided into calm, and his thoughts hastened again toward the pictures of the future, which incessantly reflected themselves in his fancy, and which were far less dark than he could have believed some months ago. Gunnar had never, from his childhood, been his own master; had never had the management of his own time; he had, in a word, from his boyish years, been a servant; he had never been able to turn to the right hand nor to the left, according to his own pleasure; had always been compelled to obey commands or prohibitions. He now, on the contrary, saw a time just before him, when, in the intervals of active and zealous labor (and labor never frightened Gunnar), he could do that which he listed; could, if he pleased, go at the earliest cock-crow, with his gun upon his shoulder, out into the woods, and stroll about there as long as he chose, or till hunger drove him home with his heavy game-bag—for Gunnar was, as we know, an excellent shot; or, on the same terms, he could betake himself, in the fresh morning or the cool silent evening, in his little boat to the lake, to pull up one fish after another, for Gunnar was likewise a lucky fisherman, and understood the art very well. He had been born and brought up on the banks of a great inland lake, rich in fish, where, during the whole of his childhood, and afterward in his youth, he amused himself day and night. From this cause, therefore, he mostly managed all the fishing at Grantorp, whenever they wished to have fish to eat; not, however, in the old aristocratic way, where there was the proper fisherman of the establishment, but either it was bought, or it was taken by the servants of the house.

He would now, in the evening, do carpenter's work just as he pleased—chairs, tables, chests, and such things; he would go to church every Sunday, and every Sunday evening he would play on his violin, and sing as much and as loud as he liked. He would, in time, when he had saved money by his gun, by fishing, and other things, buy himself a horse or else a mare, which should have foals, because he had for them an inborn passion; and, in his many brilliant pictures of the future, often stood the image of Elin, who came to see her sister in some beautiful Whitsuntide holidays or at a merry Christmas. In the former case he would amuse her by taking her out upon the lake in his boat; and in the last, he would make for her a stained and polished workbox, for he had learned how to do this from a city cabinet-maker, whom Ma'msell Sara had once had at the Hall.

Another image had likewise its place in these pictures, which began to be more and more prominent as well as that it pos-

sessed a certain pleasure for Gunnar ; namely, he was very
fond of children, and when he saw the gardener's pretty little
lad of seven years old, he now often thought, "I may myself
have such a one in seven years and some months."

Strange enough was it that even Lena, whom he certainly
could not bring himself to love, scarcely to tolerate, did not
very much stand in the way of these pictures. It is true, she
was a clever, industrious, active wife, whom he but seldom
saw, and who, when he came home, had all clean and in order,
with a good meal ready for him, while she sat at her spinning-
wheel, or in her loom, which buzzed and rattled, so that he
escaped much conversation with her, to which he felt himself very little inclined, however much she sought for it;
yet at the same time he was always friendly and good-tempered toward her. And Lena, on her side, was extremely
affectionate towards Gunnar, as well as tolerably kind and
reasonable. Sometimes she had, indeed, her own particular meaning in her inquiries respecting the purchase of
the furniture and other movables. Gunnar, however, could
not greatly object to that, because, on the one hand, Lena's
meaning was extremely prudent, and on the other, the greater
portion of the expense fell upon her; for, singular enough!
although she constantly had money—constantly bought all
kinds of "things," and always paid, if not at the very time
when she took the wares, at least when the traveling merchant
came next on his rounds—constantly went to all the fairs in the
town, and always bought something "fine" there ; yet she
had still, notwithstanding, two years' wages unpaid in the
Squire's hands.

Gunnar was thus almost consoled for his compulsory marriage. Besides this, people soon accustom themselves to their
fate in youth, and adorn it with all the flowers which fancy and
hope can assemble ; and not until some time has passed do
they make the discovery that these flowers have never bloomed,
although they were even at one time so fortunate as to see
them in bud.

CHAPTER XIV.

It was now the 14th of March, that time for "flitting," when many a one leaves the *lares* and *penates* which protected him in the house, to seek for others similar in another home; for, according to *our* belief, these remain in the empty house, and never quit it.

The day for the flitting was Wednesday; and already, on the preceding Saturday, had Gunnar and Lena arranged for their movables going to the little farm, as well as for obtaining permission to go there on Sunday, together with Bengt, to get the place a little in order, as the people who were to remove thence were already gone, But when Sunday came, Lena was ill; she said she had a severe pain in her head, and was obliged to lie down, so that Gunnar and Bengt went alone.

"Ah, how splendidly and famously you will live here at Vika!" said Bengt, as they stowed away the new furniture in the new, handsome, and spacious sitting-room. "Here you are coming to live like a prince! Here you have a room both large and fine, and a washhouse; and that pretty little chamber, there, on the other side of the passage; and the little orchard, and the wood, and meadow, and all the great lake in front, and the meadows on the other side. And such a famous cow-house, and all! Don't you remember what a sorrow you made about it at first, before Christmas? Yet, there was certainly something to be troubled about. You are, however, just as lucky as if you had sat upon a wishing stool!"

"Oh! I can not exactly say so," replied Gunnar, in an under voice, because, precisely at the very moment when Bengt was talking about the wishing stool, Gunnar had clambered up to it for a little moment in imagination, and, behold! an image not at all resembling Lena stood there, in the very foreground.

"Yes, and so can I say too," returned Bengt, "and you deserve—I don't know what—because you would not take me for your servant instead of that bull-headed Abraham. I have just now thought about it, and I fancy that Lena will make a managing and a capital mistress, who will keep every thing exceedingly clean, and will give plenty to eat, though she may, between whiles, quarrel a little."

"Yes, Heaven knows!" answered Gunnar, and thought upon something quite different, and did not think that he was, by so doing, guilty of any thing which was in the least wrong.

"Yes, but look, now, how wondrously neat and handsome it is here!" said Bengt, when they had put every thing in its place, and a good fire was burning on the hearth. Gunnar set out butter, bread and cheese, and brandy; for whilst the work had been going on, the mid-day had already arrived.

"Here's a health! now let us drink to each other; and thou shalt have my thanks for every day that we have been together, and for all the help thou hast given me," said Gunnar, with tears in his eyes; and taking one glass of brandy himself, he offered the other to Bengt.

"Yes, thanks and health!" returned Bengt, striking his glass against that of his companion, "and home and farm-luck to you now, and all time! And it is very wise of you," added he, after both he and Gunnar had emptied their glasses to the bottom, "to take a drop now that you are your own master; for a man may very well take a sup now and then without becoming a drunkard, and he may very well be saved without taking the 'temperance pledge;' and they are foolish who do so, when they can, of themselves, be temperate. But, look you! for old incurable drunkards, and such poor wretches as can not stand alone, the 'temperance pledge' is very well; for, you see, then they know of a certainty that damnation waits them, not exactly for taking a sup; for I don't believe, for my part, that damnation troubles itself about that, but because they are oath-breakers, and do it when, with their hand upon the book, they swore to let it alone. Look you, that is the business, and those are my thoughts about it."

Gunnar was of Bengt's opinion, and considered himself to be such a rational fellow, that he could take a drop but always in moderation. He said he should require it, now that he must so much more frequently be in the wood, and upon the lake. They again took each of them a stout glass, but neither of them felt it any more in their heads than when one of our fine gentlemen takes a mandarin cup of tea into his.

Towards evening, the two young men having finished their business, determined to take a little sail upon the open lake, which was bright as a mirror. This year, the ice had been so slender, and had melted so early, that already, in March, it had disappeared, and the lake lay now pure and bright, and the evening sun saw itself reflected upon its waters, and smiled thereat, like a young pleasure-loving maiden.

"What a monstrous handsome boat you've got there! What did you give Nils Andersson for it?" asked Bengt.

"Oh," replied Gunnar, "I had a bargain of it with a lot of other things; for, you see, he had no use for it at Tomta, where he scarcely has so much as a duck-pond. But it is quite new and well built, and I shall not spare it; for, do you know, Bengt, I shall spend my life in the wood and on the lake."

"Yes, I see, and I might have done that with you instead of that dunce, Abraham; and if you would take me in autumn," remarked Bengt.

"It seems very nice," answered Gunnar; "but one ought never to take one's best friend for one's servant—that's my honest opinion."

Thus conversed the two young men, as the boat hastily glided, to the rapid stroke of oars, across the lake; and here he who will may easily observe how clear-sighted is Friendship, even among rude and uneducated men; while Love, on the other hand, is blind among them—and almost equally blind is he among those human beings who are first in enlightenment and knowledge.

"Now we must, indeed, turn homeward," said Gunnar, when the evening sun said Good-night, and merely left behind it a crimson light, which tinged the lake till it resembled a sea of blood. "If I were now my own master," continued Gunnar, "I should sit here till the heavens were dark, and the lake also, and the new moon began to shine; for it is the most beautiful thing I know when the moon shines upon the lake, and every stroke of the oar is like a rain of silver. See, it is beautiful, that it is! And when one sings lustily the while, it is delightful!"

"Well, sing now in that way while we row homeward," said Bengt, beseechingly.

"I don't know justly what to sing," replied Gunnar, in the same evasive tone as some of the nightingales of our drawing-rooms, when people ask them to sing something out of "Norma," or the "Huguenots," or "Lucia," or suchlike works.

"Ay !" said Bengt, "sing that one about ' Elin is my sugar deary ;' I have not heard you sing it for such a long time."

"Oh ! it is not worth any thing," replied Gunnar, and made such an irregular stroke with his oar that the boat became violently unsteady.

"What, the devil !" exclaimed Bengt, who could not swim, "I think certainly you will lay us here upon the mermaid's blue bed ; but, look you, I am not going to have that done, for I can not swim like a goose, and fly, and dive, and swing myself this way and that way, in the water, as you can."

"Ha ! ha ! ha !" laughed Gunnar, in youthful gladness, and shook the little boat more violently than ever, that he might make the otherwise so courageous Bengt scream out. But when Bengt saw that there was no danger, he sat quite silently, and then Gunnar sent the little boat gliding on again, and Bengt began to beg him once more to sing a merry bit of an old song.

"Ah ! now do sing about ' Elin is my sugar deary,' " prayed Bengt, " and don't trouble yourself about Olle laughing at you for it on the wedding-day, and singing your beautiful air in such a confoundedly stupid way, for since then you have never once sung it."

"No, indeed," answered Gunnar, and coughed, not because his lungs were oppressed with any thing, but to put some control upon his heart, which began to beat, and on the blood which began to be in a ferment as soon as he thought on the old song which he had formerly sung so often. He moved the oars in the mean time briskly, and kept time to himself as he sang, in the beginning rather tremulously, or in a perfectly new mode, but afterward evenly, and so loud and clear that the mountains listened, and Echo answered.

> " Elin is my sugar-deary ;
> Elin is my raisin-tree ;
> Elin is my sweet bell cheery ;
> Elin is great joy to me.
> Elin is my heart's best treasure ;
> Elin is my dear delight ;
> Every one and altogether,
> All in one, is Elin bright.
>
> " Elin do I love sincerely ;
> Fair as are the roses red ;
> Fairer than a piece of linen,
> Softer than a skein of thread ;

Plumper than the large sow feeding,
Rosier than our neighbor's knot,
Light and slender as a fly is,
Brisk as is a rifle-shot.

" Pike shall all be turned to bullhead ;
Oxen shall on wings advance ;
Granite stones be loaves of barley,
Stockholm shall begin to dance ;
Brunkeberg shall be a shallop,
Doctors' shops the churches big,
Ere I can forget my Elin,
For she is my roasted pig !"

" Nay, hold still, Gunnar !" exclaimed Bengt ; " that was a monstrous fine echo. Hark how it says, after you, ' roasted pig,' just as plain as a man."

" Yes, yes, it is, indeed, something more than a human being," replied Gunnar, and glanced up to the lofty mountain-shore from which the sound came.

" Now, do you really think," asked Bengt, "that it is a maiden who sits up in the mountains, and talks in this way there, and says the words after one ?"

" Yes, that I believe certainly," remarked Gunnar ; " for the mountains can not talk at all. But, look you, she never says any thing after one but what she takes a fancy to."

" Well, then, she has taken a monstrous fancy to ' roasted pig,'" remarked Bengt, and Gunnar laughed. " Have you ever seen her ?" asked Bengt further.

" No, I never have," returned Gunnar ; " but I had an aunt who once saw one when she was a child."

" And how did she look ?" inquired Bengt, with great curiosity, because the night was already at hand, and the marvellous begins to have its full force as soon as the sunlight is gone.

" Ay, she was as white as the purest snow, and had coal-black hair, and my aunt saw how she stood upon the mountain, and yawned, and constantly repeated all she heard."

" Oh, bless me ! in all my days !" exclaimed Bengt, without doubting a single word of Gunnar's ; and a great deal of that implicit belief arose from Gunnar's relating it as if he himself entirely believed it.

" It would be very entertaining if one could sometimes see either the echo, or the mermaid, or the wood-fairy, or suchlike," said Bengt, as he helped Gunnar to make fast the boat, for they were now at land. Now, however, it was almost dark, and

Gunnar's admired new moon had arisen, and looked down upon the two young men, within whose breasts at this moment, perhaps, more pure, earnest, real poetry might be found, than in the whole swarm of "Minstrelsies," and "Poems," and "Songs," and "Fancies," and "Lyrical Pictures," and "Poetic Flowers," etc.

"Bless me! have you never seen any thing of the sort?" (namely, mermaids, wood-nymphs, etc.) said Gunnar, in a certain tone of superiority, as if he himself were intimate with the whole society of spirits and elves with which the superstition of the peasantry, at this moment, peoples the sea, the mountains, woods, valleys, heaths, and even the air.

"No, I have never exactly *seen* any one," replied Bengt, as they rapidly walked homeward by a small path through the deep, thick wood, "but *heard* have I many times both spirits and other goblins."

"Perhaps it would be the best not to talk about suchlike things," suggested Gunnar, "now that we are here in the dark wood, and not a very long way from the witches' caldron and the heathen king's grave, where the ghosts are always so bold on Sunday evenings, and where jack-o'-lanterns are seen; but this much I will tell you, Bengt, that if at any time any thing comes to you which you can't understand, you need only make the sign of the cross before your nose, and say the Lord's Prayer with an honest heart, and it will instantly vanish."

"Have you tried it?" inquired Bengt, with a mysterious feeling of awe, in which, however, a great pleasure was mingled.

"That have I, certainly," answered Gunnar, "when I have so often in the night-time gone through the great, deep wood to mother's."

"No!—but have you? What did they look like?" asked Bengt.

"Why, as to that, I can not exactly say," replied Gunnar, "because I did not stop long enough to stare at them; but as soon as I was aware of them I did as I said, and then I shut my eyes, and went on with a resolute step, and said the Lord's Prayer all the while, and they never did me any harm. But, look you, I have my own thoughts, and they are these: that if a person has not done any thing wrong, he then can go safely both for ghosts and goblins; but if he has any thing bad on his conscience, then they can come and pester him at pleasure."

" Nay, but who is there who has not some sin on his mind ?" observed Bengt, quite self-complacently.

" Yes, yes; it is a matter of course," conceded Gunnar, " that we are all of us sinful creatures ; but, look you, there is a grand difference when a person does something bad with a deliberate intention or in great wrath ; and do you know, Bengt, that many a time I thanked my God when I have been going, as we now are, in the pitch-black night through the thick wood, that He has preserved me from doing what I have many and many a time had a desire to do—that is, to knock Olle on the head !—for, you see, he can incense me to such a degree with *one* thing and *another*—and, among others, with singing after me my songs ! And you may well believe that I never would have taken Lena if my conscience had not knocked and thumped within me like a stone in a churn."

" Ay, ay," replied Bengt, who was thinking more about the wood-sprites than about Lena; " ay, ay, if you had not taken her, then the necks, or the woodwomen, or some other monsters, perhaps, would have had you. Many a one who has deceived, and made a fool of a girl, goes about quite unmolested."

For some time they walked on rapidly, and in silence, which at length was broken by Bengt.

" Ah, ah !" exclaimed he ; " how solitary and lonesome it will be when you are gone ! I think I never shall get used to it ! Lonesome will it be in the men-servants' room ; lonesome out at work ; and lonesome in the kitchen at meals, where you and I always ate out of the same dish !"

" Ay, ay !" answered Gunnar, and sighed. But Gunnar was one of those who moved quickly, and such can seldom participate so much in sorrow as those who stand still. The two young men began now to talk about the future.

" I shall stay where I am for some years, and drudge for another, but afterward I shall look well about me for a nice lass—that I shall," said Bengt. " That Elin, Lena's sister, she was just a girl after my liking," added he, as Gunnar did not answer him.

Gunnar stopped, and stood still amid his quick walking, but he said nothing, and Bengt asked, " What is amiss with you ? Did you see any thing ?"

" Oh, no, nothing," replied Gunnar, for he did not feel his conscience so heavy, but that he might burden it with a lie ; and now it was his turn to talk about the future.

"Yes," said he, "Abraham (the stupid fool) will come on Wednesday, and then there will be only hard work all the spring, and, look you, so long Lena will stand on her legs; but in the hot summer, when she will need help, I will have mother to come; for I want, first of all, to see what sort of housewife Lena will be, for never could I bear that she should behave ill to mother; and when she comes to want her help, then I think that she will behave well enough to her. And in the Midsummer holidays, if all is well, then we shall have a little merriment; for look you, then—" but Gunnar did not get any farther; he came to a stand-still, but that was in his conversation.

"Yes, how was it?" said Bengt. "Did not Elin promise to come to you at Midsummer, if her mother was brisk and well?"

"Oh, ay! she certainly did talk about it," answered Gunnar, and immediately changed the subject.

Thus conversing, the two young men continued their walk hastily onward, and reached Grantorp about nine o'clock. They both went together directly into the men-servants' room, to know what time it was, and whether the others were still up, and had supped. Supper was just over, and all the servants, as well as a few of their acquaintance, were now assembled in the room, before a good fire, smoking their pipes, laughing and chattering on this holiday evening. Nobody exactly saluted Gunnar and Bengt, who had spoken, on entering, a general "Good evening!" and then "God's peace be with you!" was given in return, and the two went forward, hung up their caps, and drew near the fire to warm themselves.

"What will there be for work to-morrow?" asked Gunnar, turning to the overseer.

"Bless me! how indifferent he pretends to be; just as if nothing had happened!" said Olle, and laughed, with his hideous fiend-like laugh of derision.

"And what may that be?" replied Gunnar, in a tone of defiance; for he was always excited to anger when Olle opened his mouth.

"Bless me! What! he pretends to be ignorant! ha! ha! ha!" screamed Olle. "It is just as if he never knew such a thing could happen. Ay, now you have got something to do! Ha! ha! ha!"

"Speak out what it is, then, you devil's hound!" said Gunnar, enraged. "How shall I know what happens while I am away?"

"Do you not know," said Overseer Anders, who was an elderly, sober, and sensible man, "do you not know that your wife had a son at noon?"

"Yes, and a red-haired one into the bargain! Ha! ha! ha!" laughed out Olle scornfully.

Gunnar heard not another word. He stood for a moment confounded in the middle of the room, pale as a marble statue, and without much more life or thought; after that he rushed like a tempest toward the door, and dashed through it.

"Ha! ha! ha! Now he has some curiosity about his red-haired crown prince," laughed Olle, as Gunnar, with a tremendous bang, closed the door after him.

"Curse me, if I know what you are talking, grinning, and laughing about," said Bengt, who was not by any means of as irritable a nature as Gunnar, and who had not the same hatred to Olle either, because Olle neither envied or excited Bengt to the same extent; "I, for my part," added Bengt, "think that this is a great misfortune for Gunnar; for, look you, he has now to flit to his place on Wednesday, for then both the beasts and Abraham (the beast!) are to come. But, you see, he would do well to take the old woman to be with him till Lena is up again."

This last remark Bengt made more for himself than for the others, and nobody wondered at Gunnar's disappearance, imagining that he had gone up to Lena, to welcome his new-born son, about whose arrival they only supposed he had a little miscalculated.

All the men-servants retired to bed; the fire went out, but Gunnar did not return, and nobody thought about him.

CHAPTER XV.

BUT Gunnar! what did he think? He thought nothing. He merely hastened on, careless about bad spirits, but with all the pangs of hell in his breast; without hat, through wood and bog, scarcely lighted by that new moon which he loved so much, but which he did not now once remark; and about midnight stood before his old mother's bolted door. He paused for a moment before he knocked, and the fear of terrifying the old woman was certainly the first intelligible thought that sprang up within him since Olle had been to him a Job's messenger; who had astonished and dismayed him, and who had set every feeling within him in a state of combat. His wounded sensibility towered up to the sky, and upbraided him with his simplicity; his goodness of heart, and his easy faith, laughed to scorn by those demons which he had long since chased away from him, but which now returned; his lost freedom; Elin; in the midst of this the words of the tutor; his own unceasing repugnance; Olle's derision—all these stood before him now in frightful colors. He had, however, nobody to blame but himself; he was too proud to lay the blame on any other than his own conscience; and however pure and clear as a mirror it was, it was not able in this terrible hour to silence and appease all the anguish-pangs which made themselves felt in every part of the young man's soul.

"I shall frighten my poor old mother to death," was his first intelligible thought; and the next, a determination that while he knocked gently on the window, he would announce who he was, and thus would rouse the old woman. In the agitated state, however, in which he was, he knocked much louder on the window than he intended, and his voice in these words— the first that had passed his lips since his last angry demand from Olle that he should *speak out*—was ghastly and hollow, so that the old woman woke up in a great horror out of her first deep sleep, and exclaimed—

"Merciful heaven! Is it thou, Gunnar, or is it thy ghost?".

"It is I," replied Gunnar; and he shook at the bolted door with violence, as he now no longer feared to frighten the old woman. But that was the very thing to frighten her, and she cried out at once—

"Gunnar, Gunnar, is it thou, or is it *something evil* in thy shape, which thus comes and goes through the bolted door?"

"Oh, it is I, sure enough," answered Gunnar, entering, and throwing himself spiritlessly upon the sofa where he had slept so soundly and so calmly in his younger years.

Mother Ingrid hastened to rouse up the fire; but when by the light of a blazing stick she came to see Gunnar's countenance, disfigured by anguish, suffering, and passion, the sweat-drops upon his white, smooth forehead, and the deathly paleness of his cheeks, she again exclaimed—

"Gunnar, my son, once more do I ask thee, is it *actually* thou, or is it thy ghost, or hast thou taken the life of a human being?"

"No, I *have* not yet, but I *shall!*" replied Gunnar, in the fervor of an idea which had first at this moment lighted up, or rather flamed up within him—that a bullet would pay for his dishonor; that blood would cleanse away shame and insult. Suspicion lightened, and wrath thundered; and the object of both and of Gunnar's hatred and fury, was, and continued to be, no other than Olle.   Toward him, however, he had feelings, which, notwithstanding his northern nature, did not accord with the Corsican proverb, *La vendetta tranversale*, for he would, in this moment of madness, have been ready to fall upon even an adherent of Olle.

"Eternal Father!" said the mother, trembling to that degree that the burning wood was ready to fall out of her hand. "What dost thou mean by this horrible word?   Do not talk in that way, Gunnar, because, with the help of God, thou dost not mean what thou sayest, but God hears even the ungodly word. Recollect thyself now, and then tell me what it is so dreadful that has happened to thee."

"Me!" answered Gunnar, with a countenance the least in the world calmer, but still dark as night, "nothing has happened to me, but Lena—the beast!—the worm!—"

"Gunnar, Gunnar," said the old woman, admonishingly, "do not talk in that way of thy wedded wife; thou art doing a great sin.   What, then, has she done?"

"She has had a child!"

"Well, that you knew would happen beforehand."

"Yes, but not *now*, not *to-day*."

"Gunnar, Gunnar!" besought the mother again, "do not tempt God with thy tricks. I could see plain enough that thou hadst told me a lie, and many a time have I prayed God that he would forgive thee for it."

"I lied!" exclaimed Gunnar, and rose up hastily, "no, never *I*, but Lena, and she has lied—the basest lie which a woman can be guilty of."

"Mother Ingrid seated herself beside him, took his hand in hers, rested his burning head against her maternal bosom, and endeavored by all means in her power to calm him, as well as

E

to get him to talk about all these distressing circumstances. She obtained her object, Gunnar became somewhat calm, and he succeeded in wholly convincing her of the truth of his word and of his calculations. No representations, however, in the world, could induce him to promise that he would be quiet, and not take revenge on Olle, who was the *only one* on whom his suspicions fell. The old woman talked, besought him, reasoned with him, but all in vain. She succeeded, however, in awakening that kindness of heart which even the frenzy of his mind could not destroy; and he began to feel almost a satisfaction in forgiving Lena, or at all events in pitying her; but for Olle he had no compassion.

"Yes, mother," said he at length in conclusion, "you may say what you will, Olle shall pay the reckoning for it, and you readily can, if you will, put him on his guard against me; for should even the king himself and his officers, and whoever else, choose to stand by him, I would fall upon him, let me see him *when* and *where* I might. Let him mind, therefore, and keep out of my way."

Towards morning the mother and son began to talk a little more calmly over these distressing circumstances. The mother advocated reconciliation and harmony, the son would not listen to a single word of the kind.

"Impossible, dearest mother!" said he—"a downright and absolute impossibility that I should be able to take Lena to myself, my own wedded wife, when she has acted in this way towards me, and when I regard Olle as the father of her child. No, look you, that can never be, and a mother can never once wish or ask it.

And now they talked over and over that which he so truly believed, judging by Olle's jeering words, in which so much malicious pleasure was exhibited, as well as by his former affair with Lena, much more than by her inclination to him, which certainly never seemed very great, for, on the contrary, it always appeared as if she could not bear him.

At the very moment while Gunnar was talking on this subject he suddenly sunk into silence, and, to Mother Ingrid's greatest amazement, exclaimed at length, after a long time of silence and deep thought, as well as with a great change in the expression of his countenance,

"Mother, do you know what? Olle is innocent!"

"Well, but that I have said and believed from the very beginning," replied the old woman, not without a faint smile passing over her withered lips.

Gunnar did not see it, nor comprehend, at all events, its meaning, but continued,

"Ay, he is innocent, as you say, mother, because Olle was away from the middle of May, when he went into the militia to be drilled, for, you see, he had been excused for several years because he was not tall enough, and then he lay sick of ague in the hospital till long after midsummer; so he is innocent."

The conversation of the mother and son now took another direction, and Mother Ingrid in the end said sufficient to obtain from Gunnar a sacred promise that he would not speak with any single human being, let it be whoever it might, until she, Mother Ingrid, had had some talk with Lena; that he would keep himself quiet and peaceable, and go in a straightforward way and ask advice of the clergyman, and above all things not go and publish the whole affair before he had done this.

In the mean time the day had already advanced, and after a deal of trouble, Mother Ingrid induced Gunnar to accompany her to the Hall, where he was least of all inclined to go. The mother put his disarranged apparel in order, stroked his hair from his face, and said, in conclusion,

"Dear lad! thou shouldst really have something within thee, otherwise thou wilt never stand it. Thou hast not tasted a morsel since noon yesterday. Eat a crumb now, and then let us two go, for it's getting toward evening, the sun is fast going down."

"No, thank you, mother! I could not possibly eat any thing," replied Gunnar; "but if you have a drop or two to give me, that I will be glad of."

"Really," said Mother Ingrid slowly, while she went to the cupboard, "art *thou* now, my dear Gunnar, going to take to brandy again, which thou hast so often condemned and forsworn?"

"Oh, yes, but it was only folly," replied Gunnar; it does one no good to let drinking alone, that I can very well see; and I can very well drink a drop now and then without making a drunkard of myself; I am too old and too wise for that now, and I find that a drop tastes well when nothing else does."

"Yes, yes; so said thy father before thee and thy brother, and ill went it with them both," sighed Mother Ingrid, and thought within herself how much misery Gunnar was already suffering because of brandy, although at this moment she would not remind him of it, but poured out for him a quarter of the brandy which she had bought to give to the mason, who was to come some day to look at the poor old woman's half-tumbled-down chimney.

Gunnar poured out a draught for himself—he poured out two—and then he said,

"Look thou! now, indeed, we will go in Jesus' name."

CHAPTER XVI.

FEW words passed between the mother and son during this long walk through the woods, which was certainly not a rapid one, because Mother Ingrid was not able to go so quickly, and Gunnar did not hasten her, but, on the contrary, made long silent pauses, leaning his burning and throbbing forehead against some tree trunk, or laying a little ice upon it whenever he could find any in the rifts of the rocks.

It was already twilight when they reached the Hall, and those who met Gunnar said, with astonishment and a smile, "Well, at last!" or, "Now, you are come at length!" or, "It is well you are come—we have had such a search after you!" or the like.

Bengt came forward to Gunnar and said,

"But where, in the Lord Jesus' name, have you been? We have been seeking prodigiously for you. The minister was here, by chance, just at noon, but he was in a dreadful hurry, so the child had to be baptized full gallop. Ma'msell Sara carried it, and Anders, and Lotta, and I, we stood sponsors; and that is the reason why I have my Sunday clothes on; and the Squire set off this morning ever so early, and does not come back for several days, and that was a good thing, else you would have had abuse enough. But where in the world have you been?"

Gunnar did not look up during this address, but followed Bengt into the men-servants' room, while Mother Ingrid went up to that part of the house in which Lena was.

"What!" said Bengt astonished, "shall you not go up to

your wife, and look at your lad ? He is a big fellow, with red hair, and cry did he like a ghost when they dipped him, so that he has got your singing voice, however."

Gunnar was silent, and threw himself upon a bench, stroked his hair down over his moist forehead, and held his hands before his eyes, and ground his teeth silently and imperceptibly together.

"What in the world is amiss with you ?" asked Bengt, who saw, nevertheless, how he was suffering. "You are as ill as a dog, that I can see! Go and lie down a bit, and then you'll be better. Will you have a sup ?—I have a drop in my case bottle."

With this Bengt poured a large draught, which Gunnar, without thinking, swallowed, and then lay down upon the bench where he sate, and fell asleep in a few moments. Youth, weariness, health, and a good conscience exercised their influence upon the young man, who, after a most fatiguing day, which succeeded a perfectly sleepless night, had not taken a morsel of refreshment,—nothing but brandy, and had walked many miles in this state. He slept, and good angels rejoiced assuredly because of it.

In the mean time Mother Ingrid went up with slow steps to the room in which was Lena, and entered it with silence and solemnity. Lena was in bed; but still quite strong and well. No one was with her in the chamber. A deep crimson covered her countenance, which was somewhat paler than ordinary, and her eyes were not able to meet the old woman's stern and grave glance. Mother Ingrid walked up to the bedside, and seated herself. Not a word was exchanged. After a long and anxious silence, Lena said with a mixture of boldness and embarrassment,—

"Perhaps you would like to see the lad, grandmother ?"

"Oh, I am indifferent about that," said Mother Ingrid, with severity; "because although, to my poor Gunnar's misfortune, I have become your mother-in-law, it does not follow that I am grandmother to the lad."

Lena was silent.

"For shame, Lena!" said Mother Ingrid, after another oppressive silence. "For shame! never, no, never should I have believed it of you! I thought, on the contrary, that you were excessively fond of my Gunnar, else, you may believe me, I should not have taken so much pains to get him to have you,

so much as it went against the poor fellow's inclination.   I fancied that you loved him above any thing else on earth, for so
you seemed to do."

"Yes, God, and my Father know, that I both did and do so,"
said Lena, bursting into a torrent of tears.

"Well, then, how could you go and make a fool of him in
such a dreadful way?" asked Mother Ingrid.

"Make a fool of him!" exclaimed Lena, with averted eyes,
in which the tears were already dry, "Befooled him—it is not
me that has fooled him.   It would have been he that would
have made a fool of me, if he would not have had me—that I
know!"

"Ah, you know very well what I mean," said Mother Ingrid
dryly; "it is not worth your while to try to throw dust in my
eyes.   Blood is thicker than water, and I know whom I can
believe best."

"Yes, God knows what Gunnar has been talking to you
about," said Lena, but still without looking the old woman in
the face.   "The lad does not remember, I reckon, what took
place, and many things which happen when folks are drunk
they forget when they are sober."

"Oh, be quiet with such talk," said Mother Ingrid, "and
don't tell me such things.   Your own words prove that you
have your senses about you, and that you understand what I
mean: and as to what you say about folks doing things when
they are drunk, I don't believe that of Gunnar, for I *know* that
he never told me a lie, and that he never got drunk more than
once in the autumn, and unlucky was the time!   But now, look
you again!   There are some people who can tell a lie before
God and the priest, and such can also tell a lie to an old wom
an body; and this I can tell you, that you have no more shame
in you than I don't know what; and that Gunnar is not one to
be played with, and that he will take it to the assizes, for he is
not bound to burden himself with other folk's children, and to
slave and strive for them."

With this Lena began to cry distractedly, and to wring her
hands, and to say that she would go and drown herself (a threat
which the peasant often uses, and which others believe after it
has taken place) if Gunnar cast her off; said she should be the
most obedient and devoted wife in the world, if Gunnar would
only show her mercy, and, in the end, acknowledged to Mother
Ingrid the real fact, and besought her with clasped hands to

set every thing straight; assured her—asseverated and swore by all which was sacred—that nobody in the whole world but she, and *one more*, knew the honest truth, so that Gunnar would never be brought to shame for "his goodness in showing her mercy;" such was the expression which Lena used in her affliction.

Mother Ingrid sate in silence, and listened to Lena's prayers and representations, irresolute as to what was right or what was wrong; what she ought to do or what to let alone. But kind-heartedness, that gift of God, which is the symbol of womanly justice, gained in the end the ascendency; and she promised, weeping silently the while, to endeavor to set all things straight between them, if Lena on her part would promise henceforth in every possible way to conduct herself correctly and to be discreet. Lena promised every thing in her time of need; she promised, as the saying is, "gold and green woods," because, carried away by the violent, unbridled love which she really felt for Gunnar, and which increased every day in proportion to his coldness toward her, the idea that she might lose him, that she might be separated from him now that she was just about to live with him in comfort, was a thought very much more dreadful to her than all the shame of her behavior, all the ignominy, all the scorn and the ridicule which she well knew would be her lot if Gunnar put in practice Mother Ingrid's threat. Wily and crafty as Lena was, she knew very well in what way to talk, so as to influence Mother Ingrid's excellent heart, and to represent the picture to her in the most beautiful and attractive colors.

"And never shall Gunnar," said she, in her zealous persuasion, "need to slave himself and struggle for the child (if it live), because I shall take sufficient care of *it*, and *it* will always bring us good friends, and we shall, perhaps, enjoy many an advantage which other peasants don't get; and I shall wait on Gunnar and you, mother-in-law, like a servant, and that for all my days: and Gunnar shall never, and you shall never, repent of your goodness to me, but I shall, all my life long, do my best to deserve it."

Thus talked Lena; and Mother Ingrid listened to both promises and advantages. When a person has striven through a whole long life, at all events through the greater part of it, into old age, with every possible kind of want; feels himself forlorn and forsaken, there is a great temptation to such a one in a certainty of more quiet and more prosperous days by the side of his beloved ones; and in Mother Ingrid's class, at least, many deviate from the *point d'honneur* which every one forms to himself, and people shut their eyes to a disgrace, the guilt of which is not their own, and which, therefore, does not weigh heavily on their conscience, and which need in no wise appear before the world; they shut their eyes to this, even when their hearts are quite right. So, at all events, did Mother Ingrid; and she promised, sighing deeply the while, to use all her influence with Gunnar, but by no means answering for her own success.

The two women had just arrived at this point in their important conversation, which was carried on in a low and whispering voice, when the door softly opened, and Ma'msell Sara entered with a plate and a basin in her hand.

"How is it with the good woman and her little son?" asked she, full of kindness. "I have brought with me a little suitable and nourishing food, which will do them both good. See! Good evening, Mother Ingrid! How goes the world with you down there in the wood? I can well understand why you should come thence to see your son's son. But you should have come a little earlier, and then you could yourself have carried your child's child to be baptized, and have named him yourself. As it was, I made free to do it all; for the clergyman was just setting out on a journey, and was in a hurry, and we did not know of a certainty that you would come, and no creature could find Gunnar, which we all thought was very odd."

"Yes, every thing happens in this world for the best," replied Mother Ingrid evasively; "and the child has certainly been better off for being carried by you than if it had been by me; and, as regards Gunnar, why—he had the goodness to wait for me, poor old body, and I could not walk fast all that long way."

"Well, and what does he think about his lad?" inquired Ma'msell Sara; but nobody gave her an answer, and therefore she continued—"Yes, poor Gunnar, he has really done himself most wrong by his folly, for now he must go and help himself alone, as he best can, for some weeks to come; for I will not hear a word about Lena going down to Vika before she has been churched, because, first and foremost, both she and the child need the quietness which they may have here, and which she, methinks, can not find there in her household; and if she went, people might think that my brother and I turned her out, as it has so unfortunately happened; and such a thing is not to be done, for the last words which the squire said before he set out this morning were, that Lena was to stay quietly here, and be nursed here in the best manner till she was perfectly recovered. Oh, no, don't cry, now," said she, turning to Lena, who put her hands before her eyes, not exactly to conceal her tears, but many other feelings; "but you must beg," continued Ma'msell Sara, "that grandmother will help Gunnar till then, and eat now of that which I have brought, for it is good, and it will do you good also. Has mother Ingrid had coffee? Not! How? What has the housekeeper been thinking about?"

And with these words Ma'msell Sara went out.

"Now, do go down, by all means, to Gunnar, dear good mother-in-law," besought Lena; and Mother Ingrid went, with a sigh, about a black business.

Arrived in the men-servants' room, she found Gunnar still profoundly asleep, and Olle standing beside him trying to lay a sham baby, made out of an old coat and a garter, on his arm, to vex him when he awoke.

"You have ugly tricks with you, Olle!" said Mother Ingrid, and took away the coat. "Be on your guard against Gunnar; he is as good as gold as long as he is not provoked, but if he is, he does not rightly know——"

"Hold your tongue, old scarecrow!" said Olle, laughing. "Keep your old toothless jaws still! It's only young lasses that have any business to preach, and not old scrubs like you!"

Gunnar moved himself in his sleep; Olle rushed out of the door, and Mother Ingrid availed herself of the occasion to wake Gunnar.

"Wake up, Gunnar," said Mother Ingrid; "I want to talk with you. I have a deal to say to you, to which you must listen with sense and calmness. Come, now."

Mother and son again betook themselves to the road through the wood, but they did not go silently as on the former occasion, but Mother Ingrid talked, and Gunnar made objections. Mother Ingrid made use of all her maternal power and womanly gift of persuasion; Gunnar combated for his dislike, long and perseveringly, but when Mother Ingrid reached her solitary dwelling, Gunnar said, in a low and hollow voice:

"Well, be it so, then, mother; for my happiness or unhappi-

E*

ness you are answerable! I will do as you would have me, let come what may. I will not seek for revenge on Lena or *that other;* may God only grant that he goes out of my way, if I meet him with my good loaded gun! My life and my youth are both wasted, let me do whatever I may. It, perhaps, would be wrong to carry the affair to the assizes, however just my cause may be before God: and if I did so, why, then, I should never come near this place, but go out with all my troubles into the world; and, look you, then I could not take you with me, and that," said Gunnar, with great energy, "*that,* look you, does not weigh lightly in the scale in which my determination is laid. Yes; so good night to you, mother. Now there is no more to be said on *that* business. God only grant that Lena will do all that she has promised to you, and God grant that she behave well to you; yet I shall keep my word, and stand by it as an honest fellow should do. Yes, and you will come to Vika the day after to-morrow, according to agreement. Good-night, mother!"

Gunnar returned with heavy and slow steps to the hall. When he reached home, every body was gone to bed, and most of them were asleep; and as they all believed that Gunnar was up-stairs with his wife, nobody wondered at his absence, or made any inquiries about him. Gunnar therefore lay down, weary, without having tasted a morsel to eat through the whole of that long, terrible day, which cut away from the life of the young man many years.

The following day he was taciturn and reserved. Toward noon, he went with a firm, calm, and almost heavy step, up to Lena's chamber. As soon as he entered she began to weep aloud, took his hands, and would kiss him, and behaved in the most humble and penitent manner. Gunnar, however, withdrew his hands, turned aside with anger and repugnance from both mother and child, and yet endeavored not to show these feelings in so strong and powerful a degree as he actually felt them. He merely said—

"God comfort thee, Lena, if thou do not keep *every single word* thou hast promised to my mother; and God comfort thee if any one comes and points their finger at me; and God comfort thee if in one way or another thou at any time deceive me, for if I get angry, I tell thee beforehand, that I do not know what I then do; such has my temper been at all times, and it is not improved now, that I know by myself."

Having said these words, Gunnar went his way.

And here we will take a leap forward in time, that is, from now till the autumn of the same year, as well as pass over Gunnar's solitary time with his mother at Vika; his first settling down there; Abraham's entrance on the scene: Lena's arrival and establishment; the small changes which, by little and little, and day by day, were made within the humble habitation.

CHAPTER XVII.

LENA had now gained her object. If Gunnar, conformably to his first threat, had gone immediately to the clergyman, and told him about the actual state of affairs, then, perhaps—so feared Lena—he would have believed him, and the whole thing might have taken an extremely unfortunate turn for her; but *now*, thought she, now he can do nothing, for it is quite too late. And, in consequence of this security, she threw off, by degrees, all her assumed character, and exhibited herself, before long, in her true form, and that was unpleasing enough. Time had produced the same change in her temper as it had done in outward nature; important changes had taken place, but it had not been all at once, but so gradually that nobody knew *when* or *how* they happened. That which had been soft and tender in spring was now hard and stern; and as we are not intending to dwell long upon this period of time, we will merely give a little example of the prevailing tone in the house.

" What in all the world," exclaimed Lena, sharply, one day in the cold month of November, " what are you mumbling about there in the chimney-corner, mother-in-law? It was a miserable thing that Ma'msell Sara should throw away upon you that wretched elder-flower tea and honey, and stuff you with the notion that it would do any good to such an old thing as you; for now you are everlastingly poking in the chimney-corner, with your messes, and kindling the fire, whether it is wanted or not! I think it would be a deal better if you were washing the cabbage, that it could be chopped for supper, if Gunnar ever comes in. What, the deuce !" continued she,

turning to the laborer Abraham, "are you got into the corner?
Have you not had your victuals, and swallowed them into the
bargain? What are you sitting there and thrusting your nose
in for? Be off with you, and go to your work, you cursed
reptile, who neither earn your clothes nor your victuals! I
must say," continued she, when Abraham had left the house
with great speed, "that of all Gunnar's schemes, that of taking
such a downright fool as Abraham for a laborer was the most
stupid. I never would say a word about it, however, if Gunnar were ever in the house, or if he ever did any thing himself;
but, look you, when he has nothing to be doing, then he spends
his time in the wood and on the lake, day and night through;
and we shall see how it turns out."

"Lena, Lena," replied Mother Ingrid, whose gentleness
and forbearance never failed her when Lena merely broke out
upon herself, partly because Mother Ingrid's temper was of
that kind, and partly because she determined to do *all*, to bear
all, suffer *all*, to sacrifice *all*, merely to be under the same roof
with her son; but she never could patiently bear to hear Lena
abuse Gunnar, which, indeed, she very seldom did when he
was present, but often in his absence, because she really felt a
sort of love for him, but of that kind which generates importu-
nity, jealousy, caprice, and anger, much more than tenderness
and actual true devotion. "Lena, Lena," therefore said Mother
Ingrid, "do think a little about what you are saying; is not
Gunnar employed both when he is in the wood and upon the
lake? Who has been eating little fish all the week, if not we?
say nothing about the large fish which he has sent up to the
hall and sold; and have you forgotten the great cock o' the
wood which Gunnar brought home with him last week?"

"No, no, Heaven forbid!" said Lena, jeeringly; "there is
not much in his bringing *something* sometimes, for he mostly
comes home empty-handed, and yet for all that he is so mad
after going and stopping out in the woods, or on that devilish
lake, that he'll stop there altogether one of these fine days!"

"Oh, Lord in heaven forbid it!" replied Mother Ingrid; and
thought to herself, "Yes, what is, indeed, the reason that he
does not like to stop at home? Not *my* fault, as I hope; I
fear at the same time."

And Mother Ingrid was right; it was dissatisfaction, that
most terrible of all home-feelings, which drove Gunnar as much
as possible from his home; and Lena was also right when she

said sometimes in her wrath, " I quite believe that the house burns him !" for there was a something which burned and tortured Gunnar merely to see Lena and her child, which he never but once had noticed, and that was when he was alone in the house. Then he had gone up to the cradle, looked upon the sleeping child for a few moments, and said to himself, " Eternal God, grant that I may never in my wrath and my hatred fall upon that poor little innocent creature !" and then he patted the child upon the cheek, and went out.

Gunnar was entirely altered in temper, and in every thing. He was gloomy and grave ; nobody ever saw him smile ; he was no longer heard to sing ; and his violin hung unstrung and dusty upon the wall ; but the old ever-loaded gun was, on the contrary, so much the cleaner, and the wild creatures of the wood were aware of it, and the trees of the wood might also have told, if they could, that many a shot of Gunnar's was merely at a mark, a pleasure, almost the only one he had at this time, of which nobody had any idea, because he himself thought that it was bad economy of shot and powder. He, therefore, was silent on the subject, but could not withstand this inclination, whence it came that he was very soon a matchless shot.

Gunnar never did his stipulated days' work at Grantorp; these fell to the lot of Abraham, and caused him (Gunnar) merely to get a glimpse of the squire two or three times in the course of the year, and then he turned out of the way, and the squire did the same.

CHAPTER XVIII

And now we say farewell for a little time to the cottage at Vika, with all its passions (for Abraham had a passion for eating, drinking, and sleeping), all the love, all the thirst for power, all the hatred and disgust, which found place within its narrow limits, and beneath its low roof. Maternal love revealed itself there in two such dissimilar forms, and filial love likewise, but then there was the love which was concealed, and the dislike which was visible, under the false masks of indifference. And now we leave this dwelling and enter into *another*, similar to it, at many miles distance, and that to the northward, where likewise a new year's May sun glanced in through the bright and not very large window-panes, and mournfully lighted up a death-bed, on which an elderly, and to us unknown, woman, struggled with the last powers of life against death, which already held her in his embrace.   By the bedside lay, upon her knees, a young girl, who wept; and when at length the dying one heaved her last sigh, made her last convulsive struggle; for the last time endeavored to live, but for the first time was defeated, then did the young girl burst forth into violent weeping, and exclaim, in her inexpressible anguish, although none but the dead heard her, "Oh, God! what will become of me, poor creature! who have lost my kind, my dear support in this world, my adored, my beloved mother?   Now have I no one— no one in all the world to care for me, excepting my sister Lena."

And now came in the weeping female neighbors; for Elin's mother, a kind, pious, right-minded, and God-fearing woman, was greatly beloved by the village in which she lived; and now those anxious operations after death were commenced— those preparations which precede decay, and which are alike painful and repugnant in cottage and in palace, especially when they are moistened by the bitter tears of heartfelt affection.

This was more than commonly the case in this instance. Elin had been the apple of her mother's eye, and the mother had been Elin's whole existence.   Now the one was cold and lifeless, and the other, fatherless, motherless, and penniless! The mother had had a little annuity and a deal of help from many quarters, and, besides this, she was a very skillful needle-woman and weaver, so that she and Elin were very well off; lived most comfortably and respectably, in a little house outside the town, which Elin's mother enjoyed during her lifetime. But now all was entirely gone at once, and Elin was homeless.

It is true, that both on the right hand and on the left Elin received offers of a home for the moment, for that she should remain alone in the desolate house with her dead mother was not to be thought of.   The nearest female neighbor, therefore, who had always been a good friend of the deceased, took Elin home with her.   She was the wife of a well-to-do peasant, who had only one son, of the same age as Elin, who had been brought up with her, and who "went and read" at the same time that she did, from which circumstance, in this class of life, a friendship generally is the consequence—frequently a bond of union which endures through the whole life. The father, a creditable, clever, but austere peasant, plainly foresaw that the portionless Elin would become dangerous to the peace of his rich son, and he was therefore silently dissatisfied with the state of affairs, yet still he received the poor girl in her great affliction with the utmost hospitality, and immediately became her supporter and her adviser.

"Now, thou must not cry so much, dear child!" said he to her, when his wife returned with her from the house of mourning, "but thou must call in thy reason, give thyself up to it, and think in this way: that thy mother could not live always, and that she is well off where she is. And now we will set about and do the best for thee that we can, and my son, Erik, shall set off and ride to thy sister and brother-in-law, and bid them come here, so that they can arrange about the funeral, and all the rest, and then thou canst return home with them, or to somewhere near their place; for, look, thou hast no other relations, I know, hereabouts, and must be longing, I can very well believe, to be with thy only kith and kin."

Elin was satisfied with all that Father Anders proposed. He was regarded as the wisest man in the place, and as one who always knew to a tittle what he and every body else ought to do, or to leave undone. His word was thus decisive; and Elin, in her great grief and necessity, actually had only one single wish, and that was to see again her sister, who in person and voice somewhat resembled the dead mother. As Elin, however, was only imperfectly acquainted with Lena, who was thirteen or fourteen years older than herself, and who had been away from home ever since her childhood, and as Elin had only seen her during one short visit, which she had paid to her mother, as well as the twice when Elin herself had been at Grantorp, she therefore imagined that she should find in Lena, if not the beloved and lamented mother, at least an elder sister who would resemble her in kindness and affection, as well as be a stay for the future. She therefore thanked Father Anders as much as she was able in her deep sorrow; and Erik, who would gladly have gone to death for his playmate, the lovely and good friend of his childhood, had, a very short time after the arrangement was made, mounted Brunte and set out upon his journey. And Father Anders had by this means killed many birds with one stone; he had, at one and the same time, exhibited his prudence, his helpfulness at the time of need, his unselfishness in sending out his own horse and son, as well as succeeded in obtaining the absence of this latter during the greater part of the time that Elin was with them; he had, besides this, devised an opportunity for her quickly leaving, and probably for always, the place in which he lived; for Father Anders, like many another father, hoped and trusted that love and absence never could go together, and that all love would be vanquished by time.

CHAPTER XIX.

Lena sat and scolded in the house at Vika.

"It is a cursed thing that I should get this deuced complaint in my foot, so that I can't go and look how that lazy fellow, Abraham, has hoed up the potatoes! Mother-in-law, you can go out and see whether he does it tidily or not, and give him a wakening if he does it badly. What now! need you put on your jacket to do a little errand like that in the warm summer? You're beginning to be delicate are you? It's not weather to get cold in! Nay, bless me! mind what you are about! Don't you see the lad standing just behind you? My word, if you'd knocked him down! Yes, come hither, my little Gustaf, and thou shalt have mother's pincushion to play with, as thou can't have grandmother's spectacles, without her screeching and screaming, and saying that thou art doing wrong. Come here to mother, my little God's angel, all the rest are cross with thee!" (Mother Ingrid returns.) "Now, what has Abraham to say for himself? Is he doing any thing, or is he doing nothing? What, then! do ye call that being industrious? I should have done that bit in half-an-hour, and he's been at it ever since day-dawn. Did you see any thing of Gunnar? That's a devilish wood where he stops so everlastingly! and that just now, when I am ailing in my foot, and can't move from the spot!"

"Yes, what would you that he should be doing that I can not

do ?" said Mother Ingrid, mildly, while she was busying herself about the fire.

"Botheration take you! do you go out and bestir yourself in the cow-house," said Lena, enraged. "It's a downright shame, when a woman who is not older or more infirm than you are can't do such things! Old Britta of Björkebo is a very different sort of body; she fodders, and manures, and milks, and looks after the cows like any man."

"Ay, look ye, she hasn't got such a weakly chest as I have," replied Mother Ingrid, as mildly as before; "besides, you know very well that I would do all this, but Gunnar won't let me—he'll hardly let me milk."

"Yes, that I believe," answered Lena, "for so as Gunnar humors you, and sets store by you, have I never seen any menfolk do, and that to an old woman! The fiend fetch me!" added she, with bitterness; "I'll never believe that he bought the mare, and made himself the cart, only to drive you to church in. It was a downright shame to see how conceitedly you two, both of you, sat in it on Sunday. But if I only get well in my foot, then things shall go on properly, both with such journeys and the rest of it."

"Thou shouldst not envy me the ride," said Mother Ingrid, "for it had nearly been my last journey. And if thou hadst been holding the rein, as thou wantedst to do, when Olle, out of wanton mischief, frightened the young horse, and if Bengt had not started forward and thrown himself before the horse, then it would have run away right down the stony hill. And as to Gunnar having bought the horse, and made the cart, just on purpose to give *me* a ride, I think it is a shame of thee to say so, thou that know'st so well that Gunnar has need of the horse for all his business, now he has got Anderson's tillage too; and thou know'st well enough that thou might'st have had a ride in the new cart on Sunday if thy foot had been well."

"Had a ride! Yes, I know very well I might have had a ride," repeated Lena, scornfully; "but then, mind ye, Gunnar wouldn't have looked as pleased and as conceited as when he set you by his side and acted as coachman."

Mother Ingrid was silent, and Lena was right. Gunnar was not destitute of a good deal of pride, and with that a little vanity. In whatever class he might have been brought up, he was one of those who would always have been seen, always have made themselves distinguished for their personal qualities; and such as these have often the little weakness of desiring that all which belongs to them may be admired. Had Gunnar been gifted with birth or riches, or with both of these, he would never have been one of our laughable and despised dandies, who will be first in fashion and show, the last to undertake any thing which will not be talked about and attract the public gaze. Gunnar would never have belonged to this class, but to that other which must have *every thing* which is theirs, from the least to the greatest, from that which is seen by all eyes to that which is visible to no eye but their own, as beautiful, as comfortable, as suitable to its purpose, as elegant as possible. Had Gunnar been a magnate, probably nobody's horses or carriage could have compared with his; he would have been unrivaled in his outfit, in his manner of demeaning himself, and in his ability to be at once the proudest among the proud, and the best toward all his dependants. As it was, he was only a poor peasant; but we will not deny that he was conscious of a great degree of pleasure and self-satisfaction when he, at length, saw his own young and able horse trot forth in the neat and well-made cart, the labor of his own hands, which cost him many a sweat-drop, and many a half-night, and which now, new painted and grand, should convey—not Lena, but his old, affectionate, and beloved mother to church. It is possible that this had constituted, for a long time, one of Gunnar's most lively desires. And now, at length, it was accomplished; now, for the first time, he helped the old woman up into the vehicle, seated himself beside her, and escaped away from Lena, and all that upon a bright and beautiful day in spring! Ah! it was too much to expect that that young mind should not be a little proud, and that this feeling should not impress its stamp upon the lofty pure forehead, the princely arched eyebrows, the fine, straight, and perfectly aristocratic nose, and the haughty and curved upper lip. Lena saw it of a truth. Olle made the discovery also, and now, as always, in his envy and spite, attempted to do all the mischief he could, but which, this time, fortunately did not succeed. But, as real merit smiles at the vain attempts of envy crawling in the dust —envy not occasioned by wrath at merit itself, but at the splendid fruits of it—so Gunnar smiled at Olle, cracked his whip at the gay young Bläsa for being so silly as to be frightened at Olle's tricks, and continued his drive to the church, not displeased with the amazement that was excited, and the admiring glances which were directed to the brisk horse and the newly painted cart.

A consciousness of his own worth and his own ability began strangely to awake within Gunnar's mind. He began to discover that he was superior to his connections in manifold ways, and a desire arose within him to rise above them in every thing. In Gunnar many glorious natural endowments lay buried, which never could see the light, and his soul was, perhaps, one of the strongest instruments of genius, of profound investigation, of science and statesmancraft, of which every chord, every tone, was clear and pure, although fate had never struck them. But when the storm raged around Gunnar's soul—when the dead calm of every-day life and the tide of petty cares ceased—when powerful emotions and sufferings urged on the wheel of the heart, then was heard the sound of that stringed instrument's tones, like those irregular, aërial, chaotic sounds which proceed from the Æolian harp.

"It would be a good thing, mother-in-law, if you would sweep out the room before mid-day; but, look you, you must go quickly about it, for it will soon be twelve o'clock."

Thus sate Lena continually, and issued her commands on that mild May morning; for, with all her ugly failings, Lena was, in the highest degree, an orderly, clean, prudent, and clever mistress of a house, who never neglected any thing, who always did more than any other two. Her annoyance was now great in being compelled to sit still, bound, as it were, to her chair, because she had trodden upon a nail, which had inflamed her foot, as well as by seeing the kind, good, but mild and slow, Mother Ingrid doing all her work; nor can we so entirely condemn her feelings, nor yet the little *mauvais humeur* which arose in consequence, though we must deplore that Lena was not able to conceal it, as well as some other things; for Lena was, in her way, notwithstanding all her violence, a mistress in dissimulation when she had any thing to gain by it. Hence it happened that she very seldom was snappish at Mother Ingrid when Gunnar was present, but so much the more so in his absence, precisely because she knew that Mother Ingrid, with her excellent heart, would never at any time complain or tittle-tattle. And Mother Ingrid never did so, not only from the real excellence of her heart, but from the wish, to which all her prayers tended, that as much happiness, or at least as little unhappiness, as possible might befall her Gunnar in this mar-

riage, which Mother Ingrid had, at two different times, set
herself, in opposition to circumstances, to compel and to demand.

"Bring here the potatoes, that I may peel them, while you
make up the fire to roast them by," said Lena; but the next
moment, turning suddenly to the window, she exclaimed,
"Mother-in-law, look, in a minute, who it is that is riding so
boldly! Can it be that deuced Abraham who is riding down to
the water at that rate? He ought to have put the horse-cloth
on, and that very carefully, for it is a great damage to a horse
to take it warm down to water."

In the mean time Mother Ingrid had gone to the window, and
stood there, somewhat amazed.

"Well, what are you stopping so long for? Was it Abra'm?"
asked Lena.

"Oh, nay! it is a strange fellow, who is coming here, and is
dismounting," replied Mother Ingrid.

"A stranger!" exclaimed Lena. "What does he look
like?"

"He looks very grand," returned Mother Ingrid, and prepared to remove from the window, and pursue her work in the
chimney-corner.

"Merciful Lord! what a cursed thing it is to be fastened
down here as I am!" lamented Lena, impatiently. "What
sort of a fellow is it? Go out, then, mother-in-law, and see
what and who he is, and learn whether his business is with
Gunnar or with me. Make haste!"

Mother Ingrid went out, and immediately returned with the
equestrian messenger of ill-tidings, young Erik, who, after a
very polite peasant's bow, with a grave and sorrowful countenance, announced to Lena her loss, dwelling still more particularly on Elin's sorrow and trouble, and her longing desire to
see her sister and brother-in-law.

Lena let fall a few tears, but began immediately afterward
to make inquiries about the effects which her mother had left
behind, and now swore more than ever at the deuced nail which
that fool Abra'm laid in her way, and which now would prevent her accompanying Gunnar to see to and take account
of every thing. But as Lena was both cunning and quick in
thought, she soon consoled herself with the reflection, that now
Gunnar could, in her place, bring back Elin with him, and that
three of them could not go with one horse all that long way,

and that it would be very convenient for them to have Elin
through the summer, as Gunnar had undertaken Anderson's
work, and they were thus compelled to find more women's day-
work at the mowing and in the harvest; then they could do
without hiring. Besides this, Elin was so quick with her
hands, could help her with one thing and another, and did not
look as if she would be a great eater. Lena thought of all
these things while she talked to Erik about her native village,
of which she did not remember a great deal, as well as giving
to Mother Ingrid directions, in part loud, in part in a whisper,
as to what was to be prepared for the stranger guest, to whom
Lena wished to offer all imaginable cottage-comforts. *Per fas
et nefas* had she, during her many years' service in gentlemen's
houses, become possessed of divers things; she had also a few
odd table-napkins, with the marking picked out, as well as a
diaper table-cloth, which she allowed Mother Ingrid to lay
upon the table in the middle window, for the handsome, spacious
room had three, one on each side. Furthermore, she let her
bring forth the best brandy which the house contained, butter,
and cheese; besides which, Mother Ingrid brought a piece of
meat and potatoes, as well as milk: for, in consequence of that
work of Anderson's which Gunnar had undertaken, Lena had
now three cows, and thus had a great deal of milk.

Just when the little meal was ready, the master of the house
entered, with his game-bag much heavier than common. Gunnar had been in the woods ever since the dawn, and had been
unusually successful. He had now brought with him a large
wood-grouse and several blackcocks, so that he was in the best
possible humor. He was at first most agreeably surprised to
see the grand arrangement of the table and the guest, who was
a perfect stranger; but singularly enough, his good-humor increased, if possible, with the news which Erik announced, and
Gunnar had never been so ready to obey Lena's wishes as on
this occasion. It was a very pardonable thing that he should
not grieve about the death of his mother-in-law, whom he had
never seen, and scarcely ever heard of, and that he should look
forward with satisfaction to a time which would bring Elin
under the same roof. It would also have been pardonable if
the heart had beaten with quickened throbs at the mere thought
—but it was really unpardonable of the heart, not of Gunnar,
who as yet had not the least idea of it.

It belonged naturally to the proud character of Gunnar that

he should be a good host, and that he also was, whenever it was required.

"A health!" said he to the young Erik, wishing him to empty a silver bowl of pure, clear whisky, with the same relish as the weary, hungry, and thirsty hunter. Erik, however, excused himself, and said that he had "taken the temperance pledge." The two young men seated themselves one on each side the table, leaving the women to take care of themselves, and allowing them afterward to eat quite unnoticed, each in her corner. Abraham also took his dinner by himself, upon his bed by the door, as was always customary.

"Yes, and it is true that you belong to the temperance people, and have taken the pledge? then I will certainly not press you to drink," said Gunnar, who regarded an oath as more sacred than any thing else. "I at one time thought myself of joining the teetotalers, but I didn't after all; for this was my way of reasoning, that I ought to have the sense to be temperate; and that brandy is one of God's gifts as well as any thing else of which the moderate use may do good, but that all those ought to renounce it, who either drink too much of it already, or who know in their own minds that they shall be unable to resist in the long run. For many years, as I have said, I never drank a drop, for I had, from certain causes, an abhorrence of brandy, although for myself I found it very agreeable; but now since I have become a steady man, and beyond this my own master, and am out so much both by day and night in the wood and upon the lake, I take a draught now and then, when I seem to want it, and I know that it strengthens the body and keeps up the spirits; but never, I trust, shall I become a drunkard, if nothing—if no great sorrow and adversity befall me, for then I would not answer for it."

Erik nodded approbation of Gunnar's words, and quietly smiling, wished that nothing might ever happen which should convert his host into a drunkard; as for himself, he said, he never thought about the matter; he never had any particular taste for brandy, but immediately adopted "the clergyman's proposition." "For, look you," said he, "he is a terrible Turk about this teetotalism, and draws into it both young and old, both men and women, and every body who is confirmed."

"In that case, then, Elin is a teetotaler," said Lena; and young Erik, whose countenance crimsoned, assured her that nothing in this world would persuade Elin to let a drop of brandy pass her "small rosy lips."

Gunnar was silent, and crimsoned also.

The young men sat there, ate, and conversed, and were outwardly actual specimens of the most beautiful models of the Swedish peasantry. Gunnar was of lofty stature, slender and broad-chested at the same time; his whole exterior, his whole being, largely exhibited both outward and inward power. The eyes were of a deep-blue and of a resolute expression, the penetrating glances of which were softened by the long black eyelashes; the eyebrows were proudly arched; the nose, mouth, and chin, were finely formed; the forehead, lofty, broad, and smooth as a mirror; while the hair, of so dark a brown that it almost approached to black, lay in heavy and picturesque masses on each side of his countenance. It was a deep conviction of Gunnar's mind, that every person who adheres to his own class in life is far higher than he who apes the manners of another; and, therefore, he had always, even from his boyhood, had an especial aversion, not to the *gentleman*, but to the peasant who imitates the gentleman in any way, and nothing could have induced him to throw off his blue peasant's coat for a peasant's surtout, or, as Gunnar called it, "a gentry-surtout," or his long, luxuriant peasant-locks, for the closely-clipped head of the gentleman and the poor soldier of the present day. Gunnar, on the contrary, took the utmost care of his hair, as he did of his person generally; in part, because it was natural to him, and in part, as the result of Mother Ingrid's delicate sense of cleanliness and order; and this it was, perhaps, which contributed so much to the violent passion which he awoke in the heart of Lena, who, notwithstanding many other faults, yet never could endure any thing which was uncleanly and neglected.

Young Erik, on the other side, sat there with his fair hair, long also, but that was in consequence of his father's strict command that he should always wear it in the manner of the old Swedish yeoman—that is to say, parted on the forehead, and falling straight down over the ears. His eyes were of a lively and gentle expression, and of a blue as bright as that of the sky on a spring day. The coloring of his agreeable countenance was that of roses and milk, and made a strong contrast with Gunnar's brown cheek and dark whiskers. Whether Erik had eyebrows or not, one could not exactly say, because they were so light in color that they could be merely seen in a bright light. He was nearly the head shorter than Gunnar, and looked as gay, sportive, open-hearted, and full of the enjoyment of life, as Gunnar, for some time past, had looked silent, reserved, and grave.

Gunnar was not by any means disinclined for the proposed journey, which it was now arranged by the young men should begin by the earliest dawn of the following day. Both Erik and his horse required this one day's rest, as he had ridden through the greater part of the night; and, for Gunnar, it was requisite that he should make several small arrangements for his absence. Abraham was immediately sent to Ma'msell Sara, who, strictly equitable and observant of the law in every thing else, had, nevertheless, the weakness of all country ladies, that of looking through their fingers at those sportsmen who shoot before the legalized time, and who gladly appropriate their booty to themselves, giving in exchange new and handsome bank-notes. This little service rendered by Ma'msell Sara was now to furnish the means for Gunnar's journey; and Lena, assisted by Mother Ingrid, prepared a good supply of eatables, which were stowed in Gunnar's blue chest, but as for the rest, it was Lena's desire that Gunnar should take nothing with him "which would lumber up the cart" in which Elin and her necessaries were to be brought home.

"Dear," said Lena to Gunnar, who was unusually kind and obliging to her—"dear, as we two are now alone for a little while, while mother-in-law is milking and Erik is looking after his horse, I will beg one or two things of thee : look well after Elin, and see that she does not keep any of the household goods for herself, but that they are all sold and go into the general amount, and that is the opinion of Erik's father, Anders Nilson. But, look you, *it is necessary* that you have an eye upon Elin, because she will, assuredly, become avaricious and selfish on this occasion—that every body can believe."

Gunnar, who had just before been in so good a humor, even toward Lena, now grew angry; his eyebrows contracted, but he made no reply, although he felt a great inclination to speak openly in defense of Elin. He now went his way, however, without giving her any answer; and the cunning Lena mistook him this time, for she regarded his silence as an assent, and was greatly satisfied.

At the very earliest dawn of day, the two young men seated

themselves in the newly-painted cart, before which Bläsa trotted with Erik's Brunte fastened loosely beside it. It was quite a handsome turn-out. The two young travelers had agreed to journey in this way together, and, also, that every time they baited the horses, these should take turn and turn about, and thus alternately draw the carriage and trot on beside it.

When Abraham had been sent to the Hall with the game, he had also been commissioned with a little private message to Bengt, that he should meet Gunnar by day-break at the place where the two roads meet. But as Abraham could not keep silence before Olle, about all the wonderful things which had happened, and which were going to happen, so now Bengt did not betake himself alone to the appointed place; Olle also went, and was marching about at the junction of the roads, when Gunnar and Erik drove rapidly up. Gunnar immediately became angry.

"What the deuce must you bring that wretch with you for?" said he to Bengt, in an undertone, as they pulled up, and while Olle was vainly attempting to frighten the horses, and shake to pieces the cart.

"It was that chattering Abra'm's fault," returned Bengt.

"Yes, I'll pay him for it," said Gunnar, and ground his teeth. He then gave Bengt a few small commissions regarding that same Anderson, whose farm-work he had undertaken, and, besides that, prayed Bengt to do him one or two other little services, which Bengt was heartily willing to undertake. All this while Olle was screaming at the highest pitch of his voice—

"And so-o, you are going, I hear, to fetch a young lass! That is fine! Yes, that, I fancy, will suit you! Now, you'll have to ask me soon and often to go and see you at Vika, for I think a monstrous deal about her, Ellika, or whatever she is called, and I got a kiss of her when we parted at Christmas, and—"

"That is a cursed lie, like every thing you say!" interrupted Gunnar; "she no more gave you a kiss than she ate the sow that goes round the corner of the dike. Farewell, Bengt! Thanks and honor to thee for what thou hast promised to do for me. Let the cart alone, Olle, else I'll lash you with the whip right across your face! Ho! Bläsa!"

Olle retreated, but continued to shout after him the same words as long as Gunnar could hear him.

F

"What sort of a fellow is that?" asked Erik, when they were at about a hundred yards' distance from Bengt and Olle.

"Which of them?" inquired Gunnar.

"Bless me! that one that bawled and behaved so horribly; as to the other, he looked like a good sort of fellow enough."

"Ay," replied Gunnar, jealously and angrily at the same time; "that is a cursed wretch with whom I lived in service for two years, but whom I never could bring myself to bear. And it is horribly stupid of me, because, by rights, a good fellow ought never to be angry with such a creature; but I can never keep myself within bounds when I see him, for he enrages me by every possible way and means. And he is a drunkard as well, and a wicked man in every way."

"Now, he ought to join the teetotalers," remarked Erik.

"Oh, nonsense!" replied Gunnar, "for then he would certainly do as old Olaus of Kärreboda, who promised, with his hand upon the Bible, that he never would *drink* brandy, but, see you, he *ate* brandy with a spoon as much as he chose. And so it would be with Olle; for there is nothing but guile and deceit in his whole body, and oaths and promises are to him like so much snuff. No, he is a regular Judas, with a red wig."

"You don't like him," said Erik, smiling.

"Nay, I have as great a loathing to him as man can have."

"Well, but if he should follow after Elin, and should be intrusive and insolent, as he said?" asked Erik, a little uneasily and hot about the ears.

"Oh, the wretch! that shall he not!" replied Gunnar; "it shall be my fault if he do not let her alone. I believe he'll never dare to come to Vika, and if he were to poke his nose in there, I'd give him such a flogging with a whip as should satisfy him."

"Yes, that would be right," exclaimed Erik, breathing freely, and never suspecting that he had a far more dangerous rival much nearer to him.

The two young men talked on a variety of subjects during the journey. Great confidence had been placed in Gunnar with respect to taking journeys and executing business, and he had in this manner, as well as in consequence of his innate desire for information, much local knowledge within the district where he had merely traveled once; and he would with tolerable accuracy tell about what lay north and south, east and

west, as well as *up there, down there*, and *out there*, and pointed
out with the handle of his whip all the remarkable objects by
which they drove, as well as described them in his own way to
Erik.

"There, do you see," said he, "Korsberga church on yonder
hill? There is a very fine tomb there, you must know, in which
lie eleven persons of the name of Fältstjerna (field stars), and
you'll never find in that family more than that self-same eleven,
and in their coat-of-arms they have eleven stars; and he who
was the founder of the family went out into the war as a simple
trooper to Karstorp, but he returned home as a captain of horse
and a nobleman."*

"Yes, that might very well be," said Erik.

"Oh, yes, certainly, in its way," returned Gunnar; "but I
can not exactly understand how a man can be a better fellow
because he has a fine name given him, and is called a nobleman. And yet for all that it would be agreeable enough,"
added he, after a short reflection; "because if one were a
devilish good and clever fellow, in all respects, it would have
its bright side, thus at once to take precedence of every body
else, and that one's children—" here he suddenly checked himself.

"Well," said Erik, "that one's children?"

"Ay," returned Gunnar, more slowly and with less enthusiasm, or, rather, with a certain melancholy in his tone, "that
they had their father's example, and that every time they heard
their grand new name, it should come into their remembrance
that they should be excellent men like their father. Ay, ay;
then it would not be any thing so monstrously stupid. But,
look ye, those only who *actually* deserved it should be distinguished, and it should be the downright noble fellows to whom
every body would take off their hats, and not a set of scamps
and villains who now carry themselves so arrogantly, and are
called *gentlemen*, only because they have property, and are able
to commit robberies with their money, partly by injustice, partly by the sweat and toil of the poor. Psha!" said Gunnar,
with disgust, "I can not endure such gentlemen, whose whole
dignity consists in their coats and their money-bags. No, a good
peasant is far, far before such, and therefore as I can never be
a nobleman nor a priest—Heaven knows, since I never went

---

* A fact. (Author's note.)

to school—therefore I am, and will continue to be, a peasant all my days, and I will not have any thing on my grave but 'honest and of good understanding,' and this I will deserve."

Thus did Gunnar converse with Erik; but amid these more grave subjects another was frequently introduced, now called forth by one, and now by the other traveler, and sometimes by both—namely, Elin. When the conversation turned upon her, Erik became talkative, praised her incredibly, and extolled her above the skies, but still never ventured to say, what he had resolutely determined within himself, and that was, that should he even have to wait for his father's death, nobody but Elin should ever become his wife.

Gunnar was more taciturn on the subject of Elin, but he listened with all the more attention, and sighed imperceptibly when he compared all the merits and the good qualities of his young sister-in-law with all the ugly faults which, day by day, revealed themselves in Lena, and which made her still more and more abhorrent in his eyes.

CHAPTER XX.

By noon of the following day, the two travelers arrived at the end of their journey. A day and a half had been occupied by it, although it was not much more than seven (Swedish) miles, but we must bear in mind they were not two of our young lieutenants, who fly with the wings of post-horses and whipcord, but two young peasants and farm-workers, who traveled with their own horses, and about their own business, although their burning desire to arrive at the end of their journey could match itself against that of our lieutenants, which is often small enough in comparison with the rapid flight which they so much love in general.

Gunnar and Erik first put up their horses, and gave them something to amuse themselves with, and then entered Father Anders' large, well-to-do peasant's house, in which Elin sat alone, sewing some piece of mourning against the funeral. She was not now the blooming, merry, lively, dancing maiden, who at the wedding, a year and a half before, had delighted all

eyes, and constituted the single point of light in Gunnar's remembrance of this wedding.   Now she was the daughter, pale
with weeping and sorrow, but as perfectly lovely and agreeable.   She sat there, looking so neat and elegant, in a black
every-day dress, with a little snow-white kerchief on her shoulders, and her light-brown hair braided closely and smoothly on
her temples, and fastened up behind in a thick and glossy plait,
much in the style of our most elegant ladies—(N.B., if they
have any to fasten up).

She arose hastily, and went toward Gunnar; extended to him
her hand, and burst into tears.   She thanked him for having
come; thanked Erik heartily for the great trouble he had
taken, and was much grieved that Lena was prevented from
coming by such a sad accident.

"Oh, yes," said she, warmly, and in an under voice to Gunnar, "all my hope and trust is in you, dearest brother and sister, for I have now no other support in the whole world."

Elin spoke thus, because she knew very well that it was
only now, during her first period of sorrow, that she was invited to spend a few days at Father Anders', and she estimated
both Father Anders himself, and the dextrous but yet simple
Mother Karen, according to their full value; but she knew
sufficiently well that in the end they would do nothing for her;
and, as regarded the son Erik, she was much attached to him
as the friend and playmate of her childhood, but she never
thought any thing about him when she did not see him; his
image did not stand forth with any particularly bright coloring
in her mirror of the future; and she thus made a sufficiently
ill return for the honest and ardent tone of Erik.

Gunnar did not say much.   He felt too deeply for that; but
he entered with Father Anders into the various circumstances
which connected the little and now deserted dwelling, where,
after the interment had taken place, an inventory should be
made of the property while Gunnar was there; and this Father
Anders promised to put up to auction, as well as to conduct
the sale himself, because he was the most esteemed auctioneer
in the whole town, or the district.

Toward evening an elderly peasant-woman came in and
whispered some words to Elin. Elin again began to weep,
nevertheless did not leave Gunnar, but, on the contrary, asked
him if he had any inclination to accompany her down to the
house of her deceased mother, and to see the features of the

departed before the coffin-lid was fastened down, as the dead, according to the account of the woman who had shrouded her, was not at all changed.

Gunnar accepted the proposal immediately, and took his young sister-in-law by the hand, took that small peasant-hand firmly into his own, and accompanied her through the pretty and neat little town.

"Oh! how many a time have I walked and run along here, both in joy and sorrow!" sobbed Elin, "and now, perhaps, it is for the last time that I am going down to the pretty little house, which you can see there among the blooming cherry-trees. Ah! what happy days have I not spent there! and now, what will be my fate?"

"Thou shalt live with us—thou and we will live happily," replied Gunnar, and pressed her hand firmly.

Elin returned his hand-pressure, but not his words, for they were now at the door of that little house where Elin was born, and had lived twenty years of happy childhood and youth. She wept much when they went into the little entrance, and then opened a door to the left, where a large room, or the so-called house-place, was situated. In the middle of this room stood the open coffin. Elin started back, and let go Gunnar's hand; but afterward recovering courage, she soon led the way, and conducted him to the beloved corpse, over which the last beams of the evening sun, trembling through the waving leaves of the cherry-trees which wreathed the window, cast a beautiful light —a marvelous radiance.

"Ah! she lies there just as when she was alive!" sobbed Elin; "see how beautiful and how good she looks. Oh! it is exactly as if she were going to speak. Look, she has not a single gray hair; and how like she is to Lena about the mouth. Dost thou not think so, dear Gunnar?" (Gunnar made no reply.) "Ah! my God! that death can thus come and put an end to the life of an excellent being. And *she* lived only to make people happy and do them good."

After this Elin remained some time standing in silence by her mother's side, but at length she went away to some flowers which stood in the window, broke a little rosebud, as well as a few sprigs of blossoming geranium, placed them in her mother's hand, kissed her forehead, and then said softly, weeping the while—

"Now, Gunnar, we will go."

Yet, once more she threw herself down by the coffin; and now it was Gunnar who compelled her to act the reasonable and prudent part; he lifted her up softly from the floor, pressed her closely to his throbbing heart, and said—

"Do not weep so, my good, dear Elin! I will be to thee both brother and friend, and—"

He could say no more. His full heart felt more than it had words to express. He carried Elin out into the entrance-room.

"Thanks, dear Gunnar," she then said; "let me be; I shall now indeed be rational again."

When, however, they had gone out through the little entrance door, she suddenly stopped.

"Ah," said she, "perhaps I shall never come hither again while it looks as it has done, because after the funeral every thing will be cleared away! I will just once more take a peep into my little summer chamber, which mother always let me have for myself through the whole summer, as long as one could do without fire."

With this she opened the door in the middle of the entrance, and conducted Gunnar into a little room so neatly and elegantly arranged, that no young lady could have one much more so, although the habitation itself was old and poor. There stood in the window pots in which were growing many kinds of flowers; above these hung a cage containing a little warbling linnet, and before the window stood a table, the drawers of which were locked. Outside the window ran a clear brook, among cherry-trees, and close beside it a little flower-garden, which had constituted Elin's delight and pride, and upon which she had spent many an hour and many a thought. She opened the window, sighed, and looked down upon the fresh flowers; looked up to the blossoming trees, and again down to the clear little rapid brook; gazed upon all these with melancholy and tearful glances, but said nothing; she afterward looked round the room, but fixed her eyes again thoughtfully on the window and all it contained.

"Ah, in that window said she, "I had all the little which was dear to me! and now, perhaps, I shall never more see these trifles!"

"And why not?" said Gunnar; "why should you not see them again?"

"Oh, heavens!" said Elin; "how can I take with me my

little bird, my flower-pots, and my little table, which would sell so well?"

"What's the use of selling them?" asked Gunnar again; "and if you would like to have them altogether with you on the journey, why should you not? On the contrary, they can go exceedingly well."

"But then I have a little chest besides," said Elin.

"Well, yes, that will stand behind in the cart, and then you can have the table beside you, and we can set the flower-pots as we can, and the cage with the little bird you can hold on your knee."

"But then, how will you manage to drive?" inquired Elin, well pleased at Gunnar's proposal.

"Oh, I shall manage well enough!" replied Gunnar, and laughed so charmingly; "I have walked beside a cart many a time before now, and carried a load heavier and worse to carry than *that*. Don't trouble yourself about it; you shall have all your little property with you, that I answer for, and it will go capitally."

Elin thanked Gunnar with all her heart; and in order that she might have all her little possessions in one place, they determined immediately to carry them down with them to "Father Anders'," where her chest was already. Gunnar took the table, a little footstool, and a myrtle in a pot. Elin took the birdcage, her beautiful London Bible, and some other devotional books which she had upon a little shelf, together with such small flower-pots as she set most value on; and, thus burdened, they returned to Father Anders' house, after that Elin had cast a long and sorrowful glance at the door which led into the room where lay the last remains of her beloved mother. On their way they met Erik, who was glad to help Elin with the whole of her load, with the exception of the bird-cage.

"That you may carry yourself," said Erik, who wished to enliven her; "for I will not go and carry that ugly little thing which cost you so many tears."

"How was that?" inquired Gunnar, who felt an extraordinary interest for every thing which concerned Elin.

"Why," replied Erik, "I caught the little bird, and gave it to Elin, with the cage and the fountain and all; but God knows how it was! the window stood open, and the cage in it open too, so the bird flew out, and was away for a day and a half, and Elin cried all day and all night, and the next day I had the good luck to catch him again and entice him into the cage; but Elin would not believe that it was the same before she actually saw that it was, and that he came and took hemp seed from her lips; then she believed it was hers, and it made her happy again."

CHAPTER XXI.

THE interment took place with silence and solemnity, because Elin's mother had been universally beloved; and every one reverenced Elin's sorrow. There was scarcely any who did not say, "Look what a handsome and agreeable brother-in-law Elin has got! He looks much more fitted for her than for that cat-like Lena, for she was as bad a piece of goods as ever grew up. God grant that she may behave well to her sister-in-law! Yet the brother-in-law is a fine fellow, that one can see plain enough!"

The inventory was made out; and Elin left all to Gunnar and Father Anders' pleasure, that they might do just what they thought best. She wept much at parting from her friends and the place of her birth; and also when, at the commencement of the journey, they drove past the churchyard where her mother lay interred, and where the newly-cut, green turf pointed out the spot, she covered her face with her hands, and wept bitterly.

"Ah, do not weep so, my dear, sweet Elin!" said Gunnar, who now felt it was his duty to console her. "Thou wilt ruin thy lovely eyes, and make thy head ache, and then I shall be so distressed."

This last argument operated most. Elin endeavored to put a restraint upon her emotions, and she succeeded; and before long, if she were not exactly cheerful, still she was most kind and conversable.

The two travelers talked a great deal about the future; and already might any observant person have perceived how in these conversations they thought much more about each other than of themselves. Elin said that she had not the slightest inclination to take a service, but would much rather remain with her sister, and live with her as a maid-servant, considering that they must have one, it being necessary on account of Anderson's work. Gunnar represented to Elin that she, who had never done any thing but sew, and spin, and weave, and such-like sedentary employments, would find it very difficult to have to go into the cow-house, and to make herself useful in the meadows and fields, to gather twigs, to thrash, etc. Elin, however, said that she would attempt to do all this, and declared that she ought to learn to do them, for that she was turned twenty; and she concluded by laughing, and saying—

"How should I ever manage, if I should any time become my own mistress?"

A pang went through Gunnar's heart at these words. He called to mind Erik's parting from Elin. How he had shed tears, and accompanied them along the road; how he had caressed and embraced Elin, and how she, on her side, was friendly toward him both now at parting, and many another time during the day. Gunnar was silent for a long while; at length he said, with a certain effort:

"Ay, ay, Elin dear. Thou think'st a good deal about that Erik, and Erik, too—that I can very well understand—why not?"

Elin looked at him with her clear blue eyes, and Gunnar looked at her with his dark eyes. They bewildered themselves for a moment in each other's glances; and their hearts beat quicker, and their cheeks glowed with a deeper crimson, but neither of them knew why.

The journey was not a rapid one. Gunnar had no longings for his home, and seemed, therefore, to have great doubts about Blåsa. Singularly long silences often succeeded to earnest and animated conversation. Gunnar and Elin felt themselves for a while unspeakably happy, and then again—as if they were in want of something, but they looked one upon the other, and then—all want seemed supplied.

"But," said Elin, after a silence of an unusual length, "thou never think'st about your little Gustaf. It seems to me that it will be so delightful to see him and to play with him. Is he a sweet little child? Is he like thee or like Lena? He ought to be like thee as he is a boy, for thou"—but she did not finish the sentence.

"Oh, yes, the lad is a nice child; there is no fault to find with him." Having said thus much, Gunnar talked about something else.

They had to spend the night at the house of a peasant with whom Gunnar was acquainted; there they seemed to be most heartily welcome, for Gunnar was beloved every where, and Elin became so the moment any one saw her. The kind and affable peasant-wife set before them the best she was able, and showed them in the evening into a pretty double-bedded room, where they were to pass the night, wishing them as she went out "a pleasant night's rest." Elin sat down for a moment considering, and then said with great simplicity,

"Dost thou know, Gunnar, thou must certainly go out and find another sleeping-place for thyself, that I may have this room; for I never can accustom myself to sleep in the same room with a man. I have never yet done it, although I know well enough that it is the universal custom among the peasantry."

Gunnar left the room. And, however weary and sleepy he might be, for he had walked nearly the whole of the day, and that keeping up with Bläsa the whole time, yet still he lay pondering on various things before he went to sleep. In their sitting-room at Vika, there were two "curtained beds," as they were called, to which there were handsome blue-striped hangings, which had been woven by Lena, and trimmed with white linen fringe, the remnants of the weaving, which she had collected during her years of service. One of these belonged, as a matter of course, to the husband and wife, and in the other slept Mother Ingrid, and where also, Gunnar had always heard, "the new servant-girl," whom they were to take in the autumn, was to sleep. Away by the door stood the wooden press-bed, where Abraham sat every evening, and out of which he turned every morning. Thus was it, but how was it now to be? Gunnar, at first, could not at all discover how they were to manage, but he thought a deal about it. Where was Elin to sleep, "who would not sleep in the same room with the men-folk," which was otherwise so extremely usual among the peasantry in Sweden, where the houses contain seldom more than one common room for all purposes.

"Hist!" a light flashed upon Gunnar's mind. Could not Elin have that small wardrobe-chamber, which was of so trifling a use, and in which there was even a little fire-place. They lived also in the middle of the wood; and when winter came, he would take care that she had fuel to burn; there was no danger of that, even though he himself might have to cut it at

night.   He fancied that he could do *every thing* for Elin, at this
moment; he had, nevertheless, a presentiment that Lena would
not do any thing which did not promote her own interest; and
he had an instinctive feeling that, as regarded her, it would be
better to go to work in a diplomatic sort of way than to
attack her directly.   Besides this, he hoped that the old
proverb would be true which says, that blood is thicker than
water ; and, therefore, that Lena would make an exception
as regarded Elin, in her constantly selfish mode of pro-
ceeding.

Gunnar went to sleep late, and awoke early.   Life was again
worth living for.   When Gunnar was dressed, he went out in
the first place to look after his horse, and, after that, he took a
turn round the house in which Elin slept, and could not possibly resist the temptation, whether he would or not, of casting
an inquiring glance toward the window, where he knew, of a
certainty, that she was.   How astonished he was, then, to see
her standing, already dressed, and smiling at him through the
open window, bidding him good morning, but giving him, at
the same time, a warning sign with her finger, when he was
about to utter aloud his joyful surprise.

"Hist ! then," said she.   "Do not let us wake our excellent
host and hostess ; but if you are impatient to set off, we can do
so easily, without waiting till they wake, or without breakfast;
for when we rest a little we can refresh ourselves from our
store of provisions."

"Oh, nonsense !" replied Gunnar, who had quite another design ; "we need not be in such a desperate hurry.   The horse
requires time both to eat and to rest, and it will be much better for us to drive a little quicker.   And you, dear Elin, you
require some good coffee before we set off; and that I know
we shall get from Mother Britta, where we are.   And I, too,
can do very well with a good warm breakfast.   No, we need
not hurry so very much; but now, do you come out for a little
while, that we may take a walk, and look about us this glorious
and lovely summer morning."

Elin did not see any thing objectionable in Gunnar's proposal ; she threw, therefore, her black shawl over her head, and
stole softly out of the house to him.   Hand in hand went they
around the peasants' fields, which were particularly beautiful
and pleasant, and, at length, came up to the top of a steep hill,
from which they had a most extensive and beautiful view.   This

little farm, where they had passed the night, lay at the extremity of the lofty, beautiful, and wood-covered mountain of Billing, which elevates itself in the midst of the most lovely and fertile plains of West Gothland, like an immense giant, green almost to its very summit, and blue, and bluer still, the farther one removes from it.

"Oh! I never before saw such a beautiful and grand prospect!" said Elin, and pressed Gunnar's hand.

"Yes," replied Gunnar, who was bewildered with the view of the unrivaled landscape which lay below him. "Yes, I always seem to lose my breath when I see this fine plain, which, after all, is certainly not a plain, when we come to it, although it now looks like one, with all its churches, and towns, and gentlemen's seats; and see, there, Elin dear, there are the two church towers of Skara; and look, there is Kinne hill, so beautiful, and round, and dark-blue; and that light-blue stripe down there, which glances so in the morning sun, that is the Venner lake. It is a great lake, thou mayest believe; but not so inconceivably beautiful and bright as the Vetter lake; for there it is only fresh water. Hast thou ever been on 'the hill,' dear Elin?" (Elin shook her little head by way of negative.) "Then, some Sunday, this summer, we will drive there, thou and I, if we go nowhere else, for *that* thou shalt see. It is really the finest thing any body can see, I think. There thou wilt see the great lake lying just like the plain here before thee, and glancing and shining like thy hair, or else foaming and whirling, and of a gray-blue color, as if it were enraged like an evil beast. And then thou shalt see Leckö Castle, which lies out in the lake like a gray goose on the waters. Thou mayest trust me, all these are most remarkable, when they are seen, although it sounds almost stupid when one describes them. I lived in service a year on the hill, before I was 'confirmed,' and I never shall forget how strangely the lake affected me sometimes. Yes, do you know, Elin dear, it was just as if the mermaid, or the neck, had decoyed me to her, and I shut my eyes many times when I stood upon the shore of the lake, that the water-spirits might not have power over me, and drag me to the bottom; for I had an indescribable desire to throw myself in, and thus, perhaps, I might have remained there with them."

"Yes, but then thou canst swim like an eel," observed Elin, and held Gunnar all the firmer, as if she feared lest this sin-sprite could come even through the air, and carry away Gunnar before her eyes, to "the narrow and shining stripe."

"Oh, yes, I can swim," replied Gunnar; "but what would that avail against the mermaid, if she *would?*"

"What dost thou fancy that she looks like?" asked Elin.

"Oh," replied Gunnar, "she is certainly handsome, like thee."

"Fie!" exclaimed Elin, laughing, "that thou should compare me to a witch!" and, with that, she gave Gunnar a little blow with her hand; and Gunnar took her hastily round the waist, and drew her to him. Elin, however, as hastily escaped from him, and said gayly and kindly,

"Nay, come now, Gunnar, otherwise they may fancy that we have run away from them when they wake."

"Yes, and left the horse and cart, and all the things," observed Gunnar, somewhat annoyed, for he had no idea of returning. He was now too much excited by what he had seen, what he heard, and what he remembered. The past days of his childhood stood so vividly before him in this beautiful sun-illumined present, that it was a vexation for which Gunnar was not rightly prepared to have to descend again to every-day life, with all its petty cares, some of them, it is true, not more than an inch in size, but, on the contrary, of many hundred pounds weight. Still, however, these were not so *just now;* they were all as light as feathers, and hardly an inch in size; and Gunnar followed Elin almost like a shadow.

During the rest of their journey they conversed incessantly. When one person willingly talks, and another person still more willingly listens, then may the conversation be called lively; and few things will bear any comparison in delight with a lively conversation between two persons suitable for each other; it is like the divided apple, of which each side bears a different color.

Toward afternoon the travelers found that, notwithstanding the good feed which the horse had in the morning, the slower he went the nearer he approached the end of his journey. When the old "gentleman's seat," the old gray "nest," that Grantorp, which might tell us so much about ancient times if it could talk about such things—when this old house came into view, Elin exclaimed,

"Look, there is the great stone Hall! Never did I see such a large house! And it is only of stone. Bless me! how mysterious and gloomy I thought it was in the winter, a year ago, and now it looks almost cheerful. Look how beautiful and grand it is, standing there in the midst of the woods just bursting into leaf! The squire asked me whether I would not come and live in the family as housemaid in the place of Lena; but I could not then have done it for half the world, and that for many reasons," added she, sighing deeply; "but now, you see," continued she, in a livelier tone, "it might do very well."

"Oh, no, no! In the name of Jesus, shall it never be, Elin!" said Gunnar, and became deathly pale at the mere thought. "No—promise me that. Swear to me, Elin, that you never—no never, in all your days—will enter into that robber's den."

"Bless me! but why dost thou speak thus of such an excellent place, with such a good family?" said Elin, a little indignantly and reproachfully.

"Ay, I know very well why," muttered Gunnar, half aloud, and became gloomy and silent. Elin questioned him no further on the subject. She already thought of something else.

But now they turned off from the great high road, leaving Grantorp to the right, and traveled on by a narrow path through a deep wood. This path wound beautifully among the gigantic growth of firs and pines, and the evening air began to give that fragrance to the wood which is so agreeable, yes, so irresistibly delightful, to all dwellers in the woods. Gunnar, with his lips apart, the nostrils extended, and his head thrown back, inhaled large draughts of this glorious wood air.

"Oh, how delicious it tastes, after all the dust of the high-road!" said he, and looked up to the tree tops, as if he were observant of some bird. He then looked down to Elin, who was unobservedly wiping away a tear from her eye.

"Ah, do not weep thus, heart's dear Elin!" besought Gunnar. "Thy hot tears always burn me. I think thou art so much to be pitied. Only rely on *my* power; thou shalt be well off with us, and never shalt repent the day thou set'st foot on our door."

"Yes, God grant it!" sobbed Elin.

God himself knows best whether at this moment he sent a presentiment to Elin, or a warning, or both; but she wept bitterly, and Gunnar hardly drove at a foot's-pace.

"Now, cheer up, Elin dear," said he at length. "The road winds round a very little to the left, and then thou canst see both the lake and Vika, and our meadow, and our wood, and the new boat which I bought at the midsummer fair, and every thing which we have."

"Bless me! may I go out in the boat?" asked Elin, with all the gladness of a child, and dried her tears.

Gunnar, extremely delighted, took her hand, and stroked his cheek with it, and pressing it warmly at the same time, he said,

"Yes, yes; thou shalt go in the boat! Thou shalt sit and sing one of those lovely old songs, which thou singest so well, and I will row thee far out into the lake, on some beautiful and calm evening. And then thou shalt go out with me to lay the long lines; and early, by break of day, thou and I will go out and examine the nets, before the sun is up. Asch! what delightful sails we will have!"

With this he gave the horse an animating little cut with the whip; and look, now—now there lay spread out before their eyes, the beautiful lake, bright as a mirror, surrounded by grassy meadows and hills covered with wood. Upon the nearest shore lay the beautiful little farm of Vika, which had probably derived its name from a long, narrow headland, wooded with birches and alders, which, running into the lake, formed a creek (vik), and upon this headland the house of Vika was built. This headland constituted the finest pasturage land on the farm; and at this time a few cows and sheep were grazing among the trees, and thus giving beauty to the scene. The house itself was entirely new-built, unusually lofty, large, and neat, for a farm-cottage. The barns and farm-buildings also looked new and flourishing. The whole place, indeed, had a pleasant and comfortable appearance, with its little garden, in which were green shrubs, and blossoming fruit, and cherry-trees. Just across the lake might be seen a church, and several farm-houses, with their shining red-tiled roofs. The picture thus represented was one of unusual beauty, seen in the light of the descending sun, which at that time seems always to cast a twofold splendor over the earth, as if she would that this, her child, should miss her, should wish for her during the darkness of night, and not forget her for the moon and the thousand stars, whose delights she seems to envy.

Thus does graceful woman often fly from the glances and

blandishments of man, and precisely at the last moment of her tarrying, heightening her powers of fascination, that she may leave behind her that sun-bright memory which may defy every dangerous rival. Do you not recognize yourselves, you good and beautiful ones, who, even in this, resemble your glorious symbol—the sun?

"Oh! how beautiful! how beautiful!" exclaimed Elin, and Gunnar's passionate glances seemed almost to devour the words from her lips. He felt himself, at this moment, to be inexpressibly happy, because it was Elin whom he had conducted here, and because it was to his home, "and to _her_ home," that he had brought her. He could have kissed the very earth, so lovely did it seem to him at that moment. But we, ah! we will weep, because we seem to hear those unhappy words breathed through empty space, those words of a suffering human being, who had learned too truly the uncertainty of all earthly happiness.

> "Know, smiler! at thy peril art thou pleased;
> Thy pleasure is the promise of thy pain.
> Misfortune, like a creditor secure,
> But rises in demand for her delay;
> She makes a scourge of past prosperity
> To sting thee more, and double thy distress!"

Thus exclaimed Young, some time in his dark nightly despair; and _where_ can be found the happy mortal who has not, sooner or later, chimed in with his sorrowful lament?

"Welcome, dearest Elin," said Lena, and dried her own eyes, although they were scarcely perceptibly moist; "but now we will have no crying," added she, and that wisely enough, because it would have been difficult for her to shed tears now that she was not angry—for then she always cried.

Elin's tears on the contrary, flowed abundantly; and she thought Lena, now, more than ever, like her deceased mother, except that her mother had looked far milder and kinder. Elin, however, did not say so; she spoke merely of the resemblance, which filled her with joy, and yet which caused her to weep.

Gunnar nodded at Lena, but afterwards hastened into the house to salute Mother Ingrid, who had not heard of the arrival of the travelers.

"Good day, fallé,"* said little Gustaf, in a clear, childish

* A familiar contraction of _far lille_, or dear father. (Author's note.)

voice, and came bounding towards him so gladly and affectionately, that Gunnar felt a sad and oppressive feeling in his heart at not being able to clasp him in his arms, for at this moment he could willingly have embraced the whole universe— but not, however, this child, whom otherwise he would have loved as tenderly as his own.   But with a heart like Gunnar's it was impossible, but that *notwithstanding*, and spite of *every thing*, he should feel a tenderness for this little child; sweet-tempered, good, and lovely as it was, and which grew up, day by day, under his own eyes.

"See, there's something for thee, poor little thing!" said Gunnar, and gave him on the spot a hard and dry biscuit which had been left at the funeral, and which had withstood all the disasters of the journey, commonly so destructive of every kind of pastry—and which had remained entire and unscathed in the pocket of his coat.

"Thanks, fallé," said the boy, and immediately began to nibble at the gift, whilst Gunnar patted him on the head.

"See, thou art a good lad, my Gunnar! and a thousand times welcome home," said Mother Ingrid, who alone had seen his behavior to the child, and she wiped away a tear, an actual tear, from her old eyes.   Her son embraced her, and asked her how she had been for these many days.

In the mean time Lena and Elin had a little conversation together.   Elin about the departed mother, and Lena about "the effects" which were left.   Now, however, they had come into the neatly arranged sitting-room, the floor of which was scattered with fir-twigs.

"Oh! how nice you have every thing here!" said Elin, and looked round her with great delight.   "What an exceedingly handsome, lofty, and spacious sitting-room you have!"

"Look, in that bed thou art to lie with mother-in-law," said Lena.

Elin and Gunnar exchanged glances.

"Oh, no!" said Gunnar, with great decision of tone, "I have faithfully promised Elin that she shall have the little chamber to herself, and there she shall sleep.

"Oh, it is impossible!" replied Lena, in a tone of some displeasure; "there is no bed, and we have no bed-clothes at all; and all our garments are hanging there, and—"

"Nonsense!" interrupted Gunnar, "I shall, some of these days, before the mowing begins, put together a nice little bed

—that I shall. I can have elm-wood enough, and mother has both a pillow and a quilt in her chest up in the garret, that I know, who helped to pack them up."

"Yes, and Elin is heartily welcome to the loan of them," said Mother Ingrid, who would much rather sleep alone in her bed, and who was at the same time kind-hearted, and glad to be helpful.

"Yes, but it is a great sin to wear them out," said Lena, who immediately remembered that when Mother Ingrid died those things would belong to her.

"Oh, I shall not wear them out so very much," said Elin beseechingly, and embraced Lena. Lena promised to give her consent, all the more, as she had it in her mind to get an infinite deal of assistance, and many a useful thing done, by the quick and dextrous Elin, though, at the same time, she should give her neither wages nor any thing else.

The evening was uncommonly agreeable, and Lena in the best of humors, more especially when she saw how little Gustaf nibbled at his biscuit, as well as that he had got it from "good fallé." Elin took the child up in her arms, kissed him most affectionately, for he was both clean and sweet, as well as handsome.

"Ah! thou sweet little angel," said she, "thou art as sweet as sugar! But I can't make it out who he is like: it is neither Gunnar nor Lena."

Lena busied herself assiduously at the cupboard, and seemed not to hear. Mother Ingrid looked down at her knitting, and Gunnar went out. Some time after, when he returned, they were talking about something else, and he again became happy and cheerful, happier and more cheerful than Lena and his mother had ever seen him since they had removed to Vika.

"And you have, besides, a farm-laborer!" said Elin, who was thinking over all the affairs of the family. "My word, but you have people enough to feed, and now you will have me besides."

"That won't make much difference," replied Lena, "for thou art nothing of an eater in comparison with Abr'm."

"Abraham is a magnificent fellow!" said Gunnar, waggishly, and glanced significantly at Lena and his mother, that they should not gainsay him. "He is now out doing day-labor at the Hall, I reckon," continued Gunnar, in a jocular tone, and with difficulty keeping himself from laughing; "but he will very soon be coming home, and *then*, Elin dear, *then* thou wilt see a monstrously handsome, and pleasant, and smart young fellow, just such a one as has taken thy fancy."

"Just such a one as has taken my fancy!" repeated Elin, rather indignantly, "I have taken a fancy, certainly, to nobody."

"Well, what of Erik, then?" returned Gunnar, and held up his finger in a merrily threatening manner.

"Yes, what of him, then?" replied Elin, and blushed a little.

"Ay, ay!" said Lena, laughing aloud. "Now we shall see our Abr'm pulling Erik Anderson's nose out of joint, let him be fine and rich as he may; for you may believe Abr'm is something of a *calvalier*, that is he!"

Lena had learned some fine words and phrases during her many years of service in various gentlemen's families, and she often made use of them when she was in a good humor: but she always mangled these words dreadfully, and Gunnar could never refrain from laughing at her, and imitating her.

"Yes, Heaven help me, exactly a true *calvalier*," said he; "fine and elegant as a doll, and quick, and clever, and nimble as a magpie, and intelligent, and—"

"Ah, you shall not make a fool of the poor fellow," said Mother Ingrid, smiling, but nevertheless with a grave manner, "he is to be sure moderately *schangteeler*, as Lena says, but he does his duty, and that doesn't consist in strutting and swaggering about like a turkey-cock, as you other young fellows at the Hall used to do, thou Gunnar even in former days, and Bengt, and Olle, and many another."

"Yes, look ye; they were altogether laboring-men at the Hall, and such as they always have a little more of the *pettermätrar* in them," remarked Lena jocularly.

> "If you'll take a look at the gentlemen's servants,
>   You'll see, though they're fine, they've no substance at all!"

sang Gunnar, in his clear, pure tenor, and looked waggishly at Elin.

"Well! that was a treat to hear Gunnar sing!" said Mother Ingrid; that I did not expect to hear for a year and a day."

Gunnar cast his eye up to the wall, where his dusty and unstrung violin was hanging by the side of his gun, and said,

"Now, how stupid it was of me not to have bought myself

some violin strings when we drove through Sköfdt, for either at Råberg's or Lagerstedt's I could have got them ; but I can, after all, send for them very well from our own town, by the postman from the Hall, and that I will !" added he, with gay animation.

The evening was particularly delightful to every body. Elin took possession of her new apartment, and already thought how she would adorn it with curtains, and a little blind for the lower panes, that she might keep Gunnar and "that laborer" from peeping in. Gunnar assisted her in setting every thing in order ; knocked in a hook for the bird's cage, the small inhabitant of which amused little Gustaf indescribably ; he carried in her chest of drawers, her table, and the other small matters which they had brought with them. Lena looked at, and carefully examined, every thing, and inquired whether "the table and the bureau" were Elin's property *before* her mother's death, which Elin honestly declared to be the case. All the articles of clothing which had hitherto been hung in that room were carried up into the garret, and Gunnar promised that the next day he would drive in some hooks to hang them upon. They arranged a little temporary bed for Elin, scanty enough, it is true, but with which she was perfectly satisfied till better could be obtained.

When Abraham at length came home, Elin could not help laughing, because she had actually in part believed the description they had given her, or, at all events, she could not imagine to herself that she should see such an ill-favored, clumsy, crooked-legged, and mean-looking young man of twenty. His hair was rough and ill-kept, his clothes worn and neglected, and he seemed hardly gifted with half the intelligence of ordinary men, although he had double their capacity for eating. When Elin, however, had had her laugh out, there was an end of it ; and from that day forth Abraham had *two* defenders, for Mother Ingrid had always done this against Lena, who was incessantly scolding and abusing "that *brute* Abr'm," and Gunnar, who often lost patience with his stupidity and want of sense. He was, nevertheless, a strong and clever laboring man, and as patient as he seemed to be ; and was, besides that, as entirely devoted to Gunnar, as much so as is the so often ill-treated dog. Elin, however, thought to herself, " Good heavens ! what a delightful thing it is to escape having to be always in the same room with such a one !"

CHAPTER XXII.

A SEASON of comfort and enjoyment now commenced. The summer sun seemed not only to shine through the unclouded and brilliant firmament, but into every heart beneath the low roof of the peasant's dwelling. Elin shed a few tears now and then, but every body tried to comfort and enliven her, and, if they are beloved who make these attempts, then are they mostly successful. Lena's foot was become well again, and she could now, therefore, go and look after every thing; and never had Gunnar been so kind to her and the boy as now, and never had he done so much work, or made such good bargains before. She was, therefore, in an especially good humor. Mother Ingrid was unusually free from the weakness in her chest during this warm, pleasant season of the year; and, besides this, she was made so happy by the general good temper that prevailed, and by her son's return to the light-heartedness of former days. Gunnar was now, at all events he often was, in tolerably good and cheerful spirits; he sung now and then at his work, although it almost always was in an under-tone; felt a new and extraordinary life within him, which diffused its powerful influence over all his undertakings. He attended industriously, and with much more zeal than he had formerly done, all his occupations; but the pleasure he took in home-work prevented him from going out as much as formerly to the wood or upon the lake. He principally was engaged in a small shed, at work on "a neat little bedstead, which he was making for Elin," as well as just such a chair as she had in her former chamber, and a little "book-shelf." Elin often went out to him there, and watched his work going on with great pleasure: she always, by his desire, put aside his long hair from his face, because he was at work with "both his hands," and then heard him say, "Bless me! what a little hand! and how delicate and white, like a young lady's!" and, deeply crimsoning, she would draw away her hand from his lips.

Elin's usefulness in the family began the very day after her arrival, because Lena had "stuff" by her to make up; she had "stuff for a dress for Gustaf," and a "waistcoat-piece" to be

made up for Gunnar; and all these were to be done by Elin;
and Elin did it, not only well, but quickly and with pleasure;
besides this, she said that she must "of necessity endeavor to
do" out-of-doors work in summer, for, without any preamble,
she immediately confided to Lena, that it would be very repugnant to her feelings to go into any other service; and that she
would much rather remain with her relatives, if she could only
give them satisfaction, and do all that any ordinary servant-girl
would do. Lena was perfectly well pleased with this proposal,
and Gunnar—overjoyed, but he laughed, nevertheless, every
time Elin talked about her future "out-of-doors work," until
one time, when Elin really seemed a little hurt at it, and then
he determined and fixed that when the great "hall-farm mowing" began, which was now just at hand, that Elin should go
with them, and make an attempt at hay-making. In preparation for this time, Gunnar made for her a small rake of
the very lightest kind of wood, and with so much delicate
ornament about it, that little Gustaf believed it was a plaything for himself, and he cried terribly when they took it from
him.

"Dear Gunnar," said Elin to him, when she saw the child's
distress, "do make a little rake for little Gustaf."

"Oh, I don't trouble myself about it," replied Gunnar, looking gloomily.

"Oh, yes; do it for *my* sake!" said Elin.

And now, behold, Gunnar made a little rake for Gustaf; and
Lena, and Mother Ingrid, and Elin, and, most of all, little
Gustaf, were delighted at it.

Little Gustaf now spent most of his time with Elin in her
own pleasant room, which was adorned like a doll's house, and
where she sat and sewed, and by this means little Gustaf became gentler, cleaner, and dearer to Gunnar. Every body had
found their advantage in Elin's arrival. She was the sun which
diffused mild and warm beams around—beams so healing, so
invigorating, and yet—which burned. Even Abraham seemed
to have a feeling thereof. He might now be seen standing
with his face bent down to the waters of the lake, that he might
wash and adorn himself—an operation which Lena had hitherto
insisted upon in vain, but it now was done without any admoni-
tion. He even now combed his hair on Sundays; and one day,
during the allotted rest at noon, when Elin went out for a breath
of fresh air down to the beautiful shore of the lake, she saw

Abraham sitting behind a bush, busy mending his working jacket, which was sadly out at the elbows.

"What are you doing, Abraham?" asked Elin, kindly, but with great difficulty to prevent herself from laughing to see how awkwardly he set about it.

"Oh!" replied Abraham, confused; "I was trying if I could not put a patch on my every-day jacket, that they should not laugh at me so."

"Give it here," said Elin, and took from him his work. "You can not do it, that I can see. I will help you. Now, do you go to my room—the key lies over the door; upon the table there stands my thimble, and the scissors and thread are there too; bring all these with you, and some pieces of blue woolen cloth which lie upon the chest of drawers."

Abraham immediately obeyed, and sprang up the hill joyfully, like "a nag galloping," as Gunnar always said of Abraham's movements; and, in the mean time, Elin undid all that Abraham had sewed. Abraham was back, with the speed of an arrow, and it was not long before his jacket was, at all events, *whole*, though we regret to say that we can not add *agreeable* also.

Abraham, who had never spoken during the whole time, wished very much to pat Elin when the jacket was finished, and attempted to do it, but Elin withdrew herself from his touch.

"Nay, fie, Abraham!" she said; "don't trouble yourself about that, but take all in good part. I will gladly help you any time when you will tell me, and if you will keep your hands off me."

After these words Elin went down to the shore of the lake, and, stripping up her sleeves, washed her hands and arms—washed also her thimble and scissors; and when she returned to her little room, put on a clean neckerchief and apron, because Abraham's jacket was very dirty.

In the mean time there beat, under this dirty jacket, a heart which hitherto had lain entirely torpid.

CHAPTER XXIII.

The hay-harvest was now just at hand; and one evening, during supper, when they were all making merry about Elin, who felt that it was *necessary* that she should try her powers in this "out-of-doors work," Abraham, after some coughing and clearing his throat, lifted up his voice, a most unusual event, and said,

" Yes, I shall not mow so monstrous fast, and so she can keep with me, if she likes, and rake."

" You !" exclaimed Gunnar, enraged, and curled his upper lip, and contracted his eyebrows as aristocratically as any lord of the realm; "you! and do you think that Elin will go and rake after you? No, don't think of such a thing. I shall mow myself, and you must stop and do something at home !"

Abraham was silent, and consoled himself with a dish of porridge. This change made Elin indescribably happy; Lena also thought it was a good one; but Mother Ingrid, like Abraham, remained silent, and what her thoughts were, God alone knows, who has himself given to woman's eyes, ears, and feelings, the ability to be sometimes almost omniscient. She heaved an inaudible sigh, and watched, from her dark corner, the beautiful countenances of Gunnar and Elin, which smiled so lovingly at each other, while, amid joke and talk, they ate out of the same dish, and fed little Gustaf with their spoons, while Lena was busied at the fire.

———————

CHAPTER XXIV.

" The great mowing will begin on Monday," said Abraham, one Saturday afternoon in July, when he came home from the work at the hall-farm; "for so said both the inspector, and Overseer Anders; so now you have got something to think about."

" Indeed !" said Gunnar; " yes, and to-morrow we also go to

G

church, as we said, if it continues as beautiful weather as it is to-day. Mother and Lena can drive in the cart, if they like; and I and Elin shall go the direct road by the side of the lake."

"And who, then, is to look after the lad?" inquired Lena, rather snappishly.

"Abraham can do that," replied Gunnar.

"I can very well stop at home with little Gustaf," said Elin, "and then Abraham can go to church as well, for he has not been ever since I came here, I believe."

Nobody made any reply.

"Can not it be so?" inquired Elin, after a little silence.

"Oh," said Lena, heartlessly and coldly; "Abraham can not read, nor has he any Sunday clothes."

Elin looked astonished.

"Poor Abraham!" said she, at length, in the most compassionate tone, and went up to him. "Can you not read at all? then, indeed, you are not able to go to the Lord's Supper. Poor, poor lad!"

Abraham was silent, and looked down sorrowfully.

"Can not you read at all?" asked Elin, again with the utmost compassion.

"Oh, I can blunder out a little," replied Abraham.

"Listen, Abraham," returned Elin, in an under voice; "come with me into my little room, and let me hear what you can do."

And they two went out immediately.

Lena burst out into a loud horse-laugh.

"Let them be put to shame and perish," said she; "I believe on my soul that Elin will teach Abraham to read, which nobody else could, neither schoolmaster nor minister. It would be much better that she kept her reading skill out of sight, till little Gustaf begins, for that is what I never could do, for I never was so much given to reading as mother and Elin were. Look ye, Elin has read the Bible right through over and over, and that is really a horrid waste of time."

Gunnar was silent, and felt, for the first time in his life, a spark of jealousy, and that of Abraham. But at the same time he felt that admiration, that sacred reverence for a beloved object, which alone makes love for a woman take firm root in the heart of a man. Mother Ingrid looked at him, penetrated his feelings, and sighed—and that was not the last time either.

After a considerable time Elin and Abraham returned, and joy beamed from the eyes of the latter.

"He does not do it so very badly," said Elin; "and now I have promised Abraham that I will stop at home to-morrow, and that I will read with him the whole day, and that afterward at all his spare time I will read with him also, so that he may be able to go to the Lord's table, he as well as any other good Christian people, at some future time."

"Yes, there you'll get out of your depth," said Lena, and laughed.

"Thanks, Elin, my good, sweet Elin," said Gunnar, taking both her hands and pressing them in his, without troubling himself about what Lena said.

Abraham had vanished, but a little while afterward they heard the sound of clapping down at the water side, and as Lena was dreadfully inquisitive, she stole down the little hill to look, and quickly returned, ready to burst with laughter, and told them that Abraham was down there washing and scrubbing a shirt.

"Yes, that is quite right of Abraham," said Elin, laughing at the same time, and blushing a little, "because, as the truth must come out, I told him quite kindly, that I shall be very glad to read with him, only that he must keep himself clean and decent, well combed, and neat in every way, otherwise I could not do it."

"Yes, yes," laughed Gunnar, "we shall see that Elin will very soon convert Abraham into one of those *pettermätrar* about which Lena talks, because Elin can do what she will with people."

But now all went to rest, and, wonderful enough, Abraham was the one who had most to think about; an art which he otherwise never exactly profited by, or, indeed, very much practiced.

Gunnar was obliged to go to the church the following day, because it was a particular day on which the parishioners met on business, and he, on account of "that Anderson's tillage," must be there, as he had something to announce. Mother In-grid and Lena drove there with pleasure, as it so happened that the horse was not out, nor could they have the use of it again soon, because when the hay and corn harvest once be-gan, church-going and pleasure journeys were not to be thought of. Elin and Abraham remained thus alone, and he who has seen the opera of "Sargine," knows how love can do more than abilities; and he who saw Abraham's newly-awakened mind and attention, as well as how anxiously he studied every word, every look of Elin's, could never have been mistaken in the sentiment which gave life to his hitherto soulless and dull existence.

He made already astonishing progress, and when he at dinner only ate half a dish of porridge, and left a piece of his bread, Lena laughed, and said,

"I fancy of a truth that this reading feeds Abr'm, for I never saw him eat so little before for dinner."

"Yes, it very well may be that it feeds," said Abraham, "meat to me is nothing at all to it; but I would gladly read in the afternoon, too, if Elin is so good as to hear me."

"Good Lord!" said Gunnar, half aloud to Mother Ingrid, "I really believe that Elin has put both sense and understanding into the poor lad; did you hear, mother, how sensibly he answered?"

"Yes, yes," sighed Mother Ingrid, "it would be good if she did not take sense and understanding *from* somebody else."

Gunnar looked at her in astonishment. He did not comprehend a word of what she said, and he pondered a deal about it.

Oh, these men, how amiable they are! and how intelligent and knowing! and what intellect they have, and what a great and glorious capacity for thought and investigation; but how little they can *understand* sometimes!

CHAPTER XXV.

ELIN could not sleep all night for thinking of her first day in the mowing field. At half-past three o'clock she was already up and dressed; she wore a striped woolen skirt, and a little black boddice which belonged to her mourning, and which was laced up in front, and with nothing on her arms but the snow-white chemise sleeves, because the day promised to be extremely hot. She stood thus, looking at her new rake, when Gunnar tapped at her window, and asked her to come out, because it was now time for them to be setting off.

"I only just want to get my hat," replied she, and the next moment she joined him.

Gunnar looked at her for some minutes with that pure delight which every one has felt when they see the most beautiful thing they know.

"Dear Lord! how charming thou look'st to-day!" said Gunnar, who was also quite gayly attired.   He, too, was in his long, snow-white shirt sleeves, with a new broad-brimmed straw-hat on, a handsome homespun waistcoat, and new summer trowsers, ready for "the great mowing at the Hall-farm."

"Thou wilt be," continued he, "the handsomest and the neatest girl among them all, that I will answer for.   But, sweet Elin, take, by all means, a pair of gloves with thee, else thou wilt have blisters on thy dear little hands, and then they will make all sorts of rude jokes; for delicate, and white, and slender as they are, and handsome as thou art, they will come about and stare at thee in all kind of ways."

"Would to heaven that I were the most active and the most hardy among them!" said Elin smiling, and sprang back again for her gloves.

After that they set out.

"Never before did I go to a mowing with so much pleasure," said Gunnar.

"Why so?" asked Elin, innocently.

"I don't exactly know why," replied Gunnar, "but it is such gloriously beautiful weather, that may be it.   Didst thou ever see such a splendid summer morning, dear Elin?"

"Never," replied the maiden; and then they stood for a moment to listen to the lark which was singing high up in the air.

"How beautiful God has made our world, after all!" said Elin, and fixed her eye upon Gunnar.

"Ay, and all that are upon it; and all his human creatures can be happy sometimes," returned Gunnar, and drank in Elin's glance with delight.

"Yes, but then they must be good, and do that which is *right* in all things," continued Elin, as they again rapidly continued their walk.

"That as a matter of course," assented Gunnar, "for if the conscience only just begins to murmur a disapprobation about any thing ever so long ago, then it immediately becomes cloudy in the soul.   No, one must go on one's way uprightly, and honestly, and in the way that God appoints, if one would be happy.

"Ah, Gunnar!" said Elin, and looked up again to her tall companion on the narrow wood-path, "how mother would have liked thee! how glad she would have been if she had known the man whom Lena had married! I tried, indeed, to describe thee to her after the wedding, and told her that thou wast the very handsomest and the most agreeable lad I had ever seen; but she said, what really is the truth, that goodness does not consist in beauty; and when I told her what a thoroughly good character thou hadst, she sighed, and said, 'that it would be well if it always remained so.' But ah! I at that time could not know how excellent and how kind thou wast? *Now*, however, now I know it, and *she* knows it too, and certainly she can see both thee and me here upon earth from heaven, where she assuredly is. What is thy opinion, Gunnar?"

Gunnar's heart was full of holy gladness because of Elin's innocent encomium. He made no reply; he said not a word; he merely took her hand in his, and she did not withdraw it; and thus silently, hand in hand, they came to the great meadow, where already many mowers and rakers were assembled.

Every body looked at Elin. Overseer Anders arranged and directed the mowing, and every one took his own place in the rank of mowers, and Elin followed faithfully every step which Gunnar took. They scarcely had any talk; but they often looked at one another, smiled and nodded, and then their hearts beat still stronger than before.

While they were taking their so-called noon rest, Bengt came up and renewed his acquaintance with Elin. Olle also came, and attempted, in a narrow turning, to put his arm round her waist, and "steal a little kiss," as he himself said. Gunnar, however, came up with his scythe, in desperate haste, and with a lightning glance of wrath in his eye.

"Have a care," said he, "of touching Elin, else I'll give you that which you shall never forget!"

Olle sprang away as fast as he could; but when he got to a distance, he waved a kiss with his hand to Elin, and bawled, and laughed, and made a disturbance, as usual.

Elin got quite well through her first day's work, but she was horribly tired in the evening, so tired, indeed, that Gunnar wished to carry her home, which, however, she laughingly prevented. Nevertheless she begged, when they had gone half-way, that she might sit down for a moment and rest herself on a mossy stone.

"Thou canst very well go on, dear Gunnar; don't let me keep thee here, for I know the road by myself," she said.

"How thou talkest!" replied Gunnar. "Dost thou think that I would go away and leave thee here in the intricate wood, and so late in the evening? No, before I will do that, I will stop here, standing against this tree, all night."

Elin only looked up to him, with her thanks; Gunnar only looked at her, and they could not satisfy themselves with looking at each other, but they knew not that these looks were wrong.

As long as the mowing was at a distance from the Hall, Gunnar and Elin went to it together, in the same way that we have described, and the other haymakers and mowers said in the mean time to each other, "Have you seen Gunnar of Vika's sister-in-law? How dreadfully delicate she is! She is a handsome lass, but she looks so proud! And would ye believe she wears gloves! and has such a grand hat, and white woolen stockings and shoes—Heaven defend us—this hot weather!"

When, however, it came to the carrying of the hay, and the storing it in the barn, then Gunnar was compelled, as he said, to make an exchange with Abraham, for he must think about his own affairs. Lena helped him with these, and the old woman looked after little Gustaf, and prepared the victuals. It was a sort of torment to Gunnar to see Elin and Abraham setting off together to the hall, and yet he could not keep his gravity when Elin in a morning said, laughingly,

"Well, come now, Abraham! You are not ready, as usual, are you? Yes, then I must go on before you." And then Abraham, well washed and trimmed up, made his appearance, and with the most joyful of awkward grimaces prepared to run after her. Abraham was in the mean time become quite a different being, and that which Gunnar could not be sufficiently astonished at was, that Elin could persuade him, all the way there and all the way back, "to chop the Catechism," as Gunnar phrased it.

"It is very wrong of thee, Gunnar, to laugh at this," said Elin once, though she was not able to prevent a smile from playing about her own mouth.

"Good Heavens! I'm a long way from laughing at *the thing*, dearest Elin, but I am amused that thou or any body else in this world could produce this effect on Abraham, and persuade him to it.   But if any body could do it, it would be thou."

"Oh! any body else, who would have done it, might," replied Elin.   "Thou shouldst see him; he is as pious as a lamb, and as devotional as a priest, with his hands clasped together, as he answers my questions; and now he knows the greatest part of the little Catechism, and I try to explain it to him as well as I can, and in the same way as I remember our pastor used to do to us communion-children four years ago."

"Yes, yes; thou wilt be explaining the word of God to him," said Gunnar, "till one of these fine days he will be explaining his love for thee—so think I."

"Ah, you menfolk! you are all like one another as pea to pea! you always will be talking about love and such stuff," said Elin, with a little disgust, and half laughing, and went into her chamber, while Gunnar, delighted and captivated, looked after her, and Mother Ingrid sighed.

One evening Elin and Abraham came home from the work at the Hall.   They had carried the hay, and Elin had stood upon the rick with one of the other young girls.   Elin had a deal to say about the day.   Ma'msell Sara had been out, had treated them to a luncheon, and at various times had talked a deal with Elin; had called her up to her room, and given her a cup of coffee, biscuits, and other things.   In going down she had met the squire on the stairs, and he had also had some talk with her: "And he will above all things," said Elin, "that I should go and live in service at the hall, either as parlor-maid or house-maid.   He is a handsome and agreeable gentleman, the squire," continued Elin, "if he had not that hideous red hair, and then if he would only let one be."

Every drop of blood boiled and raged in Gunnar's veins, but he kept silence, and left the room.

CHAPTER XXVI.

A Sunday was now near at hand.

"To-morrow Elin and Abraham shall really go to church if Abraham gets his new clothes," said Mother Ingrid.

"Elin and Abraham!" exclaimed Lena, laughing; "it sounds just like a married affair, as if they were going to be wed."

"Ay, believe me! they would be made fools of, that they would!" said Abraham, with great simplicity, and licked his lips, while Elin alternately blushed, and was dying with laughter.

"Yes, my good Abraham," at length she said, "we don't trouble ourselves at all because they make fun of us; we shall go to church for all that, and read our Catechism all the way; shan't we, Abra'm?"

"Ay, to be sure," replied Abraham.

"Yes, but, look you, I will hear how that goes on, and so I shall go with you," said Gunnar.

And he did go with them; and, what was still more, he did not disturb their reading, but walked silently and softly behind them, and thought that Elin looked like an angel of God, as she went before him and expounded the word of God to the poor and hitherto half-witted youth, who now, partly in his own, and partly in some clothes of Gunnar's which Elin had borrowed for him, walked beside her so clean and orderly. By his answers he proved of a certainty that he was extremely simple and stupid, yet still that he was not without feeling and a small grain of understanding.

"What dost thou think of our good clergyman?" inquired Gunnar from Elin, when they came out of the church.

"That he is an excellent servant of the Lord!" said Elin, who had shed warm tears as she listened to the simple and truly heart-reaching words of the worthy minister.

"Yes, he is a servant of the Lord and a good man," said Gunnar. I will always testify to that."

Abraham was to go from church to a sister of his mother's, who had promised him a summer coat, and thus Elin returned alone with Gunnar.

When they had turned out of the high road, and thus parted

from the other church-going people, who had observed with inquisitive glances the young, handsome, and neatly-attired maiden, whom they had only seen once before at church, they both walked on for some time in silence.

"Elin," at length Gunnar began, "dost thou know that I have *something* on my heart which *must* be spoken? I am about to beg something from thee, which thou *must* promise me."

"What can it be?" asked Elin, standing still, and gazing at Gunnar, whose voice was unusually grave and deep.

"Ay, come and sit down here a little while," besought he, "I have something to beg of thee."

They seated themselves upon a soft and inviting tree-stump.

"Yes, Elin," continued he, and took her hand in his, "thou shalt promise me—promise me sacredly, that *never*—never in all thy life, thou wilt take a service at Grantorp."

With these words, his dark eye flashed both with rage and jealousy, and with—love, and was also dangerously irresistible.

"I promise! I promise!—although I do not at all understand why thou desirest me to leave undone that of which I have never thought about," said Elin, quite bewildered by his glance, and with her head almost laid upon Gunnar's breast.

"Ay," said he, with flashing eyes, closed teeth, and pressing Elin to him, incited to this by many dissimilar feelings—"Ay, I will tell thee, Elin, the squire is the greatest villain and coward that I know, and he merely wishes to have thee in his service to—to ruin thee!" and, with this word, he clasped her to his heart, as if he would defend her from the prince of darkness himself.

"Oh, fie, how thou talkest!" said Elin, and escaped from him, rose up, and again commenced her homeward way. But her heart beat dreadfully, and a spark of light had opened her eyes, and sparks of love had kindled a thousand-fold in her heart.

The two walked on together for some time in silence, and then conversed on indifferent subjects. Elin was silent and reserved the whole day, and avoided meeting the burning glances of Gunnar; she read a long time with Abraham in the afternoon, when he returned with his new summer coat, thought much upon her departed mother, and was happy to think that she now saw her continually. In the evening, however, when she laid herself down upon her new little bed, and said her customary evening prayer, she thought no longer on any thing, but slept as soundly and as calmly as usual, and resembled in this respect, although so unlike in others, not the worst of our young, accomplished, and well-read young ladies, who have their heads crammed full of romances and novels, operas and dramas, ballads and canzonets, in which love reveals itself in all its variations, colors, and tones. Elin was as equally ignorant of the symptoms of love, as of those of the most inexplicable powers of nature, and knew just as little of her own heart as of the stars which circled over her head at night; she was as little acquainted with its irregular and wild throbbing; and she would have been as much amazed, if any one had said to her that she loved Gunnar, as if they had told her that the earth went round the sun, and not the sun round the earth, and yet the one was equally true with the other. But Elin knew it not; she, therefore, felt no repentance, no pang of conscience, and did not get up in her own imagination a whole torture-history or tragic-romance about criminal love, a sister's jealousy, slander, separation, tears, anguish and suffering without end, nor at last upon the dagger-stab, pistol-shot, poisoning, death, and burial.

No, Elin thought of nothing of this kind, because she thought not once upon the subject—of *love*, namely. She merely felt it, and feared it, and avoided it; but when it no longer stood beside her and startled her, when Gunnar's glances no longer set her heart beating so violently that it threatened to leap out of her breast, then she forgot it altogether and was tranquil and happy. Thus it was with her on the following morning, and for many days afterwards; and Gunnar,—who was not so incessantly at her side,—was kind and brother-like, but not so violent and passionate as on the former occasion. He seemed, as it were, to have recovered himself, whether from good instinct or from resolution, we cannot rightly say; because sometimes men revenge themselves upon our great penetration by becoming incomprehensible, and such was the short trance, the short tranquillity, which Gunnar now seemed to enjoy, but out of which he was so soon to awake, when the lightning of chance circumstance began to flash, and arouse him from his slumber, or his good resolutions, we know not rightly which.

The glances of Gunnar and Elin did not meet and melt together: they no longer rested for moments lost in each other,

as they had done formerly; but if their eyes met, one or the
other cast down his, or turned them aside; and if they each
felt that the blood mounted up into their cheeks, the eye of the
other did not see it, and therefore it produced no effect. Elin,
at all events, thought not of it, and we have said that we do
not know what Gunnar did.

CHAPTER XXVII.

TIME sped on softly; and one day, during the noon-rest,
Elin was sitting down by the shore of the lake with her sewing, and Abraham was kneeling before her, reading aloud a
lesson from the Catechism. Elin went on with her sewing,
and needed not to look at the book, because she knew it off by
heart. Gunnar stood leaning against a tree, and resting, at the
same time, on his gun, with which he had just shot a cherry-
eating magpie. He stood thus silently observing the group,
but said nothing, and disturbed not the lesson. Abraham
scarcely boggled at all in his reading; but if he did so, then
he first looked up at Elin, and then at Gunnar, as if to beg
pardon for his fault from them, the only human beings who
ever had shown him kindness, sympathy, and pity—the *only*
ones he ever loved.

"Yes, that really is so very well done," at length said Elin,
"that if you continue to go on in the same way for some time,
I certainly think that you may go to the minister, and ask him
to admit you soon to the communion. What dost thou think,
Gunnar?"

"I did not rightly hear what thou saidst—I was thinking of
something else," replied Gunnar. But Abraham! he sprung
up with a joyful and heavy-footed bound of delight, and before
either of them heard a word of it, he took Elin with one of
his strong arms, and Gunnar with the other, and pressed them
both at once to his newly awakened heart. Unprepared as
they both were for this sudden manœuvre, they made no re-
sistance, and Gunnar's and Elin's cheeks met together, and
almost their lips.

"Let me go, Abraham!" exclaimed Elin, and dashed about

her like a young foal; but when she did get really at liberty, she burst into such a hearty fit of laughter that Gunnar was almost obliged to join, although he at the same time felt grateful and angry with Abraham.

Which of you, ye romance-crammed and stuffed young ladies, would, on an occasion like this, have burst into laughter? Not one of you! You would have wept, blushed, not even have been able to look up or to move; others, perhaps, with a little more experience, would have made a great noise, —would have been supported,—would have steeped themselves in *eau de Cologne*,—have drowned themselves in cold water, and have choked themselves with *eau de luce*,—would have puffed, and panted, and thought—thought—thought— Heaven knows what!

But Elin laughed, concealed, by that means, her blushes, stroked her hair from her face, took up her sewing materials, which, during "this earthquake of the heart," had nearly fallen into the lake, and desired Abraham to be so good as to be a little less energetic in showing his joy another time. Gunnar was silent, and would have been very glad to have kissed his own cheek, but as he could not do it, and was not able to kiss Elin's, he therefore went on his way.

"Thou hast so many times wished to have a sail on the lake," said Gunnar to Elin, in a very calm and brotherly tone, which he had assumed—Heaven knows how—that same evening during supper; "thou hast wished for it, dear Elin, but there has never yet been exactly time for it; now, however, as I am going out this evening to lay some night-lines, that I may take a little fish, both for our eating and for the pocket, I shall be glad to take thee with me, if thou wilt."

"Oh, that I will, certainly, so gladly, so gladly!" exclaimed Elin, and clapped her hands with delight. "I have never been on the water but a few times when I was a child, and then Erik rowed me on a pool in the wood, in a little old boat which the boys of the town had at that time, and which afterward fell to pieces."

Gunnar's countenance visibly darkened every time that Elin mentioned Erik's name; and Mother Ingrid, who always saw things, sighed unobserved, as she sat there in her dark corner— there in the dim corner of life's decline.

"Then shall I go with you, and row?" said Abraham, in a business-like tone, for he now never needed to be told his duty, unless when he was busy over his eating; now, however, he hastily rose up and laid down his spoon, because he saw Gunnar get up.

"Oh, no," replied Gunnar, who certainly did not wish to have Abraham in his boat—"oh, no; there is not occasion for that. Eat your supper, and then go to bed, for Elin will help me to lay the lines—that is not so difficult a matter, and I can row myself."

Mother Ingrid sighed more deeply, and Abraham sat down to his dish of porridge, which was less agreeable to him than usual this evening, so that he entirely forgot to scrape the dish with his spoon.

"Take something more about thee; it will be rather cold on the lake, however still and warm it may be on the land," said Gunnar to Elin, and went down to the shore.

Elin ran into her chamber, tied a handkerchief over her head, and threw a woolen shawl over her shoulders, and then hastened after Gunnar. When she came down to the shore, Gunnar stood already in the boat, and offered her his hand. It was many days now since she had taken his hand. She trembled perceptibly, and Gunnar from that believed that she was afraid.

"Do not be afraid," said he, "my sweetest little Elin. There is not the slightest danger here with *me*. Come and sit here;" and he placed Elin in the middle of the boat, opposite to him, took the oars, and began to pull with long, powerful, and manly strokes.

"Oh, I really am not afraid!" replied Elin, who neither wished to tell a falsehood, nor did so, for, least of all, did she fear his love, which she did not at that time understand herself. "I am not afraid; on the contrary, I think it is delightful," added she, and began to feel ashamed, because instinct whispered in her ear that laughter and shame are very often an antidote for love; as silence and gratitude, again—but what is the use of saying it? Ye who will read this, ye romance-crammed young ladies, you know it beforehand, perhaps far better than we who write.

"Now, don't sit there laughing and jesting, but make thyself of some use, my dear Elin," said Gunnar, half vexed at the maiden's pleasantry in this glorious moonlight.

And now Gunnar showed Elin how she must bait the hook before she threw out the lines; and she did it as well as she

could, and pretended several times, not without a little unconscious coquetry, that she should fall into the lake. Gunnar,
however, was wise, and saw plainly enough that she was only
making fun of him.

"Yes, throw thyself in," said he, therefore, "and I will
plunge in afterward, and fish thee out, or else stop with thee
at the bottom of the lake."

Elin became silent. "At the bottom of the lake with Gunnar!" thought she; "oh, that could never be so very bad!"
Death had not any horrors for Elin; and who knows whether
it might not have had a great attraction for Gunnar in this wonderfully beautiful evening hour. It was now the beginning of
August; and this August moonlight, more glorious than that
of any other season, fell broadly over lake and land. The lake
lay like a silver sea, tranquil and pure as the blue vault of
heaven, and its surface rippled sometimes with a soft motion, as
if it were occasioned rather by the restless spirit of the water,
than by any thing else, even by the lightest wind. The shores
extended themselves so marvelously around the lake; they
seemed as if they were changed; as if the moon had laid a
spell of enchantment upon them, which alternately threw them
into the most brilliant light and the blackest shade. They were
not at all like that which they seemed to be in daylight. The
lake, the heavens, the earth—nothing resembled itself in this
mysterious, enigmatical hour. Not less so the human heart,
the human mind. Gunnar was silent, Elin was silent, and no
other possible sound was heard, excepting the regular stroke
of the oars.

Gunnar rowed into the middle of the lake, and when they
were come there, Elin said—

"Now I have laid all the lines, what more shall I do?"

"Sit quietly, and look at me," replied Gunnar.

"And what would be the good of that?" asked Elin, and
cast down her eyes.

"It will please me, it will delight me, while I row," returned
Gunnar.

"Oh, nonsense!" laughed Elin. "No, do thou tell me a
story such as thou dost sometimes. I fancy that I should just
now like to hear a child's story about giants, and witches, and
such things, because when I am *with thee* I never am frightened, not even in the middle of the night."

Poor Elin! she could have had no idea how much she

betrayed in that one expression, *with thee*, upon which she laid an emphasis.

"Indeed!" said Gunnar, and then, after a little thought, he continued, "Oh yes, I know many stories, and one which surpasses them all. It is called Frithiofs Saga; it was one I borrowed from the tutor when I was ill of the scarlet-fever some years ago. Ah, if I could but tell it thee! At that time I knew long pieces of it, nay, whole pages, by heart; for it quite fixed itself there if one only read it once. But now I have nearly forgotten all the parts I knew, and if thou dost not know the story, thou wouldst not perhaps have thought so much about them. There was a king's daughter, who was called Ingeborg —and ever since the time when I saw thee first at the wedding-dinner, I fancied to myself that she was like thee—and she loved a peasant; for thou must know that in those times there were no proud noblemen and fat citizens, but only kings and peasants; and Ingeborg loved the son of a peasant, and they two were brought up together in a temple, and the temple lay in a lofty grove, or, as the story calls it, in Balder's Pasture; and, dost thou know, Elin, I have only just to row round to the other side of the lake, to show thee a meadow which I always imagine to myself is like to that 'Balder's Pasture.' The meadow belongs to a pretty little farm, which is the property of an old major, a horribly stern but fine old gentleman, who has a very beautiful daughter, almost as pretty as thou art."

"Ah, yes, but that is not telling me the story," interrupted Elin, who never liked to listen when Gunnar or any body else said that she was pretty.

"Nay, that I know well enough," remarked Gunnar, smiling; "and I never really had any intention of telling thee the whole story, for that I neither could nor would I exactly, but I will show thee 'Balder's Pasture,' as I always call it to myself."

The boat now glided under some tall alder-trees, which hung over the lake; and as these were thick and leafy, and it thus all at once became dark, Elin grew afraid and crept toward Gunnar, who now no longer rowed, but merely guided on the boat with one oar into the shade of the alders.

"Yes, come hither to me," said Gunnar, with a tremulous voice; "thou art now a little bit afraid because it is so dark, but thou shalt soon see something so grand, so grand!"

Again the boat glided out into the moonlight, and there lay

before their eyes a lovely meadow, in which the fragrant hay was now piled up into large haycocks, amid the lofty and branching oaks, luxuriant, white-stemmed birches, and other trees of still finer kinds ; for here might be seen elms, maples, and ashes, although the oak was the most general. Here and there, also, grew thick and branching hazel-bushes ; the trees, however, stood apart, scattered here and there, and the moon threw down masses of light amid the night's envious masses of darkness. Elin thought that she never had seen any thing so beautiful and glorious, and could not sufficiently admire this 'Balder's Pasture,' as Gunnar called it ; and just then, all at once, both she and Gunnar heard a rustling, as if of some one walking, and then another sound, as of two persons quietly conversing.

"Hist !" whispered Gunnar to Elin, and shoved the boat noiselessly under some alder-bushes, which perfectly concealed them from the sight of those who approached, but, at the same time, did not prevent Gunnar and Elin from seeing and hearing what occurred on the shore, which was here quite low.

"Hist !" whispered Gunnar again to Elin ; "I would not that they should see us ; gentlefolks always fancy when we poor folks are out in the evening, that we have something bad and unlawful in hand."

"God forbid it !" said Elin, and drew herself, influenced by some inexplicable feeling of fear, still nearer to Gunnar, and he did not repulse her, but put his arm around her waist ; and, thus sitting, silent as spirits, unobservant of their hearts' still more violent and rapid pulsations, they heard the following words :

"Oh, my August !" said the voice of a young lady—and they saw at the time that it was the major's daughter—who stepped now forth into the moonlight, leaning on a young man's arm. "Oh, my beloved friend ! This is the last evening, the last hour of our glorious summer ; for, when thou art gone, it will be only autumn—autumn in nature, and autumn in my heart !"

"Do not say so, my dearest Elfrida," replied a smart, well-grown youth, whom Gunnar recognized as her cousin. "Oh, do not say so ! By these words thou wilt embitter my whole life, and make still more heavy the hour of parting. Ah, if it were only *I* who suffer, but that thou also shouldst do so ! That I, the wretch ! should have destroyed thy happiness and

thy angel peace!—I who, nevertheless, knew so well that thou
wast no longer free, that I never in this world could hope to
possess thee, even if thou couldst have released thyself from
thy plighted word; because Poverty—that hydra which de-
stroys every thing—has, indeed, caught me within his talons,
and *another*, endowed with all that Fortune has denied to
me, will soon, soon clasp thee in his arms. Thought of despair!"

Elfrida sobbed upon the youth's breast, and the lovers again
returned by the way they came.

Gunnar and Elin sat long silent and motionless.

"Poor lad!" said Gunnar, at length, in an almost inaudible
whisper close to Elin's ear, so that not even the air, but only
she, and scarcely *she* was able to hear the words, "Poor, unhappy youth! he loves her so dearly, and he shall never have
her, and I—I shall never have—thee!"

"Now, let us really go home," said Elin, pretending that she
had not heard Gunnar's words. She hastily resumed her seat
in the middle of the boat, laid the oars in Gunnar's hand, and
made a sign that he should row.

"Wilt thou not go on the land a little?" whispered Gunnar.

"No, thank you," replied Elin; "row home at once."

He rowed at first with unequal and ill-timed strokes, but
afterward briskly and without intermission. They were very
soon at the shore, and opposite to the cottage.

"Thanks, Gunnar!" said Elin, as she sprang out of the boat.

"Good night, Elin!" replied Gunnar, and secured the boat.
During this operation, Elin reached the house, and was within
her little chamber before Gunnar had left the shore. She
opened the door, and then fastened the hook with a strange
excited feeling, or as if she had been pursued by something—
by a *something* which was not Gunnar, and which was a spirit
of evil. She undressed herself hastily, and lay down, and began immediately to think of her mother; to think whether her
eyes would be gloomy—whether they would look darkly and
with displeasure upon her, or not.

"Ah, sweetest mother, be not angry with me!" said she, half
aloud and with clasped hands. After that she repeated all her
evening prayers, more audibly than usual—repeated them yet
a second time, but with great rapidity; and when, after the
second time she found that she had not been thinking about
them, but had merely hurried through them while her heart

was beating violently, she went through them all yet a third time, more slowly and deliberately ; and endeavored with all her might to think upon every word she uttered. After this she shut her eyes that she might sleep, and said to herself, " I will never go on the water any more, it makes one feel so uneasy."

But she could not sleep. She had heard that when a person in a wakeful state desires to sleep, he must think upon a softly heaving lake, or else on a gently waving cornfield, but this experiment she had never tried, because she had never been sleepless before, excepting at the time of her mother's death, and then she would not sleep ; now, on the contrary, she wished to sleep to be rid of " foolish thoughts." She began to experimentize. She thought upon a heaving lake, but it soon became a sea of moonlight upon which a little boat glided, in which she sat, and the boat was rowed by—— " No! a waving cornfield would certainly, be better!" thought she, and she turned her mind to such a one, but there immediately came to her fancy the cornfield where, on the preceding day, Gunnar had gone to reap, and where she had tried to bind up after the reapers, but could not manage it, although Gunnar had attempted to teach her.

The little sod-roof at Vika covered, small as it was, many restless and perfectly sleepless beings. The human sufferings below it grew and shot up, as if in emulation of the weeds above ; and like these also, neither autumn nor winter, cold nor snow, would be able to prevent their growth.

Mother Ingrid lay sleepless in the depth of her curtained bed. She did not weep, but she sighed. Age and indifference had made her almost both deaf and blind to all the rest of the world, but for her son she had the quickest ears and the most delicate sight, and she—she alone, who knew him so well, saw in what danger he wandered, on the brink of what a deep abyss he stood.

Lena, also, had been now for a long time relapsing into her former sour and crooked temper, scolding threatening and commanding. She had began to grow weary of Gunnar's man· ner, which was so much more friendly and unreserved than it had been before Elin's arrival. She began to think that this was not by any means sufficient. She desired to have his love also ; Gunnar, however, seemed to be dead and buried, deaf and blind to her demands ; and she now began to beat her brains to discover some mode of accomplishing her wishes, and asserting her power over his heart, for her love awoke and flamed up in proportion to his repugnance to her. Even with Elin she began to be dissatisfied. The pleasure of novelty was now over. Elin was too cheerful, too kind, too refined, too independent in her ideas, and, at the same time, too submissive in her disposition; besides this, she dressed herself too smartly, she took too many holidays, however much and industriously she might work, and all that without any wages at all. This last circumstance, however, prevented Lena, at the same time, from venturing openly to scold and grumble, during this last summer month, at all events, because if she did so, it might determine Elin in haste to act independently, and take another service for the following twelve months. Nevertheless, Lena was testy and perversely tempered toward her, found fault with many things which she did, as for instance, teaching Abraham to read; constantly studying in the Bible and other books herself; and not the least, this evening's sail on the lake. In Lena's opinion these things were so unnecessary; were of no profit—were childish and foolish; besides, to all this must be added, the commencement of a dark, and from this time rapidly growing jealousy, which now and then shot forth sparks that kindled into flame her violent and choleric temper. This night, therefore, she lay awake, and wept from envy and passion. When Gunnar returned, he pretended not to notice it; perhaps he really did not; at all events he pretended that he was soon asleep, but he was awake, and now for the first time looked correctly and honestly down into his own heart, and found there—nothing else but Elin—she, and nothing besides, in the very innermost of his heart's core.

Abraham lay on his press bed, breathing aloud, and tossing over every minute. Never since he was born had he till now been kept awake by any cause connected in the remotest degree with his soul; now he could not sleep from the vexation he felt because he had not gone with them on the lake—more especially as he fancied that Elin had laughed at him; Elin, who never once thought on the subject—and, therefore, he now repented that, after all, he had not eaten up his porridge. These thoughts occasioned him to be still awake when Gunnar returned, and he began to make inquiries from him respecting the sail and Elin, and the long lines, upon which Gunnar merely replied, " What the deuce are you lying awake for ?

Only lie down and be still, and go to sleep, and don't trouble yourself about me and my long lines!"

Little Gustaf lay in his crib, and whined, and moaned, and cried, because he had a pain in his stomach; and as we have just mentioned the little fellow, we may as well say that he was a little darling to Elin; that she kept him with her nearly the whole day; that she once or twice upbraided Gunnar with being so cold and indifferent toward "his little lad;" that Gunnar on these occasions was silent, but nevertheless, when neither Mother Ingrid nor Lena saw it, he would caress and amuse him, for he cared so little about Lena as not to have the slightest jealousy, and regarded the boy as any other child, becoming attached to him because he saw him daily, and because he saw how dear he was to Elin; and the little fellow, by some inexplicable contradiction of nature, was fonder of Gunnar than of any one else in the family, because even Elin gave way to him.

Such was the general state of mind during the night; and when the morning came Gunnar went and examined his baits, taking Abraham with him, who now would have given all he had if he might but have lain still and slept. Mother Ingrid sat in her corner with her spinning-wheel, Lena racketed about at her household work, Elin sat at her window sewing with the utmost industry. Out of doors it rained; people could neither go to work in the corn nor the hay. The whole of nature was clouded, and men are, indeed, a part of it.

At half-past three o'clock, after a perfectly sleepless night, Gunnar went down to the shore, in a gloomy state of mind, and Abraham followed him, half asleep. When they came to the boat, Gunnar was the first to enter it, with that lightness and grace which was peculiar to him; still, a close observer might have perceived on this particular morning an unusual slowness and indifference in all he did. After him Abraham tumbled clumsily and heavily into the boat, so that it rocked from side to side, and then immediately seized upon the oars.

"No," said Gunnar, "let the oars alone. I shall row myself, and you can examine the lines." Abraham looked pleased and astonished, like a child who finds some important piece of business confided to it which had never before been done. He had never once before been trusted even to touch the lines, much less to busy himself about them when set.

"There, sit down in that place, and don't stand wagging the

boat," said Gunnar; "Ah, no, in that place, not there! and there's no need for you to keep staring into my face in that way. Sit down as you should do."

Gunnar wished to be as much alone with his thoughts as possible. He had not been able to disentangle them during the whole night, because, beside Lena, he could only despair and feel dislike. But now, forgetting the whole of the gloomy scene; the rain which soaked through his clothes, the morning air which chilled him to the bone; forgetting all besides else, he riveted every thought upon that Elin whom he loved beyond every thing else—fervently, frantically, with his whole burning soul and passionate heart, and yet with a certain degree of reason. He, indeed, gave himself up (for the first time, it is true) to this love; but he said even then within his heart, "It is wrong, it is improper, it is criminal. Lena has sinned far, far more toward me, but I have forgiven her, and it does not belong to me to punish her by committing an offense against her. I cannot at all endure Lena; I can never make myself do so; and now still less, I fear, than ever. But that is no reason why I should love Elin; I must endeavor, with all my might, to overcome this feeling for her, and, above all things, I must not drag Elin down with me to destruction."

With these good resolutions Gunnar returned home that morning, but with a poor booty of fish. As he passed Elin's window, he saw her sitting at her work. He nodded coldly to her, went on his way, and did not speak to her through the whole day.

Elin, who, during the night, had felt the bitterest contrition, entirely lost this feeling in consequence of Gunnar's coldness, which caused, in its place, anguish and anxiety. She began to love; and without thinking upon, or once having a presentiment of danger, she sucked in poison from a feeling of which she had no knowledge. She had felt herself gay and happy in Gunnar's affection, and in the thousand little proofs of attention and devotion in which she hitherto had not imagined any thing wrong, improper, or dangerous. Only for one moment, in the boat on the preceding evening, had a feeling of anxiety come over her—an uneasiness as to whether her mother's spirit, which might hover around them, would not condemn her for thus going out alone with Gunnar; but then, thought she, "Gunnar is so odd sometimes." Now, however, when Gunnar was cold and displeased with her, all her trouble of conscience was gone, and nothing remained but sorrow of heart. This Elin felt to be very heavy and very bitter, and yet she did not understand herself!

During supper, which always used to be lively, and diversified with pleasant chat, there now prevailed an unusual silence and dullness. Gunnar sat thoughtfully at the table, looked down, ate, indeed, but took as small a quantity in his spoon each time as if he had been Elin's bird. Elin sat there on a low stool, and gave little Gustaf four spoonfuls for every one which she herself took. Lena, in a sour and angry temper, busied herself at the fire; threw about the pot-hooks and the fuel with a great noise, and in a rage, at the fire-place; swore at the wood, which was too wet, and at the meat, which was too dry, and which ought to have lain in pickle till Sunday; and at the rain, which poured down just now when she had to go for water; and at the bucket, of which the handle was broken; and at Abraham, who had not brought it; and, lastly, because, as she said, "there sat four folks, who very well knew how to eat and cram till they were as full as they could hold, but who were not willing to do a single turn to help her!"

"Bless me! I will help thee," said Elin, most willingly, and got up instantly from her little stool.

"Ay, methinks I shouldn't get a deal of help," said Lena, angrily, and with a loud laugh, "if *ma'msell* is to go and fetch the water in that big, heavy, cursed, broken bucket."

"I went and fetched water for you to-day, and many another time," replied Elin, mildly.

"Yes, that I believe, but it was in a pail that little Gustaf might have carried," said Lena, tauntingly.

"There is a water-tub," said Elin; "if you will come with me, I will gladly try to help you with it, if we did not bring it quite full, because it is too big to carry up the hill from the lake, and I am not used to it."

"There is no need of that," said Gunnar, and rose from his seat. "Come, now, Abraham, let us two go and fetch the tub full, and then there is an end of all the trouble for this evening, and to-morrow, if it rains, I will mend the bucket."

Lena, like all ill-tempered and unreasonable people, did not pay any attention to the reasonable and and helpful spirit which all this evinced, but she merely took hold of Gunnar's first words:

"Ay, indeed!" said she, incensed; '*there is no need* that Elin should be of any use to me! Did not Gunnar say so? Nay, she shall, indeed, sit like a princess, I reckon! but, look you, if *she* wants help she must have it on the spot. If she wants a flower-garden, then both Gunnar and Abraham are up and digging; and if she will have a fence round it, it must be done; and if she will have a flower-stand, Gunnar is up at night to make it; and if she will have pine-twigs to lay on her floor, and leaves to stick in her ceiling, Abra'm runs all the breath out of his body to get them! But, mind ye, as for me, I must go and do every thing for myself! I never have any body to make such a baby and such a pet of me!"

The two men had been out of the house a long time, so that they did not hear more than the very commencement of Lena's angry complaints; Elin, however, wept silently, and little Gustaf stood beside her and dried her tears, and whispered to her, "Mother is cross; leave off soon, Eli'—Eli' shall not cry; mother soon will be kind again!"

Mother Ingrid, who had scarcely spoken the whole day, now said, "I think you are unjust in what you say, Lena. You know as well as we all, that Elin will gladly help you with every thing that she is able; and as to that little flower-garden with the fence round it, it was mostly done on Sunday afternoons in the early summer."

"Yes, and they might have found something more useful to do at such hours," replied Lena, yet at the same time a little mollified, or a little sorry that she had scolded Elin before the Michaelmas changing of servants was over. She went, therefore, as if accidentally, past Elin, and made believe that she now, for the first time, was aware of her tears, although little Gustaf had shouted it aloud, and was now crying with all his might because Elin cried.

"What in all the world are you crying for?" said Lena to Elin. "There is no need for you to take on so because I scolded Abra'm, the fool! because he had not mended the bucket, and did not help me, nor——"

But now Gunnar and Abraham returned with the water-tub, and Lena set to work with it, besides which, she thought it better not to scold any more that evening.

CHAPTER XXVIII.

SEVERAL days which succeeded the foregoing were all cloudy and rainy out of doors, and cloudy and discordant within. For a long time a certain degree of gayety, cheerfulness, and comfort, had prevailed, and no one had really enjoyed it more than the old personified experience, Mother Ingrid, in her corner. Now every body except Lena sighed, and *she* grumbled ; but as she, after all, neither would nor dared to grumble at Gunnar, and as she considered it not to her advantage, *at this présent time*, to find fault with Elin, and as she never scolded Mother Ingrid when the others heard it, there now remained only Abraham as her victim ; and he, poor fellow, when she did so, always took up his Catechism and read aloud, that he might thereby drown her voice ; and if any of the others were present, she was ashamed of abusing him, when he was incessantly reading in his Catechism, and never forgetting to repeat to himself—"*Question !—Answer !*" as if those words were a part of the edifying matter of the book.

If any one of the family during this time felt a spark of joy, it was this poor Abraham, because in the chance of being examined by Elin, and praised by her, he read really with as great satisfaction as was possible for him to be conscious of; and when Elin kindly encouraged him, and represented to him the happiness and the holy joy which he, perhaps, would soon experience when, like other good Christian people, he should go to the Saviour's table, and there celebrate His memory, give thanks, pray, and promise—then Abraham wept for joy, and made some of his very strangest gambols in the water-puddles for very delight.

One day Elin said to Lena, because she felt too shy to speak to Gunnar, since he had shown himself so cold and indifferent toward her—

"Dearest Lena," said she, "wilt thou beg of Gunnar, that he will very soon go with Abraham to your dean or rector, as you call him, that he may hear how the poor lad has improved himself in reading, so that he might, perhaps, at some future time, let him be confirmed. That would be such a happiness

H

for him, and such a pleasure and satisfaction for us all, I think."

"Stuff! what good should we have of it?" said Lena, vexed; "and Gunnar has something else to do, than to run off with Abraham to the parsonage. And if he were so silly as to take the fool with him, then they would see Abra'm stand and stare like a billy-goat, and not be able to read a single word. No; believe me, all this reading is nothing but childishness, and waste of time. He is, and he will still be, an ass, let one do what one will, and let him poke his nose ever so into the Catechism."

Elin sighed, and was silent. She began already to discover that the peace of the family was jeopardized if any one contradicted Lena in the least. Mother Ingrid, however, sate in her corner and spun, and heard all that went on, and pondered out a way of adjusting matters so that every thing might turn out for the best, if possible. Among other things, she determined that poor Abraham should go, and let their universally respected pastor hear his (Abraham's) progress in sense and Christianity. For this reason, the next time she was alone with Gunnar she began to speak on the subject.

"Dear Gunnar," she said, "now that the rain and the bad weather prevent thy working, and, I am sorry to say, thou canst do nothing either with the hay or the corn, canst thou not find time enough, either morning or evening, to go to the rector with Abraham, and let him hear how he can say his Catechism, and ask whether he could not let him be confirmed in a little time?"

Mother Ingrid's words were, as we may very well remember, law to her son at all times, and therefore he felt himself obliged to comply, and promised immediately to go the next morning. The same evening he mentioned this to Abraham. Accordingly Abraham, in the morning, put on his best holiday clothes, and assumed a most important and dignified demeanor.

"What does all this mean?" said Lena, spitefully and contemptuously; "what folly have you got in hand now? What stupid nonsense is this? Who is going to make a fool of himself on working day?"

Thus said Lena, while the men dressed, and made themselves tidy. No one answered a single word, but when they were ready Gunnar said to Abraham,

"Come, now;" and they went.

"It is *my* doing," said Mother Ingrid, when they were out of the house; and this she said that she might avert the storm from Elin; and then she began spinning so busily at her wheel, behind her rock of flax, that she could scarcely hear Lena's scolding and grinding.

CHAPTER XXIX.

GUNNAR, on his way to the rector's, was gloomy and full of thought; this was now always his mood: and when the worthy rector, and good pastor, after he had heard with pleasure Abraham's improvement, and had granted his request that at some future time he would admit him at the Lord's table, he began to inquire from his former disciple and favorite, the young Gunnar, about his domestic affairs; to all of which he received monotonous and few-worded replies.

"And thy respectable old mother is well, and gets on well with thy wife?" asked the clergyman.

"Oh, yes," replied Gunnar.

"And thou has only one child yet?"

Gunnar was silent. The rector took his silence for assent; but Gunnar thought, with despair in his heart, "I have indeed *no* child. I have indeed *nothing.* When mother dies then shall I be alone, and——*one* word, *one* single word at the right time to this same holy man before whom I now stand, and I should have been free—free as the bird of the air." And in the midst of this freedom's sun shone Elin's bright image before the young man's thoughts.

"And who was that young girl who was with thee at church a few Sundays since?" asked the rector, still further; "I did not know her. She was not of our communion."

"With permission, that was my sister-in-law," replied Gunnar, bowing in a most confused manner, and crimsoning so deeply, that the clergymen remarked it.

"With permission," said Abraham, and bowed like a clown, in imitation of Gunnar, but without any embarrassment, "with permission, that is she who taught me to read so well; for she is just like a reading priest, and the best girl that ever was; and she is, with permission, before any one else."

The rector could not help smiling at this speech, nor could Gunnar, although his heart beat; for now, standing thus beside his confessor, he knew how he loved Elin better than every one else, and also how great was his sin in so doing. He avoided the glance of the holy man, which was keen and penetrating, but at the same time gentle and consolatory. One might almost have believed that he both understood and pitied Gunnar; if he did, he locked this knowledge and this pity within the remotest sanctuary of his thoughts, until a resolve attained there its maturity.

CHAPTER XXX.

GUNNAR bore incessantly within him a terribly bitter feeling, and felt constantly the ague and cold without; for he was now scarcely ever to be seen in the house. He had thus a sort of excuse to himself, that he now, far oftener than formerly, sought an especial friend to deaden his pain; for the moment warming and cheering, consoling, and calming; I mean, unhappily, the brandy-bottle. Gunnar, in the early period of his sad marriage, when cold reason guided all his steps, had taken one, and at the most two drams a day. In those glad and gay times which preceded these, he had, indeed, too often given way to the taste of the hour and the inspiration of the moment, and had taken two or three; but now! overcome by the pain and passion of a hopeless attachment, which he strove in vain to extinguish, he endeavored to drown his anguish, and took often his five and six draughts, sometimes two at once; and Lena, the wretched Lena, low and brutish in all her feelings, testified her little refined and true affection for him, by rather exciting him to this transgression than endeavoring to restrain him from it; and Lena was a striking example that it is only the wicked, low-thoughted, and contemptible woman, in whatever station she may be, who, without loathing—yes, often with a certain revolting pleasure—can see and associate with drunken fellows.

To Lena's astonishment, however, Gunnar never became in-

toxicated, though she herself provided the strongest and best
brandy in the country; and this because he bore far more than
any one else through his strong and uneffeminated constitution.

Elin saw nothing of all this, for she kept herself almost constantly, during this rainy weather, within her own chamber,
weaving a piece of delicate stuff for Lena, out of which Gunnar
was to have clothes made. But, with a mournful heart, she
strove with continually breaking threads, and continually out-
breaking tears. Never had Elin had such need of her dear departed mother; never did she seem to see so little likeness between herself and Lena, and never so great a difference between
the commands and advice of a good and upright person and
those of a harsh and unreasonable one. Lena insisted repeatedly
that it was Elin's fault that the weaving succeeded so ill; and
as Lena, in practical life, was a thoroughly clever and knowing
woman, and well understood all her business and affairs, and in
her perpetual remarks on all that went on about her was mostly
in the right; and as Elin was, in the highest degree, good and
conceding, and without sufficient self-reliance; and as Lena,
moreover, had still much of her mother's voice and her mother's
look, although hers were sharp and hard; so, Elin bore all in
silence, but with heavy sorrow at heart, and thought almost
incessantly of the changed manner of Gunnar, and pondered over
the inexplicable cause of it—often fancying that it was owing
to something which she must have done, though she knew not
what, but which gave her cruel pain.

One day came Lena, and protested that the web was all
awry, stood awry, was woven awry, with many other awries.
She seized on the loom with the strength of a man, and dragged
it hither and thither; wrath gave her an altogether amazing
power—pushing and jamming the great heavy loom to and fro.
Thread after thread snapped asunder; and Elin, who knew
that she would have to piece them all again, only sighed.

"Yes, but it makes it none the better to stand there sighing
and staring at it," said Lena, flying up and down, and athwart
and across in the loom, "without taking a pull here—no! *there!*
Ah, speak, milksop! Go, look for Gunnar, who stays down in
the shed chopping wood!"

Through the drenching rain Elin rushed forth to Gunnar, and
felt even a refreshment from the heavy shower, compared with
the lightnings of wrath and the storm of words.

"Dear Gunnar!" said Elin, timidly, "be so good as to come

in to Lena, and help us a little with the loom.   There is something awry which Lena can not herself set right."

"Shall I bring some tools with me ?" asked Gunnar, without
looking up.

" I don't know," answered Elin, and her heart beat so violently that she did not know what she said.   They went in, one
following the other at a considerable distance.

"See here !" began Lena, the moment she set her eyes on
Gunnar; " see here, what a piece of work Elin has made of
the weaving !   Had I not come in, she would have ruined it
outright and for ever.   See, *here* it is awry; *here* it is awry;
and here it is warped : and if thou hast not got thy hatchet, I
must e'en go after it, while thou lookest on.   Come here, Elin !"

Lena hastened out, and did not return before they heard her
call to Abraham to bring the forgotten axe.   In the meantime
Gunnar set the loom right without saying a word, and Elin assisted, in the same silence.   But at length, when she thought
she heard Lena approaching, her oppressed heart admonished
her to avail herself of the opportunity, and with a tearful glance,
she looked up to Gunnar timidly, and said, " Good Gunnar, art
thou also angry with me ?"

" One can not well be angry with God's angels !' answered
Gunnar, hastily, and with an open, clear, affectionate look, and
as not considering how *much* those few words implied.   But
Elin *felt* it, for she became instantly consoled, joyous, and cheerful, bore without vexation all Lena's chidings, did promptly
what she required, and sat for an hour afterward alone, singing
to herself, piecing all the broken threads, but without a single
tear in her clear blue eyes.   She was so joyous, so kind, so
playful, and cordial, that even Lena became pacified ; and at
evening, as the family were at supper, and the sun went down
in great splendor, Lena, said jeeringly, and with a sort of malicious joy, yet laughingly,

" Mark me, if we are not invited to a mowing-help at Lars
Carlsson's, now the sun shines so bright.   I know that he designs it, and waits only for the weather taking up.   I wonder
how his meadow looks which lies yet uncut.   The hay will be
nothing but dry bents, it's my notion ; and he will not get half
the value of the crop.   But they are all alike, the scrubs and
sanctified beasts, who think themselves better than every body
else, and wiser than God the Father."

" Ah ! he is neither a scrub nor so conceited as thou thinkest," replied Gunnar; "he is a dashing fellow, yet knowing and clever, only he has plunged overhead, and taken too great a farm; and so he can not manage it just as he ought."

"Ay, ay, and therefore he is just a scrub; and, therefore, he has to make great mowing-helps, while all other people mow their own rye!" retorted Lena, half laughing.

"Ah, well! never mind, so that his harvest-supper does come off!" exclaimed Elin, joyously, and clapping her hands. "I have never in my life been at a harvest-supper. That my mother never allowed me, and in those days I never got a rake into my hands. But see now! Oh! that will be delightful!"

Elin had not uttered these few words, before a youth of some fourteen years of age stood in the room, and made his father's best compliments, who hoped that the whole family would do him the honor to come to-morrow to the harvest-supper.

Elin leaped for joy, and made all sorts of odd faces at Abraham, who also took a few of his "swine's capers," as Lena was used complimentarily to call his lubberly leaps. Lena laughed, and poured out a full dram for the boy, who swallowed it at a draught, and took his departure to issue more invitations, and drink more drams.

"Did not I say it?" cried Lena, before the boy had well closed the door behind him. "Yes, I knew to a certainty, that, if the weather only took up ever so little, we should have a prompt summons to help at the mowing, instead of his doing his own work when it wants doing."

"Thou canst stay at home," said Gunnar, coolly.

"Yes, I should think so, indeed!" answered Lena, angrily; "and thou, and Elin, and Abra'm, and whole troops with you, can go. No, thank you! I shall go with you, though it does vex me thoroughly. But at what o'clock must we set off for the morrow's attendance? That must be done at midnight, I fancy?"

"No," replied Gunnar; "I shall row thither, and then it will not be necessary to set out before three o'clock."

"Well, that is, at least, early enough to my thinking," said Elin, laughing, and skipping hastily away into her chamber, to look after apparel for the morrow's fête—to make use, for once, of two phrases out of the language of the saloon.

Elin had a little fault: she was vain of her dress. Both her mother and herself had been industrious and clever, and had, in fact, earned no small sum with the needle, and all had gone for Elin's dress and little fancies. She was, moreover, very affectionate and compassionate, and gave her left-off clothes to the poor and needy, and thus had herself very often new and handsome ones, and had always a great quantity of them in proportion to her rank and condition. She took the greatest care of them, so that they always looked as though they were wholly new. Among her variety of apparel, she had a particular holiday dress of light pink print, which she thought she might put on, although she continued in mourning for her mother, for she had heard that it was allowable to wear pink in mourning; and, delighted as she was at the prospect of going to the harvest-supper, she must, for no consideration, put on gay-colored clothes.

In the morning she arose at the first peep of dawn, and began humming to herself for joy over the lovely weather and for something else, to comb out her long auburn and glittering hair, clean and soft as that of a maid of honor; and, platting it into a large, thick plait, she finally fastened it in the most approved style with a neat little comb and a large hair-pin. Sighing, she next put on her gold earrings, the last she ever received from her departed mother, securing them carefully in their places that they might not get lost. She then clad herself further; and when her toilet was complete, in her light handsome gown, with black apron, and black silk scarf, she looked as neat and spruce as a little doll, for her clothes sat well and gracefully on her slim and yet full figure.

"One can not well be angry with God's angels!" she exclaimed repeatedly to herself, and sung it over to herself in a low, soft tone. There was something heavenly and enchanting for Elin's heart in these words of Gunnar; but she regarded it merely as a little innocent exultation that her brother-in-law was not angry with her. "He is certainly annoyed by something," she thought at the same time, and drew a deep sigh at the idea; but the egotism of affection, the greatest of all, made this reflection vanish before the other. "He is not angry with me! He compares me to the angels of God! If I were but one, I would hover continually around him, and gladden and inspirit him!"

"Now, then, Elin!" screamed Lena, shrilly, when it was about half-past three, "art thou sleeping yet? Up with thee in an instant, or we shall row away without thee. The men are already down by the boat. Bestir thyself, and fling round thee thy wrapping-shawl, for it is cold on the lake so early in the morning."

All this screeched Lena as she hastened along the passage, and without opening Elin's door; but Elin heard it, obeyed her summons, caught up her clothes, threw over herself her great wrapping-shawl, and hastened, skipping and joyful, after Lena.

"Ah, no! I must kiss little Gustaf before I go, and say a kind word to 'mother-in-law,'" said she, when she had got a good way from the house; turned at once round, flew back again, hastened to the child's cradle, kissed him so that he woke, and then called laughing to Mother Ingrid, who already was up spinning in her corner, "Good-bye, mother; amuse yourself with Gustaf, whom I have wakened up for you;" and with that she hastened out, and was scarcely out of the house when Lena was at the strand. The old woman ceased her spinning, and, smiling sorrowfully, looked after the good and happy maiden.

"Yes, *such an one* should she have been!" said she, half aloud, sighed deeply, and began again to spin; at the same time that, with the other foot, she rocked Gustaf's cradle, in order that he might sleep again. It was, however, neither with the excited tenderness of a father's mother or a mother's mother, the rays of which go right up out of the innermost depths of the heart, but with the care of a good and gentle nurse.

In the mean time our four bounded over the light crisp waves, stirred by the summer wind, and breathed into their lungs the brisk air of the lake and the morning, which was changed into the fresh joy of life in the soul, and a soft melancholy in the heart. Even Lena was less stern, less sharp and cross than usual, and Abraham himself got a half-friendly word from her. Her good humor expressed itself now, as at all times, in loud laughter, and satirical, half-spiteful, but frequently by no means stupid reflections on all that passed around her in the world—the works of God as well as those of men. She spared no one, and was abashed by nothing. She had now almost all the talk to herself in the boat, and pretty much in this manner:

"Bless me, Abra'm! Thou lookest altogether like a new pot-cuckoo, that one sees in the market, as thou sittest idly in that red-brown summer dress, with that red-brown face, and

H*

those red-brown fists. Or some one has dipped thee in alder-bark dye, and then rolled thy head in herds. What the deuce, Hans Mattsen! I think thou hast white stockings on thy-legs! Bless my soul, what extravagance! But, Heaven help us! Why I actually believe that they are the bare legs that are so clean and white. Ha! ha! ha! Well thou hast scoured them! Thou must have had both sand and ashes to them—ha! ha! ha! What a stupid lake is this, which takes so many turnings and twistings, and has so many promontories, and islands, and un-necessary things, that are merely lying in the way of people who want to get straight on. But, there! how plain Holma church is to be seen! that is because they built it so prepos-terously large that all the money was gone before it was half finished, and so that nobody can go thither in winter, lest they should be frozen to death; for the whole· congregation can sit in one corner of it. Have you heard, *apropos* of the church, that they begin, both girls and little boys, to preach in the island congregation there? So the turn will now come quickly to us; but I tell thee, and swear, that if thou beginnest to preach or to make a noise, I will strike thee dead; for thou lookest, in-deed, as if thou wanted to preach! And Abra'm there, he must, since he has picked up a word here and a word there out of the Catechism; perhaps he will next mount the pulpit and cry, 'Repent!' But that shall be but a moderate sermon, I promise you, for I shall preach myself as much as is neces-sary."

"Yes! God knows, I both *can* and *will*," muttered Abra-ham; but Lena did not hear it, or affected not to hear it, but proceeded:

"Well, now, I begin to be hungry, but, thank God! we shall get enough to eat and to drink in the course of the day; there is no fear of that, for there is nobody so proud, ostenta-tious, and lavish, as Lars Carlsson and his wife. Goodness! they are genteel to madness; and they would now spend their last farthing, or part with their last morsels, though they should starve all the rest of the year, for there is nothing like consist-ency in these sort of people. One thing to-day and another to-morrow; they live and they have nothing, and vagabonds are they altogether. In every thing new and preposterous you are sure to find Lars Carlsson. Should not he, think you, be the very first to enter that new fire-assurance company which Gun-nar praised so exceedingly, and must, of course, have a finger

in, were it only to let Lars befool us into it? as though we had
not taxes, and impositions, and misery enough, without laying
more on ourselves!"

Amid all this gossip, Gunnar and Elin sat silent, and gazed
at each other, for they sat so near and so opposite to each
other that they could not avoid it; and Gunnar said to himself—
"Perhaps there is some sin in it"—and Elin said nothing.
But presently the morning sun began to cast his warm beams
upon the voyagers, and Elin unfolded and opened her great
checked wrapping shawl; perhaps impelled to do so by the
sun, which shone and warmed her from within.

"What in all the world!" exclaimed Lena, as Elin opened
her shawl. "Why I trow thou hast been tricking thyself out
in fashionable muslin! Never did I see the like of that at a
harvest-supper before! What is the good of that? Mercy on.
me! I never caught a sight of this folly till thou just now
opened thy shawl; for thou hast taken up thy gown-skirt so
that I only saw thy petticoat. Bless me! What an absurd
and vain apparition!"

"Oh, gracious Heaven! how vexatious!" said Elin, wholly
cast down. "Am I now too grand again? Ah! only think if
they laugh at me, and mock me! Ah! that I did not take
care to ask thee, dearest Lena!"

Hard-heartedly and scoffingly replied Lena, "Ay, why didst
thou not? Thus it is to be so wise in one's own conceit!
And now thou must put up with being well laughed at."

A tear rose to Elin's eyes. Gunnar had hitherto kept
silence: but now it was no longer possible.

"Don't fret thyself, Elin, for such a trifle!" said he, with a
glance so mild and kind, that Elin's tears quickly returned to
their source. "Be glad and light-hearted as before," continued
he, "Lena only quizzes and jests with thee. If thou art as
fine and neat as a doll, well; don't trouble thyself about that,
let them do it who are not so. Console thyself with that."

"Oh, yes! that is a fling at me," said Lena, reddening with
envy and jealousy; but Gunnar began to rock the boat and
busy himself with the oars, and spoke in a high and overpower-
ing voice to Abraham, bidding him steer, and not be so stupid;
and then he began, clear and loud, to whistle a lively polka;
the way in which for hours he answered Lena's outbreaks, and
which were thus most frequently compelled to silence. It was
so now, and within a few minutes they lay-to at the strand,

and began to advance towards Lars Carlsson's shop, which was, perhaps, a furlong from the shore, but to eight such legs as those of "our four" such a distance is but a few steps. When they arrived, many were come, and many were not come.   The mowing and entertainment began almost immediately, and the work continued with little interruption till six o'clock in the evening, when it for the most part concluded, and all turned homewards to take the only regular meal of the day; for till then they had only bread and butter, with or without cheese, ale, brandy, and the like.   The labor of the day, and the consequent appetite, made the place of the supper at first not perfectly silent, but calm and quiet, and each one thought only of himself and his wants.   Elin had taken her place at the table among some other pretty young peasant girls, who all, in the most zealous terms, praised her neat dress and her general appearance.   Elin was silent, and felt far more ashamed than gladdened by it, though she thought that she could not by any means perceive that quizzing which Lena had foretold her, but met rather general good-will and kindness, for *thus* did Elin interpret the admiration which was excited by her attractive exterior, her joyous disposition, and her tasteful attire, which nothing but Envy found unbefitting; and it is not to be imagined that this black lady—Envy—does not seat herself at the harvest-supper, amid the peasantry, as certainly as she does at the royal table amid its guests, and casts her poison into the brandy-flask as surely as into the champagne-bottle.

Presently the first hunger was appeased; and then the company, for whom the long and well-covered board had been spread in the court, began to be loud in their discourse; and the host, with his sons and servants, went round and exhorted the guests to help themselves, and to spare his entertainment as little as they had spared their strength in the meadow.   He was an admirable host, was this Lars Carlsson, a perfect example of hospitality; paid the most incessant compliments to his guests, though somewhat grotesque ones, but spiced with great country wit, and found continual reason to bid them eat and drink, be merry and lively.   When he came to Elin and the young women, he reached her first of all a silver cup of foaming ale, and then holding it to his own lips, said—

"A health, thou little blossom of beauty, who this year, for the first time, hast burst forth in our fields—a health, my sweet one. I should really lose my heart outright, only that all the boys here would go mad, play the deuce with me, and murder me out of sheer jealousy. And yet, see there!—may I not one day come to be your father-in-law, eh, my sweetest?"

Gunnar, who did not sit far off, looked at him with a pair of eyes in which might be plainly read both thunder and lightning; for Lars Carlsson had another son, older than the one who had brought the invitation to Vika, and who showed himself one of the company's handsomest and most attentive attendants, and at the same time one of the first of rural dandies. His name was Oskar, for Lars Carlsson was an admirer of antiquity, and had, in keeping with this taste, named his children. One daughter was christened Maximiliana, another Eugenia, who were commonly called Maxa and Eugena; and, in the same manner, his Nicholas was obliged to creep out of his Russian skin, and into that more Swedish one called Nisse.

Elin looked up, and received the friendly host's compliments with a pleasant and jocose manner; not at all confused or disconcerted, though she blushed beautifully. Elin was one of those favorite children of nature, of those lovable, womanly beings, who are sometimes, if not very numerously, found in every possible nook and condition of life, and who display in whatever they do, a tact, a charm, and a power of fascination which no one can readily withstand. The effect of this in these women is an augmented charm; for the consciousness of being observed and admired by men becomes so familiar, and a matter of course to them, that they retain their self-possession, it never forsakes them; they never wholly forget themselves, looked confused or surprised, are at a loss what to say or to answer, flash open their eyes or close them, titter or look affected, as do others—that is, the many who only now and then display a little paroxysm of beauty, only sometimes awaken a feeble admiration.

When the son Oskar came to Elin and desired that she should also drink a health with him, she declined this, and jested with the youth in a wholly different tone to that which she used toward the father; so prudently, and with such regard to her maidenly dignity.

"Oh!" thought Gunnar, and that nearly for the first time with perfect ingenuousness—for the rapid libations had thrown a light mist around his delicate conscience, though not altogether around his brain—"oh! if I had but hit upon this treasure, this jewel; if I could have pressed her to my bosom, and called her mine—then would I willingly have labored in an anchor-smithy day and night—or——at least from sunrise to the latest hour of evening."

When the supper was over, the dancing began immediately, to the sound of several brisk country violins, and out on a little lovely green grass-plat, surrounded by lofty and shady trees, and where some benches were placed for the occasion. Scarcely had the dance commenced, before one, two, three carriages of the gentry, and some chaises, drew up before the stately farmhouse, and out of them stepped the family from Grantorp, the major and his young daughter, Miss Elfrida, and with her an older gentleman in their company, with the clergyman of the parish and his whole family—all invited by Lars Carlsson, "to have a peep at the dance on the green grass a little while in the evening;" and every one had been obliging enough to show much pleasure in complying. They were now served with both coffee and tea, the former strong and excellent, the latter somewhat flavored with powdered cinnamon; and, further, they were offered city biscuits, fine bread, and with these wine in tall slender glasses. The appearance of the gentry occasioned some little interruption to the dance; but after a few minutes this went on again with redoubled spirit, and soon were seen the major, who resembled one of Charles XII.'s blue troopers, and the young ladies, the young people from the parsonage, the tutor and boys from Grantorp, mingled in the glad and lively dance, and commenced a little polska; and a black cloud passed over the senses of Gunnar when he finally saw Elin whirl round, gay and gladsomely, with the master of Grantorp himself! This sight was more depressing to Gunnar than any other that he could conceive; and he noticed with demoniac glances how charming this gentleman found the young and handsome Elin, who, amidst all the gentry, formed the chief topic of conversation.

"My faith!" said the elderly gentleman who was with the major, and took a huge pinch out of his box, "this damsel would create a sensation in the great Stockholm itself! She is actually a *Taglioni champêtre*. See only how lightly and gracefully she revolves, exactly as Taglioni, in the Sylphide, pirouettes round her sleeping lover. *C'est charmant!* Bravo!"

"Yes, but our distillery servant, Olle, does not look, methinks, much like a sleeping lover, but one right widely awake yet!" said laughingly, and somewhat spitefully, Ma'msell Sara, who frequently answered with a peculiarly caustic and laconic irony, the old *précieux* chamberlain's eternal Stockholm common-places.

Gunnar this evening experienced all the pangs of jealousy in his heart, every one of which was different to the rest. One cut deep, one stabbed maliciously, one tore it up violently, another rent it to and fro. When Elin whirled round with the master of Grantorp, Gunnar had the strongest desire to send a bullet from his rifle through his skull. When she, contrary to his wish, waltzed with Olle, till he ceased to drag her about, he felt a burning impulse to pay him off in the same way; when, gladly and lively, with chat and joke, she danced with Bengt, with whom she was so well acquainted, as he generally spent his Sunday afternoons at Vika, Gunnar closed his eyes; and when Elin—as Gunnar thought, though he did not express it in our fashionable phrase—coquetted a little with the son of the house, the conceited Oskar, then Gunnar went his way, and leaned against a tree, as if he was dizzy with dancing; for he had, in fact, been dancing, in order to forget his suffering—and had performed an impetuous polska with a young girl whom he had often waltzed with in his former gay and happy days of sport and pleasure, but for whom he had never felt much attachment.

Elin, with all the quickness of a woman's eye, had noticed this violent, and almost maniacal dance, noticed Gunnar's excitement, and the damsel's contentment, and finally Gunnar's leaning against the somewhat distant elm. Without pausing to reflect, she abruptly brought the dance with young Oskar to a close, and hastened away to Gunnar, took him gently by the arm, that he might perceive her—for he stood there with closed eyes—and with a tone so sweet and tremulous that a person must have been made of lead not to detect in it all the disquiet and sympathy of affection, said,

"Gunnar! what is amiss with thee? Look up, or I believe I shall faint with terror, for thou look'st so ill."

"I ill!" replied Gunnar, unable to control himself—"Oh, no! *Now* I am better than ever; and still better shall I be, if thou wilt only dance with me a little half hour!"

"If I will!" said Elin, who had suffered inexpressibly from Gunnar's coldness and repulsive mood for many days past, and his avoiding her now during the dance. But such a dance as there now took place! Yes, that was worth witnessing, for the poor young creatures now danced, not upon mortal feet and legs, but upon the frenzied wings of love. They flew! Their glances melted into one, and time flew for them equally swift as themselves. Gunnar had merely aimed at dancing some moments, and half an hour had already flown by, and he believed that there were yet some left of the brief instants.

The air was clear—night had already fallen; and when Gunnar and Elin at length terminated their dance, the dusk of the evening, and the general confusion, caused no one to see Gunnar press Elin for a moment to his heart; he loosed his hold, and hastened again to his tree, but with a hundred-weight's oppression on his conscience. Elin stood still and speechless, and neither heard, nor saw, nor answered, when Lena came, and, hastily clutching her by the arm, said with a sharp tone,

" That was what you came to the dance for, eh, good-for-nothing! Thou thought to seduce Gunnar from me, that I can believe. I will away home from these wretched, abominable goings on. They that will, can remain standing here, but Gunnar shall row me home. Thou and Abraham can stay here if you will, and go round by the road."

" Nay, I shall accompany you," answered Elin, both lost in thought and full of thought.

Lena's wrath, for it was in rage that she now really spoke, had not flamed up of itself, but the Still-man Olle had both kindled it, and blown it into a blaze with all his might. Lena had been sitting and gossiping with some others, middle-aged women and girls, who had already quitted the dance, when Gunnar began the mad waltz with Elin. Lena had not at all noticed it till Olle plausibly and maliciously, as was his constant habit, came to the group of gossipers, and, screaming and laughing, made these remarks on " the horrible dance."

" See you, Lena!" he shrieked, " how Gunnar dances with your sister? He likes her famously, I can see, and she is just as crazily fond of him; so that it is not so much to be wondered at, if he thinks more of her than you, Lena! Ha! ha! ha! Take care, Lena! that may become a foul fish for you to scale. Your sister may soon become the mistress of the house, and rule you, and you may go as maid-servant under her into the corner. Ha! ha! ha! I should be amused to see how angry you'd be if your sister supplanted you, as—the

devil take me!—I believe she has already. Ha! ha! ha!
See how they whirl round! See how passionately they gaze
on each other! And there! I verily believe that he kissed
her before they parted, for so, at least, it seemed. Ha! ha!
ha!"

Lena needed to hear nothing more to make the fiendish
madness of jealousy blaze up in her; she flew at once from
her place, and fell upon Elin as we have seen.

We have said that Elin stood motionless and speechless
where Gunnar had left her after the dance. She did so still.
She did not rush away now to the tree where Gunnar was
leaning—she *now first* woke to a full consciousness. She felt
now that degree, that excess of affection which we call love,
and which no woman can feel for any other than the man
whom providence has destined for her consort, without crime,
especially when that object of affection is the consort of another. All this now stood clear to the mind of Elin; and she
was conscious how inexpressibly she loved Gunnar, and how
wrong it was. She no longer heard or saw, or took leave of
any one, or spoke a word, but followed Lena mechanically,
when she went up to Gunnar, seized him by the arm, and
asked him whether he stood by the tree and slept—whether he
had had enough of his wild dancing—whether they should not
row home.

"Ah, certainly!" answered Gunnar, rushed away from the
tree, and hastened down to the shore where the boat lay, altogether forgetful of Abraham.

Lena and Elin followed; and when they arrived at the boat,
they saw, with some wonder, that Abraham lay and slept in it.
But all were silent, for every one was in a mood of mind difficult enough to describe. When they had entered the boat,
Elin wrapped the shawl about her head, and pretended to
sleep. Gunnar, on the contrary, rowed with tremendous long
pulls, as if he would fly from some one; but the evil accompanied him, for it was fixed in the center of his conscience,
and bit keenly and deeply into it. Lena attempted to wrangle
a little, but as no one answered, she was compelled to be silent.
At length she spoke thus to Abraham:

"Never did I see thee before do any thing that was not precisely stupid. But it was sensible enough to go and lay thee
down in the boat; much more sensible than some others who
danced and flung, both in season and out of season."

No one replied; but, after a moment's silence, Abraham said, in a low tone, " Yes, the dancing has not fallen very much to my share—that God knows; but the fact was, that, as Elin would not dance with me, I was resolved not to dance with any one else."

Elin did not hear Abraham's remark, and it was well that she did not; for her heart was oppressed before, and it would have become more so if she had perceived how she had wounded another human heart. Women have, at least, a spark of compassion in such cases, especially if they are good, pure-minded, and incorrupt. All were silent, and Lena's wrath began somewhat to allay itself, especially as Gunnar said a few kind words to her, asked her whether she was cold, and whether she would not have his Sunday coat to wrap herself in, as he was rowing without it, and it lay in the boat. Lena, however, was not cold, but was, at length, weary of keeping silence, and finally began to express her discontent in the following manner:—

" That was really a horrible feast and tumult! Such things are enough to make any one poor, who is not richer altogether than Lars Carlsson. It is horrible how set up the whole family is by a bank! the girls and the boys too. And what was the use of inviting the gentry? It was nothing but downright pride! Ma'msell from Grantorp sat there, I saw, in her most fashionable summer hat, for I know them all well enough; and Miss from Svanvik was as grand in her mousseline-de-laine as at the banquets of the gentry. That is just an ass, that major, who wishes her to have the poor scarecrow from Stockholm, the chamberlain, or chamber-servant, or whatever his title may be—that old, long, lean, hell-cat, from Stockholm, who does nothing but take snuff in church on a Sunday. Him she will be compelled to have, whether or not; for so says Anna Lisa, who is cook there."

Elin sighed, partly on her own account, partly on that of the poor young lady. Gunnar merely rowed without rest or pause, either for body or mind. It began to dawn before " our four" landed at Vika; and, silent and out of sorts, went all to their beds for a short sleep.

When Elin found herself alone in her chamber, that terrible anguish and disquiet fell over her which every right-minded being *must* feel when he has a great reproach to make himself; who has done something which is not only sinful and unjust, but which is hopelessly irrevocable; and all this Elin seemed to herself to have done. " If I had stolen, if I had lied and calumniated some one," thought the young girl, whose sin-register was so short, and made up according to the popular notions—" if I had done any of these things, I could readily restore the stolen property, recall my words, weep and pray for forgiveness, from both God and those whom I had injured, and none but myself would suffer for my fault; but now!—now I have done too grievously wrong, and know not how I shall repair the mischief."

She wept bitterly, and implored God, and the spirit of her mother, to strengthen and counsel her. But the Most High is, as we well know, deaf and silent to such prayers, so long as we do not listen with open ears to the voice of conscience, through which alone He speaks loudly and clearly. Elin was, perhaps, not wholly able to comprehend this strong and inter-nally-written law, but she listened to it, nevertheless; and when the morning came, she shunned every glance at Gunnar, every possible meeting, and humbled herself to Lena's minutest wishes. And now first became Lena thoroughly intolerable. Her suspicions of Elin and Gunnar were fully awakened; and though she did not openly express her meaning, she sought in-cessantly for occasions to, at least, torment Elin, to chide and reprimand her, and blame her on the most absurd charges. Elin bore all. Gunnar was rarely within, and when he entered Elin went out. Lena saw nothing which could properly excite her jealousy, but it seethed, nevertheless, suspecting that she had cause for its existence.

So passed whole days—yes, even weeks. Hay and corn-harvest went on, and drew near to their close, and the earth began already to look yellow and stripped, like a heart which had no longer any hopes. The earth, however, will soon be-come white, in order again to become green; but the heart!—ah! that neither grows lighter nor greener, but parches up, freezes, withers away, till, finally, the green blades are plucked up by the roots.

But the hearts of neither Gunnar nor Elin froze, or were parched up, but they burned with a flame which strove to de-stroy every sense of honor and of duty. When Gunnar saw Elin, he felt only one desire—to press her to his bosom, and tell her how dear she was to him; when he did not see her, his vivid yearnings, and his consciousness of his infidelity, persecuted him, and he was devoured with remorse for his unhappy passion, yet he was strong enough to seek to surmount it, and he avoided Elin with all possible care.

Elin, on her side, had no longer any thought for any thing but Gunnar. No creature on earth did she love more than Gunnar; for the slight degree of affection which she felt for the other three was merely the consequence of the relation in which they stood to Gunnar. If she caressed little Gustaf, she thought of Gunnar; if she submitted to Lena's ill-temper with mildness and submission, it was now merely for Gunnar's sake; and if she showed herself helpful and kind toward Mother Ingrid, it was almost wholly from affection to the son. This affection had drowned all other feelings, and yet gave itself not a moment's indulgence; for she avoided Gunnar, on her part, attempted the impossible, which was, not to think of him, and gave to her boundless love nothing but tears. But these flowed often, and copiously; and many fell on the slender threads in the loom, whose strokes kept time to the throbbing of her heart for whole days together. The loom was at once Elin's comfort, refuge, and sole confidant. In this she lived. Gunnar must have clothes made from this web; he would bear and wear every thread which she wove together; and this thought was enough to give to her labor that charm which nothing else could possess. Lena saw with what zeal she labored at it, and what patience she displayed over it; but Lena was not endowed with a single fine feeling, or she had altogether outworn such, and therefore she did not comprehend the real cause of Elin's zeal and diligence, but ascribed it merely to good habit and disposition; and, without commending her by any means, she felt a miserable strife in herself between the desire to keep Elin with her, and to have her away; for here jealousy and selfishness came into a revolting contention, and no one could yet say which of these feelings was the Goliath or the David. But this was soon to be determined, and that from many occurring circumstances.

CHAPTER XXXI.

WE have said that Gunnar was seldom at home, and it was seldom indeed; for whole days together he would take his meals out by himself; and often he came home merely for a moment, swallowed a little food, with the usually accompanying brandy, and then hastened out again, frequently seeing no more of Elin than a glimpse through her window, but always listening to the quick stroke of her shuttle, and that with a melancholy kind of pleasure, in the thought that it was for him that she wrought. But one day he was at home at a regular meal-time at noon, and all the members of the family were assembled in the room. Gunnar sat solitary at the table and ate. Elin had long before abandoned the custom of eating out of the same dish with him, for she fancied that she could perceive that it troubled Lena; but she now sat upon her little stool, with her earthenware basin on her knee, and imparted plentifully to little Gustaf of her food. Abraham sat, as usual, in his corner by the door, Mother Ingrid in her nook, and Lena busied herself with preparing the food, eating, ever and anon, out of the same spoon with which she stirred the pot. Thunder had muttered all the morning, but now it gloomed tremendously. It became at once almost pitch dark; and while they sat in astonishment at the cause of it, the lightning, in turbulent and manifold flashes, blazed in through all the three windows, and a crash as terrible accompanied it. The window-frames were dashed in on one side, and the room was instantly filled with rolling smoke. Every one believed that the thunder-bolt itself had fallen into the room; and Elin, following the simple impulse of nature, cast herself, in her terror, with Gustaf in her embrace, into the arms of Gunnar.

"Gunnar, Gunnar, we shall all perish!" she exclaimed.

Gunnar clasped her a moment to his heart, but released her again instantly, and said, with much feeling,

"Don't frighten thyself so, Elin dear; don't tremble so, dearest mother, the danger is over now. The lightning fell just by us, in some tree probably, but the deluging rain will soon extinguish it."

And it did rain terribly! Hail and rain rattled and rushed like fire, round about and over the house. None ventured to look out, or go to the window, much less to go out, except Gunnar, who did not hesitate to go into the court and look round, and at the same time to gather up some hail, perhaps not so big as hens' eggs, as the city newspapers had it, but quite as large as walnuts. When he brought them in, Elin expressed her astonishment, never having seen hailstones so large; and Gunnar bade little Gustaf take them, and he took them, but he started when he felt how cold they were in his little warm hands. Abraham laughed aloud at this, and Elin joined the laughter, with the constant disposition of youth to laugh, so long as it has no cause to weep.

"Bless me! thou stupid, senseless thing, as thou art, Abra'm," said Lena, with an appearance of anger, and turning towards Elin, against whom she was embittered since her involuntary movement at the explosion of the thunder, which by no means escaped her jealous and inquisitive eyes, "One," continued she, "is astounded with some hailstones, which she never saw the like of, and the other laughs at a little child which is frightened. Come here, then, my little boy, let mother take him, and don't let them make a fool of thee. Come, then," continued she, and offered to take little Gustaf from Elin, but he clung to her; and in the midst of the contest, the door of the room opened, and a beggar girl entered, more than usually ragged and forlorn, and at the same time thoroughly drenched with the deluging rain, which still continued.

"What, in Heaven's name?" said Lena, repulsively, "is that thee, Lotta? So, of all things, art thou and thy mother, the thievish slut! again in the country here? They said that you both were safe in the tower of Mariestad! Well, it is best for you that you take heed to yourselves, for you, ye witches, are like the bewitched hen, which draws eight stivers out of the house every time she goes in and out of the door, for wherever you get your noses in, there something is missing, that is certain. Don't stand staring in at the door, I say. Thou hast no business to stand there, so shabby and wet as thou art, and dripping as the rain does from thee."

This was Lena's welcome to the poor girl, whose teeth chattered in her head with cold and hunger, for the rain and the wind had almost pierced through her.

"Go forward to the fire and dry and warm thee," said Gunnar, "and ask the mistress to give thee a bit of meat."

"It is all gone," said Lena, angrily, and flung with the pot out into the kitchen, but dared not contradict Gunnar. She did, however, what she could, for she put out the fire at which she had cooked.

"There is a piece of bread for thee," said Gunnar, and took Elin's bread, which she turned to and fro in her hand, but dared not herself give to the girl.

"Thanks, many thanks," said the forlorn girl, and, becoming assured by the compassion of Gunnar and Elin, she asked of the latter some little article of dress to cover herself with. But now came Lena back out of the kitchen, and said angrily, as she saw the girl put the bread into her wallet, "Pack off— go thy way to the eternal pit, or I will help thee!"

"I have allowed her to warm and dry herself a little," said Gunnar, "and she need not go till the rain is a little over."

"Oh, it is so, is it?" muttered Lena. "No one shall obey me, but every one shall house here that will, and I must go by myself and drudge—and—"

But Lena's wrathful speech we do not trouble ourselves to complete, for even they to whom it was applied did not trouble themselves much about it. But it cut deep into Elin's soul, for she always split the words of Lena on the edge of conscience, fine as a hair, and seemed ever to stand in debt to her, yet could not help feeling how unreasonable, harsh, and unjust, she was towards all others. She stole away to her little chamber, and Abraham rushed out, wild as it was, for the mistress's thunder terrified him far more than that of heaven; but Gunnar remained behind to avert the rage of Lena from the poor girl. As soon as the rain would permit, she too went her way. When she closed the door, Lena listened after her a while, and then sprang to the window, which looked out upon the road, and stood there some minutes, when she started hastily forward, and with an oath exclaimed, "Nay, that shall not be!" and darted out of the door.

Gunnar was sitting with his head bowed on his hand, and giving no attention to Lena's movements, till she banged the door after her in her wrath. He looked up, glanced at Mother Ingrid, as if he would ask some explanation from her of the cause of this last outbreak of Lena's anger; but as the ancient dame did not lift her eyes from her wheel, but spun on, sunk, as it seemed, in wholly different thoughts, he looked out of the window, and now saw Lena returning with a little bundle under her arm. Like an arrow was she again in the room,— the rain still, though more lightly, continuing,—and cast the bundle with great violence on the bench, and exclaimed, fiercely and bitterly,

"I fancied that the stupid Elin had something in her head. That I suspected; but see, this shall not pass, to throw away clothes upon the pitiful beggar girl. She met her there in the entrance, and gave her them. Nay! sooner than that shall be, I will have them *myself*."

The fact was, that Elin, compassionating the poor, half-naked girl, had caught up in haste an old gown and neckerchief, which were ragged, though not much soiled, but neat, as was every thing which Elin possessed. These she had given to the poor girl, calling her to her as she was going away; and all this the cunning Lena had heard and comprehended; and, flying after the girl, had snatched from her, without ceremony or right, the little which she was so thankful for, and which had made her so happy.

"What is the meaning of all this?" asked Gunnar, who did not clearly understand Lena or her wrath, nor whence the bundle really came; for he believed the beggar girl had been gone away some time, and had nearly forgotten her.

"Ay, that I will relate," said Lena. "There goes the silly and stupid Elin, and gives to Banka-Lotta such of her clothes as are good enough for any body here. But, mark! I snatched them from her altogether; and now will I take them, and never again shall Elin see her gown or her neckerchief, when she has so completely thrown them away."

"Fie, thousand fiends!" said Gunnar, jeeringly. "Thou art always alike, Lena, that must one confess; thou never hadst a heart in thy bosom; and therefore nothing ever goes well with thee in the long run. And who authorizes thee to take from Elin? And what dost thou give her? Why, *nothing*— not so much as I can lay on my nail, although the girl drudges for us the whole day. And I have seen clearly enough that thou meanest to give her nothing the whole year round, nor the next neither. But, mark, that shall not be! I am master here, and can both command and forbid, when I please; and if I rarely exercise my power and authority, it is none the more extinct, understand; but now, I say—" and here Gunnar struck a hard, but determined blow on the table—"she shall have full servants' wages from the day she came, and these shall be the first stivers that I can scrape together. Let me see," he continued, and took down the almanac, which always lay on a little shelf over the window. "Let us see: she came here fourteen days before Midsummer, and at least, till quitting time, she will have a third of a year, and then full wage and board for the next year. And that say I for certain, and let no one grumble at it."

Lena dared not actually grumble against it; for when Gunnar grew angry enough, or took his master's authority up, and did not merely keep silence and go his way, then Lena grew frightened, and dared not properly oppose him; but still she murmured, and as jealousy now, too, blended its poison in her gall, she said,

"Yes, do it. Willingly for me; but then I say that I will have another maid for a servant—a stronger and abler—for another year; for now I go and slave with all my power, and Elin merely concerns herself with what is grand, and with sitting occupations. No, that will I endure no longer, but let her see after another place, and soon; and I will see after a more useful servant."

Gunnar was dumb; he was slain with his own weapon, and perceived now clearly where lay the bounds up to which he might command, and where he could not. He felt himself well admonished by his conscience to declare peremptorily, that Elin should have her full wages, but not to command that she should remain in the house. But he made conscience retreat; and, stung by the cruel thought of parting from Elin, of not living at least under the same roof with her, and being able from time to time to gratify his eyes with the sight of her, he said, resolutely, but without all passion, under the influence of the most powerful motive:

"How canst thou talk so, Lena! Does not Elin do all that she possibly can? She can not well do two things at once, that we know. She weaves from sunrise till late in the evening, and when she has done weaving she helps thee willingly with all sorts of out-of-doors matters—that hast thou just said."

"Yes; but she can not do that, and hold it out, for she has not been accustomed to it from her childhood," said Mother Ingrid, who for many reasons was desirous that Elin should, in all peace, leave the peasant's hut, and take another service, although Mother Ingrid, better than any one else, saw how amiable the young girl really was.

Gunnar answered not a word, cast only a glance—darker than any one had ever seen from him—toward the old mother, that met not hers, which rested fixedly on the thread which she spun. He started up abruptly, and hastened out to his work, but this seemed to him heavier than ever. Gunnar had never attempted to acquire so much power over himself as that he should part from Elin. He would not literally break his marriage vows, and, above all, could not drag Elin into perdition, but he would see her, hear her, live daily in her presence, be consoled and calmed by it, and love her " as a brother ;" a sentiment which all those who love for the first time, and do not thus clearly know the obscure identity between love and friendship, believe that they shall be able to hold in subjection with time and good-will.

·CHAPTER XXXII.

From this day Lena became intolerable toward Elin, and her ill-feeling did not fail to break forth against her whenever the smallest opportunity presented itself. Incessantly did she talk how " fine and delicate she was," what " milk-fingers" she had ; of what little use she was, and how discontented she was with her. Elin merely kept silence, and worked all the more diligently at the weaving, in order to get it quickly done, and then show that she could do what she wished, and possessed strength enough, as she herself believed, and which she intended to exercise to the utmost of her power ; for Elin, too, wished to remain where she was. She did not properly make the thing clear to herself why she should, but she had courage for any thing but separating from Gunnar. He was her sun, her life, her sole thought in the world. She knew not what she wished. She knew two things only ; she would not take Gunnar's love from Lena, but she must keep that which he had given her—Elin, and would herself love him with all her heart, as indeed she did.

A few weeks went on from this time, and Lena became worse

and worse; began to talk loudly of the *necessity* there was that Elin should procure another and more fitting service, and that she herself was looking about for another maid; abused her bitterly late and early, and at the same time, when no one was by, cuffed her, and called her sundry nicknames, from which Elin might conclude that she was jealous of her.

This wounded Elin cruelly; and she began to reflect, if she were ultimately compelled to quit Vika, how severely it would wound her. She had no one to ask, to counsel with; and even in Mother Ingrid she fancied that she perceived a certain coldness which painfully afflicted the poor, friendless girl. Abraham alone was the same toward her, with his everlasting loving-kindness, which Elin had a method of so keeping within proper bounds, that he scarcely dared to peep at her, much less to touch the very hem of her garment, and so he continued at every vacant moment to come and chat with Elin; and she always asked him immediately where his catechism was; persisted in knowing, whether he would or not; and then heard him in it, clearing up for him what he babbled by rote, without further interruption. Thus Abraham, whenever he met Elin, had no time to say more than, " Yes, yes, thou Elin! Thou art a rare girl, and that thought Ostekar, or whatever he is called, that Lars Carlssa's eldest boy." This would occasion a little embarrassment to Elin, but she always smiled, and then Abraham would willingly pat her on the arm at least, when Elin would give him a push, and say sharply, " Go immediately for the catechism!" and therewith all courtship was terminated in the most serious hearing of the catechism, which resulted in Abraham soon having this at his fingers' ends, and in getting a promise from the clergyman that he should soon " go forward," as Elin always called going to communion—that sacred occasion which she, with the most unfeigned and most unshaken faith, with the hope of innocence and the pure heart of affection, portrayed to Abraham in such beautiful and attractive colors.

The end of September had now arrived. The weary web was not yet finished, but kept Elin the whole day imprisoned; and by night she lay often awake, weeping and pondering on *what* and *how* she ought to do, for Lena now gave her daily to understand that she was resolved to be rid of her; that she was useless, etc.; which pierced deep into Elin's self-respect.

One Friday evening she had not lain down to think over all this, but sat up, and, lighted by some splinters of pine-wood which Abraham had privately given her, she worked at a so-called night-cap, that is, a shirt-front for him; since he had now obtained a promise from the clergyman that on the next Sunday he should receive the sacrament with the rest of the congregation. Toward two o'clock in the morning the work was finished, and required only starching and ironing. This was accomplished by means of some small dry sticks, which Abraham had procured in all secresy, and of a little smoothing-iron which Elin possessed; and when the clock in the house struck three, Abraham's shirt-front lay neatly plaited upon the pole of the loom, and Elin cast herself upon the bed in her clothes, in order at the very earliest break of day to recommence her weaving. At this she sat assiduously at work the whole of the next day, which was Saturday, although she was both sleepy, weary, and had a pain in the head. At noon Abraham came, got his front, expressed his thanks, and bowed and scraped in token of his gratitude, and stood a moment by the beam of the loom; during which time Elin heard him a few sentences in his catechism which he never could rightly make himself master of. Just as he accomplished this, in came Lena, and, turning to Abraham, bawled at once—

"Dost thou stand here, thou good-for-nothing thing, instead of going to the threshing-floor and doing what I have told thee! Is it not enough that thou hast lamed thyself with all this running to the parsonage? Out with thee, this instant!" And with that she gave him such a push that he went headlong out of the door. Then said she to Elin, "There never surely was such an ignorant thing as thou, and so mean-spirited as to take up with such a creature as Abra'm! Fie! the thousand! That would I never have done when I was a young girl! It was much better that thou shouldst weave out the web than be gossiping with him, and consuming both his and thy time."

And with this she flew out again, for Lena had now for some time been wonderfully busy with doing something in the kitchen, nobody rightly knew what.

In the evening, the air was heavy and gloomy; Elin had woven and wept many hours, but at length she could no longer guide the threads, but leaned against the framework of the loom; and before she was aware, sleep fell over her swollen eyelids, and she lay with her head sunk on her arms, and her arms propped on the loom. But just at this instant Lena required the help of Elin to bring in a water-tub, and as

Elin showed that she was able to do such things, she was
called on as often as possible for such purposes, especially as
Lena kept up a dreadful to-do with a mysterious boiling and
splashing about of water, in the aforesaid kitchen.

"Now, my eternal God!" said Lena, and struck her hands
violently together, as she entered and saw Elin asleep! "Dost
thou actually sit and sleep in the loom? Well, that is grand,
however! but I comprehend it well enough. Abra'm, the
swine! steals into thy room by night, when we are asleep, and
there will soon be mischief there, that I can tell."

"No! such language I can not submit to hear," said Elin,
bursting violently into tears, and threw herself in indignation
out of the loom. "Every thing else I can endure from thee,
but not such vile, abominable words, as I never deserved."

"Yes, thou deservest what thou gettest," answered Lena,
and seized on Elin just as she flung herself out of the loom,
and threw her back into it with a force many times multiplied
by rage. She grasped the poor young girl in her arms, and
threw her headlong and recklessly into the loom; so a part of
the wood-work struck against one of her temples, and caused
the blood to stream down her cheek. When Lena saw that,
she went her way, swearing and blustering, but said not a word
about the water-tub, but banged-to the door with a tremendous
clap.

Stunned and confounded by all this, Elin remained for a
long time deprived of consciousness; but when at length she
opened her eyes, she felt a sharp pain in her arm and temple,
saw that the day was gone, the night fully set in; saw the new
moon arise, and diffuse a constant and strong light; listened
anxiously for every sound, but as she perceived none, she stole
silently out, and softly took the way down to the lake, partly to
bathe her throbbing head and bruised arms, partly, in undisturbed quiet, to weep and think over what she ought or ought
not to do; for now she felt perfectly satisfied that things could
not continue as they were. When she arrived on the shore,
she descended to the very farthest stone, sat down, oppressed
with anguish, on one of them, took a handkerchief which she
had on her head, dipped it in a softly-approaching wave, for
the evening was calm and beautiful, and began to wipe away
the blood from the temple, and bathe the whole head, which
ached and throbbed, at the same time pouring water on the
swollen arm. Not a sound reached her ear, except a gentle

sough in the trees, the bland murmur of the lake, and the cry of a bird, which the peasantry of our province call "haruggla," and which is heard of autumn evenings, with a strange, melancholy voice of wailing, but by no means so wild and harsh as that of the night-owl. All these sounds, not loud, but combined, in addition to the splashing in the water as she wrung out and again wetted her handkerchief, caused her not to hear another, namely, that of a man's step which approached, but was nearly inaudible on the smooth grassy bank.

It was Gunnar, who came from the wood, and took the lower road home along the shore of the lake, with his gun on his arm, and a number of young birds in his game-bag, which he intended to send to Ma'msell Sara, for sale, so that he might be able, in some degree, to reward Elin for all her diligence. The shooting of these birds had been a pleasure to him—they had been easily killed, and when the shot penetrated their little hearts, Gunnar's own had beaten with a peculiar disquiet, for it was for Elin that the shot was fired. But now he stood dumb with astonishment. Was not this Elin herself sitting there at the water's edge. Did she not seem softly to bewail and lament herself? And did he not see in the moonlight that the white handkerchief which she held to her head was bloody as she withdrew it again? For some moments he watched in silence this singular apparition; but at length he advanced toward the stone where Elin sat, saying at the same time—

"Elin, dear, is that thee? and what dost thou there?"

At first Elin was terrified; then she was filled with anxiety; but immediately these sensations gave way to joy; and all this change took place in a second. But she did not answer Gunnar before he had repeated his demand, adding—

"Hast thou wounded thyself that thou bleedest so?"

"Yes—no—ay—yes!" answered Elin, who did not wish to speak the truth, and who yet was very unskillful in feigning. "Yes," said she at length, "I *have* wounded myself."

"With what was it?" asked Gunnar, who now stood close to her.

"With—with—with—I really do not know with what."

"Where was it?"

"Oh, up in my little chamber."

"Was nobody else there?" inquired Gunnar, who now began to suspect something.

"Yes—no—yes; there certainly was somebody else there," answered Elin, evasively.

"And that was Lena," said Gunnar; but Elin was silent.

"It was not Lena?" asked he again, after a short pause.

"Yes, certainly, it was Lena," replied Elin, with a tremulous voice.

"Was she angry?" demanded Gunnar, warmly. Elin was silent.

"Was she angry?" repeated he once more; and then Elin, no longer able to contain herself, began to weep bitterly.

"Ah, yes—yes, I understand!" said Gunnar, with closed teeth, and placed himself by the side of Elin, on a stone which was mossy and soft, and large enough for them both; but his wrath passed in a moment into the most tender compassion for the weeping maiden. He put his arm round her waist, and pressed her softly to his bosom, and she leaned for a few tender and happy moments against it, during which, however, she never ceased to weep. But quickly she raised herself, withdrew herself gently from Gunnar's arm, and, taking his hand between hers, said, sorrowfully—

"Yes, my good, dear Gunnar! we must part one of these days. This state of things will not answer in the long run. I am of so little use to you," continued she, and blushed at having been near taking the affair from a wholly different side.

"Thou dost us too little service, thou little indefatigable ant! whom I hear at the loom as long as God's daylight continues!" said Gunnar, tenderly, and pressed Elin's hands between his own. "Nay, my dear, good child! it is no want of vigor, but thou *wilt go away* because she is wicked and outrageous toward thee; and Lena—she is thus because she sees that I can not bear her—but thee all the more."

"Oh, no!" said Elin, bitterly weeping, and yet feeling in those tears a relief which conscience was not wholly able to diminish—"oh, no! if it be so bad, then is Lena truly pardonable. Perhaps I should be the same in her place. If she now loves thee, Gunnar, so immeasurably, as one *can* love thee, and yet seest that thou——Ah! she hates me not for my own sake, but for thine—and I blame her not. But an unlucky day was it when I came hither!" continued she, and wept more bitterly. "I have caused strife between you, without wishing it, and before you were happy and united, and had nothing to reproach one another with."

"Ah, thou knowest me not!" replied Gunnar, with inward emotion. "To tell thee the truth, I have never loved Lena for a single day, but, on the contrary, thee; from the hour that I saw thee at the wedding."

"Fie, Gunnar, that thou canst and wilt talk in that manner!" said Elin, and let go his hand. "Ah! how would thy mother grieve if she heard thee speak thus of thy wedded wife!"

"Yes, yes, Elin!" exclaimed Gunnar, and rose to his feet— "*all* is not as it seems, and as it *should be,* here in this world. Lena has more upon her conscience than I have, and it is not necessary for thee to go away on account of Lena; but, *I beseech thee!*" added he, with tenderness and melancholy, and seated himself again at Elin's side—"I beseech thee, remain here with me. Ah! I need this small consolation. In all duty and honor will we entertain a regard for each other, and if I am only allowed to see thee, then am I satisfied, and will willingly bear my cross with patience; but when Lena is harsh with thee, then think only of me, and bear it for my sake."

And, in the midst of this very talk of Gunnar merely *looking at* Elin, and that Elin should *merely think* of Gunnar, he took her hands, raised them to his forehead and his eyes, kissed them, and lavished on them all those caresses which he would so willingly have bestowed on Elin herself.

"No, no!" said Elin, and extricated herself from Gunnar— "ah, no! that will never do! Lena will never forgive thy loving me, were it ever so little; and thy mother will never forgive me; she looks coldly upon me, although I endeavor to please her, and to gratify her in every little thing that I can. No!" continued Elin, weeping, and let Gunnar again take her hands—"no! we *must* part, but it will be dear to me all my life that I have seen thee, Gunnar!"

She could proceed no farther. The word which she did not speak, but which her heart uttered in a sorrowful joy, was the only consolation for Elin's sick soul—the only star in her dark heaven; for she too well knew that she, alone and friendless, should be cast out into the world, without a single object on which her heart could repose, except the affection of Gunnar.

Oh! they were sweet and glorious hours which the poor creatures dreamed there by each other's side, while love borrowed something calm and mild from friendship, for Elin now confided all her little griefs to the friend by whom she sat, and

Gunnar spoke for the first time out of the depths of his heart and his soul (and deep were these found in both), without, at the same time, betraying the foul secret which he, Lena, his mother, and one person more, only were possessors of. But to quiet Elin's conscience, he yet said many times, "Thou canst trust me, Elin! thou know'st that I never yet lied! thou canst readily be convinced that Lena has done much greater wrong than I do her, in having a regard for thee, and that our catalogue of sins can never possibly be so black as hers!"

"Yes, God grand it!" sighed Elin, but the sigh was not one of the heaviest; love had made all smooth, and she looked into the future not so gloomily as in the beginning of their conversation. She should—so they agreed—make yet another attempt, by diligence and labor, patience and obligingness, to appease Lena; but if this did not succeed, she should then procure a service not far off, but so that, occasionally, she could see and speak with Gunnar. They therefore agreed, also, so to act in the presence of Lena, the mother of Gunnar, and Abraham, that they should not be aware how dear they really were to each other, but to keep this little precious secret to themselves.

"But now will we go, my dear, good Gunnar!" said Elin, who equally with Gunnar enjoyed the pleasantness of the present hour, but now only first bethought herself that they might *possibly* be taking the time along with them.

Gunnar, now for the first time also during the evening, cast a glance at his dearly beloved moon, which at that moment shone down on two solitary lovers, without their observing her, and, as if somewhat offended on that account, and regarding herself as too near, was hastening over the azure firmament much more fleetly than usual—at least so thought Gunnar, for now he was just about to say, "Good-night!—Sleep well!"

"What, in heaven's name!" he exclaimed, glancing in amaze at this nocturnal torch, which so many other lovers have sung— "What is the stupid moon about? I actually believe that she shone in the evening, for now she is already hastening behind the mountain, and so the clock must have struck nine. Nay, that is utterly impossible, that can never be!"

"Oh, yes! but," said Elin, smiling, "it is quite right, though; and the moon knows better than we what she is doing. But, see thou, my good Gunnar, thou must certainly go in first, and take no notice of having met me, and then I can steal into my little chamber, and no one hear me."

" I never meant to do otherwise," answered Gunnar, and Love stood beside them, and laughed, and clapped his little cunning hands, for he had already brought the two, with their eyes open, to go along crooked ways instead of the open and direct ones. And this they the soonest became aware of themselves, as may be perceived by what follows; for just as they were about to rise from the stone where they had sat, to which Elin had repeatedly exhorted, she said,

" One thing would I ask of thee, dear Gunnar, before we part." Elin already felt the blessed enjoyment which every woman experiences in being able to lay in a manly bosom all her little and great troubles, for a manly bosom can have an answer to all her questions, can have comfort, counsel, and guidance. " What shall I do with poor Abraham? I have for a long time promised him to accompany him to church, on the day when he shall for once be so happy as to go forward to the Lord's table. But now I can not well do it, since Lena—"

She blushed to speak out, and it was only in hasty words, and half laughing, that she informed Gunnar of Lena's absurd suspicions, at which Gunnar nearly burst into open mirth, adding, somewhat waggishly, that Lena might be more than right if it depended on Abraham alone.

" Elin," said Gunnar now to her, but with all seriousness, and taking her by the hand as if he had been her father— " Elin, dear, think only in this case, as in all others, what is *right* and *wrong*, distinguish carefully between the *good* and the *bad*, for that is the first of mortal duties, and thou wilt soon find, now and always, both what thou shouldst do, and what leave undone. Hast thou promised the poor, wretched, but good-hearted Abraham, who has not another being in the world who cares to be near him, when he stands forth before the countenance of the Saviour, and prays to Him for His grace? then thou must certainly keep faith with him, for God regards the word-keeping and the tender-hearted, be assured; and much rather ought'st thou to keep thy promise to him into whom thou hast instilled reason, truth, hope, and love, than trouble thyself about some foolish words which Lena uttered in her wrath, and which she, perhaps, never again has thought of."

"Then I shall go to church in the morning," said Elin, who was blindly disposed to follow every word of Gunnar's, and even his slightest thought.

"And I too," said he—kissed her softly on the brow, and went his way. She remained sitting some seconds, and looked after him as he went, he who constituted her heart's whole earthly world. She stretched forth her arms toward him—but, luckily for them both, Gunnar did not happen to look back at that instant, though he did so at the next, and then continued his hasty course. Elin delayed yet some moments, thankfully but sorrowfully happy, and then stole away to her chamber, where she immediately went to bed, without troubling herself about food or any thing else.

When Gunnar entered the house, Mother Ingrid sat and slept, or at least was motionless and silent; Abraham sat sleepily by his well-emptied and scraped out porridge-dish, but Lena was still busy at the fire.

"It is well that thou art come at last," said she, "it is horrible, thy long staying in the wood now."

"Take the game into the cellar," answered Gunnar, and pulled out of his game-bag one young bird after another.

"That is a brave booty!" said Lena, who saw that Gunnar looked gloomy, and dared not anger him then, but, on the contrary, wished to appease him by praise of his fortunate shooting. But as she passed Elin's window, she struck sharply upon it, saying harshly, "If thou wilt have any supper, come into the house, and that immediately."

"No, I thank you," called out Elin.

"Well, then let it be," answered Lena, and the day was at an end.

CHAPTER XXXIII.

THE Sunday morning dawned calm, clear, and beautiful, as did almost every day during that splendid summer and autumn, when September offered not merely one, but many, real July days." Elin dressed herself immediately in Sunday attire, after she had asked timidly of Lena whether she could do any thing for her in the morning, as she passed her window, but got a short and negative reply. When Elin issued from her chamber door, Abraham stood already dressed, in the entrance, with book in hand, which he had procured from Elin, as she had two. He looked in thoroughly holiday trim, washed and combed, with his hair still dripping wet, but still, of the old fashion, standing erect. Of the waistcoat lent by Gunnar, he had buttoned only the lowest buttons, and displayed the new shirt-front, so that the whole of it should be seen. His boots were greased with a piece of bacon which he lately got, and of which he ate up the remainder with a good relish. His hat Gunnar had bought him out of his wages, his clothes were free from both clay and mud, and his hands scoured, first with sand and then with ashes, but still of an unusual human colour, for they were blue, just like the color of coats which Titulus Kaeding some years ago called purple-blue.

Elin's first feeling, as she became aware of Abraham, was an involuntary disposition to smile, but the next to sigh, devoutly and from the heart, for in Abraham's eyes beamed a light which good spirits instantly made palpable to the finely sentient and clear-sighted Elin, as one which religion had kindled in this dim chaotic soul.

"Good-morrow, dearest Elin!" said he. "See now, how gallant thou goest to accompany me to-day, on this great occasion, for I see thou hast thy church clothes on ; and if master and mistress would but come we might be off at once."

"Do they *both* go?" asked Elin, gladly. She thought that if Lena was disposed to go to church, she must be in a kind and gentle humor; for she could not unite thoughts of hate and wrath with going to God's house, hearing His word, and speaking with Him. "Lena must indeed be kind," thought

Elin, "and I will not show the least resentment of yesterday's occurrence, not even that I remember it."

But now issued Gunnar and Lena from the house door, and Elin advanced immediately toward the latter, and in a most friendly manner said,

"It is charming, Lena, that thou goest with us to-day, and particularly joyful for Abraham, on his day of honor."

"Yes, I still mean to take a little leisure now and then," answered Lena, tolerably friendly; for the knowing Lena had much sense, if she would only have used it, and felt now, moreover, a spark of remorse for her proceedings the evening before toward Elin, particularly when she saw that Elin had been obliged to draw down her auburn hair much farther than usual, in order to conceal the wound in her left temple. She was, at the same time, by no means kindly disposed toward Elin, but her ill-will to her she yet desired to conceal, as far as possible, from Gunnar, from a dark obscure feeling that the opposition might place her in too ugly a light before him, whom she yet loved deeply in her own rough way. The uneducated *feel* nearly all that which we educated *know*, and can put into words. That is the difference.

All went silently on the way toward the church; no one was disposed to talk; and even if this disposition showed itself in any one or more, then there was always one pair of ears too many, and so all were silent. Ever and anon the glances of Gunnar and Elin met; and an almost imperceptible movement of the mouth, a slight twinkle of the eye, was the only pleasant morning greeting; the only observations were on the beautiful summer day, for summer still lingered in that delightful year, as some women continue to charm us, whom Time has adopted as his foster-children, and therefore hurries past them without even touching them with his hard, reckless hands, and sharp devouring teeth.

"Oh, how glad and frightened I am!" whispered Abraham to Elin, just as they entered the church.

"Yes, glad and happy ought'st thou to be, dear Abraham," answered Elin, softly, "but frightened need'st thou not be. He who has done no evil, but always the best that he knew, has no occasion to tremble before God. Be thou, therefore, of good courage, and think only of what is good, and courage will come of itself."

The people now entered the seats; the women on one side,

the men on the other. Elin sunk down, absorbed in holy thoughts; Lena looked around her. The confession was not yet begun; but now the church doors were closed, and the voice of the pastor, at once powerful and gentle, awoke Elin, and perhaps Gunnar too, out of their own dreams of devotion, where probably many a light and dark object of this world stood forth.

This priest, this utterer of the word of God, had a manner usually of speaking to the people so that they listened, comprehended, loved and believed in his words, and at the same time endeavored to establish their faith in their works, their love in their mode of life, and to build their hopes in a pure and good conscience. We will not say that his preaching had this effect on all, but it produced far more good than that of many of his brother preachers did; and the consequence was, that his congregation was one which nobody talked of, which seldom or never gave example of gross crimes, great misdeeds, discord, excessive vanity, lawlessness, and indifference to God's message, or of fantastic religious movements. All such things were shut out of this congregation. All the young and unmarried, and many of the younger married people, who now began to have children growing up, were all his confession-children, or had, as the peasantry express themselves, "gone and read" before him, and were by him formed into a class, which it is difficult to describe, and which, moreover, can not be imagined, except by those who, with their own eyes, have seen how inconceivably much good a worthy and, for his true duties, zealous shepherd of souls can effect, and *vice versâ*, unhappily. Thus, all the young—and these always constitute the soul of every human mass—had so high an opinion of their pastor, put so much faith and trust in him, that he led them where he would, which was best seen when the so-called "Preaching Epidemic"* approached even this congregation, for there it was upset; not by stern prohibition and the civil power, but by intellectual indifference and coldness to all similar excess unproductive of advantage. Not a single member of the whole congregation fell of himself into this preaching sickness, the cause of which is still unexplained, and involved in a wonderful darkness. A few wandering peasant girls only, of doubtful character, were attacked by it, and, singularly enough,

---

* See Howitt's Journal, vol. i. p. 38, for an account, drawn from authentic sources, of this extraordinary psychological manifestation. (Translator.)

found out just one village on the boundary of this parish, where
drunkenness and looseness of morals had been ever the most
difficult to uproot; and here they settled themselves down
among an ill-informed people, and began their convulsive falls
and preachings, which were witnessed only with a certain degree of curiosity, and found no imitators. The rector at first
let the affair take its own course; did not deny his own house-
servants to go occasionally to hear "preaching-girls.;" but
one evening he presented himself suddenly and unexpectedly
among a little observant audience, who were listening to one
of these preaching peasant maidens. The girl came quite to a
stand when she perceived him enter, but he urged her to proceed, which she eventually did, but with great embarrassment,
having nothing at all to say but what she had uttered many
times before, namely, broken, short, and mutilated exclama-
tions out of the sacred writings, as, "Repent ye," "make yourselves ready, "turn ye." She called on them to repent, and
declared that if her hearers did not do this they would be
punished with the most terrible punishments that could be
conceived; spoke always of thousands of small and great
devils, which she, with an actually astonishing invention, knew
how to place and introduce where they certainly had never
been before.

Thus had she, on another occasion, before the rector heard
her, amongst other things, spoken of the village maypole,
which, since the primeval times, had its place in the most
open part of the village, was furnished with a weathercock,
and was in this manner of positive use as a weather-prophet
the whole year round, till the Midsummer was again at hand,
when the maypole was adorned by the youth of the village and
neighborhood with leaves and flowers and blown eggs, and for
the time afforded a great and truly innocent pleasure for the
old, and still more for the young. But this poor innocent maypole the preacheress denounced to the lowest root, and into the
deepest pit of perdition, declaring that the weathercock only
pointed to devils, and that the pre-mentioned empty eggs were
altogether choke full of small devils, and that the like sat in the
dry leaves and the blown and broken-off flower-garlands, and
rained down, like a thunder-rain, upon all those who went
under the pole.

She had, moreover, before the pastor heard her, apostro-
phized with great disgust, an old disbanded hussar, who was

at a loss how to do himself a service except by here and there playing a lively tune to the dance of the young people in the country, upon an old and cracked fiddle, and thereby winning a trifle for the support of himself and children. Him, all imaginable musical places of amusement, and the poor innocent fiddle, she had doomed indiscriminately as the devil's invention and delight, and declared that the arch-fiend would take both player and dancer; that within the fiddle was to be found a whole play-place of mere imps, who there amused themselves, and crept in and out through the sound-hole, scarcely visible to the preacher herself, totally invisible to all her sinful hearers, who all were slaves of sin, and both lived and died, went, stood, lay, and danced, in utter sin, over head and ears. In like manner did she condemn, in a high degree, all crooked combs, and declared that the devil would therewith comb all those who wore such, when they came into hell.

The consequence of this attack on the maypole, the fiddler, and the crooked combs, had been, that the villagers had sold the maypole to another village for three quarts of brandy; and that the old hussar broke his fiddle—but immediately resolved, in all secresy, to glue it together again; while all the village girls went for a little while with their hair carelessly hanging about their ears, having burned their crooked combs; but that a carpenter soon after prepared dozens of new ones, of the like pattern, made of stained wood, as those were which were burned.

The first act of this drama was already played out some time before the rector became the hearer of this peasant girl. She now perspired dreadfully, was obviously oppressed by her spiritual hearer, and repeated the same thing many times; and when the ideas were altogether exhausted, she took a long psalm, and made her audience sing it from beginning to end, when she began once more to repeat the very same words she had used previously to the psalm. When she had done, she withdrew; and now the rector stepped forward, and asked the assembly if they had heard any thing essentially new from the preaching-girl?—if he had not told them the very same things before, though in a different order of arrangement?—whether they were dissatisfied with his ministry?—whether he neglected his duty, or ill fulfilled his mission, etc.; and at every query all answered in a breath, "No! Heaven forbid! far from it! God only grant that we may be able to live as we are taught by our highly-respected pastor," and the like ; and on that an old peasant stood forward and declared, on behalf of himself and fellows, "that the congregation had such ample instruction from their excellent minister, that they had no need to listen to any revival sermons, whether from girls or ranters, but believed they would always be pious enough were they only able to practice all that their venerable rector taught them, both in church on Sundays and on many other occasions, while he, both in life and every thing else, served to every one as a perfect pattern and reproof."

All, in one breath, acquiesced in this ; and, in their enthusiasm for their pastor, the assembled ploughmen insisted that he and no one else should preach to them a little while. But the rector declined this very graciously, saying, that there, in that narrow room, he had not space to preach, but bade them right welcome to his church the following Sunday to hear him, at the same time remarking, that family devotion is best exercised where each, with collected thoughts, takes the Sacred Writing, and reads some passages therein, the younger asking of the older explanation of any thing that appears doubtful ; and that each household within itself ought to exhort each other to the fear of God, and a Christian walk in general, but should leave to their neighbors to do the same within themselves. "For," said the pastor, "if any one fulfills his *own mission*, within his *own* circle of operation, he has no need to do any thing more than to endeavor to satisfy himself that his neighbor does the like as well as he, though it may be of a different fashion, and so neither condemn him, nor desire to set up for his teacher, till he is thoroughly certain that he himself stands before God higher than him whom he would dictate to and set right."

"Ay, there is our minister quite right! God bless the worthy rector, now and forever ! Good-night, good-night !" resounded from all sides, and every one went home in peace with himself. And from that time it became a point of honor never out of curiosity to run after and listen to ragamuffins ; but every one to look after his *own* affairs, totally indifferent to *preaching-girls ;* and these soon saw themselves compelled to seek their congeners in other quarters, or where they had not to contend against the real superiority which lies not in word or phrase, but in sound faith, hope, and love, and the power of imparting to these the most attractive and inviting forms.

Such was the clergyman who now in the parish church raised his voice in the pulpit before his attentive audience—such the man whom we have endeavored only by a few strokes to portray, and whom people never accused of any thing, except that, spite of persuasions, he would never become provost (rural dean), but persisted in continuing, being, and being called, the pastor of his church and of his sheep. His words were neither new, nor at any time very many, or grandly put together, but simple and direct from the heart, and going to the heart; and to-day he concluded his address to those who were about to communicate with the cheering tidings, that a youth in his congregation, who had for many years been excluded from the Lord's Table, not exactly for erroneous conduct, but for entire lack of Christian knowledge, now at length, through his own desire, and the assistance of a good person, had passed his examination admirably. That this had been many times repeated; and therefore to-day he would enjoy the great satisfaction of accompanying the rest of the congregation to the Lord's Supper, and there enjoy the means of grace which he had now first made himself worthy of.

A low murmur arose in the assembly, for every one who did not know whom the youth referred to could be, asked his neighbor; and soon all eyes were fixed on Abraham, who trembled both with joy and confusion; and then these looks were turned on Elin, for every one had been informed by Abraham that she had been his only instructor; and she now, inwardly rejoicing, with blushes and with cast-down and tearful eyes, awaited the result of her exertions on his behalf. All thought how sweet and sensible she looked; and Gunnar—he thought she looked like one of the angels of God which hovered in the old church's painted ceiling, and which from his childhood had been to him the type of every thing that was beautiful and holy; and in this moment he made a solemn vow to God *never* to drag down this angel of heaven to earthly sin and misery.

"Thanks for *this*, dear Elin!" said Abraham softly to Elin, as they went out of the church; and in this simple word, streaming out of a joyful heart, lay the whole of Elin's reward for all the unwearied labor and care she had had with the poor youth.

On the way homeward, our four, at the commencement, said nothing; but, finally, Lena threw open her conversation-box, for as the people came early to church, and had also lingered a little after the sermon, she had not neglected to lay in a whole freight of news from the congregation, and this must now be unloaded, that is to say, related, talked over, and expatiated upon.

"Bless me, in all my days! have you heard," she began, "what has happened at Grantorp? There has been a terrible robbery in the course of the night, and therefore they have sent for the constable, and are holding such examinations and making such a stir about it! But it is utterly unpardonable of thee, Abra'm, who wast there when it occurred, and obeyed the squire's summons, and yet never said a word, or talked of it to us. I stood so stupid and foolish—we who are tenants on the estate, and not to know a syllable about it; and those who talked about it before me would not believe me when I said that we had not heard any thing of the matter. It was that Kajsa, from Masbo, who related it before me; and, good-for-nothing as she always is, I saw clearly that she did not believe me, but took it to be only a cunning trick, and that I would not let her know how much I knew about it. And then I saw her go and speak with the Still-man Olle, and point at me, and say something of some kind."

Elin sighed deeply; for it seemed to her that all this was so sad and sorrowful.

"What have they stolen?" asked Gunnar.

"Oh, they have stolen a quantity of corn out of the barn; and they have broken into the brandy distillery, too, and stolen brandy; but this was so cleverly done, that it was merely by chance that the squire discovered the fact, and now he makes such a terrible stir about it!"

"It is remarkable that no one spoke of it to me," said Gunnar; but quickly began to think of other things, while Lena related at full all that she had heard, and a little more, about this theft, and many other things. Elin and Abraham went on a little in advance, and the latter found occasion to say—

"I heard by chance on Saturday night about this robbery, but I did not trouble myself about it, and forgot it. But dost thou know, Elin dear, that I trembled in every limb, so that I thought I should fall on the floor, and get the preaching sickness when I had to go to the Lord's table; but I became like a new man when the curate just gave me heart; and then the rector came with wine, and I felt really that it was the body and blood of Jesus Christ that I received at that moment, and that after this I should become a totally different creature."

"Ay, God grant it!" sighed Elin, who, on this Sunday, was in a disposition of so much meekness, but still of melancholy. But this melancholy soon changed into the gayety of youth; for as Lena looked less than ordinarily cross, and as Elin had now pleasure enough in simply looking at Gunnar, and as Abraham was so glad, the weather so beautiful, little Gustaf so merry, and the relaxation from labor so exhilarating, after a whole week's uninterrupted drudgery, she gave herself up to her natural cheerfulness, and the sun of gladness spread its ruddy beams yet once more copiously over her. But, alas! it was the sun in its setting—it was blood-red!

CHAPTER XXXIV.

Late in the evening of this Sunday came Bengt, but his countenance was far more gloomy than usual; and, staying only a few minutes, he requested Gunnar to accompany him a little on the way homewards, and answered dubiously when Lena eagerly, and Gunnar, with some indifference, asked him particulars of the robbery. When Gunnar came back, he too was unusually gloomy, said next to nothing, and pushed little Gustaf somewhat rudely from him when he sprang toward him and clasped him by the knee. But this immediately caused him regret; he lifted up the boy, kissed him, but set him down again, and sate—sunk in deep thought.

Lena had almost uninterruptedly continued busily engaged in the kitchen during the Sunday afternoon, with her eternal boiling—as she now said—preparing traveling provision for Gunnar, as he must early in the morning set out on his own business for Anderson's tillage, and remain away some days. This struck Elin a little strangely, but she did not think much about Lena's checking her whenever she attempted to go into the kitchen, and always held the front door, as well as the door into the sitting-room, whenever she passed in or out. This struck Mother Ingrid quite as strangely, for she was kept back in the same manner; but *she*, on the contrary, thought *much* of the affair—for it did not seem to her that it was ale-wort that she smelled from the kitchen, but something very different ; and yet Lena persisted that she was brewing ale, but that the first quantity was spoiled ; for the malt was bad, and the yeast equally so, but that now it would be famous.　This she had also said to Gunnar, who liked beer, but who was easily put off, never pried into the kitchen, seldom was in the house, never troubled himself with matters of cookery, but took blindly on trust whatever was told him about them.

Gunnar actually took his departure on the Monday morning ; Elin toiled again in her loom ; Abraham went forth to his day's work ; Mother Ingrid span, and sighed ; and Lena was still busy with her boiling, and that most hurriedly ; but toward evening she dressed herself, almost as for church, stopped the boiling, took the key with her, and hastened away, no one knew whither.　And we, too, must now leave the peasant's hut at Vika, to enter for awhile within walls, and under vaulted roofs, in the old gray-stone house at Grantorp.

CHAPTER XXXV.

In this old country seat, Grantorp, sate the squire at home, such as we have already known him, neither one of the good, nor of the thoroughly wicked, but still growing more distrust-ful, cunning, and malignant every hour.　He was finding out the robbery ; and some words of Olle had caused his thoughts to fall upon Gunnar, whose hate of him he suspected, whose present gloomy temper he feared, and whose readiness of hand and dexterity he knew.　There was a piece so cleverly sawn out of the door of the brandy warehouse, and again inserted, that only a skillful hand could have done it ; and then there was a little taken out of each brandy-tun, and that so managed with the pump, that it was clear that it was some one who was well acquainted with the concern who had done it ; for the pump was somewhat out of order, and required a hand that had often used it.　Again, of the grain which had been taken from the place, there was seen some spilled as through a hole in a sack ; and thus they could track the thief a part of the

way, and this was exactly on the road to Vika. Olle had not
omitted, and that by a few clever words in the right nick
of time, to make the squire observant of this; and the squire
really began to suspect Gunnar—the more so as he believed
that Gunnar possibly would hold himself secure of not being
suspected; that no one would accuse him, or make search
with him and Lena; and little to the credit of the squire, it
must be confessed that these proceedings might bear very much
against him if they should involve Gunnar; and he determined
to go politicly to work, and, in the first place, to hold a sort
of accidental police examination of Abraham, when he met with
him at work on the Monday at noon.

This took place much as follows:—

The Squire. Well, what does thy master now-a-days?

Abraham. What?

Sq. I ask what thy master, Gunnar, at Vika, does with himself now?

Abr. I don't know.

Sq. Knowest thou not what he does? That is impossible.

Abr. He is generally away there at Anderson's work, or in
the wood with his axe.

Sq. Does he go into the woods of the estate?

Abr. Yes, to be sure.

Sq. Ay! but that is forbidden; I will let him know that;
and that thou canst greet him with from me.

Abr. No; I mistook. He never goes there.

Sq. Hem! No, that thou wilt not persuade me. Is he not
often away of nights?

Abr. Yes, sure, sometimes.

Sq. Well; have you any good new thrashed grain down
there at Vika?

Abr. Oh, to be sure! Lena both thrashes and winnows,
and seems to have whole sacks full when I go to help her.

Sq. Does she do this herself?

Abr. Yes, sure; she can do work for four; for such old
womanish scrubs are good for nothing else, and Elin can not
help in such things.

Sq. Well, have you good brandy to make you merry?

Abr. Ay, sure; I often get a sup of Lena when she wants
me to work beyond my power, and wants so much water for
her cooking, and so much wood-chopping for her fire, and that
often happens.

Sq. What does she boil so much ?

Abr. Why, that I can't tell very well. Lena will, perhaps, say it is beer ; but I have my own opinion about that.

Sq. Well, now, what is thy opinion ?

Abr. Oh ! nothing.

Sq. Well, does thy mistress make malt ?

Abr. Oh, to be sure !

This Abraham said laughing ; and now the squire went his way, and believed what he believed ; and Abraham said, much pleased, to himself, " Ay, pish ! dost thou think thou hast found it out ?" and fancied that he had preserved most excellently his own private knowledge of the matter. " No, pish, indeed ! neither the squire, any more than Olle, shall get to know it," thought he further ; for Olle had on the very same day questioned him nearly in the same way, but with a totally different object.

The squire went now and pondered on what was best to do ; but Olle knew already what *he* had done ; for when he had, on the Saturday evening, sent the constable home from Grantorp, he had said before him that he was almost sure that the culprit was Gunnar, at Vika brandy distillery ; and the constable, brought up as a child with Gunnar, a little older, and much stupider, had had a pique against him almost ever since they went to school together ; for the constable always prided himself that he belonged to the gentry, because his father was an old rogue of a bailiff, who stole so long and so much from his employer, that he eventually became possessed of the whole of his estate. In later days, though Gunnar and the constable had not had four stivers' value of transactions with each other, they had always looked askance on each other ; and once, a few years ago, the constable, riding toward Gunnar, knocked off his hat with his riding-whip, as he went by. Gunnar was going briskly, but in perfect quietness, along the road, though he certainly did not take off his hat when he saw the constable coming. The constable having struck off the hat, tried to get away, but could not effect this before Gunnar, always very alert, quick, and sudden in his movements, had seized on the bridle with one hand, and on the riding-whip with the other, with which he gave the constable several good cuts, and then let him go at his leisure. But this little occurrence each of the actors had kept pretty much to himself, although they had had no other witness than the dumb horse. The affair had by no means cooled their feelings toward each other ; and if Gunnar had laughed in his sleeve at the " man of the gentry," he, on his part, had secretly vowed vengeance on Gunnar whenever opportunity should serve. And now was his opportunity at hand, and Sir Constable smacked his lips over it, and resolved to avail himself of Olle's hint as soon as the way opened, which, alas! was immediately, in connection with other most important events.

When the squire had questioned Abraham on Monday about his employer, and was led by his simple answers to far other than the truth, Ma'msell Sara sate alone in the great house, somewhat annoyed about a parlor-maid whom she hired in autumn in the place of little Lotta, who was about to marry, but whose leaving was prevented through some intervening hindrance. Such little troubles are common enough in the country, where there are no register and commission offices, and no great superfluity of servants; though such as are to be got are far better, and more trustworthy, than city ones. Now Ma'msell Sara was much more troubled than very many others, for she was so seldom accustomed to change her maid-servants; understood so little how to visit in the neighboring houses of the gentry, and entice away their servants; and had never any so-called old char-women, but when she was in need she called in the help of an ancient, decent, and honorable dame, the sexton's widow, and formerly in service at Grantorp. This last she just sent forth into the country, but without hope of finding any very likely candidate for the place so late in the season; for in the earliest summer, yes, in some districts, at Easter itself, both masters and servants began to look out, and engage for the following year.

Ma'msell Sara now sat and cut out shirts for the boys, and wondered, with an every-day sigh, from *whom* or *how* she should get any help to sew them, when the door softly opened a little, and Lena put in her head, inquiring, "whether she might be so bold as to walk in."

"Certainly," said Ma'msell Sara, but heaved another every-day sigh, for she had never thought of Lena, and was moreover only too certain, from old experience, that when she came it was to ask for something; and however kind and helpful a lady may be, she is always much better pleased when her help, counsel, and good offices are not needed. Ma'msell Sara had also heard some words of the suspicions of the squire and of others against Gunnar whispered about, but was extremely indignant at them, and declared that she would venture to pledge her life and property to the honor of Gunnar. But now she thought Lena too was come to complain of this rumor, or something connected with it, and it fell on Ma'msell Sara with at least a feeling of annoyance.   But Lena looked so calm and glad, and—so far as the robbery was concerned— so perfectly innocent, as, indeed, she felt herself, that Ma'msell Sara, as soon as she saw her, and heard her speak of it, could swear that she was so—for Lena, altogether ignorant of any suspicions against Gunnar and herself, talked of the theft so freely and naturally; lamented in bombastic phrase the "gracious gentry's injury;" but added, flatteringly, that it is well when misfortune happens to the *rich*, and not to the *poor ;* and hoped that the thief would speedily be discovered, whom the shrewd Lena, like every body else, set down to be well acquainted with the place, and therefore not far from it.

All this she could not have spoken off-hand, thought Ma'msell Sara, had they been in the smallest degree concerned, and heaved a relieving sigh, much more from the heart than those which we call every-day sighs.   But ma'msell experienced, on the contrary, a real satisfaction when Lena at length, after some little prelude, brought forth her actual errand, which was nothing more and nothing less than to offer her sister Elin as chambermaid, having heard at church that this situation was vacant.

"I will tell you candidly how it happens," said Lena, who, when she really was in a good humor, and called her cunning and dissimulation to her aid, did not appear so repulsive, and had a great power of well disposing her words, "Well, the matter is, that Elin, my sister, is delicate and somewhat effeminately brought up, and is fitted for a rich and nice situation in a gentleman's house; but among poor peasantry, as we are, if she were obliged to do hard and rough work, out-of-door labor and the like, she would soon fall into consumption—weak, and slim, and small as a withe, as she is; for she is at least willing and zealous, and when she carries a tub of water with me, I perceive how she totters, though she will not let go; and for out-of-door labor she has neither hand nor strength; and as I am now in place of a mother to her," added Lena, and wiped a little the eyes dry as powder, "I would so willingly recommend her to where she was fitting and would do well; and I know that I can with a good conscience place her *here*, for weak as she is for heavy work, she is just, clever, diligent, and excellent in fine work and sedentary occupation.   And now

K

she weaves a web that I would not work for any thing; for it goes ill and heavy as shame itself, and dark it is too; and yet she labors at it so bravely, and works it as thick together as a skin, and as level and smooth as one, without a single knot either above or below, although constantly a whole score of threads break at once. And sewing of all kinds she does like a dress-maker. This dress of mine she has made for me, and these gloves too; and in this neckerchief she has marked a single flower in the corner, and here on my bonnet she has made a darn so fine that the eye can scarcely perceive it, for I chanced to tear out a check on a bush last summer."

Ma'msell Sara smiled at this catalogue of accomplishments, but was on the whole thoroughly pleased, for she had always liked Elin much more than her sister, and agreed entirely with Lena, although a little selfishness was at work in the affair. Ma'msell Sara declared that she would most gladly take Elin, and bade Lena send her on to the hall, the sooner the better, so that she could give a countermand to Madame Smedman before she had engaged another, for before any one did Ma'msell Sara desire to have Elin. She bade Lena sit down, entertained her with coffee and rusks, gave her a whole bundle of apples and pears to take home, and biscuits for little Gustaf; inquired after this her little godson, and told Lena to bring him out with her before it was too late in the autumn.

No one could be more delighted than Lena. She returned home quite elated, for she had now killed a whole score of flies at one blow, as she thought. She had got rid of Elin in an honorable way, who was in reality a " nail in her eye;" she had procured her a really good place—and there she knew that Gunnar never went, whatever the reason might be. And as for the squire, Lena feared nothing for Elin, for no one knew better than Lena how matters had really stood in former days, and she thought, moreover, that it was every body's business to take care of themselves. Gunnar, she further thought, could not for shame's sake do other than sanction this arrangement, nor Mother Ingrid either. To Ma'msell Sara she had done a service—that she had distinctly avowed—which might be useful to her in many ways, and she had a capital servant in readiness for herself: for Lena had effected a variety of concerns on the preceding Sunday at church, and all this had she further got done in Gunnar's absence, for we have already said that he was gone for a few days on business of his own.

When she reached home she was in the very best humor in the world; and then Elin, equally glad, met her with the finished weaving, folded properly together, and with many hanks of thread which remained over, so that she quite overwhelmed her with praise and caresses.

Elin, in the utmost delight at this unusual tone of mind in Lena, and at her resemblance at this moment to her dear departed mother, threw herself into her arms, wept, and bade her always be thus, and then she would willingly die for her.

Lena thought rightly that now was the opportunity to repre-sent to Elin what a wise step she had taken for Elin's own profit and advantage; and when they had seated themselves in the house, Lena a little weary with her rapid walking, and Elin with her zeal in finishing her web, Lena began, and related the result of her visit to Mam'sell Sara, the causes of which, however, she twisted a little, for she now made it seem as though she had received the offer, and not that she had herself offered Elin.

Mother Ingrid stopped her spinning to hear the matter, greatly interested in it, as we can well conceive.

" Yes, Elin dear," said Lena, in her most winning tone, " that have I truly done for *thy* sake, and not for *mine*." (Mother Ingrid thought her own thoughts, but thought, too, that what Lena had this time done she had done well.) " And thou wilt thank me for having procured thee so splendid a service," continued Lena; " for a better mistress than Ma'msell Sara was never found in the world; and with the squire, as parlor-maid, hast thou plainly nothing to do, for the house-maid attends on him"—(this Lena said peculiarly for Mother Ingrid's satisfaction)—" and now I shall come terribly to miss thee, who art so clever and willing; but thou hast never been accustomed to this drudgery, nor ought I to wear myself out with it; but I shall take a coarser, stronger girl, and do the sedentary work myself. Thou hast, it seems to me, so thoroughly helped me, that I have nothing either to weave or to sew, before I spin afresh.   And fine wages wilt thou get—far more than we are able to give thee; and immensely more vails, for the parlor-maid has the best guest-rooms in her department, and I know when Lotta got as much as two and three rix-dollars at a time; and Christ-mas-boxes thou wilt get, too, and coffee every morning, and many a time after dinner; and there need be no tearing of thy clothes, which thou art so much afraid of, for thou hast no concern with any heavier work than the fine wash, and for that thou gett'st off with only a single pail of water; and the scouring is mere child's play, for all thy rooms have painted floors, and so thou wilt be sure to be happy, and wilt thank me many and many a time."

Elin was silent. One tear chased another, but she was unable to utter a word. Her doom was now pronounced. She should, she *must* separate from Gunnar, and Vika, her new El Dorado. Lena's anger she could well have withstood, but not her kindness. Before this she must yield, and when Mother Ingrid also added her approval, and kindly and affectionately counseled her to accept this good offer, she answered, with sighing and with tearful eyes,—

"Yes, my kind, dear Lena, God knows that I am thankful for thy kindness and motherly thought for me, poor child, and I see plainly enough that I could not do for you all the service that I so fervently desired; and I shall entirely follow thy advice, and remove to Grantorp, since thou hast wished to place me there; but thou wilt pardon me" (and here the tears ran copiously down her cheeks), "that it is a severe trial for me to separate from you all. Remember, that I never have been any where but with my mother, and brother and sister, and have always shrunk from the idea of a service in a great house, among gentlefolks and many companions. But I see plainly that this must be my fate, and that I am afraid of that for which others would thank God. But thou shalt see," added Elin, and wiped her eyes, "that thou wilt not have thy recommendation disgraced; for I shall do all in my power to do honor to it, and comply with the commands of my superiors, and the wishes of my companions."

"Nay, by the powers!" said Lena, laughing, and glad to find her victory so easy, "before them shalt thou not stoop, but 'have the skin upon thy nose' from the very beginning; and set thyself upon thy high horse, and so teach them respect for thee, for otherwise wilt thou never stand right with them."

"Ah, yes, but," said Mother Ingrid, "with kindness, civility, and equableness of temper, people get on better, both with comrades, masters, and all other persons in this world. That ought thou thyself to have experienced, dear Lena, for when thou art so kind and sympathizing as now, both I and many others are ready to go through the fire for thee: but—"

"Ah, yes, mother," interrupted Lena, "now is the question

not about me, but about Elin; and I am certain that both in one respect and another she will conduct herself well at Grantorp, and do that which is most genteel."

"I certainly shall try," said Elin, with a sinking heart, and drew not an "every-day sigh;" for this hour, she thought, had settled all her little fate.

With the same oppressed heart she went to rest at night. When she entered her little chamber, which, a short time before, in her great joy at having finished the web and got it out of the loom, she had swept and adorned with foliage and boughs in the best manner, she looked most melancholy and full of trouble, thinking, Ah! here I shall not be many days longer, but out in the deceitful world, alone and abandoned. She wept now over all that she must leave—relatives, friends, freedom, her own little sanctuary and asylum in this chamber; and, more than all this—far, far more wept she at the mere thought of Gunnar. She should never again see him—he would soon utterly forget her. Elin thought she had heard that men were apt to forget; and what could he say—what could he think? She once half promised him never to take service at Grantorp; but that was in the glad, happy, altogether merriest days, when she did not intend to take service any where, but to live and die by the side of her brother and sister. But now the times were so changed that to think of such a bygone promise would have been the highest ingratitude to Lena for her kindness and motherly care. "No, no," thought Elin, while the tears streamed over her cheeks; "it is quite the best that I am compelled to go and take the earnest-money in the morning, before Gunnar comes home. Perhaps he might oppose it; and this would look ill, and cause unpleasantness. No, I will indeed go, and he shall not get to know of it before it is done;" and again the tears flowed freely.

The next morning she was pale and downcast, but did not weep, but set out in the forenoon, with a heavy, care-worn step, toward the squire's estate; and Lena, who had lain the whole night felicitating herself on her management, and on much besides which lay in joyful perspective, bustled about more than ever in her kitchen; and Mother Ingrid spun and sighed, and shook her head sorrowfully, as one fume after another of freshly rectified brandy reached her experienced nose.

Abraham, altogether ignorant of the object of Elin's going away, went and lay on a bank by the way-side, and offered to accompany her a part of the way; but Elin thanked him very kindly, and requested him to allow her to go alone, at the same time wishing him to hasten what he was doing at the fence there, for Lena was wanting him; and Elin continued her way, oppressed with sorrow, and Abraham his labor, a little vexed in his mind. But about eleven o'clock in the forenoon, Mother Ingrid was awakened out of her deep thoughts, and Lena out of her spirituous occupation, by a singularly angry clamor and barking of Gunnar's hunting-dogs, which stood bound in the stable, by the sound of horses' hoofs, and the rattling noise of a hasty carriage.

Abraham hurried into the room, shrieking shrilly, " Mistress, mistress! quick! for Jesus' sake, quick with you! hide it! thrust it away! the constable is coming!"

And the sheriff's officer was at his very heels, and stood at the same moment in the doorway, and heard every word that he screamed out. Lena had, however, presence of mind to put out the fire, bolt the door into the kitchen, and calmly walk into the sitting room to meet the constable.

"Where is Gunnar Hakansson?" demanded he, peremp- torily, and without taking off his hat; while his accompanying witnesses, two old men in blue-collared coats, who had ridden along with him, stepped in, with their riding whips in their hands.

"He is away," said Lena, with the utmost self-possession.

"Well, what have you got up here at home, good folks?" asked the constable, in the same loud, authoritative tone.

"Oh, a variety of things," replied Lena; and wiped a seat with her apron for the constable to sit upon.

"Nay, I have something else to do here than to sit," said the constable; went across the room, looked about, and tried the kitchen door. "We must go into the kitchen there, and see first what there is afloat."

"Oh, heavens! the worthy sheriff's officers can not go there," said Lena, officiously, "it is so miserable there! I am just busied with boiling some clothes, and told Abraham, the stupid servant there, that I distilled brandy, that he might help me to carry water cheerfully."

"Ay, ay!" said the sheriff's officer, going toward the door, though Lena in a civil way withstood him. Ah! what would she not have given at this critical moment to have been " the man called Bosco," and who could at once conjure away any thing out of a kitchen, and any thing else into its place? But this could not be; she hoped, however, to be able to talk the thing away, and began to attempt it; but the constable "let no one play with him," he said, and so he never did—that is, when a person had not that plaything—gold—for the play. He went quickly toward the door, spite of Lena's opposition and Mother Ingrid's still anxious sighs, and Abraham's assurance that there was no brandy distillery there, or any thing else. And now the constable stood in the kitchen with his witnesses, thundered and swore, and plucked the little pan from the fire and asked what that was.

"I did not know of that," said Lena; "I have never seen that before. That Abraham has set there, I can well believe."

Lena thought—*Prima regula juris est: negas.*

"Ah, nonsense!" said the constable. "What will you make us believe next? Ay, this will be be very pleasant for Gunnar, your husband! I shall give him a clawing, I think, that will make him remember me. Go for him immediately, or—"

"I can swear by the holiest that he is away, and that he has not been in the kitchen to-day as I remember," said Lena, who believed that the business would probably fall through, if it could be proved that Gunnar had not been concerned with it.

"Oh, stuff and nonsense!" continued the constable, "he is at home, and knows all about it, just as well as you."

"Nay," said Mother Ingrid, who stood at the kitchen door with the poor mother's heart in her very throat, "nay, Mr. Constable, by the good God! my daughter-in-law speaks the truth: Gunnar is absent, and has not known the least about—"

"Silence, Satan's hag!" said the constable, and began to seize the pan, the still-head, and several small ankers of brandy, which he caused to be carried out to the chaise, and then used very little ceremony, but after some fierce threats against Gunnar, and curses of him, and a little taunting laughter besides, away went Mr. Constable in his rumbling vehicle, and the witnesses went bumping away on their bob-tailed horses, and the dogs yelled more than at their coming. And Lena now first burst forth into a loud, desperate weeping and gnashing of teeth. She tore her hair, flew to and fro, and cried out about every thing, " Merciful God!" (for he who is over all, is also in all, whether good or bad.) "Great, merciful, God! The devil

take the like! My brandy! my brandy! my brandy! and all
my grain, and the potatoes and all! and Erick Olsa's pans,
which must all be paid for. We are regularly ruined, and
what will Gunnar say?"

"Yes, that is the very worst of all," sighed Mother Ingrid.

"Ah, but that, at least, costs no money!" added Lena.

"Yes, yes, but that which it will cost him is far worse than
the money!" bewailed Mother Ingrid; "and in thy great
trouble, dear Lena, it is, perhaps, a sin to upbraid thee with
any thing, but ah! why didst thou do this unknown to him?"

"Because he would *never* have allowed it," said Lena,
weeping.

"Yes, and that proves that it was wrongly and foolishly
done," added the old woman.

"It was nothing of the sort!" screamed Lena. "When the
wagoners are here in the winter, passing to and from the
wood, then I should have had brandy for them, and sold it, and
we should have won inconceivably by it, and now that dog of
a constable here has clutched it.

"Oh, indeed! so you meant to keep a public-house? Well,
if thou hast persuaded Gunnar to enter on that, then I was
wrong."

"Poh!—one enters readily enough upon any thing that one
has any profit in," thought Lena, and wept and bewailed herself at the same time. Abraham had totally vanished, did not
come home to dinner; but, on the other hand, Elin came about
one o'clock, softly and silently, and with the heavy earnest-
money wrapped in her handkerchief, in which she had also a
little delicacy for Gustaf, and had no presentiment of the fresh
cause of sorrow and trouble which she was soon to experience.
But scarcely had she got within the door, before Lena, shrilly
screaming, related all to her, but that so hurriedly and con-
fusedly, that she at first comprehended but little of it, and
asked several simple questions, as—"Bless me! canst thou not,
dearest Lena, distill brandy? that is what many people do.
Hast thou not distilled brandy there in the kitchen? Can not
every one do what he will with his own grain and his own
potatoes? Canst thou not get thy pan and thy brandy again
from the constable?—the pan, at least, if thou sayest that it
belongs to another!"

"Ah, thou stupid sheepskull!" said Lena, in her vexation,

"thou understandest nothing that is of any use!" And she wept again, and went on as before ; but at times put to rights both kitchen and sitting-room, which testified her natural and inbred love of order, which in the midst of her very deepest troubles never wavered or forsook her.

From Mother Ingrid, Elin procured somewhat more intelligible information of the affair, and now mingled her present with her past tears, distilled from Lena's unlucky brandy.

" Ah! dear Lena! why hast thou done that unknown to Gunnar?" said Elin, more in sorrow than in real reproof.

" Ah! be still only, thou sea-pike there, that can sit and ask about things that can't be helped, but could not lend a hand where it was needful, or the distilling might all have been ended, and all this spectacle avoided," screamed Lena, beside herself; for the more she thought of the affair the more enraged she became. She began with being frightened and anxious, then sorrowful and troubled, but now she was wrathful as a fury; and when once little Gustaf came in her way, and cried when she kicked him from her, she seized him by the hair, and was about to give him a severe beating, from which, however, the united prayers and protestations of Elin and Mother Ingrid rescued him. Elin took the child into her chamber with her, and set herself sorrowfully to clear the web of knots and hanging threads, and Mother Ingrid went out to see if the poor, unprepared Gunnar was coming, but he did not appear.

The day, in the mean time, approached its close. No one had eaten any thing at dinner, and toward evening the household began to appear from their different retreats, and assembled in the sitting-room ; but Abraham peeped carefully first through the window, to see whether Mother Ingrid and Elin were there, which he felt instinctively was very desirable.

Lena, in the midst of her trouble, yet made groat porridge, and every one took theirs. No one said a word, as Lena was silent, but finally Abraham was pleased, altogether contrary to his custom, but calmed and emboldened by the stillness of Lena during the meal, to open his mouth and say—

" Yes, it was too bad that there should happen such a loss to mistress. And I know *best* that it was not I who talked about it, for, see! when some one asked me what mistress did with such unaccountable quantities of wood and water, I *always*

K*

answered—'Oh, tist! get thou to know it!" for I suspected well enough what it was—I did."

Lena had sat speechless during this discourse of Abraham's, but when he had done, she exclaimed—

"Who asked that?"

"Both the Still-man Olle and others did."

Lena had not heard the word out before she started up like a whirlwind, threw from her porridge-spoon and basin, flew at Abraham where he sat in his corner on his usual seat, and, without saying a word, seized with both her hands on his bushy, oakum wig, and dragged him a long while to and fro, first in silence, and then incessantly repeating—"There, we have it! This is the babbler, then! But I'll teach thee to babble! I'll teach thee to prate out of time, I will! That hast thou for thy tittle-tattle. I will pay thee for——Ah, tut! I will," and so on.

It was strange enough that Abraham did not emit a single sound, but let his head obey every pull, just as if it stood loose on his shoulders, like that of one of the plaster rabbits; but, whether silence proceeded from Abraham having wept inwardly, or that he really had no feeling in his bushy, shaggy hair, or whether with a certain stoical cold-bloodedness he sustained Lena's frenzied dragging by the hair, that can we not positively determine; but this is certain, that, as soon as Elin had got away from little Gustaf, who sprang screaming to her, she hastened to the battle-field, and implored Lena, by all that was sacred, not to do so; but could scarcely abstain from laughter, when Abraham merely said—

"Ho! let her willingly tug, it signifies nothing!"

Lena was actually dumbfoundered by this answer, and went away to the fire. Abraham took advantage of the chance, stole quietly out, and up into the hay-loft, where he lay down and slept well after the day's many changes of weather, and the circular and rotatory swinging of his head.

Elin went softly to her room, but did not lie down. She continued sitting by the window, now looking out on the heavy and restless lake, now on the highway by which Gunnar should come, for the full moon illuminated it.

In the sitting-room all was still, though neither Mother Ingrid nor Lena lay down, for both waited with oppressed minds for the arrival of Gunnar, who had said that certainly he should come home, however late it might be. Toward eleven o'clock there was the sound of wheels driving swiftly, and shortly afterward was heard Gunnar's rapid step, by which the almost omniscient, or, at least, all-comprehending mother's heart already descried that he knew of nothing unpleasant, but, on the contrary, came home glad and satisfied with the result of his journey. This time, however, the mother's heart mistook somewhat; for Gunnar's journey had been successful, but a sense of mischief, and mortification from a wholly new cause, now, however, hastened his steps.

"Gracious Heavens! how sad it is to tell!" said Lena, when Gunnar entered the room; for she had now again fallen in her spirits, and was no longer furious, but timid and anxious. The moment Gunnar was in he began to ask for some food immediately, at the same time saying—

"Have you heard the current report that Olle spreads concerning me? That I am the perpetrator of the robbery, it is so well done, he says. But I will give him something that is well done, that I promise him; but it shall be on his carcass—the hangman!"

Gunnar was angry. It was not agreeable now to bring forward some new trouble, but—it must out. Mother Ingrid began to relate to Gunnar something disagreeable, and Lena assisted; and within a few minutes stood the foul naked truth before the young man. At the commencement he was silent, but at the end he exclaimed, in a high degree of subdued grief—

"A fig for losses, and injuries, and fines, and all that;—but shame! shame! Ah! Lena, why hast thou inflicted that on me? Never didst thou cause me any thing but disgrace and infamy!"

And now Lena only wept; for if Gunnar had been angry and scolded, she would have done just the same; but this terrible calm, and this terrible reproach, expressed in a deep, manly voice, and so rarely uttered as to have lost none of its effect, was annihilating for one who was even so little sensitive as Lena.

"Ah!" said she, sobbing, "I thought of doing a real good. I thought that we should gain such a profit, and that thou couldst have as much brandy as thou wouldst, without having to buy the dear trash; and it was so excellent and fine flavored, and I was so glad because I had procured Elin a good service, and made the bargain for another in her place, and——"

"What is the meaning of that? What place is it that thou art talking of?"

"Elin has been so prudent as to take earnest of Ma'msell Sara at the Hall," said Mother Ingrid, who was now desirous to help Lena a little, and knew that it was necessary.

"Has she?" said Gunnar, and left his food standing before him untouched, and stared at the moon, and clasped his hands silently and firmly, till the blood almost was forced from them, but—that was for the squire's reckoning.

"Soh! that he should really succeed in enticing her thither!" exclaimed he at length, after a long silence, which Lena almost took for indifference, but whose wildness Mother Ingrid better knew. "Soh!—and that through thee, Lena? Well, well! *He* knows well to whom to confide his proposals. Give me the brandy-bottle. That is the last drop, if I mistake not. Food I will not touch."

And he put the bottle to his mouth and drank. He said not a word, but went, not to his bed, but flung himself down on Abraham's bench; yet after a while he said, "Hu! here I am stifled altogether with the heat!" and went out of the room and up to the hay-loft—as Mother Ingrid and Lena believed—but they deceived themselves,

Elin, who sat silently in her window, and who heard part of what had passed in the next room, now heard Gunnar go hastily out, and saw him advance with long, heavy, but resolute strides down toward the lake, and that he did not return thence; so that at length fear and love, and a desire to console him whom she so boundlessly loved, seized on her to a degree which caused her no longer to resist its call.

Silent as a spirit she stole, therefore, out of her chamber, and took her course in the same direction as Gunnar. The moon shone quite reproachfully clear, and Elin saw already, a long way off, that Gunnar sat on the strand, on the same mossy stone where they had a few days before sat together. She stopped, and hesitated whether she should proceed, but a moon-beam fell full upon her, and Gunnar became aware of her, and in an instant was at her side.

"Elin! Elin!" said he, with a melancholy and painful tone, but more than usually reproachful; "Oh how couldst thou do that to me? Had I not sorrow, and shame, and misery enough before?"

"Ah, Gunnar! Gunnar!" sobbed out Elin, and let him conduct her to the mossy stone. "Thou wilt pardon me. I *could* not do otherwise. I had, indeed, no other counsel. Both thy mother and Lena bade me accept this good offered service. I had no power. I could not, and I *will* not ask thy advice in this matter. Done is done, but thou must pardon me, if we again are to have a single glad, or a tolerable hour."

"Oh, yes! I pardon thee willingly, thou angelic creature!" said Gunnar, and clasped her convulsively to his heart, and with a feeling of terrible suffering. "But hear thou! there are some that I *never* can forgive; one who has done me more evil than if he were the foul fiend himself! one who, to all eternity, will place himself between thee and me! And let *him* take heed that I do not meet him in the wood, with my good gun; that do I vow and swear!"

"Oh, do not talk so!" implored Elin, who would so willingly calm and soothe Gunnar, rather than by any means exasperate his mind.

"Yes, but thus must I talk!" he replied, vehemently. Thou knowest not *all* about that devil; and now will he entice thee into his snare—he, who already has done *me* all the evil which one man can do to another."

"Dost thou fancy that it is the squire who informed the constable of this miserable brandy distilling here?" asked Elin, who imagined that it was this, and such like, that he meant.

"Oh, yes!" answered Gunnar, "who both informed of it, and, perhaps, befooled Lena into it; and who describes me as a thief, and sets the brandmark of shame on my honorable name, and who will, moreover, snatch thee from me; but that shall not be, if thou wilt do like me, Elin," continued he, in the utmost excitement and agony of mind. "So, then, let us trouble ourselves about the world no more, but do like two other poor creatures, who loved each other above all measure, and never could come together in this world. They tied a cord round them, and a stone to it, and cast themselves headlong into the deep lake, and, at least, *died* together."

"Fie! my good, dear Gunnar!" entreated Elin; "talk not so unchristianly and wildly. I dread to sit near thee! Oh, no! calm thyself, and be once more reasonable. I do not know thee again, thou art so strange this evening."

"Ah, well! give me a kiss! one only, only kiss, for the first and the last time!" implored Gunnar, with flaming glances.

"Nay, my good friend," answered Elin, "not *now*, not *here*, in this nocturnal hour, but another time—some other day, per-haps."

"Another time!" exclaimed Gunnar, with a cold laugh of scorn. "Who knows if one has such a thing as 'another time!' That may be determined to-day. Give me a kiss now, girl, or—"

"No, Gunnar!" said Elin, firmly, "that I will *not*, now! Moreover, thou dost what thou never didst before; and I am almost ashamed to say it to thee, but thou smellest dreadfully of brandy."

"Oh yes, I do!" said Gunnar. "Well, give me only one single kiss, and I promise thee never again to taste brandy."

"No, my good Gunnar, not NOW, that is certain; but if thou wilt promise never again to taste this trash, and keep thy word a year or so, then—"

"Ah, Elin!" interrupted Gunnar, "don't talk thus about a *year*, and a *future time*, and such nonsense. I believe that I stand at my goal, on the world's uttermost margin, and the whole world spins round me, and I around the world; and when I think rightly of the matter, thou dost well to deny me a kiss, for I vowed to God in the church never to tempt thee— never to drag thee down into sin; and a perjurer will I not *yet* be, whatever may become of me. And now, good night to thee, Elin! Place thy hand upon my brow, which burns like fire and brimstone, and its pulses beat like sledge-hammers. Didst thou ever see an iron forge, Elin dear?"

Elin answered not. Silent, and weeping quite softly, she dipped a handkerchief into the lake, and wrapped it round Gunnar's head; and then took his hand and led him past the shed up to the hay-loft, and bade him go thither and lie down. Gunnar did all that she desired, and went with a firm, steady step, though his head was so scorched with internal pain.

None of our six at Vika slept this night, except Abraham and little Gustaf; and when morning came Gunnar went softly into the house, took his gun, loosed his dogs, and went to the wood.

This was for him what reading, music, the theatre, and the like, which we educated people have as a resource, are to us when grief and despair strike their talons into heart and soul, and we endeavor to obtain at least a palliative for the pain which we feel so dreadfully. But as these means often only aggravate the evil, often instill fresh poison into the wound, so Gunnar returned, both this evening and many others, only

more and more depressed in mind from the dark, deep, and
gloomy woods, where the autumn winds dragged the tops of
the pine-trees as mercilessly to and fro as Lena had dragged
the head of Abraham. Every feeling rather grew and raged
more vehemently, more agonizingly, in the heart of Gunnar,
than were calmed by time and the solitude of the woods. Love,
hate, thirst of vengeance, the wrongs of innocence from false
representations, shame from disgrace which one has not brought
upon one's self—and therefore almost a bitterer shame, because
this feeling irritates a pure mind more than a corrupted one—
the domestic life a failure, the wretchedness of the present, and
the hopelessness of the future, seized at once on the soul of
Gunnar, attacked it on all sides, and generated in him not
merely an indifference to life altogether, but an actual loathing
of it. He looked on it as having out-bloomed itself, that the
pulp of life's fruit was already enjoyed and exhausted, and he
would fain fling away the shell—but this remained, lived, and
quailed him every moment.

With knowledge and accomplishment he would assuredly
have been among those numerous elect, who, when they find
the life of life at an end, build themselves a new one in the
ample sphere of imagination, which allows the unquiet spirit to
float on fantastic tones, by themselves only *rightly* understood;
or who draw from the canvass pictures which they once dreamed were realities; or use the pen as the instrument of these
creations; who effectively fashion a rich originality out of all
that is *new*, all that is real, all that surrounds us, all that is evil,
all that is torturing and miserable; and by this faculty are enabled amply to compensate themselves for the loss of youth,
health, possessions, peace, and joy; to elicit only the sweet
memories and expel the bitter; to weave a thick and invulner-
able covering over all their disappointed hopes, that they may
no more beam forth into the night of hopelessness; and who,
in a word, live in air, in fire, in water, after the life upon earth
has become altogether too dull.

But Gunnar had not one of those powers which tranquilize
and refresh, while they dilute the individual feelings with others
new and strange; but the most violent agonies of mind, in their
genuine, undisguised forms, not poetized away, lamented away
in song, or ground away in colors, assailed him night and day;
and he did not *sing* woe and perdition over the being, the demon in human shape, whom he regarded as the sole cause of·

all his sufferings, but he *swore* woe and perdition to him; and if ever a single spark of joy yet flashed up in his darkened mind, it was when his sure eye directed the muzzle of his gun toward a careless singing-bird in the pine-tree's highest top, and the shot resounded, and the bird in the next instant fell heavy and dead to the earth, struck in its little heart or little head, but never more singing, never more moving a single light feather. Then felt Gunnar a certain satisfaction, a something which was to his taste. "Thus hast thou shot me down, thou coward!" he thought to himself, "and I was equally innocent, equally glad and young, and thy fellow-man moreover. But thou hast shot sorrow and destruction into my soul, and therefore I will shoot some good wolfs'-hail into thy red head, so that thou shalt fall to the earth like this bird, and I may go and look on thee as I look on it now."

Such thoughts often fell into the heart of Gunnar; and if in a calmer hour he cast them a little aside, yet they returned oftener and oftener in the dark autumnal nights, and the long sleepless hours of suffering, or in the gloomy forest—deep, vast, and wild, like Gunnar's own mind. When to this is added that he ate little, but by degrees quickened his body with a dram, which, perhaps, never was able to intoxicate him, but which, on the contrary, he considered to be the only means which yet infused some life, some elasticity, into all the powers of both soul and body, we may readily conceive in what mood of mind he was.

CHAPTER XXXVI.

A WHOLE week after the eventful day passed altogether without variety. Gunnar was in the wood often till late at night. Adversity had somewhat broken Lena. She was neither so ill-humored nor so insulting as before, but bustled about like fire, in order, by diligence, and labor, and care, to make up that heavy loss which she saw that she had occasioned. Mother Ingrid sate and spun, but the old mother's heart accompanied her son every where, and suffered and grieved with him, although it did not outwardly appear. Elin worked like a little ant by day for the benefit of Lena; by night, upon a watch-guard and watch-pocket, which she would give him at parting, as an eternal and innocent remembrance of herself. No one can tell, but those who have experienced it, how much labor, how many tears, and how much sleeplessness such a work can cost a young woman; but also what a melancholy pleasure, not without its great charm, it is able to afford her. "This he will see, this he will wear, when I am no longer here; and by its means he will preserve the recollection of me and my affection." Thus thought Elin; and worked and watched, and with tears felt it light and sweet, for—shall I speak it out?—for among a hundred such works, at least ninety-nine are thrown into a scrap-corner, or are given away, or destroyed with indifference, or—God best knows what; for *He* accepts the good intentions, and in them lies such love, often such real, such pure, such infinite love, that God will probably, *sometime*, *here* or *there*, recompense the poor things for it.

But *this* watch-guard, and *this* watch-pocket, will neither be forgotten, despised, given away, nor be trodden under foot by indifference. Ah! a totally different fate awaited them.

Abraham went every day out to day-labor, and said every evening—

"Olle and the others say that it was our master who was the perpetrator of the great robbery, and that the squire says so; but I say that they lie."

Every such word, yes, every such thought, aggravated Gunnar's dreadful rancor against the squire, whom he looked upon as the sole cause of all his misfortunes, all his dishonor, and Olle merely as a tool in the squire's hands; and Gunnar felt really ashamed when he looked any one in the face, at merely thinking that people could suspect him to be a housebreaker; and that his own clear conscience was not enough to allow him to look boldly into the eyes of any one, be he who he might. This, perhaps, Gunnar might have done, had not his mind been gloomed and cast down by other cares and troubles; and perhaps these very shy looks of Gunnar contributed to give to the ugly rumor yet more strength and circulation.

On Saturday, Sunday, and Monday in the first week in October, Abraham was away on the hall-farm, and nothing was heard thence at Vika. Gunnar, as was well known, was seldom or never at home; and if he were there, he sate or moved in a perpetual disquiet; glanced toward the door at the least noise, and waited, in a word, with a certain impatience, that they should formally accuse him and arraign him for the theft, that his innocence might be brought fully to the light. But nothing was heard of this, and his temper became gloomier every day. On the Tuesday morning, just a week after the brandy day, he betook himself again to the wood, and wandered away to the wildest, dreariest part of it, which was traversed by only one narrow footpath. Gunnar had come thither almost on business. The October morning was clear and beautiful, and he wandered on thoughtfully, with a somewhat considerable burden of "fire-water"—as the American Indians so expressively call their worst enemy, brandy—and with a still gloomier mood than usual. He went on now so absorbed in thought, and looking down before him, that in his haste, and most unexpectedly, at a sudden turn of the wood, he met a rapidly advancing person; and we may ourselves imagine what was his sensation, nay, his thousands of sensations, when, looking up—the squire stood before him, not, as so often before, in his moody imagination, but in clear and palpable reality. His first movements were to clench his teeth, and put his finger on the lock of his gun. The squire paused also abruptly at some paces distant, somewhat confounded at this meeting, and not in the best of humors either, as we shall probably hereafter see. Neither of them gave way—the path was too narrow for them both.

"What dost thou here in the wood, my dear Gunnar, and with fowling-piece in hand?" demanded the squire, after a momentary, but deep silence. "Thou knowest better than any one that it is forbidden, and that, moreover, I do not like it," added he, with a tone more of warning than exactly of menace.

"Talk not *here*, and *now*, of *forbidding* and *commands*, thou hangman and scoundrel!" said Gunnar, and made a movement forward, as if to seize the squire by the throat. *Here* it is *I* who *command* and *forbid*. At *this* moment it is *I* who am *lord*, and *thou* who art the *slave ;* and I shall for once in life show thee what a strong arm can do when hate and vengeance strengthen its sinews."

And with this he approached still nearer to the squire, who was also a strong and bold man, although from his years he was far from being able, either in strength or activity, to match himself with Gunnar. But he had yet the instinctive and inbred faith that his quality of lord and master would even now go for something, and therefore he did not give way a hair's breath, but, on the contrary, advanced upon his opponent, and with both hands seized Gunnar himself by the throat. He was strong, precisely because he was cool-blooded, and would fain see whether in all points he could not contend the matter with Gunnar.

"What mean'st thou, Gunnar?" exclaimed the squire; "art thou mad or drunk, or seest thou not who I am? Hold thy tongue, and go thy way quietly, if thou dost not wish that I should punish thee according to thy desert."

"What dost thou dare to say?" shouted Gunnar, wildly, and made a tremendous clutch at the squire's throat. "What gabblest *thou* about my holding *my* tongue? Have I not held it long enough? And what pratest thou about punishment and desert, and the like stupid stuff? *Here* the question is to punish *thee*, not me; and for once thou shalt get what thou hast deserved so long."

"Let me go!" cried the squire, in a bellowing voice; but Gunnar did not loose his hold, but took a fresh and stronger gripe, by which the squire came wholly into his power; and when Gunnar perceived that, he said,

"To send a bullet through thy red noddle at a good distance, and see thee tumble head over heels like a dead-shot sparrow, that had been my pleasure; but, on the whole, thou art not worthy of a shot from my good honorable gun, but of a few raps from its butt-end."

And with this he put his words into effect.

Whether Gunnar at this moment would give his deadliest foe a severe token of remembrance, or kill him outright, is not easy to determine, and Gunnar did not know himself; but he let passion, and revenge, and hate, overcome every better feeling, which, however, would speedily have returned, when at this moment he heard a sound as of some one who, running heavily, approached the spot, and so, with one powerful blow, he was compelled to quit his prey, and—light as a fawn—to hasten aside, where, hidden by the thickets of the wood, he could not be seen by the coming one. His conscience now immediately re-awoke, and he felt a certain satisfaction in the arrival of a third, who, perhaps, hindered him from committing murder, and who could assist his enemy if it were necessary. Gunnar listened a moment, and heard distinctly—for to see was impossible—that the person coming had stopped at the place where he had left the squire, and when he perceived this he hastened farther, and went with rapid steps toward home; so that by two o'clock at noon he was again at Vika.

When he entered the sitting-room he was covered with a cold perspiration, and scarcely knew what he did. He threw the gun down, contrary to his custom, on Abraham's bed, instead of hanging it up, and felt a painful stab through his heart, when the only living creature who was in the room, little Gustaf, glad and familiar, came running to him, and stretched his little arms, and little rosy mouth toward him, and, with dimples of joy in the small and blooming cheeks, cried,

"See, fallé! fallé! Welcome! welcome!"

"I have no time for thee," said Gunnar, moving away, but not pushing the child. The child went his way downcast, and approached the gun, at the lock of which he pointed with his little fingers, exclaiming many times—" What is that, fallé? What is that?"

Gunnar neither heard nor saw it, for he had thrown himself on a stool by the side of the table, and, propping his arms upon it, rested his heavy head in his hands, with eyes closed, and strange thoughts careering through his brain. But the little Gustaf still louder and more earnestly continued his question, "What is that, fallé? What is that?"—He looked up, and now *for the first* time saw a large drop of blood on the gun! A horribly strange feeling passed through him; he hastily snatched the loaded piece from the boy, wiped off the blood with what came first to hand, and said to the child, " That is nothing." Yet it was in fact so *much*, that it was the child's own blood!

Gunnar was not in condition to cast from him all thoughts of atonement for his blood-guiltiness; he did what he could at the moment. He took the boy in his arms, pressed him to his agonized bosom, and said,—" Thou poor little thing! To *thee* will I show that I am neither hard-hearted nor unjust; and that I will not punish the child for the father's sins, for that befits only the Most High, the Almighty, since the Scriptures say so, but not us, sinful men."

He caressed long the little one, and somewhat calmed by his talk with him, he went at length out of the room, paused a moment at Elin's window, and saw her at work, without her observing him, and then went further, for he descried Lena in the chamber. Gunnar felt the need of sleep and rest, which he had not enjoyed for long; for his nights all this time past had been almost wholly sleepless; and a little ashamed to go and lie down in the middle of the day in the sitting-room, he withdrew softly to the hay-loft, where we will leave him, and let a tolerably good and calm sleep press down his eyelids, and shed some hours of rest into a soul so unquiet and stormy as his; for who can know how briefly, if ever, this, the tranquil genius of sleep, shall yet again visit Gunnar? What know we, poor mortals? *Nothing*—till the hour arrives.

CHAPTER XXXVII.

While Gunnar slept this "calm sleep," to which we could give another name were we inclined to anticipate affairs, we will turn one step toward Grantorp, and observe with astonishment how every thing there has changed and broken itself up, or, as people are accustomed to say, " has turned itself on the spit,"—which means, that the imagined sweet ale-wort has become a little sour.

Through the servant Olle had this change come wholly about. Ever since Gunnar quitted Grantorp, by means of officiousness and eye-service he made himself a sort of favorite with the squire, although this method by no means succeeded with Ma'msell Sara: and, building on this favoritism, he had actually succeeded in putting it into the squire's head that it was Gunnar, at Vika, who had committed the great theft, while a number of little coincident circumstances appeared to witness against Gunnar. It was known that he was, as people are wont to say, of prosperous and able management, much taken up with himself; had wide-stretching plans, and great speculations; appeared to be now here, now there, and was quicker, cleverer, and more ingenious than any of his neighbors. But Olle saw also that although his master really began to suspect Gunnar, yet he would not openly accuse him, before he had by some means certain proof; but this was not so easy to get; and while people sought after this, Olle gained time, and this was of the utmost importance to him. In the mean time, Olle

leaped into the wrong tun when he sent the constable to Vika,
unknown to the squire ; for when the constable returned from
the search, he related the matter to the squire, but was obliged
to confess that, on the evidence there found, a single trace of
the stolen goods could not be discovered, although the constable had pried into every corner, without betraying his suspicions, because he knew that the squire would not wish it
before they had legal proof. He must admit the brandy was
just distilled, and not of the squire's old year's stock, and that
no thrashed corn was to be found.

The squire scratched himself behind the ear, and knew not
what to do. So passed all the days of the week in which
the visitation had been made at Vika ; but on Saturday
evening, when the squire began to talk with his sister,
Ma'msell Sara, and to express suspicions of Gunnar, in
which Olle regularly supported him, declaring that Gun-
nar· and Lena were too cunning not to have concealed
the stolen goods, and not to leave them at Vika; then the
old honorable ma'msell became really angry, and declared
roundly to her brother that she had long mistrusted this
Olle herself, and bade him call up the overseer, an elderly,
honorable and sensible fellow, and inquire and take counsel
with him, rather than with the good-for-nothing Olle, " whose
aspect I can never bring myself to endure," said Ma'msell
Sara. The squire, who often enough was accustomed to
counsel with his sister and to follow her advice, because he
found himself the better for it, called, therefore, on the Sunday
morning, the Overseer Anders up, and asked him on his conscience, if he could give any information regarding the theft.

" With permission," answered Anders, " as the squire asks
me, so I can outright and on my conscience say, that I believe
Gunnar at Vika to be as innocent of the theft as the child that.
is born to-night, and Bengt also, because I have heard Olle cast
suspicion on _him._"

" Yes, but Bengt was really away on the night that the robbery happened," answered the squire.

" With permission, that was a great lie," replied the overseer,
positively. " I know well enough that Olle said that ; but, as
it happened, Bengt lay in the same bed with me, in the adjoin-
ing building, that night, both when we lay down in the evening,
and when we got up in the morning, and in the middle of the
night, too. But he was away last Sunday night, and danced and

acted in a play; and at another time he went to hear the preacher-girls; but the one was before, and the other after the robbery."

"Well, but what thinkest thou of the robbery itself?" demanded the squire further, but after a little while in silence, during which he himself began to reflect on Olle's pertinacious insinuations; "for," said he, "I understand sufficiently that thou acquittest Gunnar and Bengt, but thou must yet have thy own opinion concerning some one else."

"With permission, that I keep to myself."

"Ay, but that is wrong and ill done, when thy master questions thee privately."

"Yes, but, with permission, it would, it seems to me, be ill done to utter loose suspicions against people, and proof I have not exactly yet against him that *I* suspect."

"And that is— ?" queried the squire.

"Yes, that is just what I will not say; for I may make a mistake as well as another."

But now the squire began most seriously to represent to his servant, that it was his bounden duty to tell his thoughts to his master, in order to enable him to come on the traces of the thief, if it turned out that his opinion was correct: and if, on the other hand, the Overseer Anders was mistaken, no harm was done to him on whom his suspicions fell, for he must clear up his innocence.

"Yes, but, nevertheless, it is not pleasant, whether he be guilty or not guilty, to him who accuses a comrade," said the overseer, thoughtfully.

"Pleasant, certainly, is nothing in this affair," said the squire; "but if thou wilt tell what thou believest, I will, on the other hand, promise thee that no mortal shall know from whom I obtain my information; but I will then prosecute my inquiries myself, and thou shalt not come into question, whether thou art right or wrong in thy ideas."

"Well, when the squire promises me *that*, and that altogether unconditionally," said the Overseer Anders, "I will no longer hesitate to tell the squire that there are many who saw Olle in company with that low fellow Rönn, who dabbles a little in masonry, and has accomplices at Ringberg's, and goes there to carry on his practices. And he was at the market at Kampavall, and sold corn there, and had Ringberg's cart, but all knew well enough that Ringberg has no grain to sell; and that Rönn boasts what capital brandy they have at Ringberg's; and Olle has it, too, for his flask is always full, every mortal day, and yet he drinks and treats continually: and money has he too to swagger with, which he says he gets as wages."

"So that is it?" said the squire; "and this nobody has thought fit to tell me, till I should inquire after it myself!" added he, in a somewhat menacing tone.

"Yes, because he that offers what is unasked gets no thanks for his pains," answered the Overseer Anders; "and he who runs before he is bid may readily be suspected of wishing to accuse people falsely."

"Well, well," said the squire, "I fear the business is but too much as you say with Olle, and I thank thee for thy revelation; and now I myself will try to bring out the truth, let it lie never so deep."

Neither on Sunday nor Monday did the squire do any thing, but merely watched Olle pretty closely, and saw many matters which gave him room to believe that Anders, the overseer, had by no means wrongly judged him. On Tuesday morning early he called up Olle into a remote apartment, bolted the door, and, without any further prelude, took out a formidable Russian *kantschouk*, or a cat-o'-nine-tails, and promised Olle a taste of it if he did not confess all that he knew about the robbery; "for," said the squire, "I am indignant at thy casting suspicion on Gunnar at Vika, and begin to have my own solid reasons for believing that thou hast only been casting dust in my eyes through this."

Olle, cowardly and terrified, denied the charge at first, but a single blow brought him to confess something; a second, something more; and still more clearly the touch of the third. Rönn and he had, in fact, the day before the market, committed the theft, and Rönn had immediately sold the grain, but all the brandy they had still there away at Ringberg's, except a little that Olle had in a bottle, which was hidden in a place that he mentioned on the estate itself.

The squire said next to nothing to Olle after this confession, but hastened to secure him in this same room where they were, and of which he took the key, and hied away at once to Ringberg's, to get speech of Rönn before he could possibly be instructed by Olle of what had happened, and taken his measures accordingly; for the squire was too wise not to know that Olle would deny every thing again, if there were no witness and legal proof to confront him. In the utmost haste, therefore, he ordered the Overseer Anders to take a few other men with him, and go into the neighborhood of Ringberg's, in order, at the first signal from the squire, to establish themselves there. He himself determined to go by the very nearest cut through the wood, and it was exactly on this route that he encountered Gunnar, both to his own and Gunnar's misfortune.

Olle, shut up alone in the remote apartment, began immediately to repent his stupid cowardice and terror having compelled him to confess the truth, which, otherwise, neither threats nor bribes could have drawn from him. But he began, too, cunningly to reflect that he had been alone with the squire— that no third person had heard his confession; and that, could he but escape out of his clutches, he could deny the thing altogether; and now his first fear was, that the squire would go at once to Rönn, and get the truth too out of him; and as Olle supposed that the squire would send for Rönn, while he was aware of nothing that had transpired (for Rönn had been sometimes helpful with sundry pieces of less important masonry with which he bungled occasionally), it was Olle's most earnest wish that he could slip out and get beforehand, to prevent Rönn coming to Grantorp, for Rönn was free from any power of the squire except through the law, and against that they could defend themselves sufficiently by hardy denial.

He looked round, and quickly discovered, to his great joy, that he could very easily make his escape out of the window by means of a rope that luckily was in the room, especially as the window was not very far from the ground, for Olle was as poor at leaping as he was at every thing else. In a few seconds, but not without a certain bumping of the heart, under the brief hanging process, Olle was on *terra firma*, and on his two feet, which were never so nimble as when they were urged to flight by some danger. With this assistance he fled away as rapidly as possible, but as he must run close past the hiding-place where lay his beloved treasure, the brandy-bottle, he could not resist the desire to see whether it was yet there, and to his great joy he found it undisturbed; he set it to his lips, and drank a desperate draught, and then ran again as fast as he was able, and was the heavily running person who chased Gunnar from his purpose with the unfortunate squire, who, in reality, was far less deserving of Gunnar's unmeasured hatred and abhorrence than he supposed; for neither in the brandy seizure, nor in Elin's engagement, had he in the least degree his finger.

L

Equally innocent, too, was he of spreading suspicions about Gunnar as to what concerned the robbery. On the other side, however, it must be admitted for Gunnar, that he believed all this, and that he believed that he who could do him so much injury in *one* respect, could do it in *every other*.

But now Gunnar lay and slept that nearly tranquil sleep up in the hay-loft. A kind of reaction had taken place in him. The desire of revenge that had hitherto incessantly grown was now appeased, and mysterious spirit voices said to Gunnar in his sleep, that the revenge which he cherished had been, for the most part, unjust and precipitate. " How well," thought he, in his sleeping state—which, in great and agitating moments of life, is but one unbroken continuance of the waking one—"how well that I did not send a bullet through his forehead or his chest, but merely gave him an impressive memento of me!— for *something*, and much *still*, ought he to endure for all that I have suffered and do suffer through him."

After three hours' unbroken and almost dreamless sleep, Gunnar awoke, rubbed his eyes believed in the first instant that all together—the rencounter in the wood, the arrival of a third—all, in a word, was merely a lively and distinct dream. He would so willingly believe that; but, by degrees, the nimbus which sleep draws around the soul parted and dissipated, actuality and dream sufficiently distinguished themselves, and stood naked by each other's sides, sufficiently resembling each other, but still with their prominent differences; for the reality was, and remained what it was, and the dream had infused itself into Gunnar's present mood of mind, which, strangely enough, was far more tranquil and peaceful than before.

He seemed, to himself at least, to have made a truce with life; would not make war on it on any side, but called to mind all that it offers in reconciliation. He began, as he lay up there in the hay-loft, to retrace the occurrences of the morning, and swore to himself at the thought of the great quantity of brandy which he had swallowed before going out, and which rendered his recollection of particulars obscure enough, for he was not in a condition to satisfy himself whether he had struck the squire heavily, or only in a very trifling degree. His mind at that moment had been in such a bewilderment, that every power of distinction was lost, and there lay a cloud over his memory which Gunnar, sighing, thought that time could best dissipate.

In this disposition he arose, felt himself heavy and chilly, but determined to shake off these sensations, and went at length into the sitting-room. Lena, who believed that he now first came home, offered him food and brandy. Gunnar accepted the former, but rejected the latter with great disgust; and the thought stood before him, clear and sincere, that every moment of his life which he had to regret, had invariably been, more or less, bedewed with this loathsome brandy.

Gunnar forswore it now and forever, although silently within himself; ate with almost a better relish than for a long time before, and, from a curious contradiction in human nature, was unusually friendly and mild toward every one, and took, for the very first time in Lena's presence, little Gustaf up on his knee, and gave him part of his own late dinner. But if any thing stirred, was the smallest sound heard, he looked round expectingly, and with a certain disquiet, at the door, as one who apprehended that *some one*, he knew not rightly *who*, would come and say *something*, he knew not rightly *what*.

He went, in the mean time, out; worked actively for some hours; and when the day closed, all the household was assembled in the sitting-room, except Abraham, who was not yet returned from the Hall, where he went daily to work. Lena wondered greatly that he was so late, but Elin, glad to see Gunnar with a countenance so composed, thought not of that, but sat in a shady corner of the room, sunk in contemplation of this man, whom she so boundlessly loved—whom she would soon see no more; and who, every now and then, threw upon her a long glance, coming direct from the heart, which said far more to Elin than any words could, and which caused her heart to beat violently, and her eyes to fill with involuntary tears. When she looked down, then Gunnar also looked down, but his looks divided themselves between Elin and the door, and he said several times, "It is inconceivable that Abraham does not come; it is already pitch dark."

And pitch dark it was. The moon did not rise till toward morning, and the only light which there was in the room came from the fagot on the fire, which Lena had put on so skillfully that it would last the whole evening. But this was nearly burned out, when a rapid step was heard—yes, so rapid, that all listened, none of them believing that Abraham could ever put his clumsy legs into such nimble motion; and Elin was unable to refrain from laughter when, to their general amazement, however, Abraham it proved to be, who rushed into the room, as if pursued by something invisible. He banged the door behind him, and looked round him in confusion.

"Well, has Abraham been out among the ghosts?" said Elin, laughing, for Abraham had run till he was out of breath, and could not get out a word.

"What, the cat! hast thou been doing so long? Now is the porridge ice-cold; and why dost thou come running like a mad ox?" demanded Lena, and held a burning brand toward Abraham, who was pale as a corpse.

"Now, then, make some answer," said Gunnar, in a deep and rather hollow voice.

"Hosch! I can not! Hosch! I am so out of breath! Hosch! I am so nervous! See! I met him when they brought him! They have sought him the whole day, but at last they came right upon him; for Olle is quite beside himself with drink, and they can not make him sober, though they ducked him in the well. Hosch! I am so tired and hungry!"

"Speak a single word with some connection, thou fiery-head there!" said Gunnar; and Elin saw that he was deathly pale, and that his lips trembled and his eyes flashed, and Mother Ingrid marked this more distinctly.

"Bless me! it is not so easy to preach a sermon when one has run so!" said Abraham, and stopped again for breath.

"I have, at all events, a mind to preach thee a sermon on the ear," said Gunnar, "and will do it, if thou do not speak properly, so that people can understand thee. Whom was it that thou met—that they were coming with? Answer! or otherwise thou shalt get a fillip."

"Hosch! it was the squire, I know," answered Abraham, starting wildly, and terrified for his four-inch-long ears.

"Where had he been?"

"Bless me! in the wood, I know."

"Was he only just now coming back?"

"Bless me! in all days! a corpse can not go! He is just dead, I know."

"Dead!" all exclaimed, except Gunnar.

"Is he dead?" said Gunnar, finally, in a deeper and more hollow voice.

"Yes, sure, as a stone!" answered Abraham.

"How has he come by his death?" demanded Mother Ingrid, the only one who properly retained their self-possession, for Elin was still so young, that she easily lost hers when she heard that one was dead whom she had recently seen alive; and Gunnar had his reasons for being silent.

"Olle has murdered him in the wood," answered Abraham.

"Olle!" cried Gunnar, vehemently. "How do people know that?"

"Oh, why Olle went early in the forenoon, running to Ringberg's, like one mad, and asked after Rönn, and said there was now no cause of fear for them, for now had *he* gotten what *he* deserved, and lay murdered in the wood."

"What *he*?" asked Mother Ingrid.

"Bless me! the squire, I know!"

"What had Olle to do with Rönn?" asked Mother Ingrid farther, adding, with some vexation, "thou talkest in such a manner that nobody can understand thee."

"Bless me, in all days! they are the people who have robbed the estate last week, now every body knows that; and Olle drank a whole half measure of brandy [a pint and a half] for very joy when he came to Ringberg's, and sung, and waved about the squire's red pocket-book, in which were many rix-dollars, and said, 'Now he is dead in the wood, God be praised! and can no longer threaten one with a drubbing!' For, let me tell you, Olle had got his skin well dressed by the squire in the morning, to make him confess the truth; and therefore he was enraged at the squire, and knocked him on the head, though he says that the squire lay there dead when he came; but there are none so stupid as to believe him, for he was bloody, both hands and clothes, when he came to Ringberg's, and waved about his pocket-book, and was so glad of it. But Ringberg's wife understood how it was, and that Olle let it out in his drunkenness; and she was afraid lest they should be brought in, and therefore she stole out, and ran quickly to the constable, and gave Olle up; and when the constable came, there lay Olle, and slept like a swine, and so they threw water on him, and ducked him in the well to waken him, that they might get to know whereabout the squire lay. But Olle did not wake; and now they have searched the whole of the blessed day in the wood, for no one could believe that he lay openly on the footpath itself, away by the gray hill; but there he lay, and there they found him late this evening, for they went with torches; and I was so frightened when I met them, that I thought I never should get home."

Gunnar had not listened to all this : he was gone out into the dark night.

CHAPTER XXXVIII.

"And thou didst not merely go," said Elin to Abraham, when he had concluded his story of meeting the corpse, " but thou ran as fast as thou couldst. Thou believed firmly that the dead squire was after thee, poor Abraham."

"Yes, I was dreadfully frightened," added he, swallowing another spoonful of his porridge.

Lena went out quietly, looking aside at little Gustaf; the boy slept the angel sleep of childhood, amid lily dreams.

Elin fell into a melancholy mood of mind, and it was time to go to rest; but Gunnar did not come, and the door of the house must therefore remain open, although Abraham proposed to bolt it, and promised to open it when Gunnar came.

"Thou waken!" said Lena: "nay, sooner would the press in the corner there awake. Thou know'st well how roughly thou hast to be roused. Nay, bolt the door, and I will watch myself."

Lena knew well enough that she could not sleep. Gunnar still did not come.

"Certainty! certainty I must have!" exclaimed Gunnar to himself, with a terrible and demoniac impulse to rush on toward it; and he hurried away, through wood and night, as if he had been chased, and stood in an incredibly short time at the door of the servants' room at Grantorp. No one there had retired to rest, and no one was astonished at the appearance of Gunnar on such an occasion, as in every one curiosity and thirst of information, sorrow, and terror, were excited to their utmost degree. He quickly met with Bengt, and Bengt did not once observe how pale the inquirer was, but gave Gunnar direct and clear intelligence of all that Abraham had gone round in so confused a manner.

" But how is it *known with certainty* that it was Olle who—who—who was his actual murderer?" asked Gunnar.

" Oh, good heavens! that is not difficult to know," answered Bengt. " He had received some blows in the morning to compel acknowledgment of the theft, and had been locked in, but broke out, and he was full of wrath; and God knows how it happened when they met in the wood, for Olle is so malignant, so thorough a rogue, as thou well know'st, that his wickedness makes up for his cowardice; and I never can believe that he knocked the squire on the head in open encounter, but that he came softly after him, and fell on him from behind, so that the squire did not observe him, for to a certainty the squire would have dealt with such a miscreant as Olle; and it seems the squire has a wound in the head, as if made by something of iron; and Olle, it seems, had a great window fastener, or something of the kind, in his hand, as well as the squire's common red pocket-book, which he showed when he came to Ringberg's."

" Who gave him up?" asked Gunnar.

" That was Ringberg's wife, as soon as Olle laid down; and this he did directly, for he aggravated his drunkenness with a full half measure of brandy, and deadened all that remorse which a man can not avoid having who has murdered a fellow-creature, eh, Gunnar?"

Gunnar *spoke* not in reply, but what he *thought*, that is best known to Loke, and to him, at once the happy and unhappy skald, in whose soul every rapture and every pang develops itself with equal truth.

Gunnar had heard enough. He wandered, with steps of hundred-weight heaviness, homeward, and gave not the least attention to the wild gloom which, in the autumn-night, surrounded and reigned over the old desolate Grantorp, within whose gray walls, rich with the events of the past, the last possessor slept the eternal sleep, in a remote chamber of the tower (whether calmly or not, that we know not; God and man's conscience know that alone), and where the aged M'amsell Sara shed bitter tears of grief at the strange and sudden rending away of the only prop which she possessed in life; the only brother, who—we have said it many times—was neither entirely good nor utterly bad, but just one of our most ordinary squires, such as a good sister may become much attached to, for neither sisterly love, nor any love here upon earth, meets with a perfect object, but loves more or less out of the elasticity of its own loving nature.

Gunnar went, and his shadow stole along, black and vast, at his heels, and both vanished together in the pitchy darkness, for the moon was only just rising at midnight, and great thick clouds were ready immediately to intercept and thoroughly to obscure it.

In the room at Vika reigned, in the mean time, a heavy disquiet, and no one slept well except little Gustaf, for scarcely was Abraham asleep when he started up, and waving off something with his hands, exclaimed, " Nay, nay ! for Jesus' sake, cast it not upon me. I will have nothing to do with it. Carry it to the church." And another time he shrieked out in his sleep—" Fie ! he peeps and stares, although he is a corpse !"

" Won't mother go to bed ?" said Lena, who paced to and fro in restlessness in the room, and peeped through every window. Mother Ingrid, whom she addressed, sat silent and shrunk together, with her head leaned in her hands, in the very darkest corner of the room, which at this moment was not much darker than the rest, for only a few blackening embers glimmered from time to time fitfully on the hearth, and entered into rivalry with the miserable moonlight. The storm raged without, and the window panes rattled in the blast.

Mother Ingrid went softly and laid herself down, in obedience to Lena's recommendation, but far was she from sleeping. No, she lay and thought of so much ! and, among other things, on the little bloody rag which was in the room that day at noon, and which the little Gustaf was playing with when she came in.

" Hast thou hurt thyself, dear child ?" the old dame had inquired. " No, mother," the boy had answered ; " father wiped the gun with the rag."

" Is your father come *already* from the wood ?" she again asked of little Gustaf, and he answered, " Yes ;" but, on the contrary, " No," when she inquired whether he had brought some birds in his game-bag.

When Elin entered her chamber that evening, she had not lain down, but sat at the window and looked into the dark night, where Gunnar was abroad wandering, and she pondered on what change in her own little fate the death of the squire might occasion. " Perhaps," thought she, the whole set of servants at the hall will be dismissed ; perhaps I shall *escape* altogether, and may be able to remain here !" And she drew a light and happy breath, but felt instantly horrified that so dreadful a murder should be the cause of her joy.

To subdue the evil demon, she said half aloud the Lord's Prayer for the squire, but listened at times whether Gunnar came back, and could not conceive whither he took his way in such a coal-black night; and because she did not fix her whole attention on her Lord's Prayer, nor undividedly on the dead for whom she prayed, she repeated another for the squire, then one for herself, and, lastly, one for Gunnar; but that was the warmest.

Lie down she could not, but continued sitting at the window; when, however, the night grew late, she sunk her arms down against the window-sill, her head fell upon them, and she quickly slumbered, but lightly and uneasily, ready to awake every moment at the least sound.

But for Lena the sitting-room became at length too close; she must go out into the cool night air, and listen whether she could hear Gunnar approach, for she guessed very well whither he had directed his course. The clock had now hummed its stroke of one; the moon was totally hidden behind a cloud, but the storm danced with wood and lake, so that the branches cracked, and the billows leaped high upon the strand, like young and restless maidens, and the waves muttered and murmured like old and anxious mothers, far out on the waters. Leaf and bough were tossed incessantly to and fro; Lena thrust her hands beneath her apron, her teeth chattering and her limbs quivering with cold, and still listened, but started in terror aside as an owl close to her shrieked forth its dismal "klavit."

"Fie, thou miscreant!" exclaimed Lena, half aloud, becoming somewhat warm about the ears, but as suddenly cold again, and then troubled herself not in the least further about the owl, but merely listened. At length she heard a man's step. "Those are a man's; they are Gunnar's, but they are unequal. They are not Gunnar's." Lena knew Gunnar's step. Love, however ordinary it may be, has still a fine ear. "It is Gunnar! Is it Gunnar? No, it is not Gunnar! Yes, it is Gunnar!" So had Lena thought some hundreds of times when the coming one was at length quite near to her, and she called out, "Is that Gunnar?"

The sisters had voices greatly alike, especially when they half-whispered; and Gunnar said, with a voice in which new

L*

joy and old pain were so blended, that it struck Lena with surprise, "Is that thou, Elin ?"

"No, it is *I*," answered Lena, too much occupied with other
thoughts to have room in her bosom for any jealousy. "It is I,
dear Gunnar," replied she, more mildly than usual; "I could
not sit quiet longer in the house; how is it now, altogether ?"

"Oh !" answered Gunnar, with a hollow voice, "he is—
dead !"

"Dead, really !" exclaimed Lena, slowly, and the tears beginning to flow.

"Don't weep, Lena, said Gunnar, "I shall work enough for
Gustaf."

"Oh, thou angel of a man !" said Lena, become quite meek
of mood, and fell sobbing on Gunnar's neck ; and Gunnar, for
the first time, did not push her from him. Gunnar had need to
reconcile himself to somewhat—to make expiation to some one.
But Lena—she crept back quickly again into her every-day
soul, which, for a moment, gives way before the heart, for that
is bad in no one. Either there is found none, or it is *good;* a
wicked heart means the same thing as a vacuum, where a heart
should be.

"Heaven have mercy upon us !" she burst forth, weeping
aloud ; "What will become of us now ? It is a fact that I received a handsome sum from him from time to time, and he
promised always that little Gustaf should go to school, and study
for the ministry ; but now that is all over."

"Didst thou receive money from him ?" said Gunnar, with a
mixture of mortification and pain, but yet without any wrath.

"Yes, certainly; many's the Lord's time !" sobbed Lena,
who now thought that, the secret being out, she need no longer
be under the necessity to spare Gunnar's sensibility. This latter idea would probably never have passed frankly through her
mind, but yet she had acted upon it instinctively ; for the uneducated act often more finely than they are able to think, while
the educated, on the contrary, do just the reverse.

"How could we possibly have done so well without ?" continued Lena; ah, indeed, many and many a two and a three-
dollar banco did I get from time to time, and this went to thee
and others beside little Gustaf, although I never dared to talk
of it before thee or thy mother."

Gunnar's heart was crushed together ; and, strangely enough,
he who would have raged over these words some few days be-

fore; he who would have disdained Lena for this meanness; *he* pitied her now in his soul, and said consolingly, "Don't weep so, thou dear Lena! We shall get enough by our labor. I shall henceforth work like seven, and thou know'st what I can do when I will, and Gustaf shall yet be a minister."

"Oh, my God! how golden good thou art!" exclaimed Lena once more, and clasped her arms about Gunnar's neck, and drew him with her into the house.

But neither of them had thought that during this half-whispered and sad conversation they had stood close beneath Elin's window, which lay in the gable of the house, very near the corner at which Lena stood to wait for Gunnar.

How many significant words had Elin now heard; for she awoke out of her light slumber on the window-seat when the owlet screamed, and had already shuddered several times, when she, moreover, saw against the black heavens something white repeatedly hurry past the window, and which, in fact, was only Lena. But as soon as she heard this call—"Is that thou, Gunnar?"—Elin knew her voice, and then understood all—the whole of this conjugal conversation, one thing excepted, which she could *not* understand; and in this melancholy night, for the very first time, jealousy struck its angry talons into the heart of the young Elin, which pure love had hitherto wholly filled. Hitherto she had always seemed to feel, with a deep pain, that Gunnar did not, no, in the slightest, love his Lena—he had declared it himself. And now! now it was plain that he did. He had, then, spoken falsely to Elin—he tenderly loved his wife! So, at least, now thought Elin; and the honey of compassion was converted into the bitterest wormwood of jealousy; and Elin wept, and felt herself alone—alone in the world—and now alone, with words that she could neither explain nor inquire about—with thoughts which she could not comprehend, for she did not conceive that she was jealous of Gunnar's love for Lena; she merely felt it, and suffered from it—suffered, was wounded, wept, endured remorse, and despaired—alone.

At length she threw herself on the bed in her clothes, chilled through, and exhausted with weeping; for, to listen better for the arrival of Gunnar, she had let her window stand open the whole of that cold October night, and, moreover, lay warm and excited against its edge. Toward morning, she slept—awoke late, and in high fever.

This morning, not many of the others had awoke, who,

under the roof of that little peasant's dwelling, had sought rest for the night. Mother Ingrid had never slept, nor Gunnar, nor Lena. But still lay they all, and many a heavy sigh passed through the bosoms of these three individuals. An inexpressible anguish and fear had made itself master of the old mother; an icy coldness, a kind of stagnation and insensibility, the young son. He no longer loved Elin with that burning and devouring flame; he no longer hated Lena with that terrible abhorrence; he despised no longer the silly Abraham. There was so much within him that had leveled itself, that had reconciled itself. Brandy and stimulating drink he had forever abjured. All his severe sufferings lay and slept as if they were dead. He had but one single object in life, if life were permitted him, one wish, one motive; he would bring up little Gustaf, and educate him *well*; and for that would he labor day and night—for that live and breathe.

As for Lena, her adversities, and the destruction of her hopes, had already conspicuously subdued her; and the daily intercourse, under the same roof with kind, pure-hearted beings, somewhat touched and operated on her stubborn mind. Evil had certainly dug a deep gulf in her soul, but this gulf was not altogether bottomless, and might possibly yet be filled up with something good. This was far from being the case at present, however; but, upon the nethermost ground of her soul, there already stirred some good feelings. She saw no longer with ill-will and vexation that the old mother-in-law still lived on and moved about, although death seemed to wander, step by step, with her. Some bright, clear, and pure sparks of devotion and respect for her husband began to raise themselves out of the dark fire, with which she glowed for him. A slumbering sisterly affection for Elin began even softly to awake, amid jealousy and distrust. Sometimes she threw a compassionate, half-humane glance toward poor Abraham, whom hitherto she had regarded and treated as a mere animal, which has no other merit than its capacity for labor; and in her maternal love for little Gustaf, which before had been merely the she-wolf's raving and bestial attachment to its offspring, she began to mingle particles of reason and reflection.

With these remarks, we rush away to times somewhat in advance, and speculate beforehand on what they will bring. Every thing, however, has its beginning, although many of them seem to have no end; and, therefore, we may say, that the state of mind of Gunnar, and of his aged mother, took their origin from this unhappy night and the preceding day; but this was not the case with Lena, for she had before this felt herself bruised, and began to humble herself mentally ever since that detested day of the seizure of the brandy, which destroyed so many of her delightful brandy and brewing hopes; and especially since, of late, the squire's suspicions of Gunnar had made him less liberal than formerly.

CHAPTER XXXIX.

As soon as morning dawned on the gray and humid October day, Gunnar sprang from his place of rest; threw on his clothes; awoke Abraham, and hastened to the barn, where he thrashed without pause, the whole day, with the strength of many men in one.

Mother Ingrid sat gloomily by her work, and the wheel went heavily and more slowly round than usual.

Lena bustled, as was her wont, in and out of doors, but came, at length, into the room, and said, " Dear mother, be so good as to stir the porridge, that it may be ready for breakfast, while I run and milk our ewe, to make a little beer-posset for Elin, who lies so ill within; for I took all the morning's milk for the cheese."

And with that she sprang out. Mother Ingrid looked after her, and thought that it was like a vernal gale in an autumnal night, to hear Lena so kind and friendly, and that in the midst of her trouble: for Mother Ingrid understood more than well —had long, in silence, observed and known that the prosperous state of affairs at Vika could not arise out of Gunnar's and Lena's diligence and labor altogether, however great that might be, but that Lena *must* have some other source of income which Gunnar was not aware of, and what that was, was not difficult for Mother Ingrid to comprehend.

Mother Ingrid skimmed the pot as desired, and set out the breakfast with all its little accompaniments; and went then to poor Elin, who lay, and was delirious with violent fever; talked of her dead mother, called upon her, and wept bitterly that she did not come; talked of Lena and Gunnar, little Gustaf, the deceased squire, Ma'msell Sara, and her new service; but. all in such confusion, and so fragmentarily, that you could not from all that arrive at her inmost thoughts; for that which properly tortured her soul she did not utter; and it was now a crushing feeling of agony to experience envy and torment in the discovery of Gunnar's devotedness and love for his wife, though she had always prayed to God for that very thing more fervently than for all besides.

"Ah! I am a wretch!" said she in the frenzy of fever; I am not worthy to live and breathe under this roof, with good, virtuous people. I am a monster whom God rejects, and that I became when my mother died, and left me, and no one any longer explained to me the Scriptures, and the word of God, as she and our pastor did. And I, conceited child—I believed that I could explain them myself, both for myself and Abraham, and therefore I am indeed punished."

Thus, and often more obscurely and disconnectedly, did Elin ramble, and distress herself; but felt herself calmed when she received from Lena's hand the little mug of beer-posset, and was able, amid her tears, to kiss and press her hand.

"Now must thou go and compose thyself, dear Elin, and not lie and prate such trash," said Lena, who did not listen much to Elin's discourse, or draw from it the slightest conclusion. And after this Lena went with a sad countenance, but kindly, altogether amazingly kindly, to her many duties and avocations; for such, inconceivably many such, has a country-man's wife, who will and can fill well her post; for it almost always happens that the well or ill doing of a peasant's house depends on the mistress, and far less on the drinking of the husband, on which all the blame is usually thrown; both of the numerous evils that *do* thence come, and of those which do not.

When the evening arrived, after this long, silent, cloudy day, and all ate their supper without Elin, who lay alone on her sick bed, then Abraham betook himself to his nest; but Mother Ingrid, Lena, and Gunnar, sate silent, each in their corner of the room. Deep stillness reigned, and then a quick step was heard coming at a distance.

"It is Bengt," said Gunnar, rising from his seat; "I expected him. He promised it me."

Bengt entered the room.

"Well?" said Gunnar, inquiringly, and without greeting Bengt.

"Good-evening! Fie! it is really frightful to go in the dark night through the black wood," said Bengt, the moment he entered the room, closing the door behind him, and seating himself.

"Well ?" said Gunnar once more.

"Oh, now you may imagine that things go on excellently on the estate," began Bengt. "No one knows what he must do, and what he shall not do ; therefore no one does any thing. All run round one another. Overseer Anders does not mind what the steward says, and the workmen don't care what Overseer Anders says. Every one thinks himself master, and I the same —to the very dog."

"Ay, well, but the other ?" said Gunnar, with a very inquiring tone, but without naming the name that he wished to hear.

"Oh, yes !" said Bengt, "about the corpse. Yes, indeed, that have they been busy with the whole day. The dean and the major at Svanvik, and the constable, of course, and the king's bailiff, have been there since the morning, and the doctor did not come till this evening, for he was away attending a patient when the messenger went for him ; and now they have *obstructed* on him, or how do they call it ? but, for my part, I think they have cut him up, as they would cut up a hog, or a head of cattle."

Mother Ingrid shuddered audibly, and Lena the same.

"Well ?" said Gunnar once more.

"Well, they say that he was as fresh and sound as a nut-kernel, and might have lived for many a Lord's year, and that he is now dead by actual violence ; suffered death from hard blows, or *a* hard blow, but at all events with something hard, of iron, or the like."

Mother Ingrid cast from her dark corner a sad and gloomy look on Gunnar's gun ; Gunnar did the same ; the fire on the hearth blazed up at that moment, and the eyes of the mother and son met in a single glance, but turned away as quickly, and were cast down toward the ground.

"Well, but what says Olle ?" asked Lena.

"Oh, he is arrested, as you well know, and shrieks and laments, and swears and implores, and takes God and the devil, and all the angels and all the fiends, to witness that the squire lay there stone-dead when he came up ; and that he took the pocket-book merely to preserve it for the squire ; and that he never once knew that he had that Satan's window-bolt in his hand, which had loosened itself, and given way as he let himself down from the window; and that he never should have been so stupid as to go himself and tell himself that the squire lay dead, if he had killed him; and much more stupid stuff, which nobody pays any regard to, for Olle has killed the squire, and that is certain. As sure as two and two make four, I will stake my neck upon it, willingly as I would keep it."

"Ah! but never be sure of any thing except what you do yourself," said Gunnar, with a hollow, deep tone, and more to himself than exactly to the rest. "And there," added he in the same tone, "there we have a proof, perhaps, that a liar is always believed to lie, even if he *for once* speak the truth."

"Amen!" said Mother Ingrid, softly.

"Troth!" exclaimed Bengt, "dost thou believe that that imprisoned hangman's man can speak a single word of truth? No, not if it concerned his own soul's salvation; that I will stake my life upon. And so believes every one; and he may say what he will, and do what he may, but his head will go off his shoulders as sure as mine sits there; and that the constable says himself."

"Yes, but he can not be condemned to death, and no witness against him," said Gunnar, positively.

"I fancy thou art mad to-night, Gunnar!" said Bengt. "Is it not evidence enough when every thing witnesses against a man? And if they only get a man to confess, off will go his head as in a dance; and if they can only get a single witness, it will be perhaps struck off yet, say they."

"It is *impossible!*" muttered Gunnar to himself, "and it shall *not happen* either!" But no one heard this, at least no one answered.

"Well, but what says Ma'msell Sara? He has, perhaps, not remembered her in any will or so?" asked Lena, with a trembling voice, and with a faint hope that even she might be remembered.

"Ah, bless me!" answered Bengt, "one can get to know nothing of that yet—that comes when the funeral and all that is over. I heard them talking, by chance, the girls and Magnus, who goes among them, that the major at Svauvik will be guardian for the boys, and that Ma'msell Sara has said that she could never endure to pass the winter alone in that great and desolate place, but that she will go to the city or to Upsala, where the boys are now with the tutor."

Lena asked yet much more, and Bengt answered; but Gunnar sat with his head bowed in his hands, and appeared almost to sleep. At length Bengt took his departure, and all went to rest.

CHAPTER XL.

DARK and gloomy was the time which now followed. The days became ever still shorter, the nights ever longer. All were silent, each from their own motives. Elin, although recovered from her severe fever, through weakness and faintness could not leave her room; and Lena worked like four, and had now no other subject for her occasionally-recurring wrath than poor Abraham, who, at the same time, most luckily for him, cared less and less for this wrath and its eruptions; felt very little Lena's slaps on his handsome, well-fed cheeks, or her lugging n his thick and matted hair. Lena had long ago discovered that she had now no occasion to take that boasted "able maid-servant," but was quite satisfied to keep Elin, while she was allowed to retain her earnest-money, and obtained several other small gratuities from Ma'msell Sara, which caused Elin wholly to renounce any wages from her relatives, so that she could only be with them, and render them all the little service that she could; since in this illness she had cost them much both of care and expense.

Love, in Gunnar's heart, had, as we have said, for a while slumbered, giving way before other and mightier feelings; afterward it again awoke, remained subdued, but ultimately revived actively, and took its ancient place in the young man's heart. He had one night, during Elin's illness, and when she was at the worst, gone into the city, and, by one means or another, had induced the skillful but somewhat slow doctor to accompany him to the sick-bed of the maiden so dear to him. On the way, he had inquired of the doctor much respecting the death of the squire, and of the inspection of the body, and the inferences thence drawn, and with a feeling of horror

did he hear what the doctor many times repeated : " Yes, he
was knocked on the head by Olle, but I will declare on oath
that he did it not with the window-bolt which he had in his
hand, as every body believes, but with something else, which he
afterward cast away." What words for Gunnar !

Gunnar did not go in to see Elin. This he had laid down to
himself as a strict law ; but, on the other hand, he took little
Gustaf with him wherever he went, as far as the weather
would allow, by which it came to pass that the boy clung in-
separably to Gunnar; and the kinder and more affectionate
Gunnar was toward the child, the more friendly, accordant,
and acquiescent was the mother toward him ; and now, for the
first time, did both of those unequal yoke-fellows rightly reflect
on the words of Scripture respecting unity and working together in wedlock, which consists simply in this—that each
does not his own will, but that of his consort; goes not his own
way, but that of his consort.

From all this was spread over the whole of the house a
certain mild tranquillity, a certain peace unknown before.
But in this calm lay, however, a hidden lightning. Each had
within himself a something gnawing like a canker, including
Abraham, but that in him was hunger; for now very often
Lena, with the best will in the world, could not set out a roast
equally rich, food equally good, as formerly, before her family;
and no one remarked this more than Abraham, but simply in
that he attempted to scrape away the very glaze from the
empty dishes, and therefore Lena was obliged to give him his
food on a wooden trencher; and when he by scraping broke
this, she let him make himself another in his leisure hours,
or go without one.

But Elin had undergone a great change. She had been ill,
far more so than she had complained of; for if in the commencement she talked in her delirium, she afterward continued silent under her sufferings. She had seen death close
before her eyes, but behind the grim specter she had seen
heaven open, and God and the angels beckon to her. She
had no longer any fear of death ; on the contrary, she saw in
this her only deliverer from all that oppressed her in life ; and
her yearnings ascended from earth up to that world where
suffering is no longer found—where conscience becomes silent.
During her illness she had cast up her account with the world,
and, relinquishing all its pleasures and advantages, retained

only a certain tranquillity, a certain achieved peace of mind, both hard to win, and easy again to lose. But so Elin did not think. She conceived herself now to be born again; and if her body was pale, and thin, and transparent, she felt her soul and heart to be the same. She had searched her bosom through, in these long, dark, autumn nights, when the bed of rest was converted for her into a bed of sickness. She had examined herself, and sensibly felt the presence of God, who helped and elucidated to her all that lay dark and obscure in her soul and mind. He had purified, and by His Spirit strengthened both. He had spoken loudly and honestly;—sin had spoken the language of a slave. Elin believed herself actually to have heard all this. She knew now most clearly, that she had in her pure thoughts committed a heinous sin in having loved, with a warm, earthly, sinful love, a married man, another's wedded consort, and that her sister's. Nor was this all; she felt within herself that she, in every imaginable manner, had sought to win a return of this love; that she received it with transport (although she had before endeavored never once to confess this to herself), and treasured it as her greatest, her only earthly treasure—as something without which she had thought, in her bewilderment, she could not exist a moment. In her self-accusation she forgot altogether that if these thoughts concealed themselves at the bottom of her soul, yet had every action of hers been in direct opposition to them. Self-abasement forgets such things; and the truly repentant never avail themselves of an advocate. Elin sought not a single one of that kind within the whole storehouse of her thoughts, but let them all arise in the form of accusers, and accusers of herself only. All blame she regarded as on her own side. "I am the wicked spirit which allures them," said she repeatedly to herself; "*him* have I allured to unfaithfulness and criminal love for me; I have angered my sister by it, and awoke hatred and wrath in her; the mother, who saw well through me, I have compelled to feel the pang of grief for her child, and contempt for the criminal stranger. At the same time I have allured the little Gustaf from the heart of his mother, and the poor, wretched Abraham have I, with high-soaring pride, above those who know better than myself, endeavored to illuminate in hope and truth, but obstinately denied him the only thing that I could give, which was love; and with repugnance, scorn, and contempt, threw from me that he would fain have given me.* The memory of my mother have I sometimes feared; and trembled before her spirit which hovered around me (although at other times I often called upon it), but rather have attracted Satan and his followers to me. My old friends and the playfellows of my youth I have altogether abandoned. My teacher, the good pastor, I have not indeed forgotten, but too many of his most excellent instructions; and I am now terrified at the thought of again approaching him, lest he should see down into my heart, as he did when, pure before God and him, I kneeled at the foot of the altar, and received the means of grace which Jesus himself imparts to his children."

So probably would have sounded one of Elin's many self-accusations; and as her frame renewed its strength, her soul also raised itself in vigor and animation, and at the same time in unceasing enthusiasm for amendment, penitence, and renunciation of all earthly good, so that she might but win the heavenly good, grace and reconciliation, a holy death and an immortal resurrection. For this she prayed to God for herself; for this she still more warmly prayed Him for—Gunnar. Was that a sin ?—

Toward the middle of November, health, appetite, and sweet sleep at night, began again to revisit Elin, and after some days she felt herself so strong that she desired again to go among the others. She made the attempt one evening, and when, with weak and sufficiently tottering steps, she approached the sitting-room, and there heard not only the family but also some one else, in fact Bengt, zealously talking with Gunnar, then began her heart to beat violently, and the blood to mount into her cheeks. "That is the effect of illness," thought she; for now, just as little as before, did Elin know herself in the present hour—the ever new, the never foreseen—however she might be able to explain that which was past and gone.

Gunnar, too, grew pale, then red, and felt his heart beat with both joy and pain when Elin entered. In Lena's heart something stirred, but neither loud nor painful; and through Mother Ingrid there ran anew a fear which for some time past had lain and slumbered. The old impulses once more lifted their heads, and wished to become the rulers—would place

---

* Elin forgot that she infused love to God into that vacuum which the soul of Abraham was previously.

themselves in rivalry with the new ones, and measure strength with them; for we are always ruled over by some one or more of such. But so much had the new ones operated, that Lena, who first advanced to meet the enterer, said, with tolerable friendliness,—

"Well, God be praised! at length thou art on thy legs again; so that thou canst come out of thy chamber. It is well indeed that thou canst; for I was sometimes quite persuaded that thou would starve out and die; so bad wert thou."

"Bless me! how thin thou art become, Elin dear!" said Gunnar, who was desirous to say something.

"Ay but, the old one take me, she is just as handsome and fair as ever!" exclaimed Bengt, who at the appearance of Elin fell altogether out of the course of his story.

"Well, Bengt, how goes it with Olle at the assizes?" asked Mother Ingrid, who, like Lena, had often been in the chamber with Elin, and therefore found nothing particular to say on her entrance.

"Ay, bless me! I was at the assizes myself, for I wished to see the trial," said Bengt; "and, do you know, it was horrible! The very hairs would stand on end on your heads to hear him so obstinately and pertinaciously deny. But, see you, he snared himself; for in order to gain belief, he retracted all that he had before confessed, and convicted himself several times, by prevaricating and disagreeing relations. At one time he said, 'the squire only just moved,' when at the very first time he had said, that he saw the squire lie dead; and that he, Olle, had a bloody hand, because his nose bled; and another time he said that Ringberg's wife and all the other witnesses lied; and that it was they themselves that went talking about, before him, that the squire was dead. And the miserable window-bolt which he had in his hand, and which tallies with those up in the tapestried chamber at the hall; *that* he said, at one time, he had found on the way; again, that he picked it up from the bench at Ringberg's, as soon as he came in; and had played with it, and had so forgotten what he was about as to put it in his pocket. By that we can see what faith is to be put in his words. But, do you know, my friends, that sometimes he looked so honest when he protested that he did not kill him, that I quite started, and thought that I stood before the very fiend himself! Yes, I shut my eyes altogether, that I might not be compelled to believe him."

"Did not there come some witnesses on his behalf?" asked Lena.

"Not a single one," replied Bengt, "and therefore he received his sentence at once."

"No!" said Gunnar, and glared with a startled look upwards.

"Yes, and that was to lose his head without any delay," replied Bengt; "and when the doom was read aloud, he both screamed and danced, and was as violent as a madman ; and was so furious that no one, no, really no one, had any pity for him."

All sat in silence.

"He won't die, though!" said Elin, with a strange and highly-excited expression in her speaking countenance, perhaps somewhat thinned by illness, but with eyes beaming with a wonderful fire; with cheeks of the deepest crimson, and with a brow of such ivory whiteness, that her auburn hair, more carelessly dressed than usual, but also more beautiful than usual, falling around, seemed almost black.

"He will not, however, *die!*" she repeated once more, laid her hand on her heart, and advanced into the middle of the room, and spoke, rather to herself than exactly to the rest. "Poor, unhappy child of the world! He lies, then, under the feet of Satan; and no God, no motherly spirit, no illness, no foretaste of all the punishment of sin in a coming life, has opened his hard and fast-closed eyes, and shown him the gates of heaven standing wide open for the remorseful, the repentant, the sincere seeker after amendment, were it at the cost itself of this wretched life; but *this* has still for him so much value, and——"

"She has got the preaching sickness! The cat take me if she has not!" screamed Abraham from his corner; and all the others, who had been equally seized on by that strange astonishment, or what the French call *enchantement*, which a beautiful, unexpected, and inexplicable display of mind always produces, at this starting forward by Elin, so unlooked for, so unlike her, and so impressive—startled still more by Abraham's abrupt outcry—sprang up; and Gunnar's first involuntary movement was—we are ashamed to say it—to strike Abraham in the face, but Bengt rose and mildly warded off the blow. Bengt again, although not in so high degree as Gunnar, taken with the lofty beauty of Elin, in which now lay something heavenly, and by her simple but heart-seizing words, exclaimed instantly—

"Yes, see; that is something different from the nonsense of that Annika from Götheborg! Yes, *such* should preacher-girls be, if they would effect any thing, and not stand like that untutored Annika, and babble about amendment, and amendment, and amendment, and a thousand times of devils and the like, while she herself was so unamended a devil, that she stole a shawl, and that from Nils Pärsa's at Marby, before she went away."

"Ah! I have by no means preached, and *will not*, in the slightest degree, like that Annika," said Elin, with a peculiarly solemn and intellectual dignity, which came from the only pure source out of which such a feeling can ever flow; namely, that sincere and pure sympathy, enthusiasm's wonderful inspiration, which of itself wells up, and, as if it were the very word of God himself, whispers into our ears things that we may appropriate and proclaim.

"I spoke indeed, merely what I thought about this Olle," continued she. "I could never be so presumptuous as to desire to cry amendment to any of you, ye good, virtuous, and God-fearing people, who are so wholly superior to myself, and far better than I, poor sinner as I am. But to him, Olle, I could wish to speak; to him I could wish to represent, how he, with hasty obstinacy, denying his crime, makes it only the greater and more terrible! How he——"

But here Mother Ingrid took up the conversation, who otherwise for many days had not opened her mouth for any other than the most needful questions and answers; and now, with the voice and gesture of a sybil, interrupted Elin, saying—

"And 'judge not, that thou be not judged!' says the Holy Scripture; and how canst *thou* know whether he be so guilty, as all believe? How canst *thou* know whether truth may not for once flow from the liar's lips, and the crime lie concealed with *him* whom no one in the world suspects, but to whom the finger of God points day and night?"

All gazed in astonishment at her. Yet not *all*; for Gunnar rushed out of the room—out into the autumn night, driven by the most conflicting feelings and impressions. Elin's outburst, this revelation, which beforehand he had not dared to think upon, but all the anticipations and contemplations of which he had chased from him by a mighty effort, until the hour in which the very reality stood before him—this now operated upon him only the more powerfully and deeply.

All that a man thinks vividly of, represents to himself, lives over, and makes familiar to himself by his imagination, when it meets him at length, in reality, produces a far less, a far feebler impression. And among us educated and half omniscient people, this is so often the case! Every day, every minute, every object in nature and in art, show examples of it. Where do we find any one among us who is astonished, filled with wonder, thrown off his guard, carried away? We *admire*, but we are no longer surprised at any sublunary thing, and other things we do not see.

We certainly—we for ourselves, at least—should not fall from the clouds in astonishment, if men were immediately to begin to fly; we have so long looked for it, and thought upon it. "What great, what splendid talent!" we exclaim, when the accomplished actor, or the producer of tones bordering on divine enchantment; or the work of the master on canvass, with pencil and colors; or the labor of the chisel on blocks of marble; or the conversion of masses of stone into light, bold forms, columns and arches—beautifully reveal themselves to our minds! We *admire* the great and splendid art, but we are not *imposed on* by it. We do not believe the actor to be the person he represents; we do not suffer and enjoy with him; we are not at any moment ready to spring up and declare ourselves as his champions, if we find the right on his side, or as his destroyers, if we find that he is wrong. We feel no overwhelming impulse to rush over bench and orchestra in order to embrace him, let his art captivate us ever so much. We feel no irresistible propensity to wander among those woods, mountains, and valleys; climb those lofty pinnacles of rocks; sail those clear and billowy waters, bright with moonlight, which we see in the scenes; we merely say, "A matchless piece of decorative painting! A great and admirable illusion!"

We think instantly of the word *illusion*, exactly because it for us is no illusion, but painted wood and painted canvass; just because the word illusion is *found* where the thing is not *found*. But all that which the accomplished do *not*, the child and the uneducated *do*. They *believe*, and *enjoy* immensely in consequence; they are agitated deeply, and with effect never to be forgotten, by art; and yet do not admire it. And if a lovely countenance, a lovely view of a splendid country, suddenly presents itself to us, we exclaim, delighted, yet calmly, or in a tranquil rapture, "What a masterpiece of the Creator, of nature !".

But, ah ! we fall not down in the dust and worship; for in our completely accomplished, and too rich anticipations and preconceptions, we have always sketched something in our imaginations like it; and it is certain, that if the well-planned, well-meant, much thought over and talked about people's schools, people's instruction, reading for the people, in a word, the people's education, ever come into play and bear some fruit, it will be found to consist in a great and essential diminution of foul and hideous crimes; in greater social order founded on knowledge—much morality, much thinking, much speaking, much good, perhaps; but—a great decrease of sentiment, instinct, illusion, and poetry; and through this means, this last will probably vanish from the earth, for it is found in our thoughts only where it is not talked about; for with poetry, as with illusion, where the *word* is found, the *thing* has, in a great measure, already disappeared.

But thus far may it, perhaps, be good. In poetry there lies no actual happiness, in prose no real misfortune, so long as the latter will allow God to be God, and heaven to be heaven, and does not take this for a blue, aerial space, and God for the force of nature. But should prose ever achieve this, then will it be wretched to live on the earth.

For Gunnar, at least, God was still God, and heaven a heaven; for he hastened out into the night, as we have already said, glanced up to that high-arched, star-decorated firmament, which to him was so glorious a heaven, and seemed there to "see God," for he was "pure in heart;" and seemed through the mouth of Elin and of his mother so recently to have heard his own voice; and cast himself down in the dust, and cried to Him, and said, "God and Father in heaven, instruct me what I shall do, and what I shall *not* do."

M

CHAPTER XLI.

With dark and gloomy course autumn hastened on. Short, gray days, and long, coal-black nights alternated; and by night the blind storm raged, and by day men saw that it tore the last yellow leaf from the tree, and even branches and twigs, when it was in its full Berserker autumnal wrath. If it became more calm in the heavy air, then the cloud wept over the malignancy of the storm, and the earth sympathized as little with the grief of the one as the fury of the other, for she was wet, oozy, and repulsive, over all that surface which lately showed so beautiful and green. The brook swelled, and complained of its too narrow banks; the lake drowned its own shores, that they might serve her, in her capriciousness, for a mirror. All nature was in uproar, was an image of dejection and despair; and nothing whispered a hope except the springing rye, nothing of peace and tranquillity. Even men are repulsive in autumn, and have repulsive occupations. All that blood which flows from all the slaughter-benches; all that eagerness to collect and pile up for the winter; all that devastation which is the consequence of it in the fields; all this human contribution to the natural disagreeableness of autumn, especially in houses in the country, where autumn and excessive labor; autumn and annoying objects; autumn and the absence of all tranquillity, all enjoyment, and of every little pleasure; autumn and engrossing cares, are almost always synonymous. We do not now, indeed, speak of the autumn of the higher classes, for these have scarcely any knowledge of the seasons of the year; because in money men find a remedy for every outward evil. But we speak of the autumn of the peasantry and the poor, in which always lies something gloomy and anxious, which spreads itself heavily over the mind, and presses it down, especially if some sorrow, some trouble, exists as a substratum.

Mother Ingrid was become profoundly silent. She spun and was silent; and the great masses of tow on her old wheel were the only witnesses of the tears which, ever and anon, bitter and full of anguish, trickled from her aged eyes. Lena toiled like a horse, and Abraham like an ox. The one sighed, in the midst of those labors, over all her hopes, which had evaporated in smoke, and the, other that the food began to be so scanty, although Elin now more than ever looked glad, and nodded kindly to him, but seldom or never talked with him.

Elin, so soon as she became aware of the demons of the earth —forbidden love, jealousy, indolence, indifference, and want of aim—determined to conquer herself, took faster hold on God's hand, and made for herself a bulwark of his word. The more seducingly the evil powers spoke to her in one ear, the louder seemed the good to shout into the other; and Elin sung day and night God's praises, or expressed them to those about her in beautiful, well-sounding, sweet, and consolatory words, always as she herself understood them. And all about her seemed to have a real need of these her words; even the cold-hearted, hard Lena was thawed by them, and felt herself many times comforted and strengthened, with a fresher relish for labor, and more reliance on the future. And Gunnar toiled like a slave far into the nights; Gunnar, who renounced forever his former sources of comfort, the brandy-bottle and the chase; he, who was pursued incessantly by a dark gray specter of indistinct but wild form; he experienced no longer a single moment of peace or rest, except when Elin read to him some chapter out of the Bible, or when they sung together a psalm, or she poured out of her full heart words of heaven.

Then, but only then, that love for Elin, which raged at the bottom of his heart, changed itself into a soft and heavenly flame. At all other times it continued to corrode his soul, but in these hours all was transformed, and he wished no longer to *live*, but to *die* with Elin.

And Abraham, when he was not too hungry or sleepy, was at times greatly edified by Elin's spirit of devotion, and wept whole tubsful of tears, without knowing why. At the same time he was the only one that continued altogether like himself, and related to every one who would listen, that " Elin, our Elin, had got the preaching sickness, of a most grand and brave sort, for she preached so prodigiously well, and did not twist herself about, and screamed neither against crooked combs, nor places of amusement, nor handsome nor brocaded dresses, nor the like, but only against wicked thoughts in the heart—sins, crimes, and transgressions."

Thus much Abraham had comprehended, and great was the curiosity in the country to hear Elin; but this was not so easy; for if any came who with words of lightness endeavored to call her out, she cut them short with a laconic and negative answer. If any came, however, who said they needed consolation and help from her words, and she, with her penetrating but mild glances, believed she could perceive that they spoke from the heart, she deemed it as her duty to impart to them that which she regarded as inspiration immediately arising from God. In her communications there was so much reliance on God, and so much humility as respected herself, that even they who came merely out of curiosity went away rejoicing that this curiosity had been the visible means of bringing them to the hearing of God's own word, proclaimed by the young maiden, who convinced both young and old.

In the mean time the report flew like a running fire, that Elin at Vika had taken the preaching sickness, but that no one else was affected by it; that she never wandered about; with many more circumstances which distinguished her from the ordinary subjects of this singular epidemic, which was real in some, but counterfeited by so many others, and was persecuted and ridiculed, vindicated and admired—in a word, more stir made about it than it by any means deserved, so that a great and irregular, premature, quickly withered, and altogether useless fruit, had arisen from a small, insignificant seed, in which possibly some good might exist, had it been well grown and well tended.

Many, therefore, made pilgrimages to Vika, of whom numbers, however, were never honored with a word from Elin's mouth, or a glance from her bright blue eyes, though others boasted to have heard a miracle, which excelled all the priests in the world. The first, who offered her a little gift, she repulsed with firm but determined words; and then no one attempted to repeat any such offer. But Lena, who we know was not so scrupulous, began, quite unknown to Elin, to discover a famous meal-tub, if they only knew how rightly to manage and make themselves master of it, in her young sister's lecturing, as she called that elevated enthusiasm with which Elin embraced all heaven in order to make of it a shield for herself against every thing that was earthly. Therefore, instead of repelling those who came, with sneers, and jeering words, as she did the first day, she, on the contrary now invited them in quite kindly; but assured them, at the same time, that though her sister would be most seriously offended if they offered her any kind of gift, be it what it might, or once spoke of such a thing to Gunnar, or any person of the household, yet with equal pleasure would Elin regard any little present made to her, Lena, who both fed and clothed her, in order that in all peace, she might prosecute these devotions for herself and others.

We may perceive in this that Lena did not forsake her own real character, although its features now became very much softened and qualified by all the events which had arisen, and the adversity which she had endured.

In the mean time there took place, if not a great and noisy concourse, yet a numerous resort of people to Vika, which soon attracted the attention of the rector; but as was his constant practice, he *thought* before he *spoke*, prepared his measures, and took his resolve, before he proceeded to action for the prevention or removal of any evil. He therefore collected from many sources, differing in their kind, how these assemblings at Vika passed off; and as he that found there was not the least disorder, he therefore let the matter rest for a considerable time.

But the constable, on the contrary, always zealous out of season, and only too glad to find something to note against the "gathering at Vika," betook himself suddenly there, one Sunday evening, and found several quiet, silent people, who with great devotion listened to Elin, as, lighted by Abraham with a flaming pine-stick, she read, and, in her simple and impressive manner, explained, a few chapters in the Bible.

Mother Ingrid sat sunk down in her corner, with her hands before her face; Lena still, and apparently devotional, away on the side of the bed; Gunnar sat by the window, with his head bowed on his hand, and gazed on Elin and the Bible which was before her, and which in the whole place were the only objects lighted up, as something supernatural and holy, which he could love and worship, and did so, indeed, and that with both spiritual and pure human affection.

Elin had just closed her unpretending explanation of the fourteenth chapter of St. John's Gospel, and taken up the two hundred and ninety-fourth Psalm, and had began to sing it, accompanied by Gunnar, who, with a naturally, pure and clear voice, without any difficulty took up the second part; when in walked the constable. Elin moved her head gently by way of welcome, but did not interrupt the singing. Gunnar, on the contrary, looked him sternly in the face, and continued the Psalm with a still higher voice.

At the beginning, the constable looked blank and confused ; for, first and foremost, the company was wholly silent, kept themselves altogether quiet and taciturn, and seemed not at all to allow themselves to be disturbed in their devotion by this unexpected arrival ; and, in the second place, Elin's beauty and gentleness operated sensibly on the young man, who, in spite of his constableship, which he always carried out somewhat too *con amore*, had, nevertheless, true human feelings in his breast, which were capable of being both attracted and fascinated by beauty, and the glory which surrounds beauty, when God at times selects it as his interpreter.

But this fascination did not continue long, or, to speak more correctly, he chased it speedily and by force away ; and the constable hemmed in embassador style, and then cried in a gruff tone,

" What may this mean ?   What is the object of it ?   Don't you know, good people, that such things are forbidden ?"

" Where stands that written ?" demanded Gunnar, with a defiant tone, but not before he had sung out the Psalm.

" Where does it stand ? That, thou scoundrel, shall thou soon get to know ;" answered the constable, already angered by Gunnar's question.

" Take heed, Mr. Constable," said Gunnar, from the heat of the constable himself becoming cool—" Take heed how you fall upon quiet and serious people, who on a Sunday evening assemble together to lift their hearts to God and pray to him for grace and mercy.   Take heed how you thrust yourself into matters that the rector leaves unconcerned, and which he has far more to do with than the constable."

There are men, who, on occasion, hit just on the word which effects what is needed at the moment ; and where this is not a chance, a lucky occurrence, but almost always takes place, you may, with the greatest reason, style such a person an orator, whether he mounts the speaker's platform before thousands of hearers, or in the half-lighted peasant's hut. Gunnar was in truth an orator, and might, perhaps, have become one of the very greatest, for there are few who know so well as he did how to choose their words and modulate their voices, and who thus never seem to utter a single sentiment which falls a kernelless grain into the earth; but which springs up and produces fruit then and there required.

The constable was dumb and confused : his attendant pulled

him quietly by the coat-skirts behind; and muttering half-aloud that he would take sufficient measures against such disorders, and prohibited assemblages, etc., etc., he took himself off, and the Psalm was again struck up as if nothing at all had occurred.

Where no fanaticism, no heresy, no hypocrisy, no spiritual pride prevails, but where the soul and heart only endeavor to draw near to God, and to listen to his word, rich in solace, there toleration is enthroned by the side of the highest and most perfect devotion, and forgives every thing. All pardoned the constable, both in a short concluding prayer to God for him, as well as for the rest of mankind; said not a word respecting his hasty appearance and retreat; but separated in silence and good-humor, as they came together; and, strengthened in courage, in faith, and in all good, went each to his own home.

But the constable, on the contrary, found it advisable, the day after, to rumble away in his rattling official vehicle to the clergyman, where, no longer under the fascination of Elin's power of enchantment, he related that he, partly on business, partly on duty, found himself at the peasant's hut at Vika, on the Grantorp estate, where were many people assembled, who, among all kinds of superstitious and heretical practices, bawled and sung, and overwhelmed him, the constable, with every sort of abuse when he attempted, *with all moderation*, to represent to them the impropriety of their proceedings.—"And," added the constable, "Gunnar Hakansson, of Vika, had at the same time the great audacity to adduce, reverend sir, your permission for such doings; wherefore I have just hastened hither, to announce the affair, and at the same time to inform you that I know *positively*, that they carry thither cheese and butter, linen cloth, and quantities of wool and the like."

"Good!" answered the worthy priest, who was also a great discerner of character. "Your zeal is laudable if it be not carried to excess; but your account does not agree very well with other accounts that I hear of these matters; for you could by no means suppose that these openings for worship are unknown to me, although the good people may perhaps believe so, or take, indeed, my silence as sanction and permission. I shall know very well, at the proper time, how to deal with the fact, if I find it necessary to put a stop to these assemblings—if, that is to say, I find them in any respect mischievous.

With this answer, and with a somewhat long face, the constable took himself away, and the rector smiled with great commiseration at that unnecessary, that unseemly zeal, one might almost say that zeal pernicious to the country, which often accompanies the most thoroughly unseemly, and nationally injurious indifference. But so it is: *too much* and *too little* are the spirits of evil that most grievously assail us children of men.

CHAPTER XLII.

IN the mean time approached the rector's autumnal circuit for making domiciliary examinations—a very important time in the congregation, where this is not looked upon as an empty demonstration, and merely necessary in a statistical respect, but as an opportunity in which the people's teacher can come to see whether and how his instructions during the year have been comprehended. The rector always regarded it as one of the highest duties of his mission to conduct this examination himself; and went through it with more than ordinary seriousness. All knew this, and there was not a house in which every one, whether higher or lower in the congregation, did not for some days before the examination peep a little into his Catechism, in order to make himself more certain of his knowledge of it, and endeavor to guess the different searching questions which the minister would probably put to him.

On all estates it was the custom on these days, for the servant girls to ask for an extra light, that after the close of their day's work, they might study in " the little book ;" and in every servant's room you heard repeatedly—" Question !—Answer !" Frequently here, as in other places, this got-by-rote reading is read in a manner which makes the phrase of the peasants particularly expressive—that is, " without reading," for reading out —being too probably *without* thought or properly laying it to heart ; but God's word is a thing which must be sown without expecting that *every grain* shall fall into good ground, grow, and bear fruit. It must be sown likewise on the very rocks ; for there even are found fissures filled with suitable earth, and cherished by the warm sun ; and these too must be sown. Many a sigh coming from the heart, many a feeling of remorse, many a resolve of amendment, many holy thoughts, are awakened by this renewed acquaintance with God's precepts; and every one knew that there was no time to delay, if he did not wish to pass with shame, with the displeasure of the both loved and feared pastor, and the mockery of the spectators, from the strict and exact scrutiny which awaited them.

At Vika, there was no one who "peeped into the Catechism" more than Abraham; but he slept many evenings over it, holding a flaming pine-brand in one hand, and the book in the other, till finally, after a mighty gaping, in which the whole of his head seemed to open itself, just as when one opens a huge oyster, he laid the brand in the book for a mark, and in this manner extinguishing it, he himself was extinguished to all consciousness. Lena probably did not know her Catechism from cover to cover, but sombody must stay at home, and this she claimed to do this year. Thus, there were only Mother Ingrid, Gunnar, Elin, and Abraham, who wandered forth, one dull December morning, amid a light fall of snow, to the next village, where the household examination should take place.

"Thou freezest, Elin!" said Gunnar, who saw Elin, on the way, shiver as she went along.

Elin thought of her sins; Gunnar thought of Elin; for he saw her walking beside him, and therefore he was not in a condition to think of sin or error, but merely of her.

"Thou freezest, Elin, dear!" exclaimed he once more, "wilt thou have my coat? I can keep myself perfectly warm with walking."

"Gunnar! Gunnar!" said Mother Ingrid, warningly, "thou wilt get thy death of cold if thou go in thy shirt-sleeves in this bitter weather."

"Oh! well; but what then?" answered Gunnar, "it is mere rubbish living in this world."

"Hush!" muttered Mother Ingrid, half aloud, "I don't know thee again, Gunnar! Thou regardest neither the life of thyself nor of others, and life is still the most beautiful of God's gifts; for how otherwise should we come again to paradise?"

Gunnar started, and looked strangely at his mother.

"In truth and reality do we come to paradise even in this world?" asked Abraham, who seemed to himself to have less paradisaical feelings than ever, his being composed of hunger, after a more than ordinarily watery porridge; of fear that he should not get any thing more till late in the afternoon; of terror of the clergyman's questions of his faith; and of mortification that Elin went along so silently, and shut up within herself, and would neither look at him, talk with him, nor joke with him! However little sensibility he had, he felt that he was despised.

Elin became burning hot at the very thought of being warmed by Gunnar's offered coat; and in a hasty glance at him expressed all her refusal, and all her unmeasured thanks. But immediately afterward she shivered again with utter cold.

"Thou shalt really have my coat: for see, I have my every day jacket under, rather than that thou shalt go and freeze, and tremble, and be sick, and moan, as lately;" said Abraham, who turned and looked at Elin, and observed her shaking as with the ague; and he immediately began to put off his coat.

"No—fie! thanks!" cried Elin, who was horrified at the mere idea of Abraham's coat; "I am not cold at all."

How grateful is love! but how excessively ungrateful is indifference for an evidence of love!

Again all four wandered on with the most strangely different thoughts within themselves. Before long they reached the goal of their journey, and already at a distance could distinguish the house in which the family examination was held. The little porch, notwithstanding the cold and the snowy weather, was as though a swarm of bees was rushing out of it. There were people incessantly going in and out, who stood and talked with each other; greeted, and took leave of each other. For a considerable distance before the door it was swept, and stewed with twigs of pine, and a strong odor of pine-wood blended among other vapors, as they entered the room itself. This was tolerably large, and almost completely full of people, of whom some sate, and others stood, and all in silence. In the middle of the room sat the rector; and the dubious day, which penetrated through the room's only window, fell almost wholly on his expressive countenance, which appeared illuminated with light coming both from without and within. Before him stood a table on which was spread a white cloth, and before the table stood, as our four entered, a tall, slender girl *in her teens*, most squalidly clad, presenting a strong contrast with the rest, who turned out all dressed with marked care and neatness, as for church itself. The girl stood and pulled at the table-cloth with one hand, and held the fingers of the other in her mouth, at the same time that she was much agitated, and was very uncouth in her gestures.

With a soft voice, but clear and audible, the rector put to her a question out of the second chapter of the "Little Catechism," but by his tone you could hear that he was repeating his question, and that he had done it before.

"What does the third article treat of?" asked the pastor once again, but the girl merely trembled more than ever, plucked more eagerly at the cloth, and thrust her fingers farther into her mouth. The rector nodded once more at her, repeating a "well?" and then the girl made an inarticulate noise which was meant for some sort of an answer.

"Take thy hand from thy mouth, and answer so that I can understand thee," said the pastor seriously, but yet kindly.

The girl took her fingers out of her mouth indeed, but answered nothing.

"Gracious heaven! how grievous this is!" said the rector at length aloud. "Is there no one in the village who can look a little after this poor Lotta, since her mother does not do it?"

All were silent.

"Thus it is from year to year," continued the rector, "Lotta is already seventeen years of age, and knows not so much of Christianity as this little eight-years-old child which lately came forward. My time does not permit me to undertake myself her whole instruction, and in vain have I exhorted her to come as often as she can to the parsonage, that I may hear what progress she makes. She never comes, however, but, on the contrary, I hear with sorrow that she is accustomed to stroll about with her mother through the country far and near, little to the credit of either of them. But Lotta is now a great and grown girl, with strength and ability to earn her daily bread, and clothes, neat, if coarse, for her person. Is there no one in the village who would be willing to take her to help, and at the same time be helpful to her?—for, in a word, she is more unhappy and helpless than if she were both fatherless and motherless; for her father is confined for life in the jail, and her mother follows a wandering and disgraceful course.

A deep silence prevailed. Elin had in the mean time recognized the same poor girl to whom she gave the petticoat and neckerchief which Lena took away again. Strange feelings stirred within her. Maiden modesty and the fear of want of power contended with a desire to rescue this girl out of her wretchedness, and if all had continued silent perhaps she would have resisted the craving of her heart; but now an old man stood forward, bowed, and held his hat over his stick against his breast.

"Pardon me, worthy rector," he began, "I know very well that nobody in the village will be willing to take Banka-Lotta into their house, for see! the little they have they would willingly keep; and every one knows well enough what tricks Banka-Lotta has learned from her mother, and the more so since we have been willing to patronize the girl in the village, because she was born here, only getting rid of that Satan's mother, Banka herself. But see! ever since the dreadful great robbery of our bleach-yard last autumn—with permission— why, no one has rightly endured her; but she has gone in and out, and got a bit of bread here, and a bit there, on condition that she should go away and not soon come again."

"Gracious heaven! what a miserable creature!" said the rector, and looked up at the girl, on whose cheeks glistened several tears. These tears fell on the heart of Elin, and weighed down the scale in which lay her boundless and nearly inevitable desire to drag this helpless victim from a certain abyss of crime. All had stared about at her as she entered, and much whispering was heard during the pastor's repeated questions to Banka-Lotta; but now every eye was fixed on her, as firmly and without hesitation, but still deeply coloring, she made herself way through the throng, who willingly stood aside for her. She advanced thus to the table, and gently but distinctly addressed the pastor:—

"I am, it is true, merely a poor maid-servant in my sister's and brother-in-law's house, but I yet venture to put the question whether Lotta could not be with us a little while at Vika. Half of my food she shall have: I will work, and Lena will give her house-room. I will read with her, and give her what she needs of my old clothes."

The miserable Banka-Lotta hastily wiped the tears from her eyes, and cast a beaming look of gratitude at Elin. Elin turned, immediately that she finished speaking, toward Gunnar, in order to read his opinion in his countenance, for she now first thought that she ought to have asked his permission before she had followed her sudden, powerful impulse. Gunnar nodded to her instantly that approval in which a high degree of homage and admiration lies concealed, or rather is—very visible.   Now was Elin glad.

The pastor again measured with his glance the young Elin from head to foot, and called all his coolest reason to his aid to prevent his being dazzled by her extreme beauty, and all his profound knowledge of human nature in addition, to be able to distinguish whether this was a delusive creature, or a being filled with every good, noble, and beautiful feeling, who stood before him.

"Young maiden," said he solemnly, emphatically, and almost sternly, "with thee too, have I much to say; and as thou hast voluntarily stepped forward before me, though it was not thy turn, I will ask thee why thou believest thyself, before others, able to exhort to amendment, and to snatch sinners from their darkness, and conduct them into lighter regions, guided by thy word?"

"Not by *mine*, worthy pastor, but by the Lord's word," answered Elin calmly and clearly.

"Ay, certainly," replied the rector, "but by what right, and on what grounds, dost thou believe thyself called to proclaim the Lord's word? and how dost thou know that thou dost not confound it with thy own earthly, imperfect thoughts, and thus adulterate the word of the Lord, and lead thyself, and those whom thou wouldst improve, into that perdition which is the fruit of self-conceit, of relying and depending on one's own strength and ability in questions of the soul's salvation?"

"I explain God's holy word exactly as I understand it," said Elin, meekly, but without being confused; "I *teach* as I *believe;* and if neither the one nor the other is right, I pray God in his great mercy to pardon me, and regard my good will, and not my feeble power."

"So do I also," replied the rector mildly, and altogether influenced to Elin's advantage by her meekness and her sensible answer; "and I never utter a word without praying God to give it *his* power, *his* Spirit, and to pardon the imperfection and short-coming of my endeavor; but," added he, "I am *called* by my brethren to this office, *called* to declare the *word*, and in my clerical oath I have vowed to devote my whole life, my whole strength, the labors of the day, and the watches of the night to it; in a word, to live for my vocation, and fulfill it to the best of my ability, and—if that were required—to contend to the death for it.   But thou, young maiden! with thee it is very different: thy duties are of a wholly different kind. Thy circle of action is properly so controlled, so altogether confined to thyself or thy nearest connections, that it is a great question whether it may not be termed presumption in thee, when thou thus, self-authorized and uncalled for, steppest forth and reachest out thy hand to thy fellow-men, and promisest to drag them out of perdition, if they follow thy precepts."

" That I have never done," answered Elin, firmly and steadfastly; "and I call upon you all who are here assembled to witness for me, if you are so disposed "—and she glanced clearly and calmly around her—" whether you have so wrongly comprehended my meaning, which has been merely to exhort you to amendment of life, and Christian virtues, love to God and your neighbor, a pure and holy walk, so as at last to obtain a tranquil death and a happy resurrection."

" But how knowest thou, young maiden," inquired the rector, yet once more, " that thou, before others, art able and qualified to make these exhortations? Whence dost thou imagine that thou hast derived thy commission? Think now, well, before thou answerest me, and examine thyself whether self-love, and confidence in thy own perfection, with a consciousness of not having perpetrated such sins as thou daily seest around thee, may not have given thee this reliance on thyself, and have whispered to thee that thou hast a right to stand forward as the teacher of others, and their helper and counsellor in spiritual things.

" Take heed, and reflect seriously before thou deniest all this, that thou do not fall into a great sin, greater than all others, because it may conduct thee into all others, because people seldom observe the evil aspect of the tempter, but merely listen to his syren song."

The rector forgot for a moment that this last word was really a riddle for Elin, but he corrected himself immediately:—

" —That is to say, his fair allurements; for the gulf of self-conceit has no bounds and no bottom, and people do not fall into it suddenly, but are drawn gently and imperceptibly down into it, till the darkness becomes complete, and they are no longer able to discern right from wrong, good from evil, God's will from their own desires."

" O Lord God and Father! may I never come thither!" said Elin audibly; but upon a more direct inquiry of the pastor, " *wherefore* she stood up, and in opposition to the injunction of the Apostle Paul, 'spake in the assembly ?' " she answered, meekly and gently, and almost inaudibly to all save the pastor—

" I have this year suffered much ; much both in body and mind, have sinned and transgressed greatly ; but in my great need I have called on God, and he has heard me, and has sent down to me his Spirit ; has consoled me, soothed my tortures, given me peace, and, as I believed, exhorted me not only to a holy life, but also to benefit my fellow-men by the same revelations that I had myself received."

" Such revelations *all* those receive who with real faith and truth address the Most High," replied the rector ; " such have I many a time, in the night's silent hours, or amid the stir of the world's most moving course, deemed that I saw, heard, and understood ; and it is only in consequence of such that I open my lips and address the people.   And every one of us, who has a real faith, may indeed hear the word of God spoken immediately to himself, and *he*, he only, may be commissioned—wholly forgetting himself—to proclaim this word of the Lord ; but a person must strictly scrutinize himself, whether he really do speak the word of God or his own imaginations, and heavy will be the punishment which will befall the self-deceived, to say nothing of the hypocrite.   And therefore, young maiden, I counsel and exhort thee, but by no means command thee, to desist from thy exertions to convert other sinners—in many cases which might possibly occur, and unknown to thyself, at the cost of thy own salvation.   I pray thee, paternally and sincerely, to confine thy propensity to proclaim and to expound the word of the Lord to thy nearest connections, and merely in the most rare cases to stand forth as a teacher.   That thou wilt take the poor outcast who stands here, and who would only too soon be utterly lost, is a kind act, which no one can disapprove of or dissuade thee from ; but, on the contrary, I will recommend to my parishioners thy good example, and also that they contribute something to lighten thy good deeds, since thou thyself art a servant and dependent on others."

" Nay," said Gunnar, who stood forward quite voluntarily, " nay, she is neither a servant nor a dependent, but a sister in our house—poor and necessitous, God knows, but where she has liberty to do and let alone as she pleases, and where she is free to take Banka-Lotta, if she will."

The rector looked sharply at him, and the quick ardent glances did not escape him which Gunnar from time to time cast on Elin while he spoke.

The business was thus ended with Banka-Lotta, and she withdrew from the table with a glad, squirrel's bound, in which shone forth her wildness and want of such knowledge as is learned among men, and whence comes that decorum which is as necessary in the low dusky farm sitting-room, as in the richly illuminated saloon, if a person will have some respect among his fellows.

Elin stood quietly aside; Lotta pushed herself forward to her, and began to pat her, and to thank her so loudly, that the rector, Elin, and several others cried out at once, "Silence, be still!" and the family examination went forward.

In the meantime the mistress of the house had been out, and fetched an old stool, and wiped it, and took it to Mother Ingrid, and said, "Be so good;" and Mother Ingrid had answered, "Many thanks," and sighing, sat down, but now no longer talkative and affable as formerly, so that those standing round whispered softly among themselves, "Old Mother Ingrid from Asmumdtorp will not live long, for she looks so shockingly ill." Many, both young and old, who wanted to speak with each other, gave one another little signs, and betook themselves to the entrance room, or the porch, and some of them into the kitchen, where the mistress had enough to do with cooking meat and potatoes, boiling cabbage and beef, and roasting a sucking-pig for the rector's dinner.

In her overflowing gladness Lotta also ran thither, and in the same joyous excitement offered to go and fetch in wood, when she heard it was needed; which was remarkable, for Lotta, notwithstanding her strength, was very lazy.

"Ay, thanks!" replied the mistress, "so that nothing hangs by thy fingers in going or coming."

"Will you always think that I am out stealing?" answered Lotta, laughing.

"Yes, ever since the great robbery on the bleach-ground, we trust thee no further than we see thee," retorted the mistress.

"Nay, there I was not concerned," answered Lotta, and accompanied her words with an oath.

"Fie, girl! how canst thou stand there and perjure thyself, and that with an additional lie, and even at the family examination itself, and when people have had such compassion on thee in thy wretchedness!" said the mistress of the house, who was a sensible, discreet, and tolerably well-to-do juryman's wife, who was highly respected in her village, as well as her old husband.

"Nay, it was neither I nor my mother who stole your linen here the last time, that will I stand to the death," answered the girl; and laughing, sprang away after the faggots, actually speculating on getting, or being able to appropriate to herself, a morsel of the entertainment which was so plentifully preparing in the mistress's kitchen, though not exactly according to the rules of either Mademoiselle Nylander or Mrs. Schartaus.

In the mean time the turn had come to Gunnar of Vika. He was called, and stood forward, speaking for himself and his household, that is to say, of all the persons who were in his employ. These were now not a few; for at Anderson's farm he had also persons in his employ; and the rector said, looking sharply at Gunnar—

"Thou strikest far around thee, dear Gunnar, God prospers every thing with thee, and goes hand in hand with thee."

"Oh yes, he does!" answered Gunnar, with that look of indifference and melancholy with which he regarded the whole concourse, Elin excepted.

The pastor remarked it particularly; and after some few questions out of the Catechism, which Gunnar instantly and sonorously answered, he put some queries to him, fixing at the same time his keen glance on the young man, who stood there so tall, so gloomy, and dark of countenance, so absent from almost all that surrounded him.

"What dost thou consider as the greatest sin?" demanded the pastor, and cast a simultaneous passing glance at Elin. Elin blushed deeply. Gunnar's look also followed that of the rector; he, too, saw Elin blush, and a rapidly flitting glow seemed for half a second to light up his pale countenance; but he turned quickly again to the pastor, reassumed his whole stamp of gloomy dejection, and answered, with a hollow voice, and without the addition of a single word—

"Murder!"

"And if murder were only a sin, what dost thou call the greatest crime?" inquired the pastor, astonished and mistaken in his expectation of Gunnar's answer.

"Having committed a murder, and keeping silence so that another shall suffer for it."

The pastor paused a moment, and then asked further—

" And the highest of human virtues ; what dost thou imagine that ?"

" To avoid and abjure that which we hold most dear, if it be an unlawful love; to love our bitterest enemy ; and to give oneself up for a great crime which no mortal suspects one 'of," answered Gunnar, without any reflective effort, as if the answer had lain long, well-considered, and ready, in his soul.

The rector gazed at him, still more astonished ; fell for a moment into deep thought ; did not trouble himself, according to his wont, to go over his usual queries, and the answers he was accustomed to get ; but merely nodded to Gunnar, in token that he might retire from the table and leave room for Mother Ingrid, from whom was heard distinctly a deep sigh on Gunnar's last answer, to which she listened attentively, although it was uttered in a half voice.

" God's peace be with you, aged and worthy Mother Ingrid !" said the pastor as she approached. " You look in a suffering and declining state. How has it been with your health now for some time ?"

" God preserve the good rector !" answered the old woman ; " and thanks to him for asking after such a poor old creature as I am, and after my health. Well, I know just nothing about my body, therefore my health is very well, as we may say, though I wither away, heavy of hearing, and of——"

" And what ?" asked the pastor, gently and sympathizingly.

A solitary tear rolled down the furrows of her aged countenance, and the pastor inquired no further, but nodded kindly to her to withdraw, saying—

" A Christian, so good as Mother Ingrid has always been from her very soul, I need not, certainly, examine in the Catechism; for, if she should have forgotten the words, yet the spiritual meaning of God's truth lies all clear and bright before her, and will to her last hour; of that I am confident, who have known her so long."

Mother Ingrid was still human, and a beam of mortal joy, a little spark of mortal pride, lit up, for a brief moment, the deeply down-trodden soul of the old dame, over which regret at having, in some degree, lent her persuasion to the balance of fate which determined Gunnar's future, still lay heavily.

Elin once more came forward.

" To interrogate thee in the Catechism is quite unnecessary,"

said the rector, smiling, " for truly thou knowest it, at least, as
well as myself; but, on the contrary, I will ask thee if, now
that thou hast thought on the matter, thou wilt promise me what
I awhile ago requested of thee; for I have seen plainly that
thou hast been sunk in thought, and hast not gossiped and
talked like so many others."

At these words there was a silence, as of the grave in the
room.

" Yes," answered Elin, " I have well considered your words,
worthy father, and thank you for having awakened me to the
conviction that so great a sinner as I am can not be worthy to
explain the word to my equals, but only to such an one as
Banka-Lotta, whom none trouble themselves about; and hereafter, therefore, I shall refrain from it."

" Right, my good girl," said the worthy priest, who, both as
a man and a man of God, was desirous to retain his right alone
to conduct his flock to heaven ; but with tenderness and gentleness, not with rigor and hard language.

" Thou hast acted in this matter, I would believe," added
the rector, " according to God's own will; for it his pleasure
that every one shall exert his own power of mind, as far as it
is possible, for himself, in order to understand his word ; and
where this still continues dark, then to consult his elected
minister, if he have not, in some manner or other, shown himself unworthy of this confidence, which I hope is not the case
here."

" No, God forbid !" " No, certainly not !" " No, far from it !"
and so on, resounded both in high and low tones among the
throng of people.

" Good," continued the pastor; " and all those who of pure
devotion and desire of edification went to Vika, let them, each
in his own house, bring out the Holy Scriptures, and read them
in the manner I have mentioned ; for none of you are so poor
as not, with some sacrifice, to be able to procure himself a copy
of this necessary volume, which I will willingly lend to any
person who wants it, till he can save the means to purchase one
for himself; and then he will either not trouble himself about
the meeting at Vika, or he will be benefited by it ;—or how, my
children ?"

" Ay, that is certainly true !" " That is certainly right !"
" Nobody can deny that !" was heard murmured forth in the
room.

Elin courtesied low, and stood aside, leaving room for Abraham, who was now to be taken in hand, and who came forward awkwardly, as he did every thing, made his bow, but so ill-calculated, that he came right against the table, and, at the same time, knocked down a boy with his Sunday cap, which he stretched out behind him as he made his low bows, so that another boy was obliged to shove him, and say, "Don't push me!" By all this, Abraham became much confused, and said, "Thank you for asking!" when the pastor inquired from him whether he had forgotten his Catechism since last summer; and as the pastor again put the question, he answered :—

"Yes, sure, every single word; but Elin has taught me, and driven it into me over again, and so I know it again, let it be as long as it will."

The rector turned the leaves in the little book, and then asked—

"Out of what did God, in the beginning, create all things?"*

Abraham clasped his hands devotionally together, but still let his thumbs waltz round each other, and answered, after a short reflection—

"Heaven and earth, and all that is therein, both visible and invisible."

"Thou canst not have heard what I asked," said the pastor, "since thou answeredst so;" and he again repeated the question to Abraham.

"Silence! Let me see!" said he. "It was not so altogether stupid what I said, though; for it is only the *next* answer, it is no farther off."

"Yes," answered the pastor, not without a little smile, "thy answer is the answer to the next question, namely, 'What did God create?' but I asked thee, *out of what*, God, in the beginning, created all things?"

"Yes, bless me in all days. What in the world were they made out of now!" said Abraham, and stared at the ceiling. "It was something clever, so much I do remember; but what the cat could it be for a kind of thing? Dost thou know, Elin?" he called out, and turned round toward her; "knowest thou? I fancy thou never told me what stuff our Lord made the whole world out of?"

"Mercy! how thou talkest!" said Elin, almost inaudibly,

* The 140th question in Svibelius's explanation of Martin Luther's Little Catechism.

much confused, and gently shaking her little head, and imperceptibly shrugging her shoulders, in pardonable vexation at Abraham's stupidity and foolhardiness in wishing to throw his ignorance upon her.

Gunnar stood so that he could scarcely see Elin, but he felt her perplexity; and as he, on the contrary, stood near Abraham, he whispered in his ear, "Of *nothing* did God create the world."

"What?" asked Abraham, the first time; "What say you?" answered he, the second time, when Gunnar repeated his words; and, finally, the third time—"What do you say?" Then Gunnar lost patience, and said lowly, but audibly enough—

"Thou ass! It was really of *nothing* that God in the beginning——"

But Abraham did not give himself time to hear out the sentence, but bawled out, quite delighted—

"Ay, bless me! in all days! That is true. Now I remember it myself! Of *an ass* created he the whole world; now I remember it exactly!"

The rector stroked his chin with badly assumed seriousness; Elin gave a little cry of agony; Gunnar drew the corners of his mouth into a faint smile, the first which had lit up his countenance for a long time; but in the room there was a suppressed murmur, and some boys rushed out of the door, banging it loudly after them, and there was heard a clear and hearty burst of laughter without. Abraham, however, stood satisfied with his answer, and by no means suspected that he was the object of any laughter, or observation, but went on waltzing with his thumbs as before, and awaiting a fresh question.

"Silence there!" said the pastor, and all again became still and calm as a grave. "It is sorrowful," continued he, turning to Abraham, "that since last summer thou hast forgotten thy Catechism. If I had been aware that thy Christianity sate so loose, I most certainly should not have let thee go forward to the Lord's table, my dear Abraham."

"Do you really mean so?" asked Abraham simply, but without much embarrassment, a feeling which seldom troubled him.

"Yes," continued the pastor, with great seriousness, "for he must think and know very little indeed, who can answer that God created the world out of an ass, and——"

But here Abraham interrupted the remarks, exclaiming—

"Bless me! before every thing! Was it not of an ass, then?"

But here Gunnar stepped forward, and said, half aloud—

" Worthy rector !   I know that it is both assuming and bold, and unbefitting to step forward on a public occasion, but as this poor Abraham is in my employ, I beg humbly to say, that we, Elin and myself" (as Gunnar uttered these words, ' Elin and myself,' his lips quivered visibly, and a flush went over his otherwise so pure forehead, which did not escape the pastor), " that we endeavored most to explain to him *God's law*, and the *Lord's Prayer*, that he might thus get into his head his duties toward God and man; but as he is of so weak an understanding (this he said in a half-whisper to the pastor), we did not trouble ourselves so much with ' creations,' and the like, which he never would have been able to comprehend, but we were glad that he merely knew it by heart.   It is equally certain that Elin has told him twenty times that God created the world out of nothing, but she has not repeated it a hundred times, and that it would have required."   And with this Gunnar bowed and stepped aside.

" Ay, bless me in all days !" exclaimed Abraham joyfully. " *Now* there breaks a light entirely upon me—that our Lord created the world out of nothing at all ; and I remember that I have pondered amazingly on how he could manage it."

The pastor now explained the whole regularly to him, in the simplest manner that he could ; and Abraham answered many times, " Ay, to be sure ! Now I understand it.   Now I perceive it so famously that I could almost do it after him myself ?"

The pastor now found, himself, that it was not worth while to explain any miracles to Abraham, but instead of this put some queries to him regarding his duties toward God and man ; and here, Abraham, to universal amazement, answered correctly and rationally, and in a tone which evinced that he tolerably well understood of what the subject treated, and did not merely babble his answer by rote.   The pastor concluded his examination of Abraham with a little advice to him to seek to acquire more knowledge in such things as were not clear to him.

" Yes, certainly," answered Abraham, bowing, and scraping with both feet ; " if I and the rector live another year from this day, he shall see that I both know *who* created the world, and how he managed it, and all about it ; for now, as Banka-Lotta will read before Elin, so I shall——"

" Good, good !" interrupted the pastor ; " I understand thy good intention, and approve it, and wish that thou mayst be able

to keep thy word. And now farewell to thee," added the rector, who was glad to put an end to his examination of Abraham,
which, however discreetly people managed to conduct themselves, was rather too much of the comic order.

———•———

CHAPTER XLIII.

WHEN now Abraham had passed his examination, our four
were ready to depart, and with the permission of the rector, in
consideration of the distance, they set out at once. The pastor
gazed anxiously after them, and though he seemed to be occupied with a fresh examination, he had in his large soul yet room
for many thoughts concerning this four, and in his still larger
heart a deep and sincere sigh for them; for he, the much-seeing,
and more-knowing, he saw that here was great pain, many sufferings and griefs collected. He saw too well, that the whole
of Gunnar's being belonged to Elin, and that he in vain endeavored to combat with this powerful feeling. He saw that
Elin, contrary to her will and her determination, partook of this
passionate slavery. He saw that love for a woman was the only
thing which had power to lift, in some degree, the thick vail
which was drawn around the poor youth Abraham's slender
understanding, and pour upon it a feeble ray of light. He saw
in the aged mother's deeply furrowed countenance still more
grief than years, and traces of fresh sorrow, independent of the
old, already thrown up. He saw much more yet; for he saw
and felt that there was the odor of the burning of a crime, but
he could not discern what or how it might be.

How well is it when such a penetrating mind sometimes belongs to a perfectly good being, who does not survey through a
dark glass, men, and their thoughts and actions! Before the
mind of the pastor hovered an incomplete and fragmentary idea
of forbidden love, murder—child-murder—remorse, and torture
of conscience, with a religious fanaticism growing out of it; but
ne immediately cast away this idea as by no means agreeing
with the angelic purity and fullness of innocence in the appearance and in the brow of Elin, and which breathed in her reply
to his exhortation. He cast, therefore, these thoughts instantly

from him, as unworthy of himself and injurious to the innocent; he cast them away, as we cast away what we regard 'as that dark and demoniac inspiration by which the most clearly thinking man is often tempted, but he resolved, at the same time, to have his eye fixed steadily on the peasant family at Vika.

When our four, silently, and each shut up within himself, came out into the yard, and began to steer their course homeward, Banka-Lotta came running and hopping, like the squirrel, with which we have already compared her, and said eagerly, " I shall go with you !" Elin stopped, and appeared doubtful. The rest stopped too.

"Ought we not first," said Elin, and looked alternately at Gunnar, at Mother Ingrid, yes, even at Abraham, " ought we not to prepare Lena, and ask her leave, before we take Banka-Lotta home with us ?   Perhaps she will be altogether opposed to it, and then——"

But here Gunnar interposed, saying—

" Have I not promised that Banka-Lotta shall, for the present, be there with us at Vika, and is not that enough ?"

Gunnar was jealous of his household authority, as every fine fellow is; and Gunnar, just as little as many another of these, did not reflect always where the boundary of household authority properly terminates, when no affection, no union of nature exists to decide it.

" Gunnar may probably have right on his side," said Mother Ingrid, " but Elin is right, too; and if I may advise, Lotta should remain a little behind us, and Elin undertake to prepare her sister to receive yet another *eater;* for it is she who must prepare for us all our daily food, though it is Gunnar who must provide her means necessary for it."

" Ah, yes, that is true," replied Gunnar, who was ready to make concessions to those he loved, and was desirous to have as much peace as possible about him, since he experienced so much strife within himself.

With a wild, thoughtless, and unconcealed joy, Lotta sprang on, now before, now behind them; but when they approached Vika, Elin said to her that she must wait there till she, Elin, came back.

" Ay, but if you never do come ?" said Lotta, anxiously.

" I have already said that I shall come," replied Elin.

" Yes, but if you don't say true ? how will it go with me, though ?"

"Elin lie!" exclaimed Abraham, "Elin *never* lies! Sooner could God the Father speak falsely."

"Fie, Abraham!" said Elin, with a shrug of the shoulders: "such thoughts and irreverent expressions are wicked, and to me very repugnant! God knows how such foul thoughts can occur to good men; and good thou still art, dear Abraham, although it went badly with thee in the Catechism."

"Yes, see! I became quite confounded by the number of people," answered Abraham.

"Oh, I can not say that," observed Guunar, with a faint smile; "it struck me that thou didst not allow the people to daunt thee, or prevent thee prating and going on."

"Nay, only repeating by rote!" said Abraham; and now they were at the door of the house.

Elin hesitated a little before she stepped in. It was as if she perceived the approach of a storm: Gunnar foreboded it, and love never shrinks when it is needed to remove an obstacle out of the way, were it merely the leaf of a wild rose which should lie as an impediment before the feet of the beloved.

"Let me go in to Lena, and tell her what has been done," said Gunnar, resolutely, and went in without awaiting an answer: Mother Ingrid, Elin, and Abraham remained without.

After a minute Gunnar came back, and said—"Why should mother stay out here and freeze? Look thou after thy Lotta, Elin, dear; and thou Abraham, put off thy holiday clothes, and hang them up in good order, and get some food, and go to thy work; I will follow thee immediately."

"Ah, well," said Lena when the rest entered, "if only that Banka-Lotta don't steal the eyes out of our heads, and eat up both food and dish, and all that we besides should have, she will get her turn; and if she only work diligently; for she is strong as a horse—that is plain enough."

Now came Elin with Lotta, who was both frightened and starved through, and after a long, sharp introductory moral pancake from Lena, in which salt and pepper were the chief ingredients, and in which the questions abounded pre-eminently about laziness and insubordination, and long fingers, and pilfering, and voracity, and sluttishness, and vermin, and wicked parentage, and thieves, beggar-hordes, and running about the country, etc., etc., etc.; for Lena was at least by no means sparing in her expressions toward the new comer—she took Lotta with her into the cow-house, in order there immediately

N

to introduce her to all sorts of agreeable and disagreeable jobs, and to teach her the proper way of doing them.

Mother Ingrid and Elin in the mean time laid their heads together to contrive a bed for Lotta in Elin's chamber; and this was effected by means of an old sack, which Mother Ingrid had up among her things, and certain articles which Elin was able to furnish.

This did not accord altogether with Lena's plan, which was both night and day to have Lotta under her eyes, both for help and advantage; but when she came to learn that a little contribution for the assistance of those who took Lotta and taught her to read, was to be received from the parishioners, she allowed herself to make even this concession.   Lena was much altered, at the same time that she continued much like herself.

The very same afternoon, Elin began the governesship with Lotta, which in the first place consisted of a vigorous cleansing in the kitchen, the most thorough fine-combing, and the stripping off of all those wretched, filthy rags which made up the entire dress of Lotta.   Elin had looked out old clothes, and Mother Ingrid had even made a contribution to them; yes, Lena herself, smitten with compassion and good will, gave her, as she herself expressed it, "a right handsome and *superior* chemise."   And now Lotta's education began.   Abraham lighted them, and Lotta read, and most dreadful up-hill work it was; but Elin had the patience of an angel.

"It is very well that Elin is such a clever reading-priest, and that Abraham, who is properly good for nothing else, can prepare pine-splinters for their sittings, and light them with them," said Lena, laughing, one evening during the teaching; but the pupil did not take any notice, but went on spelling out her words in good earnest.

"Shall we have this going on every mortal evening?" asked Lena at length.

"No, heaven forbid!" replied Elin.   "I only wished to see how Lotta would succeed, and in future we shall go on by ourselves in my chamber."

"How she would succeed?   Ha, ha, ha!" laughed out Lena. "Thou meanest how she *never will!* for I take it she is just as fit to learn as little Gustaf there."

Lotta looked down, and felt herself struck and wounded. Before, she had never concerned herself about any expressions of contempt; but now she was among good people, who, with a certain good-will, had received her, and already *shame* had awakened at being so much worse than they, and an ambition to elevate herself to them. And yet people will assert that neither good nor evil example will operate. Ask the walls of our prisons, and bid them answer—they know this, best of all.

At night, when they were about to go to rest, Lotta was astonished that any one had thought of giving her a bed to herself. She was used to sleep in a corner, upon a hard bench, or upon the ground itself; and when she was in haste to take possession of her new couch, Elin asked her whether she had thanked God for his goodness, that through his command men thought of her. Lotta stood in perplexity. She did not know how to thank God; she knew only how to blaspheme and dishonor him. Elin burst into tears over this dreadful ignorance; and these tears of Elin were the first life-giving, quickening, softening dew which fell upon a mind hardened in crime and depravity. Lotta also began to weep, and for the first time, except now and then a solitary tear, or when she had wept from cold, hunger, or vexation. Her heart awoke, and Elin asked from her a little description of her former life.

"Ah, no! May I not pass that over? That is very unpleasant to talk of," answered Lotta; and Elin asked her no further.

CHAPTER XLIV.

Thus passed the few weeks which were wanting to Christmas; and when it came, all seemed to stand, as it appeared, pretty much in the same position, yet time leaves nothing really unchanged, and even where its operation can least be discerned, its strength has still been great, although not always upon the surface. Moreover, we are constantly conducted nearer and nearer to the revolutions which *will* take place, in great and in little things, in all sublunary affairs. And the nearer we approach to the great wheel which rolls along the path of business, the more we perceive the commotion in the air, the more disturbed we become in ourselves, especially if we are gifted with a mind of that quality to grasp that which is invisible, and by so many others unobserved.

Gunnar was gloomier than ever. He toiled, indeed, like a slave, but all the beautiful and delightful of the poetry of life was for him extinguished, and that is in truth the noblest light which illumines our youth, irradiates our prime, and gives a little gleam of brightness to the cloudy and dark abysses of our age ; the only thing which gives a charm to our earthly life from its beginning to its end. But for Gunnar this sunny day of poetry was closed, and the melancholy moonshine was the sole light which, now and then, broke on his chaotic, anxious, and menacing scenes. His gun, formerly, so dear to him, was hung up in the garret. The dear, old, and merry violin, little Gustaf had long ago knocked into a thousand pieces, and without receiving a word of reproof from Gunnar on that account. Never was now heard a glad or powerful snatch of a song from Gunnar's lips.

"How will it be with the Christmas dance which master promised to play for us last summer, when we were making hay ?" asked Abraham once, as he saw Lena sweeping up pieces of this violin, which was formerly so cherished, and which occasioned such a great rivalry between Gunnar and Olle in the past glad times.

Gunnar made no reply to this, except by a faint and melancholy smile ; but it stood written on his curved upper lip, for those who could perceive the reflection of the soul in the countenance, " I shall never play again, and never will any one dance to my music !"

During these weeks Lotta had made a palpable advance and retrogression at the same time. Elin had pursued her improvement with the same zeal with which she before expounded the sacred writings to her friends. It was absolutely necessary for Elin to have some great, some important object to put in the place of her unbounded love for Gunnar, which lived in a thousand-fold life in the bottom of her heart, and which incessantly lifted up its head in order to become once more regnant.

At the same time Lotta had a notion of what diligence and hard work meant ; for Lena had an especial faculty for imparting this knowledge. Lotta had, in consequence, been on the point of running away at one time, but had in the greatest kindness, been detained by Elin, yet with the assurance that it must *never* occur again ; for if she ran off, she might stay for-over where she went to. Moreover, she had purloined, and doggedly denied her theft; had thrown the blame on little Gustaf, but finally confessed the deed; had stolen again, but immediately acknowledged the fact with tears, and finally omitted stealing, even when she had opportunity for it, which, so far as concerned Lotta, was a great matter. She had, moreover, in her rude soul, in her bewildered heart, and her yet unawakened faith, conceived the idea of a God, his omnipotence and goodness. It is true, that in her imagination, Elin stood by the side of this Godhead; and it is most frequently the case, when ideas of the Most High are not received in the first gentle years of childhood, that the teacher himself, and in spite of himself, becomes placed between the late believer and God. It is only in the mind of the child that the pure image of God can arise; the more that time and experience harden the mind, the more superficial will be a new conception of this kind; and, perhaps, the consequences of this truth, if it be one, have been greater, and more incalculable, than we can hastily imagine, or than we shall here attempt to describe.

Lotta, in the meantime, had spoken with God through Elin; had learned to call upon and pray to him—to pray to him for herself, for her wretched mother, who was hardened in error and crime; for her father, who languished in chains, the punishment of his offenses. She had learned to thank God for the help he had sent her; she had wept tears of remorse, tears of gratitude, tears of joy; and these tears had still more contributed to soften and awaken her close-pent heart. But in many things she was still very much herself. The leopard never entirely loses his spots.

For the first time in her life Lotta now saw, in an orderly house, preparations for the Christmas festival, and for the first time also knew *wherefore* it was as zealously celebrated in the palace as in the hut. She rejoiced in this approaching season like a child, for her happy hours were perfectly those of the child. She leaped high for joy when she saw Lena, on a small scale of course, begin every thing which is undertaken in a great and rich house in preparation for Christmas; namely, baking, brewing, slaughtering, dipping candles, and scouring and polishing even into the most minute corners. When Lena dipped a little taper for little Gustaf, such as she had seen in the many wealthy families where she had lived, Lotta danced for delight; and when the swelling loaves, washed over with shining wort, marched majestically out of the oven, then Lotta both sung and danced. Now, that she had her daily and regular meals, she was not by any means so voracious as formerly, eating but little, and that with propriety, to the great joy of Lena, who had feared that she would prove a match for Abraham at the trencher. From the material which kind individuals of the congregation had contributed, Elin had prepared neat and suitable clothes for her, which, however, she was not to put on before the Christmas-eve itself, a circumstance which gave still more glory to Christmas, seen in perspective by Lotta. Christmas-eve fell this year on a Sunday, and the day before, on Saturday, she helped Lena to scour the kitchen, the sitting-room, and the entrance, while Elin alone scoured her chamber, notwithstanding Lotta offered to help her. The expectation of Christmas, of Christmas fare, and Christmas festivities, gave the strength of many horses to labor with. In the farm-yard she had done wonders of work, admired even of Lena herself, and received commendation from all; therefore when evening came, she laid herself down to rest with great satisfaction, and in the happiest state of mind which a human being can well arrive at. Her sleep was excellent; and when she awoke in the morning, and Elin gave her permission to put on her new clothes, and, thus arrayed, to come into the sitting room, she was several inches taller, with actual joy and pride. All expressed their pleasure, and Lena did not once begrudge her delight, since she had worked so bravely.

Gunnar only went to church. Abraham and Lotta helped to set up those unthrashed sheaves of corn which even the poorest in the country villages offer to the little birds at Christmas. Lena stood by her stew-pan, Mother Ingrid sat by the fire and stirred the porridge, with a psalm-book on her knee, and spectacles on nose. Elin had shut herself in her room and locked the door, to the great wonder of little Gustaf, who thumped at it in vain. Every where the house was scattered with pine-tree twigs, dressed and decorated, but there was no Christmas straw scattered, for that was now almost entirely laid aside, except in old, well-to-do farmhouses, where the primitive custom descends from father to son; and even there the Christmas straw is less and less in use, because it is considered " old-fashioned," a word and an idea, which unfortunately begins to be more and more " new-fashioned " among the peasantry.

This year they had real Christmas weather, for the ground

was strongly frozen under foot—all the trees stood splendidly arrayed in hoar-frost, as if adorned for the festival ; on Christmas eve, about noon, it began to snow heartily, heavily, and calmly, and to the excessive joy of Lotta, who was promised a ride in the sledge to morning service on Christmas day, if the sledging became good before that time.

"Snow more, more, dear, blessed heaven!" she cried, and nodded to the heavy snow-cloud; and Abraham laughed at every thing that she said and did.

On this forenoon the poor wandered forth with their beggar's satchels on their backs, and Lena sent them off immediately, and without much ceremony, but still gave them a piece of bread, and some of them a little bit of pudding; and Mother Ingrid made Lotta observe how thankful and glad she ought to be to escape going, like these, to every man's door this evening; and Lotta sighed, but whether it were from thankfulness, or from pure joy, that was not so easy to ascertain.

When Gunnar came home at noon, he told them that it was already good sledging on the church-road ; and Lotta then took a waltz with Abraham, in which she exerted all her seventeen years' strength of arm, so that poor Abraham's head spun round, and he reeled away into a corner, where Lotta suddenly and unexpectedly let go of him, to the great and lively enjoyment of the little Gustaf. This behavior of Lotta's had again awoke a degree of life among the inhabitants of Vika. She often uttered that good, hearty laughter, which is a consequence of all genuine, natural, and not affected *naïveté ;* something which we know how to value every where, in the lowliest hut as well as under the glitter of the crystal crown ; but which unhappily, and nevertheless, may often be of a wholly false kind, without any real worth, spite of its joyous and lively golden chime.

The brow of Gunnar itself looked a hair's-breadth more cheerful to-day; and when they, after the return from church, sate at their dinner, which on this day, according to a general custom among the country people, consisted of rye bread dipped into the stew-pan, he related various things which had occured at church, and among others, that he had asked Bengt to come and eat Christmas porridge at Vika; "For," added he, "both the lads and lasses at the hall are on board wages, now that Ma'msell Sara, to the grief of all, is gone to the city."

The afternoon was not long, for the snow fell thicker and

thicker, and therefore darkened the air. In the twilight, Elin
sat and related in beautiful,Oriental, Bible language to Abraham,
Lotta, and little Gustaf, the birth of the child Jesus on Christmas-eve, the joy of the shepherds, and the songs of promise
of the angels in the air; and the different observations and
questions of her hearers she replied to willingly and with pleasure, but adapted the answers to the capacity of every one.
All Elin's soul lay in the lively, luminous, and clear words;
and a deep sigh was heard from the corner where the old dame
sat bowed down, in silence running over in her mind how many
glad, sorrowful, and solitary Christmas-eves she had known. It
stood at this solemn and sacred moment so vividly before her
clear natural vision, how happy Gunnar would have been had
he had such a wife as Elin, and how many pains and griefs
they would have avoided which now every one had endured; for Mother Ingrid saw well how much Elin also had
suffered.

When evening came, a noble fire already crackled in the
newly whitewashed fireplace; and just as Lena had lit a tolerably thick Christmas candle, and placed it upon the table in a
brass candlestick scoured to a high polish, the door opened, and
Gunnar, who had gone a little way to meet Bengt, came in with
him, and both were requested, in tolerably friendly terms, to shake
all the snow from them before entering the sitting-room decorated
for Christmas. This reasonable request was complied with by
both of them most willingly; and immediately Lena, assisted by
Mother Ingrid, Elin, and Lotta, began to spread the table, and set
out the Christmas repast, which was abundant enough, and consisted of cured fish with its sauce, thick boiled groats, butter
and cheese, a large dish up-heaped with meat, bacon, and pudding, followed by a pancake with honey upon it. Elin stole
away, and came quickly back with a little Christmas tree, which
Abraham had helped her to make a basis for, and which she had
hung with all kinds of small ornaments, some real, some merely
for show, and on the highest top of which a circle of lights was
kindled. All this was naturally transporting to Gustaf, but
Lotta enjoyed it equally, and the rest rejoiced in their joy, and
Elin was happy in the delight that her little undertaking had
given rise to.

Ah! if all did but know at what a small cost we can make
every one happy around us, and what a sincere satisfaction this
produces, they would chase far from them that one-eyed ego-

tism, which is never able to see more than itself, and thus seldom to satisfy this only dissatisfied object.

Bengt and Gunnar in the mean time conversed together.

"Yes, as I told thee in the forenoon," Bengt said, "he is very likely to get off in the end, since no proof or eye-witness can be found, and he swears so positively that he lay dead when he came to him; and as he now wholly returns to his first statement, and will not vary a word from it, since the rector has conversed with him, and seems to have gained a power over his conscience, though he can not get him to make a downright confession.

Mother Ingrid was all eye and ear; for during this relation she watched keenly and incessantly the brightening expression of Gunnar's forehead, and drew herself a gentle sigh out of her deep and oppressed heart. The rest did not hear what Bengt talked of with Gunnar. It was to them old and worn out. They were all occupied with Gustaf and his tree.

Bengt was the only one who applied himself to the brandy-bottle; and as he demanded in vain why Gunnar this Christmas-eve did not take a strengthening drop, Gunnar answered, that neither now nor at any other time, would he taste of the cursed trash. Bengt, however, who had no such great hostility to the palatable extract of the oat, extolled it highly, and made himself merry with it, and thus made the rest merry; and as now actually good sledging was at hand, they agreed on the following morning to betake themselves in a mass to church, Mother Ingrid and little Gustaf excepted, and to ride after Bläsa, and in the new sledge, as far the sledging was good, and then to walk all together where there was not sufficient snow.

In the evening, when the whole company had sung a Christmas hymn, they went to rest. Lena slept with Mother Ingrid, and Bengt got a place beside his chamber-comrade, Gunnar. Bengt was quite excited, and talked of many a merry doing of former days, which now seemed to Gunnar to lie, as it were, quite beyond time, so long since was it.

Lotta could never go to rest with more rapture, nor awake with more joy, than on this Christmas-day morning. The drive to church was also the most charming that any one had for long experienced, as it fortunately happened, they had morning moonlight, and superb weather. The snow had fallen so level, that the whole earth appeared like a well-made bed of swelling down, which rose in luxuriant forms. All looked so soft,

N*

and pleasant, and the drive itself, in the glittering moonlight, and with the merry chime of bells, had something quite lively in it. Lena laughed, and said right jocular things, and nobody contradicted her, but laughed with her, and even Gunnar showed signs of cheerfulness. Lotta, Abraham, and Bengt rolled over in the snow the moment that they began to drive; and Elin walked by Gunnar's side, or drove at his side, "happy yet once more," as an old song has it. A genuine reaction had taken place. There was something in the air which can not be described in any way, which seemed to whistle as "of old," often the only pleasant whistling which the air has at this season.

For Lotta it was a time, too, more beautiful and splendid than she had ever experienced; and those happy hours opened still more her heart to all that was good and beautiful—pity only that the heart has as many ways out of it as into it! In church she wept much over the penetrating sermon of the pastor; and, when Elin asked what it really was that drew all those tears from her eyes, she said, to her no small gratification, "Ah! I think of my mother, how unhappy she is in her wretched condition."

"The whole of this Christmas day was peaceful, tranquil, and still; and when evening came, they went earlier than usual to rest. When Elin and Lotta lay down, Elin heard how Lotta sobbed; and on inquiring what it was which now troubled her, she replied, "Ah! I am thinking of my mother. Perhaps now she sits in some cold corner, and eats her miserable stolen bread; for no one will give her any thing."

Elin now put to her a question which she had asked many times before, but to which Lotta had always avoided giving an answer; namely, *how* her father and mother had chanced to fall into such bad ways.

"Oh, that is easily done!" said Lotta; "and I can not tell it you all, dearest Elin, because it is sad to talk of, but I could tell you enough if I would."

And then followed a dark, repulsive, confused history of a father and mother, who began their career with thieving and misery; were punished, and thereafter fell into still deeper crime and depravity; initiated their only child into it, and never associated with any but miserable and disreputable people.

"But didst thou not experience a sad and terrible feeling," asked Elin, "when thou thus in a deliberate manner took from poor people that which they earned with the sweat of their brow, and which they had much need of?"

"Oh, no, I can not exactly say that," answered Lotta. "Mother, and the rest of the gang that we had about us, always said that every body else had more than we, and that we who had nothing, were as good as they, and that it was, therefore, no great sin to take what we by right ought to have, if all were dealt out as it ought to be in the world."

"A fine doctrine!" thought Elin.

"Frightened enough I was sometimes," continued Lotta, "when they thrust me in through holes and windows, because I was little, and that most frequently in the dead of night. Still more frightened was I lest some one should come, and see me, and knock me on the head; and I was frightened, too, lest I should not accomplish what they set me about, for then, you see, I was beaten by our people. But never was I so terrified as on that last occasion, when we took all the linen from the bleach-ground."

"So then," said Elin, "thou really wert concerned in that, after all? thou hast so often sworn and protested that thou didst not know the very least thing about that robbery!"

"Ay, that I said always for its own good reason's sake," said Lotta, in a confused tone.

"Ah, there is never a good reason to lie!" answered Elin; "but it is always more or less wicked. Now what was the cause, then?" asked she further, with a certain anxious curiosity.

"Oh, well! I may, perhaps, tell you, but never, Elin, speak of it before any one, for it would occasion much trouble yet. Well, see, I may say that I was concerned in it, for there was only mother and myself that time; and the linen lies there yet, the greatest part of it, at least mother has never ventured there to look after it. See, it is *for this reason* that I tell you, Elin, about it, because I can get chemises enow there, and Elin can go shares, if she will."

"What, in Heaven's name, does all this mean?" said Elin, still more anxiously, astonished and curious; for now did she, for the first time, remember that Lotta had often, with mysterious and enigmatical words, promised her famous linen in a while; talk which Elin had not paid the least attention to, but believed it to be Lotta's accustomed rhodomontade and fun.

"Ah, yes!" answered she, in a still lower and more cautious tone. "See, the matter was this: On that night when we took all the linen, it was one of the village laborers who had to watch and keep guard, but he lay down on a heap of cloth, and slept like a stone, and it required some art to get all the linen, together with that which he had under his feet; but mother lifted his feet, and I drew away the cloth, and then he began to move, and then we pulled out another piece, and laughed.

"Hush!" said Elin, but immediately added, "Yes, but what is that thou art talking of? that the linen still remains there on the bleach-ground. That does not hang together."

"Oh no, bless me! not on the bleach-ground, but in the wood," answered Lotta, almost laughing.

"How came it in the wood?"

"Bless me! we carried it thither, to be sure."

"But have you never fetched it away, then?"

"No, certainly. There was immediately such a terrible outcry about the linen, that I and mother fled helter-skelter out of the neighborhood, so that no one should be able to see her hereabout in the days immediately after; for every body protested that they had seen her there the very day before the robbery, but they could never prove it; and mother denied it positively, and I, too, before the court, and declared that that night we were at Lexeryd, two miles off; and we left the linen and every thing lying in the wood; and we have hidden it so well, that I believe for certain it lies there still, for I do not think that mother has ventured thither and fetched it yet, but she will probably do so toward spring, when people have a little forgotten the robbery; and she does not venture at present into this neighborhood, but I came hither alone to hear what was said, and I should have gone to mother, who is up in Wassbo, when you took me, which was better."

"Gracious Heaven!" sighed Elin, "how hardened thou hast been! And thou know'st that the poor people have lost their property, which they had got together by their labor and the sweat of their brow, and which they meant to sell at the autumn market, and that it now lies in the wood, and probably rots."

"Yes, but I could not talk of it," answered Lotta, "for then they would have taken both mother and me, and the linen altogether."

The argument had weight with Elin, so far as it concerned the mother, for she felt a repugnance to her being accused by Lotta; but, on the other hand, she represented to her, that it was a great sin altogether to conceal all this, and ultimately acquired so much power over Lotta, that she promised her to go to the same woman where the house examination was held, who was a farmer's wife in the village where the theft had been committed, and to reveal to her alone where the linen lay, and together with her to go and see whether it yet remained there, and in that case let every one get his own; with the condition that neither Lotta should be taken up, nor her mother, if Lotta, with a full and sincere seriousness, promised amendment for the future.

This plan was projected by Elin, who promised to accompany Lotta on this same sorrowful expedition of confession, which should not be spoken of before any one in the house, but should be kept as still as possible. Elin in consequence made many excellent and edifying exhortations to Lotta, who wept bitterly in the darkness of the night, and neither of them awoke nearly so tranquil and satisfied as on the foregoing day.

CHAPTER XLV.

The second day of Christmas was a sorrowful day in every way. All the beautiful snow which had made so many glad countenances—for no one in the streets of a city can imagine to himself how cheering is a little Christmas snow in any country dwelling—all this pure, welcome snow now thawed rapidly away, and as it had fallen more regularly than in great quantity, this was soon done. It dripped from all the eaves of the houses, and the earth quickly peeped forth, in great black and gray patches protruding disagreeably from the wet and melted-together snow. All the trees stood again naked, with a clear water drop on every minute twig; and the good, crunching sound of a quick step on the fine snow and frozen earth had now given way to an unexpected splashing into deep mud, as often as people, with long and dubious steps, went out beneath the gray and foggy heavens, which for hours together wept over every thing in fine and almost imperceptible drops, which a melancholy southwest wind, ever and anon, drove against the already dripping panes.

Gunnar and Bengt were gone away. Even Abraham had
got leave to go to the same aunt who had given him a summer
coat, to get a pair of mittens which she had promised him at
Christmas; and Elin seized the opportunity, and said to Lotta,
that which had to be done should now be done before any
thing else; "For otherwise," added she, "thou canst never
have a moment's peace of conscience;" and though Lotta had
now rather not, she was compelled to accompany Elin, who
said to Mother Ingrid and Lena that she wished to go for a
little while to the village of Solberga, and begged that Lotta
might accompany her.

It was a genuine proof of friendship in Elin to accompany
Lotta this great distance on such a business, in such weather,
and along such deep and abominable roads. The young girls
carried themselves, however, in a very different style, so that
when they arrived at Solberga, Elin's ankle boots were scarcely
dirtied, while Lotta was wet and splashed with mud far above
the boots, though her dress was much shorter than Elin's; for
Elin had sprung and picked her way, light as a bird, over hil-
locks and stones, holding up her fine homespun woolen dress;
while Lotta, on the other hand, strode on, just as it happened,
through mud and mire, without the least regard to either feet
or clothes.

"Thou spoilest thy shoes, and thy clothes, and thou splashest
me all over, when, without any precaution, thou go'st right
through every puddle," had Elin said many times, but without
the least effect, for the power of habit in little matters is much
stronger than in greater ones. Elin seemed indeed quickly to
perceive this, and closed her exhortations regarding Lotta's exterior, and made her promise many times that on this occasion
she would speak the perfect truth, and conceal nothing, nor
equivocate, nor shuffle. Lotta promised this with tears, while
she still pushed on through the deepest mud.

"Ah!" thought Elin, "if I could only scrape away the mud
from her young soul, her boots and her petticoats might take
their chance; for when she once feels herself pure in heart,
she will soon enough come to have clean clothes too." So did
Elin believe, in the full purity of her own heart and mind.

When the young girls came to Solberga, they found the juryman's wife at home, and, what was still better, alone. She
wondered at first at the unexpected visit, prepared coffee for
the "delicate and rare Elin of Vika," who was now the type

of all that was refined and superior in the congregation; praised excessively the material of her dress, both in fineness, pattern, and texture; examined the cut of the body itself, in speculation upon a like stuff dress for her own daughters; broke out in praises of her shawl and scarf; and paid Elin a sort of compliment, in that she who yet belonged to the reading class, used both red and green, and all colors.

"Well, what has that to do with reading?" said Elin, smiling. "God's earth is green, and his heaven is blue; God's sun is deep red, and his moon yellow as gold; why should I not be allowed to wear all God's colors?"

And now began the juryman's wife also to examine Lotta, who sat silent, anxious, and timidly shrinking in a corner. Of her, she said it was now apparent that she was "among people;" she was delighted to see her look so quiet and genteel in comparison with what she did formerly; and she praised much her apparel, compared with the wretched rags in which people had been accustomed to see her.

"Yes," said Elin, "and now, dear mother, if you knew how orderly Lotta is, and how well she has learned to read in this short time, you would be altogether astonished.

Thus Elin endeavored to establish a good understanding with the juryman's wife, but delayed yet to make known the real cause of the visit, though the juryman's wife seemed evidently to expect to hear something, for she made many inquiries regarding Lena and Mother Ingrid, imagining that the young girls must have some errand from one of them.

Lotta had at length learned to feel the sense of shame. She sate, thoroughly cast down, in a distant corner, and scarcely got courage from Elin's praise; but Elin herself was obliged ultimately to advance to the difficult confession of Lotta's doings. The moment, however, she touched on the robbery of the bleaching-ground, which had been sufficiently unfortunate to most of the inhabitants of the village, since they had washed their clothes for the approaching Michaelmas, as well as their webs of linen which they intended to sell at the autumn markets, the countenance of the juryman's wife darkened deeply, and she exclaimed, striking her large hands together—

"Well, now! is not that the very thing that I have always said? I have never ceased to declare that it was Bankesa and her Satan's imp of a daughter who were the perpetrators of that robbery! and yet would they throw it in my teeth that the hardened baggage was seen the same day at Lexeryd, some miles distant; but I knew well enough what I knew; I had actually seen Bankesa throw herself over a fence, and take to her heels as she got sight of me, the very day we were talking of, and that I have always said, but nobody would believe me. And thou sittest now, thou she-thief! and weepest; and well mayest thou weep, so often as I have tried, both in anger and in kindness, to get thee to confess the truth. But mark me, she ought to have been flogged till she confessed, for it is now quite too late! Bankesa is, I warrant ye, not the woman to let such things lie and rot in a wood. She has, no doubt of it, she and her confederates, sold them at the autumn markets, and most likely drunk all the money up, for thou, thou good-for-nothing there, hast got no part of it, if thou dost not lie about it. But, however, let us go to-morrow and see after the linen, though there is little chance, for most likely she has been only filling your ears full of lies about it, dear Elin, for she is just capable of it."

Elin stood there quite cast down. All her enthusiasm for good in this business, and for the improvement of Lotta, had now been stranded on the woman's passion for her linen; and Elin now first saw, that if there was nothing found in the wood, as was very likely, it would be impossible to appease the wrath of the juryman's wife, and the rest of the inhabitants of the village, against Lotta; for, as the old dame said, it would be *absolutely necessary* that the affair should be inquired into. She repented bitterly of her undertaking, which she had resolved on, and had begun, without consulting either Lena, Gunnar, or Mother Ingrid, who certainly knew better how such a business ought to have been done. But now that it *was* done, it was too late to retrace her steps; and now there remained only to endeavor to do the best that she could. She therefore implored the juryman's wife, in the most tender manner, to pardon Lotta, and assured her, on her behalf, that she, Lotta, deeply repented all her former bad practices, and that she hereafter would become quite another creature.

"Yes, that is all fine and good, and well for *her*," answered the woman; "but I don't get back my fine linen any more *for that*, which I and my girls spun through the whole long winter; and, moreover, a piece of drugget, and those shirts for the father, and a number of our chemises, and three sheets, and all our linen stockings, and many things besides."

Lotta burst out, and cried aloud. Elin stood perplexed and downcast. Lotta had never yet truly confessed to her how great the robbery had been; and when now Lotta, in consequence of the juryman's wife's vehement warnings and subtle and deep questions, was compelled to admit that she and her mother really were not alone, after all, in the robbery, as Lotta had given out, but that they had a laborer of the parish, a fellow of an evil repute with them, armed with a huge cudgel, to knock on the head the sleeping watchman, if he should awake, then Elin herself burst into tears, and said—

"Ah, Lotta, that thou never wilt speak the truth, the real and perfect truth! Thou hast, now, so often said and protested that thou and thy mother were alone in the robbery, and certainly never did confess that you actually contemplated murder!"

"Oh, no!" said Lotta, sobbing; "Smed-Lassé (Lassé the smith) never meant to murder him, but only to give him a blow on the eyes, so that he might not see what we took away, and who we were."

"God in heaven! what wretches!" exclaimed the juryman's wife. "Yes he, that Satan's Smed-Lassé; little would he care about the life of any one that he struck, for he would take every means to prevent betraying himself, I am sure—that wicked Lassé, who never was concerned in any thing but villainy."

"Yes, but he had his face blackened, so that no one could know him," sobbed Lotta.

Elin shuddered. She had never conceived such consummate wickedness. She had heard talk, indeed, of such, but had never seen it brought so closely under her observation, or had been in the smallest degree in contact with it; and there was a moment during which she was almost ashamed of having had any thing to do with such abandoned people. But compassion for Lotta caused her soon to return to her first zeal to endeavor to put every thing in the best possible light; and when the juryman's wife's freshly excited wrath and vexation about the robbery of the bleaching-ground had somewhat allayed itself, she promised not to chide Lotta too severely, as she had been merely a tool in the hands of the mother and Smed-Lassé, and, at least, obtained no advantage from the stolen goods, as Lotta now again most sacredly protested.

It was now concluded that Lotta should remain at this house

for the night, that Elin should return alone to Vika, and that the woman, with her husband, and some other of the villagers, conducted by Lotta, should on the morrow go to the place in the wood which Lotta declared that she knew so thoroughly, and where the whole of the plundered property had been, at least, formerly concealed.

"Yes, if she only does not steal something afresh during the night," said the juryman's wife, a little harshly upon Lotta, to Elin.

"Oh, no! that I will answer for," asserted Elin; and Lotta fell weeping on her neck, and promised her once more to speak the pure truth in every thing that they demanded of her, and not to disgrace herself by any new trick: "For," said Elin, "should this happen, as certain as I live, thou shalt never come again to Vika;" and this menace Elin knew was the thing which, above all, Lotta would dread; and so it was, and more so than Elin was aware of; for Lotta had more affection for Vika than we or Elin could conceive.

Elin went at length on her way, embraced in the warmest manner by the juryman's wife, who saw into the good intentions of Elin, and her object in all this, and gave her full credit for it. She sent, at the same time, apples and biscuits to little Gustaf, and promised once more, when she had followed Elin out, both to have an eye on Lotta, and not to be angry with her.

CHAPTER XLVI.

AND now are we undecided whether we shall follow Elin on her homeward way, or remain with Lotta in the juryman's house; for there must be matters to relate in both cases, and just such matters as we believe no reader can conceive beforehand, and yet not at all surprising or mysterious. We decide on following Elin, certain that all others will go along with us.

She tripped, therefore, homewards, in the same foul weather and mud as she had to go out in, with this difference only, that now she was alone, and it began to get dark, which alarmed Elin, as she would have to pass solitarily through the same great wood in which the squire was murdered, though it was

on quite another side.   She could not, however, avoid thinking
of it, as well as of that hideous robbery, the proceeds of which
had been concealed in the same wood.   A deep wood, with
mountain-ways, and dark, deep, though small forest lakes, has
at all times something wild, though agreeable in itself, which
one may be able to express in that more and more prevailing
phrase, "horribly beautiful;" for here it would be much more
in keeping than it often is, as used by those who take a pride
in preferring the word "horrible," to every other epithet.

"Ah!" thought Elin, "if one had but a kind friend who
would meet one here, and by whose side one might go comfortably and safely!"   Imagination immediately presented Gunnar to her; and, for the first time for long, did she let her
imagination luxuriate a little in thoughts of Gunnar.

"Oh! he suffers like myself," thought Elin, "and I can not
once console him.   He dares not approach me.   He regards
it as a sin, and he has great right to do so.   But, heavenly God!
what a blessedness to dare to seat myself at his side, to put
back the long beautiful hair from his forehead, to stroke his
thin cheeks, and speak to him from the heart—speak with him
of God, and of a better life, where we may safely calculate on
different circumstances to the present; and where we shall not
be warned against holding each other dear from the very bottom
of our hearts.   Heigho! were we but there already!"

But here Elin stood suddenly still, both in her castle-building
and in her march forward; for she had already reached that
wood so much dreaded, and imagined that she heard, as she
stood, a cry like that of a savage beast.   Wolves rushed at
once into her mind, especially as these enemies of the farmer
were now committing much ravage all round the country, and
excited now, as always, terror in every one; for we do not
sufficiently reflect how rare are the cases in which wolves attack
people.   We know this by our own individual experience;
for, terrified once by the unlooked-for encounter with these
wolves, we ran nearly half a furlong's distance, with a dear
but heavy burden in our arms, an only child of five years old,
without daring once to look back to see whether the wolves
followed or not, and not at all reflecting that, probably, they
were as much afraid of us as we were of them.

Elin did, however, just the contrary to ourselves, whether
from greater courage, or from chance, we can not say; but
certain it is that she did not run, but stood still and listened,

without daring almost to take a breath. Clearly did she hear this wild howling, and heard it, to her consternation, just in that direction in which lay her way. "Oh, my God! what shall I do?" sighed she, and did not dare to move a single step. And thus she paused for a considerable time, hesitating whether she should venture forward, or turn back to the village; and in the mean time, the December darkness had fallen heavily and impenetrably over the earth. Elin could not see her way on this side or that, and had relied too confidently on her power to find the right path, now that she was alone, and had none of those who were well acquainted with it by her side. She began immediately to weep bitterly, and to repent of the whole undertaking, from which, certainly, no great advantages appeared likely to be reaped.

"Lord God! shall I stand here hesitating all night?" she exclaimed to herself, and began to advance a few steps, now onward, now aside; for she could no longer discern the path. The wood soughed above her, and the wind made the branches of the trees to crack and break. The howling of the wolves had entirely ceased; but who could know whether they were not silently stealing around just where Elin found herself? So it seemed to Elin sometimes; and her terror made her hear distinctly something which moved, and went stealthily close beside her, although she could not see it. At length she collected all her presence of mind, and set herself to shout; partly because she knew that people were accustomed thereby to frighten away the wolves, partly that she might be heard and helped by people who might chance to hear her. But this was not so easily done as proposed. Her fear made her unable to bring the slightest sound out of her throat; and she experienced the same agony in reality as we do in a terrible dream, when we fain would cry out, but can not. She attempted it many times, but did not succeed. After the lapse of some minutes, she seemed to hear the sound of human voices; and this inspired her with some degree of courage, and she began to shout ever louder and shriller. At length she heard distinctly a voice which answered her; and she therefore exerted all her power to shout, that she might guide any one to her; for she found herself totally unable to move a single step. Finally, she heard a man's step, and a manly voice, which called at a distance, "Who art thou, thou unfortunate one, who criest so? Shout now loudly, that I may hear thee, and know where thou art, that I may come to thee."

But now!—now was Elin again become dumb.   The voice which called to her she recognized right well.   It was Gunnar's —and sensations of joy and fear, and of much besides, so over- powered her whole excited frame, that with the best possible will, she was scarcely able to cry weakly, "Here—here am I!" But God best knows how her voice yet reached the fine ear of Gunnar, and she quickly heard how he drew near through trees and bushes, stumps and stones.   He was now nearly close to her.

"Who art thou, poor one, who shoutest so wildly on the eve- ning of this sacred day?" asked he, when he was quite near Elin.   He spoke, however, with a mysterious and unwonted voice, partly from his rapid running, partly from the circum- stance that he seemed to recognize Elin's voice, but considered it to be so utterly impossible, that, under the influence of the popular superstition, he believed that they might be spirits that assumed the voice of Elin, in order to lure him into some evil snare.   Elin was scarcely able to answer either, for she fancied that her ears must deceive her, for the darkness and her fear had made her quite blind.   Gunnar, on the contrary, more ac- customed to woods and darkness, could see some little, and guided by Elin's light head-dress, he came quite up to her, and seized on her arm, to convince himself that it was not a ghost but a human being, if not Elin, which he judged to be impos- sible.   Then first Elin recovered speech, and courage, and warm blood.

"Ah, Gunnar! Is that really thee?   God in heaven, how I thank thee for this!" and she sunk, exhausted by all these ac- cumulated sensations on his breast.

Gunnar now found that it really was Elin, and he could not resist this once to press her to his heart, which, like a sorrow- ing widower, so long sighed for such a moment.   But the beat- ing of his heart again recalled Elin to herself.   She abruptly broke from him, crying with womanly sensibility, "Ah, I know not what I do, so overjoyed I am that some compassionate per- son has come to my aid in this dreadful hour of need, when I really believed that I must remain bewildered here all the night, and perhaps be torn to pieces by the wolves."

Gunnar, knowing his own strength and activity, and the really insignificant danger, could not feel afraid, but only smiled at this excessive agony of Elin, in which it was impossible for him to participate.

"Ah, thou poor little girl!" said he, in the delightful feeling of a man to be the support and guard, to be *any thing* to the woman that he alone loves—"how terrified thou hast been! thou tremblest yet. Thy dress is cold and damp, and yet thy hands are so warm, and thy cheeks too. Now will I carry thee away hence, if thou wilt. Ah, so willingly—so willingly. Thou art not at all heavy—at least for me."

"No, thank thee," said Elin, and drew back, "I would rather walk, so that I may hold by thee, dearest Gunnar, that I may not again get lost, and alone, in this hateful wood."

"No, that shall not again happen, so long as a single spark of life remains in me," and he took her round the waist to help her out of the thicket into which she had strayed. When they were again upon the pathway, and going on side by side, hold each other's hand, Gunnar began to inquire what was the cause of his finding Elin so unexpectedly thus on his return from accompanying Bengt home. Other feelings had before quite extinguished all curiosity and astonishment; but now, at length, they made themselves room, or were breathed in from the air, to mingle with all those other feelings.

Elin now began to relate, in short, abrupt sentences, which she attributed to her terror, the whole particulars of her visit to Solberga, and the cause of it.

"Ay, my poor Elin," said Gunnar, "this girl will give thee no satisfaction, believe me, in that; she is bad at bottom, and falsehood and vice are rooted into her; she will never be what she ought. It is, at least, very different with her from what it is with Abraham, poor fellow! He has scarcely a spark of sense or knowledge, but he has a heart as good as gold. Lotta, on the other hand, is quicker than a fire, but has nothing in her except vice and wretchedness. I know, in fact, what I know."

Elin replied to him in mild and affectionate words. She was so desirous that he should be found wrong, and brought forward so many proofs of Lotta's improvement, that Gunnar admitted, at length, that he believed her; he wished to afford her a little innocent pleasure, but still he muttered to himself, "I know well what the girl is; serpents' eggs bring young serpents," and so on.

When they had gone rapidly awhile, Gunnar suddenly stopped, and seemed to hesitate whether he should take the right hand or go straight forward.

"Ah, merciful Heaven!" said Elin, "now we are lost again."

But ah! how little now was her fear and anxiety; far less than she would allow to be known, for Elin was still but a woman.

"Oh, no! my sweet, dear Elin, there is no fear of that," said Gunnar, but pressed hard the hand that he held. "Don't be afraid, thou dear girl," added he, "for we have only gone out of the way a little, and shall immediately come right again."

"Ah! that is well," said Elin, "but I am always so frightened and anxious. God grant that we may not come at length to the place where they murdered the squire!"

Gunnar suddenly let her hand go.

"Nay, nay, nay!" cried Elin, "don't leave me on any account!" and she linked herself faster than ever to Gunnar.

"I leave thee!" answered Gunnar, slowly. "No! death might, but the dead could never draw me from thee."

"Ay, there I could accompany thee," said Elin, softly, and almost involuntarily.

"Wouldst thou!" said Gunnar, who still heard her, and felt a ray of joy illumine his gloomy mind.

They were silent for a long time, and went on more softly than before. Gunnar at length broke the silence.

"And thou art so afraid of the place!" said he, as if they were still speaking on the same subject that they had done some time before. "What wouldst thou say to the murderer himself? Him couldst thou probably never bear in all thy life?"

Gunnar's voice was agitated as he put to Elin this question.

"No! hush!" said she, and again seized on Gunnar's hand. "Never have I spoken of him from the first moment, and from this day I could never see him without feeling quite wrathful. But, fie! we should not talk of a murderer as we are passing through this dark wood."

"But if it were not Olle?" said Gunnar.

"Well, he would still be an evil doer, and on such can I never once look," rejoined Elin.

"Yes, but now if it were some one who had perpetrated that murder, in passion, indeed, but still altogether contrary to his intention," continued Gunnar, with increasing zeal.

" Well, I still could never bear him," answered Elin, shud-dering.

" Think if it were I!" exclaimed Gunnar, impetuously.

" Thou!" cried Elin, in turn, and stood fixed to the spot.

" Yes, I say, only *think* if it were I; I, who am hasty, and often carried out of myself when my mind is excited; I, who never could bear the squire; *think now* if it were *I* who had fallen into such a misfortune in an unhappy hour."

" Oh, that wouldst thou never do, thou good, dear Gunnar!" replied Elin.

" Yes, but *think* yet, if I *had* done it, and I confessed it both to thee and to the court, and if I must die as a malefactor, what wouldst thou do then?"

" Then?" answered Elin, without a moment's reflection, " yes, *then!* then I would go with thee, and fall by the same blow as thyself."

" Oh, Elin, Elin!" said Gunnar, and clasped her vehe-mently, and with convulsive emotion to his heart, " O thanks to thee for that word! thou knowest not what good it has done me."

Alarmed, Elin released herself from Gunnar's embrace, and said, with womanly power, over every other up-springing sen-timent,

" No, Gunnar! dearest Gunnar, let us not talk of such things *now*. They make us so strange. We forget God in our foolish representations, and it is the wicked tempter who puts such words into thy mouth, in order yet once more to extract from mine how much I——" here Elin ceased.

" What?" asked Gunnar.

" Ah! thou knowest too well what," whispered Elin; and then they spoke no more all the whole long way home, but walked rapidly on, and were speedily at the house door.

" The punishment follows close on the heels of the crime," thought Elin this evening, for Lena was unusually cross and surly, exactly as formerly, neither was Mother Ingrid so friendly, Elin thought, as she had been for a long time. They both prognosticated no good of Banka-Lotta, when Elin frankly re-lated to them the cause and object of their excursion, and then how she had got lost in the wood, and finally had been helped into the right way by Gunnar, who had just parted from Bengt.

" Yes, now hast thou plunged into a terribly foolish scrape,"

said Lena to Elin, in a sharp tone, "in running off with Lotta
to the juryman's wife, in Solberga! What the deuce hadst
thou to do there? Why didst thou say nothing to me about
the business? I understand such matters much better than
thou, thou poor wench. What was the good of running off
and trumpeting it about, before any one knew whether the
stolen goods are lying in the wood or not? Pooh! there is not
a thread of them left there, that I will lay my life on. The
Bankesa is not quite so stupid as that comes to. She is, the
mischief take me! too cunning for that; she has long ago
fetched them away and sold them, and drunken the money with
her strolling ragamuffins. I know her, that do I! And where
is the use of all Lotta's confession? Not the least in the
world! but merely a scandal, that makes it next to impossible
to have her again; and she was a good worker enough, when
one could only forget the herd she came of. But I am glad of
it! I won't be mixed up any longer with thieves and thieves'
histories. Such entanglements and wretchedness one always
gets some mischief from. I don't forget that Olle endeavored
to throw the theft upon Gunnar."

"Yes, that he has got his reward for," said Gunnar, who
probably thought that Lena was not far wrong, but was desirous to help the weeping Elin, cost what it might, and to lead
the conversation to something else.

"Nay," continued Lena, who was not so easily interrupted,
"thou shouldst have told it only to _me_, and then we would have
gone and sought whether it still remained there; and if it had
luckily been so, Lotta could have had a chemise or two—or,"
added she, when she heard Gunnar exclaim—"Fie, the d——l!"
—"or she might have bargained for a few chemises for herself
before she made her confession to the juryman's wife, or any
one in Solberga. But now, if nothing at all be found—and I'll
die if that be not the result of it—then both thou and Lotta
will get but little for your running, while Lotta might have repented of her sin here at home in all quietness, instead of there
being a terrible subject for gossip, that will never cease to be
talked over; for thou canst not be so stupid as to believe that
the juryman's wife in Solberga will rest quiet in the matter,
but there will be an everlasting gossiping about the girls at
Vika, and in the end thou may'st come in for a share of the
blame, as having had a hand in the business, since thou art a
stranger, and not belonging to the parish. And what is that

O

314 THE PEASANT AND HIS LANDLORD.

which Gunnar constantly says ?—'three know what four know,'
or whatever it is."

" The world knows what three knew," answered Gunnar,
who remembered more of his Frithiof, than many of those who
think they know it by rote ! " and that is true," he added ;
" but when not only three, but many know what Elin is, and
under what circumstances Lotta came here, no one can cast a
suspicion on Elin. No, no one in the world. And as for what
concerns Lotta, God grant that she might get some other place,
but till she can do that, there is no help for it, we must keep
her if she does nothing very bad, or conducts herself very
shamefully."

Here the differences of opinion ceased; Elin gave over weeping, and Gunnar offered to assist Lena, who had now got
accustomed to be waited on both in the house and yard by
Lotta.

Abraham had sat silently in his corner and listened to them
all ; but now, as he deemed the storm to be nearly over, he took
a long pine stick, lit it in the fire, and then advanced to the
rest, casting the light in great triumph on his hands, which were
clothed in unusually light-blue gloves, the first article of the
kind that he ever possessed.

" I think they are good and strong," said he, " and as to
Banka-Lotta, I know and master knows that she is just a——"

" Oh, yes !" we know very well altogether what she is, and
is not," interrupted Gunnar, and winked at Abraham to be
silent; and while Abraham stood gaping, and inclined to ask
Gunnar what he meant by winking, Gunnar continued,—" And
now, Abraham, thou canst take the water tub, and go down to
the hole in the ice, and fill it, and I will follow thee, and help
thee to carry it in, and so we shall do a good job for the mistress, eh ?"

They went to rest in tolerable peace and quiet; but Elin
had so much to think of! Had she not, in a single moment,
relapsed into the very sin from which she had imagined herself
freed ? She loved Gunnar more vehemently, more madly than
ever ; and had, moreover, confessed this tenderness to himself !
She wept bitterly over her depravity, as she herself called it.
She wept next over the poor, miserable Lotta, and began even
to believe that she had plunged over head into trouble in
attempting her improvement : for Jealousy, that keen-eyed
demon, made clear to her certain half-uttered expressions of

Gunnar's; and Elin began to fear that Lotta also nourished a criminal passion for the young married man. And of all this, Elin was the cause—with the very best intentions, indeed, but still the cause! Every other evil Elin believed that she was able to root out of Lotta's heart, but not a feeling of this nature. She knew too well how mountain-fast it sat in her own bosom, notwithstanding all her struggles, conflicts, and prayers.

Neither could Gunnar sleep the whole of this long December night. The flame of love blazed up higher and higher, and cast a glory on every thing around it, down even to a shameful death. "Death by Elin's side! Oh, that were more delightful than any life!—except a *life* by her side!" So thought Gunnar, filled with agony, and yet still thought so. He slumbered toward morning, and dreamed so! He awoke, and cursed his life and his awakening. He longed to sleep again, thus to dream again; he desired to die, and experience it.

CHAPTER XLVII.

The third day of Christmas was a long and wretched day. Gunnar worked the whole day with Abraham. Lena was out of humor with her house affairs, which she endeavored altogether to put off during the Christmas holidays, as she did not yet wish to avail herself of Lotta in sedentary occupations, but much rather in errands, and affairs that required the use of the legs. She had now herself to sweep, to chop sticks, to clean out the hen-house, which was in the kitchen, to feed the pigs, and look after the calves, and let out the sheep awhile; and all this is not so very charming on a cold winter's day, when a person is desirous to avoid it. Mother Ingrid had put aside her spinning wheel, and sat down to her old blue woolen stockings, which she mended with gray yarn, and with her old hymn-book lying open before her. Little Gustaf went waddling about on the floor, and now plucked the very branches from the Christmas-tree, which stood there stripped of its little finery, a perfect image of all borrowed glory and greatness never attaining its end. Neither had Elin any repose. She was continually looking out into the road, to see whether

Lotta might not be coming back, both hoping and fearing it, and wondering a thousand times what had been the result of her visit to the wood. She would give, in addition to all her other possessions, that bound book, and the little work-box which she received from Gunnar, and her ear-rings, which her mother gave her, immeasurably as she prized them, so that the linen, or some of it, might still be found in the wood. She wished and she hoped it; and so strong was her faith, that she prayed to God regarding it, firmly persuaded that he was able to make that which was done, undone, and the contrary, which is the attribute of omnipotence.

And now we may proceed to the relation of Lotta's adventures. They were little like the fancies of Elin; just as little like as the two young maidens were themselves. Hate, contempt, abhorrence, lying, and cunning, with remorse and repentance in an insignificant degree, had played the chief parts in Lotta's drama. *Love alone*, on the other hand, influenced the destiny of Elin; her love for her fellow-creatures, as well as love sinful and forbidden, had led her into all these difficulties.

When Elin had left Solberga that evening, the juryman's wife, who was a discreet farmer's wife, but certainly no piece of perfection, but an ordinary old woman, who was glad to hear a little gossip from the neighbor's yard, began to ask Lotta all sorts of questions about the folk at Vika, and how things went on there. Lotta, delighted to have an opportunity of talking and telling idle stories, related in ample style both what she had seen and she had not seen, both what had happened and had not happened; for if Lotta kept pretty much to the truth in Elin's presence, yet this good genius took its flight from her almost in the same instant with Elin. Lotta related a vast deal, and Gunnar's name hovered incessantly on her lips. She exalted him to the skies, and Elin next to him, but of the rest she spoke indifferently; called Mother Ingrid a good-for-nothing old woman, Lena a regular Satan, and Abraham a beast, an ox, a stupid ass.

"It seems," said the juryman's wife, spitefully, "that thou hast most, and most willingly, to do with thy master."

"Oh, I can not exactly say so," answered Lotta blushing deeply, and pulling to pieces the ends of her new stout neckkerchief.

"Ay, ay!" continued the juryman's wife; if thou only livest

and thrivest, thou wilt be just like thy mother, and have one child after another, let the consequence be as God best knows."

"Oh, no! that will never happen, I am sure," answered Lotta, laughing, and unabashed.

"Ah, well! there is at least very little good in thee, that I can see, plainly," said the woman; "and no one can put much faith in what thou sayest; for Lena can never be a perfect devil as thou describest her, and Elin as little a perfect saint either; nor can Gunnar think so much of thee, as thou wouldst have me to believe; but when all is said, they are probably lies altogether."

And the juryman's wife talked no more with Lotta, but kept her eyes sharply upon her; and when her husband and her daughters came home, she said to one of the latter,

"Hearest thou, Anna Lesa?—keep an eye on Lotta that she does no mischief, while I speak with thy father and sister in the chamber."

And with this she went into the chamber with her husband and daughter, to relate to them the fact of the robbery of the bleach-grounds, and to consult with them what must be done; and there sat Lotta, again sunk in the deep contempt in which those whom it touches often sink, as into clay, the more they seek to get out, and who therefore finally cease to strive against it, but in despair let it do what it will. She was now again suspected, and *therefore* she took, by a quick movement, when no eye was on her, a small pair of scissors belonging to one of the juryman's daughters, which she hid in her bosom, and helped them to look for with the utmost eagerness.

Away in an empty corner Lotta lay like a dog for the night, and she was made to eat her food at a great distance from the rest. In mortification at this, she sat, and cut to pieces her new apron, and brooded on revenge, resolving not to conduct them to the right place in the wood, although she had so many times pointed it out and described it. Error and crime generate contempt, contempt generates error and crime, and, finally, sins of a deep dye: and so it goes on in an eternal and revolting circle.

The following morning they took their way to the wood; namely, the juryman himself, and two other men of the village, one of the juryman's daughters, a neighbor's wife, and a servant-maid; and not a soul in the whole village was ignorant of what was the object of the undertaking, but all excessively

curious as to its result. The juryman's wife did not trouble
herself to accompany them, making herself certain that they
were all only running after their noses.

When they came to the wood Lotta began to appear dubious
of her whereabouts, and to go hither and thither ; but then said
the juryman, who was a very solemn, honest, but blunt farmer—

" If thou dost not go straight and properly onward, but turn-
est hither and thither, and dost not show us the spot where the
stolen goods are concealed, I will beat thee black and blue."

And this took good effect at once ; for now Lotta went right
forward to a cleft in the rocks, showed a tolerable large opening between two great stones, and said—

" Yes, here we thrust them altogether ; that I protest and
declare."

Both the men and the women lay down, and endeavored to
peep into the cleft, but they saw—just nothing at all. Then
they poked down long poles with sharp hooks, which they had
carried with them, but these brought up nothing but a little
moss and dry leaves and twigs.

" Yes, thou might have had something else to do than to make
fools of us, by bringing us hither in the middle of the Christmas holidays," said one of the men of the village, and at the
same time gave Lotta a great box on the ear. " Thou liest
in thy heart, every word that thou sayest ; for I could never believe that Bankesa was so stupid as to bring the things here,
but would have a conveyance on the highway, and be off with
the whole of them together, though thou now, thou Satan's jilt,
hast hit on this scheme to make fools of us all in the village,
and lead us like ninnies with thy hoaxes. Perhaps it is only to
slip away and avoid being of some use at Vika ; for Lena is a
clever, stirring body, that will dress thy skin for thee, I
reckon."

Weeping aloud and screaming, Lotta protested the truth of
what she said, for at this time it was actually true ; and to make
it as like truth as possible, she did not forget a little circumstance which had been connected with it, and half-speaking,
half-screaming, she made the following confused relation :—

" Nay, if I should sink down this instant right through the
whole earth, then I can say no other than that there we laid
them together, and here we lay the whole night after, I and
mother and Smed-Lassé, and here we plainly saw how he was

knocked down and killed, and heard it also, although we lay as still as stones, and could not get away on account of it."

"What say'st thou?" asked the juryman, who had before made the remark that it was a dead and dismal place here in the wood; for they were close upon the spot where the squire of Grantorp had been murdered, a business which occurred exactly the day after the robbery of the bleach-ground. "What art talking about, thou wretched girl?" added he; "What was that thou saw'st of the murder?"

"Ah, bless me! that I ought not to have said!"

"Answer instantly! What didst thou see of the murder? or I will chastise thee."

"Bless me! I saw how they knocked him on the head?" sobbed out Lotta.

"Who was it?"

"Bless me! the squire—I know."

"Didst thou see it, say'st thou?"

"Bless me, yes. I saw it, sure enough."

"Why, then, hast thou never spoken of it?" demanded the juryman further, while all the rest, muttering in astonishment, ceased the conversation.

"Why, because mother and Smed-Lassé forbade it so strictly, for they did not want any one to know that we were here just then."

"Did you lie here in the midst of broad day?"

"Yes, we were here in the morning."

"But that is not at all possible, it is not," said the villager, who gave Lotta the box on the ear; "for you were all three seen in Lexeryd the same day at noon."

"Yes, because we drove."

"Well, but why did not you drive in the night, without waiting for daylight? and what conveyance had you?" asked the juryman.

"Why when we brought the lost things hither, Lassé went to fetch a cart and horse, and then, if we had traveled by night, we should have taken with us some of the . . . . stolen goods," (Lotta was ashamed to speak the word fairly out), "but the horse had got away, and he had to go after him and catch him, and we waited here, hour by hour, and so it became broad day, and when Smed-Lassé came at length, we heard people near us, and then—that was it."

"Was it then that you saw the squire murdered?"

"Yes, I saw it first, and he, Smed-Lassé, almost at the same time, although the trees stood in the way, but we laid us down and saw it."

"Bless me, in all days!" exclaimed the juryman. "Then there *is* a witness against Olle, the gallows-bird! Well, didst thou see clearly that it was Olle, and no one else?"

"I did not recognize Olle, nor Smed-Lassé either, for we merely saw his back; but mother said it was Olle."

"But she did not really see it?"

"Yes, she saw how he stood over him, and looked at him, and took something red, just like a pocket-book, out of his pocket, and put it in his own; but then it was quite silent, for then he was most likely quite dead; and so she came after us, for we, Smed-Lassé and I, had gone along the other little road to get at the cart, for he was so afraid that the horse should go off again."

"Well, but what did thy mother do when she first saw it?"

"She stopped near the booty that we left behind, and that we could not take with us in the face of day."

"But—but where in the name of Jesus did you get a horse and cart from, you good-for-nothing hussy?" demanded the other villager.

"Oh, yes, I know very well," answered Lotta.

"Well, answer, then, immediately, or the blow will fall."

"Bless me! it was Nils's in Storgaln, I know!" exclaimed Lotta, who was quite contented with the box on the ear that she had already got.

"Nils in Lexeryd!" exclaimed the juryman astonished. "He is the best fellow in all the village of Lexeryd! And *he* lend you a conveyance? Nay, that is a lie!"

"Oh no, bless me! he had broken his leg, and his son was gone to Lidköping, and would not come back for two days, and so we took the horse which was in the forest pasture with the other, and the cart stood in a shed, and we set it there again the following night. We put it there that they might not hear us."

"Bless me! such admirable practices!" said the juryman; "but now it is no use staying longer here, but we will go home, and tell what we have found, which is exactly what I saw beforehand, or what the cat laid in the malt."

So now they hastened homeward briskly, conversing zealously on what Lotta had confessed, and every now and then asking her about the matter, from which they came finally to the conclusion, that Lotta was the first who saw the squire and a fellow clad in blue (and Olle had been so dressed), but whose face she did not properly see, fighting; that Smed-Lassé also saw it, but not so long as Lotta, but that they dared not remain there longer; Lassé had first crept away, and Lotta had followed him, and immediately after them came Bankesa herself, and told the others that she had recognized the Stillman Olle, of Grantorp; and they all then had got into their conveyance, and with a young, fiery horse, they had put him to full speed, in order to get away altogether; and further, that they only met one gentleman's carriage on the whole way, and a few travelers from distant places with packs.

"But do you believe now that all this is true, that it is not almost every word a lie?" asked one of the villagers, turning to the juryman, who had a great reputation for shrewdness and sense.

"Yes, I must believe that it hangs together much as she says," answered the juryman, in an impressive tone; "for, mark you, she has really nothing to gain by putting so many lies together; and it came out altogether so unexpectedly at the beginning, and she did not hesitate, or prevaricate, as when it concerned the theft itself. Yes, yes, it is most probably as she says, and is quite correct; but now, observe, the constable ought to have an account of this without delay, and I will go at once to him, and thou, Kattrina, canst tell thy mother and the rest it has turned out just as both she and I expected, and that there is not a rag to be found there now. Adieu to you; I shall turn off here, and go the nearest way across the forest."

All together questioned Lotta, and she answered sometimes truly and sometimes untruly; for she was compelled to conceal or to refine away all that could affect herself or her wretched mother, and when it concerned any thing of this kind, it was almost impossible to get the truth out of her.

When the group reached the way that turned off to Vika, near the village, Lotta asked humbly whether she might now return home, as she could be of no further service. Lotta was anxious to avoid another meeting with the juryman's wife. All laughed, and mocked Lotta when she talked of being of service.

"Thou render any service!" said the villager who gave the box on the ear. "No! never could any one believe such a thing; and horribly simple were we ever to give the slightest

o*

heed to thy words. But see, if we could get a witness against Olle, then indeed something would be gained, and justice would take its course, as it ought."

Lotta regarded this as a permission, and without taking any leave, went her way, and was quickly at Vika, sad and downcast.

Elin came immediately toward her, and said, with an expressive inquiry, "Well, Lotta?"

"Yes, there was nothing worth going for," answered Lotta, and looked down, dejectedly.

"Was nothing at all found?" said Elin, anxiously, for she had ventured to hope to the last that Bankesa had not dared to fetch away the stolen goods, while people had their eyes so upon her. And Elin's innocent tears chased each other down her cheeks, but Lotta stood with dry eyes. She felt so happy to be again at Vika, among the first people who ever had been kind and friendly to her, and looked on her as a human being; and she was so accustomed to live merely for the hour, to be glad, sorrowful, afraid, in succession; and she did not anticipate what a reception she would meet with from Lena, when she found what the result of all this "stupid running out of reason," as she called it, had been. Then wept Lotta once more, especially when Lena said—"Lotta, if thou only dost the least wrong, or awak'st the least suspicion or displeasure, thou shalt go away from Vika, without the slightest pity;" for Lena knew that Lotta was one of those who could keep faith with a menace, if not with any thing else. But when Lotta, wearied, and escaped from Lena's sharp moral lesson, got into the cow-house, she made it speedily clean, amid glad and merry singing; and when Gunnar came and peeped in to hear what was the occasion of that unusual noise there, she came unabashed to the door, and began to joke with him.

"Oh, shame! thou good-for-nothing!" said Gunnar, and shrugged his shoulders in vexation. "What wilt thou with me? Art thou not ashamed to sing, and rollick, and come with stupid jests to men, when thou hast been had up and confessed to theft? Fie! I should weep and grieve myself to death in thy place; and I say yet what I say, that Elin does not know what thou really art, for if she did, she would never protect thee, as she now does. Take care, then, that I do not speak of it."

Struck with shame, Lotta began again to weep. Gunnar

was a man like others, and, besides that, a young fellow : he had perhaps on some former occasion answered in too free a tone Lotta's unbecoming jests, and thereby made her still more presuming ; but now he had again one only thought, one only feeling, more powerful than conscience itself, and that was Elin. Love, which some time ago was stunned by other causes, had now flamed up more violently, more irresistibly than ever ; and he who really feels its omnipotence, acquires an actual abhorrence of all others who make the slightest claims on this love.

This, at least, was the feeling of Gunnar.

CHAPTER XLVIII.

When we have once followed a human being in his undertakings, his fate, and his affairs from day to day, from hour to hour, we at length know him perfectly ; understand him down to the very minutest particulars ; and can so well conceive and comprehend the advancing of some, the retrogression of others ; the dubious and changeable circumstances which time bears along with it, and shall forever bear ; because while time for ever moves onward, standing still in any other thing would be almost an impossibility even to think of. Time advances from the greater to the less, from the less to the greater revolutions ; man goes on from the cradle to the grave ; the sun moves, the moon moves, the earth moves, every thing moves, and nothing is stationary but one thing—and that is He who propels the whole.

Therefore, every one who has given himself the trouble to peruse these unpretending sketches of the fortunes of a peasant's family, and who, in imagination, spent some time in the long Christmas holidays, and the cold winter, in their simple, lowly dwelling, may assuredly with ease picture to himself the same well-known dwelling with its grass-green roof of turf, and its whitewashed chimney, standing amid blossoming cherry trees, under a gloriously beaming May sun, mirroring itself and the surrounding green hills and their dark-green lofty pine-woods, and their light-green deciduous woods, in the lake which lay there as calm and clear as a mirror itself, so azure and transparent, without any motion in it except now and then of a light white summer cloud, which floated softly over the blue heaven, and in passing also glassed itself in the equally blue lake. Every thing around the dwelling was adorned, swept, garnished, sanded, and scattered with twigs of the fir-tree.   Before Elin's chamber window stood, in her little inclosure, two or three large, pale-yellow, fresh, vernal daffodils, with more of the like kind, half-opened, or not fully blown; and among the deep-green blades of the narcissus swelling buds already hid themselves.

But a wonderful silence reigned over all.   It was Sunday, and Sunday likewise through all nature.   The cherry blossom did not dare to snow down; the apple blossom stood scarcely blown; and no wind, no beast, no human sound disturbed the stillness and the most perfect Sabbath peace, with the exception of the ever busy bees, which softly and tranquilly murmured around the flowering, odorous gooseberry bushes, and here and there a hymn aloft, from the passing and winged musicians of the air.

If a person came, however, quite close to the little dwelling, he would become aware of the gladsome, though by no means loud, prattle of a child, and the humming of a lively polska by a young girl; and if he entered the house, he found it as carefully swept, garnished, scattered with fir-twigs and leaves, as he might have anticipated from the exterior, and little Gustaf playing on the middle of the floor with some branches of blossomed and fragrant bird's cherry, and a whole besom of *Caltha palustris* (king-cups).

Near the fire was Lotta humming, and busy about little matters, and pondering with herself whether it were yet too early to blow up the fire under the cabbage-pot, in order, according to Lena's direction, to have the greens ready just as they came from church, where they were gone to-day to the communion.

Lotta had during this half-year conspicuously advanced. Her heart had really opened toward repentance and true amendment.   It is true that she relapsed occasionally into her former laziness and bad habits, but this occurred ever more rarely, and was almost always followed by resolves, coming from the heart, never to do so again.   Elin in this, much aided by Gunnar's serious deportment toward Lotta, had really done a great work in her; and by this improvement of Lotta, Elin had sought to appease the displeasure of God whose wrath she incessantly believed herself to draw down, through her inability to pluck out of her heart her frenzied and sinful love for Gunnar. This love, in fact, grew both in the hearts of Gunnar and Elin; and hourly had it seemed, that God's good angel, which men in their blindness call Chance, stood by Elin's side, and alone prevented her giving way to the fire which raged in the suffering, and frequently vehemently excited young man, whose mood of late might often have been compared to the wonderfully transparent and azure lake, which one moment lay so calm and motionless, and the next was tossed in wildest commotion, with white and foaming waves, and this without a breath of wind stirring in the air; being therefore, stirred from its lowest deeps, beneath which people imagined there must be a volcano.

Such had been the state of Gunnar's mind, and he had now with a zeal of a different kind inspired all those about him; the aged and beloved mother; the softened and now not avoided Lena; Elin his heart's idol; and the well-disposed and devoted Abraham, to go with him to the Lord's table, saying, many times—"Who knows whether we all ever again shall do the like together?" This all of them, except Gunnar himself, believed to have regard to Mother Ingrid, whose strength daily decreased, and whose thread of life seemed reduced to the fineness of a hair. Lena had, indeed, made first one, and then another excuse for herself—spoke of staying at home, if neither mother nor Elin did—raised, in a word, little difficulties; but at Gunnar's earnest request all went together, and Lena, for the first time, gave Lotta sole care of the house and little Gustaf, not however neglecting, before she set out, to lock the chests and presses, and to hide the keys well—for, be that as it might, Lena did not now, more than ever, put much faith in Lotta's improvement. Lena knew too well how nimbly it happened sometimes, that in a quick movement a little matter could escape out of the possession of another into her own.

It now approached noon. A light, blue, and friendly smoke ascended straight and slender from the cottage, for Lotta had blown up the fire, and little Gustaf, who stood long in the window which looked on the road, exclaimed—

"There come grandmother, and Abram, and Bläsa; and there come mother and Elin, but where is fallé? Where is fallé?"

And Gustaf was right. In the car sate Mother Ingrid, with

eyes red and swollen with weeping, and the old silk hood drawn down deep over them ; and she had Abraham for driver, not a little proud of this great confidence.   A long way behind came Lena and Elin, with some other peasants, who had also been to church, and whose homeward way lay past Vika.   But Gunnar was altogether missing ; and little Gustaf, who had quitted the house at full speed, leaving the door wide open, in order to meet those approaching, did as many far wiser than little Gustaff do—forgot that which he had, and which he received, for that which he neither got nor had.

"Grandmother, where is fallé ?   Abram, where is fallé ? Mother, Eli, where is fallé ?" cried he continually ; but no one answered, for no one knew rightly wherefore Gunnar had staid behind at church, merely saying that he wanted to speak with some one.

Mother Ingrid went quickly into the house, and Abraham occupied himself with taking out the horse, but Lena and Elin stood a moment with the other church-people, or rather, slowly moved on with them.

" Well, bless me ! the poor wretch Olle is about to suffer his deserved death !" said Lena to one of the home-returning church-goers, who had told her on the way, that now at length Olle must render his last account, for now was the king's sentence pronounced, and he was doomed to die, since they had eye-witnesses, for both Bankesa and Smed-Lassé, and Lotta also, had been called up, and had not only confessed their own deed, but had given their evidence.   Their evidence was this time received, because it was so voluntary, had so little to do with their concern, though it certainly proceeded from people of no good repute ; among whom Bankesa also suffered punishment for the theft.   And, moreover, Olle's own conduct had lately tended to hasten his fate ; for he had now again begun incessantly to make fresh statements, but, as he said, merely in order to obtain mercy, and then again eating up his own words ; swore the most dreadful oaths that he was innocent ; threw the guilt from himself upon others, and heaped awful heart-shaking oaths on those assertions, while every one knew well that they were totally and fundamentally false.   He had, in a word, shuffled, and had been often convicted of telling two tales, and lies that lay as clear as the day, and relations as utterly truthless as Breitfeldt himself, and had also been pitied for his hard fate, like that poor and abandoned creature.

"Ay, in my judgment he ought to die, and that in the most shameful manner," continued Lena, "for he was always the most good-for-nothing rogue that I know, cunning and wicked every way. I shall never forget when he wanted to throw the blame of the great robbery at the Hall on Gunnar and me, the gallows-bird! No! he deserves all that he will get."

"Hu! how canst thou talk so?" said Elin in a mild, but still reproachful tone. "How canst thou *think* and *speak* in this manner, and that on this *day?* Ah! did we not learn of Him pardon and reconciliation? And ought we not to restrain ourselves from judging so harshly? 'Judge not, that ye be not judged,' say the sacred Scriptures, and if I could venture to explain those words according to my own conception, there lies in them a prohibition against our judging our fellow-men, at least too sternly and severely. Yes, for my part, I say frankly, that I do not believe that we have a right to take away the life of a fellow creature, even by judicial sentence, to destroy the image of God. How do we know, indeed—weak, short-sighted mortals, if he does not need a longer life here in time to atone for his crime—to testify his innocence?—for where men doom, there are certainly injustice and arbitrary power often perpetrated in the sentence. Think, only thyself, dearest Lena, thou condemnest the poor unfortunate Olle, for the most part out of revenge that he wanted to charge thee with a great crime; but that is not right, for every matter ought to stand on its own merits, if justice is to be found upon earth, or how, dear Lena—?"

"Pooh!" answered Lena, "I know all that well enough; and *I*, for my part, will *never* pardon Olle, let me live to be as old as I may."

Elin sighed, and entered the house, in front of which this conversation took place; the neighbor women nodded a good-by to Lena, set forward on their way home, and whispered among themselves; "Now has she begun to preach again, although the rector took her so task about it at the house-examination last autumn."

"Ay, to be sure!" answered another, "now she preaches more boldly, and with good gifts; much better than preaching Annika from Götheborg, who stole the woolen shawl from Kajsa."

CHAPTER XLIX.

"God knows what Gunnar has got to keep him !" said Lena, when she had taken up the pottage, and given their second course to all at the table. "Dost thou know, grandmother— or thou, Abraham ?"

"Don't give me any meat, dear Lena," replied Mother Ingrid, "I can eat no more to day, but lay it by for Gunnar, he will be coming, probably, later in the day. He said that he had business which would not bear being deferred, to talk over with some one, but he did not say with whom, as he helped me up into the cart, for Bläsa would not stand still. But he will be coming soon," added she, but then sate sunk in deep thought, only dallying with a few spoonsful of pottage, and then putting her plate from her.

"Is not our pottage good, mother, that you don't eat it ?" asked Lena, with unusual mildness.

"Oh, certainly, very excellent and palatable," answered Mother Ingrid ; "but I can neither eat pottage nor any thing else to-day."

"I will make you a cup of coffee after dinner," whispered Lena ; but Mother Ingrid only nodded her thanks in answer, and betook herself to her bed.

The afternoon was more than usually silent. Mother Ingrid felt herself so weary and unwell that she lay down, drew her curtains, and every one thought that she slept, except herself, who knew to the contrary. Lena seated herself with a hymn-book in her hand, nodded and read therein ; but after it had fallen several times on the floor, and had been taken up again, it wavered up and down in the reader's hand, and in this situation the back-leaning, half-gaping, and wholly-sleeping Lena, studied the hymn-book. Abraham betook himself to the barn, where he did not meditate long over the vanity of this world, but took a little sweet Sunday nap on the floor of the same, for the fodder was now nearly all consumed. Lotta had asked leave to go and see one of her reading acquaintances ; for if we have forgotten to say it before, we do it now, and announce, therefore, that Lotta went this year with the other reading

children to read with the pastor every Monday and Thursday,
and that she acquitted herself with tolerable credit, of which
the greatest part was due to Elin, and this the clear-sighted
rector also knew.

Elin had promised little Gustaf to row him, and took him,
therefore, with her down to the lake; went at once thoughtfully, and chatting with the boy, down to that very stone which
we know of old, where she and Gunnar had sat the last summer, and which seemed to Elin so wholly unlike what it now
was, although its exterior was very much the same.

"Sweet, good Elin, throw a pancake!" implored Gustaf,
and Elin gathered in her apron a whole heap of small flat
stones, and threw them into the lake, not with very much skill
or strength, for most of them fell into the water "like a
stone," without, as Gustaf wished, skipping along the surface; but sometimes, however, they made a little leap before
they plumped down, and then Gustaf rejoiced and clapped his
hands.

"Elin does it badly; fallé does it better," said Gustaf, as
Elin tried for a long time in vain to get the stones to bounce
along the surface of the water.

"Yes, what does not 'fallé' do better than any one else?"
answered Elin, and did not oppose, in this instance, the instinctive tendency that we have to praise and exalt him that
we love, as often as the very smallest opportunity is given for it.

Gustaf himself attempted to throw pancakes, but the little
stones did not fall a yard from him, and always in a direction
different to that in which he aimed. Elin smiled at these en-
deavors, and in the mean time went on gathering some large
forget-me-nots, which grew close at the water's edge. She
regarded these long, thoughtfully, and in silence, while Gustaf
played with the stones. At length, tears came into her eyes,
she did not know rightly wherefore. The heavens, the lake,
the air, the silence, these little flowers—all nature was so
beautiful, so rich in charms, that it seemed almost *too much so;*
the spirit yearned to ascend up into the higher space, glide on
from one beloved object to another; and when it felt its inability, tearful eyes, a painful oppression of the heart, testified
that man requires something *more* than mere enjoyment for all
outward senses. But this *more,* how different does it appear to
each individual! For Elin it took no other form than—Gunnar; it was he whom she missed, it was he who alone was

more than all the beautiful and noble objects that lay outspread before her gaze; it was he for whom she would have been willing to give all the rest of the world, had it been at her disposal.

"See! there he is!" exclaimed little Gustaf, just as Elin beheld, in her thoughts, the image of Gunnar in the most lively manner, and felt how impossible it was to banish it thence.

She blushed, and arose hastily.

"Fallé! fallé!" cried the boy; for Gunnar was coming along the strand, from church, and hearing little Gustaf's call, he walked straight down to the spot where they were.

"Fallé, dear, throw a pancake! Dear fallé, throw a pancake for me!" cried Gustaf, again and again.

But Gunnar did not seem to hear him. He stood erect, with his head elevated, and his eyes fixed on Elin, who stood opposite to him. His cheek was pale as the angel of death's, and all his life seemed concentrated into his eyes.

"How art thou, Gunnar?" asked Elin, at length, who could not maintain his keen and unwonted gaze, and who observed his terrible paleness.

"I am very well," answered Gunnar, slowly, "and I have something to ask thee, dear Elin."

"Dear fallé, throw a pancake! throw a pancake!" cried Gustaf, incessantly.

Mechanically Gunnar took up one of the flat stones which Elin had collected, and threw it with a strong and skillful arm into the lake, so that it leaped up six times, one after another. Gustaf clapped his hands, and shrieked for joy; but Gunnar said—

"I will throw *one* more pancake, if Gustaf will then be quick and go and pull all the yellow flowers which are near the alder bush there, and then all those white anemones, for fallé."

Gunnar threw another pancake, and when Gustaf had rejoiced over it, he ran voluntarily away, and began plucking his flowers. In the mean time said Gunnar to Elin, in a gloomy and solemn tone—

"It is well that I have met thee here, Elin, I would just ask something of thee, which thou must not deny me; for, perhaps, I shall not *so often* ask any thing of thee again. I would, therefore, speak with thee, but speak quite undisturbed by any one, and that this evening, and here on this shore of the lake.

I shall leave home to-night, on—on a matter of business; and now I have many different things to do for the remainder of the day; and in the evening, when the others go to rest, then—— I shall take farewell of them all, and——go my way; for—— I go in a carriage with another person. But, mark me! before this, I wish to speak with thee, once for all; to say to thee— Yes, yes, I know very well what I will speak to thee about; and, therefore, Elin—therefore, shalt thou not in the evening go into thy little chamber, and lay thee down, but thou shalt come down hither to the shore of the lake, and wait for me here, here on this very same stone! for I shall certainly come, only I must take leave of—mother, and the others. Dost thou hear, Elin? This thou shalt not deny me, that I tell thee."

"Yes, dear Gunnar," stammered Elin, who too well called to mind some other occasions, when Gunnar had not been so pale, or looked so tranquil as now; "yes, see, that I must deny thee! for——"

"Elin! Elin!" said Gunnar, solemnly; "dost *thou* believe that *I to-day* could implore of thee any thing wrong, had I wicked thoughts toward thee in my mind? No, but mark me! It is exactly because I know that I *can* do nothing wrong this evening, that I *pray* thee to come and speak with me, *for once only*, till—till I——set out on my journey; for, to *thee*, and *thee alone*, can I say it, that——perhaps I shall never return ——not soon, at least."

Elin looked steadily at him, and saw, what a woman can so well see and distinguish—saw that Gunnar's *soul*, and not the young man's passion, was in a powerful excitement, and that *now* there was no danger for her at his side. She had, moreover, that lofty opinion of her Gunnar which every woman has of the man that she really loves, although he may not deserve it; and she placed such profound confidence on his word, and full reliance on his promises, since he was never lavish of them, but on the contrary, often saying to Elin, "Go, thou Elin, thou who hast power sufficient for it. I answer nothing for us—for myself, far less."

Elin knew, therefore, that she might depend on his simple word, and was free from all fear for herself, but was seized with a dread disquiet on account of this mysterious departure of Gunnar, and said with a firm tone, although her heart beat violently—

"Yes, Gunnar, I will come; I will wait for thee here; but

——woe to the unhappy hour if thou failest in thy promise to me."

Now came little Gustaf with all the flowers; and Gunnar took the boy, lifted him aloft, pressed his hand to his bosom, kissed him with a lively warmth, saying then to Elin—

"Oh, Elin! *him* shalt thou protect, and lead into all good !"

But when Gustaf began to chatter and prattle with him, he put him down, and said kindly to him,

"Run now to mother, and bid her warm some pottage for fallé."

The boy immediately obeyed, and Gunnar turned now again to Elin:

"Farewell, now, dearest Elin," said he, and extended to her his hand; "see and do not shrink from thy promise this evening. If thou dost——believe me thou wilt regret it. Yes, Elin, never wilt thou have any more peace, if thou wilt not hear what I have to say to thee this evening."

During this time they had ascended the hill together, but now Gunnar walked on more briskly, and Elin slackened her pace, and then turned suddenly toward the promontory, that she might not go into the house with tear-reddened eyes.

With much assiduity and attention Lena set out Gunnar's dinner, and asked, as she did so, what had kept him so long at the church.

"Oh," replied he, "I have to set off to-night on an errand of business. I am going to drive with some one, and all this we had to settle up at the church."

Lena knew that it was of no use asking farther; for amid all the etiquette of the master, which Gunnar from the first assumed, and which he had retained undiminished, this was one main point, that Lena should not inquire farther than was convenient; and Lena, with curiosity knocking against the sides of all other people's secrets, never dared to press Gunnar. A woman who loves a man, and is not beloved by him in return, becomes forever his entire slave, and gives way before his slightest will, though she should be ever so stiff and assuming toward all the world besides.

Gunnar gave Lena all kinds of necessary directions, how this and that should be done during his absence, "in case," said he, "this should be longer than——expected."

Lena listened attentively, and asked also various questions, but did not observe that Gunnar neither ate pottage nor meat, but dexterously laid the latter in a dish in the cupboard, where Lena kept the like, and poured back the pottage into the pot, when Lena went out into the kitchen.

But the aged mother, who lay there in bed, and whom all believed to sleep, noticed every thing, and saw how deadly pale and how unlike himself Gunnar was; for otherwise he had one of those lively, changing countenances which so perfectly reflect all the impressions of the heart and soul, so that he who knew him could read his countenance just as a book. But now! now was this book altogether closed and turned to stone. Nothing was to be seen of all that passed within Gunnar, for his expressive, strongly-marked features were all like marble; and now was it first seen, in the perfect light of day, how beautiful and noble these features really were; how little need they had of the countenance's ordinary play of color, that they might serve as a model for Hector or for Ney, if imagination could form an image of these two—the heroes of the ancient and the modern times.

Gunnar then went out, and gave all kinds of orders and directions to the faithful and really sleepy Abraham, who within himself thought his master might just as well have put off his journey a while, that he, Abraham, might have enjoyed a little more famous sleep.

"Hearest thou what I say, and canst thou remember it?" said Gunnar, as Abraham answered neither yes or no, nor once looked up.

"Yes, to be sure," answered Abraham; "and, moreover, the master will probably be here again long before the things are done."

"Oh, that is uncertain!" added Gunnar; and proceeded with his orders.

Toward evening he took out some clothes for himself, but would neither have provision for the journey, nor the necessary money with him, but gave Lena the little that he possessed. When he had finished all the preparations for his going, he went with a certain disquiet and excitement round the room, fixed his eyes first on one thing, and then on another, but most frequently on the drawn curtains of his mother's bed. Once his eyes showed that he was overcome; and that no one should notice it, as all were assembled in the house to their frugal supper, he asked, "Where is Lotta?" for he had not missed her before; she who, so unwittingly to herself, yet so principally, had seized on the web of his life.   Lena answered, "I allowed her to go, and stay away till early in the morning, if she looked well after little Gustaf, and every thing else, while we were at church."

"That is excellent," thought Gunnar; for he could never yet teach himself to endure Lotta, certainly not on account of her evidence, or for the evidence this called forth, but simply because she could endure him too well.   Such are men! Moreover, he had many times during the day thought of Lotta as a cause of scandal, or an impediment to the fulfillment of his wish to get a conversation with Elin this evening.   But now this impediment was removed; and in a mind dark as Gunnar's at present, every ray of light, however feeble, is welcome. Gunnar did not eat any thing at supper, nor Elin either; nor did Mother Ingrid; but she sate up, drew back the curtains, and feasted yet once more her glance on the countenance of Gunnar, who, on the whole wide earth, was the only and last object which had any value for her.   As soon as she saw him, the tears fell down her furrowed cheeks, but no one perceived them, not even *he* for whom they ran.   They partook of the fortune of most of the tears of women—they were invisible, at the same time that they were innumerable.

"Wilt thou not lie down and sleep for an hour before thou goest?" asked Lena, when the night began to fall; but Gunnar seemed neither willing to sleep nor to set out.

"Nay!" he replied hastily; and pressed by the deep thoughts in which he sate absorbed.   "Nay, on the contrary—I shall take leave of you all, and then—go my way!"

But he still did not move from the spot.

"Good night!" said Elin, and hastened into her chamber. She thought that Gunnar looked so miserable.   She could not endure his glance.   She felt in herself that there was some great calamity in the air, which would come down and crush them all, but she could not possibly conceive what that calamity really was.

When Elin was gone, Gunnar at length arose, and went to his mother's bed, and drew the curtains quite back, seated himself on the bed-side, and took the old woman's feeble hand in his :—

"Farewell, mother!" said he; and tears came into his eyes, though his voice did not at all change.   "Farewell!—I am now setting out on a journey; God knows when I shall come

again. You, who are old, may live or die in that time; may
God be always with you, both in life and death! Farewell,
dearest mother! We shall meet . . . . . certainly soon; that I
feel quite certain of. Farewell! God be with you!"

And with this he pressed the bony hands to his face and his
pale lips. His mother did not move, answered nothing, but
merely pressed her son's colorless cheeks with her thin hands,
and then his hands to her weeping eyes, but yet not an audible
word passed over her lips. When the son arose, she turned
her face to the wall, and Gunnar again drew close the curtains.

"Farewell, Lena!" said Gunnar. "Thanks shalt thou have,"
he would have added; but the words could not out; it stood
too clearly before him at this moment, that he could not properly
thank Lena; that *all* his misfortunes came originally from her.
But he felt now no animosity against her—*would* not have any
such—but extended to her his hand kindly, and said once
more—

"Farewell, dear Lena! Promise me—Oh! promise me to
be good to mother—now and forever!"

"Yes, yes, but!—I have indeed never been otherwise;" replied Lena.

Gunnar now went away to little Gustaf's cradle. He was
already completely asleep, and the smiling mouth testified that
he dreamed of something joyous and happy.

"Good night to thee, thou poor little fellow!" said Gunnar,
and stopped down to the child. "Sleep well; and may the
angels of God guide thee when I—— I feel that I never could
hate thee, didst thou take a part of my life from me," continued
he, wholly to himself, while he gazed on the sweet and calmly
slumbering child.

"Farewell, dear Abraham!" concluded he. "Do all that I
have said to thee, and be active and clever, and then thou wilt
do well. Nay, lie still, and get to sleep, for thou need'st not,
by any means, accompany me. I am going," added Gunnar,
and now threw a long glance round the room, one more moistened glance at the closed curtains, and then disappeared through
the low door, and hastened down to the shore of the lake. On
the whole way thither he continued to say alternately to himself, "She is there! She is not there!" And we—we did exactly
the same, for we did not know that ourselves, till we peeped
into Elin's chamber, and described what was the fact.

When Elin entered it in the evening, after her abrupt " good night," she was in a dreadful conflict with herself, whether she should comply with Gunnar's earnest desire or not—go, or re-main.   She did not know whether to consider Lotta's acciden-tal absence as a sign that God commanded her to go, seeing that he took away the impediments, or as a temptation of Satan to lead her into evil.   She wrestled with herself regarding these two views of the matter, and had not arrived at a conclusion as to either, when she heard how Gunnar hastened out of the house, and saw how with quick and hasty steps he took the way down to the shore.   Then first arose love, and became more mighty than any other consideration—than all reflection, all cir-cumspection.   " He has *prayed* me, I have *promised*, and I go !" This was her first sincere thought, and the second was—" Oh, that I may not come too late, and that he, in anger at my not keeping faith, may be already gone—I know not where !"

But through the door she will not go ; it might be heard in the sitting-room, and for no price in the world would she be hindered.   She therefore opened softly the window, and look-ing back into her little maiden bower—" Pardon me, O God ! pardon me, spirit of my mother, if *ever* I go the wrong way, but—I can not do otherwise, and—and willingly take the pun-ishment for his sake !"

Elin actually flew down the hill, but when in the twilight of the night she saw Gunnar sitting on the stone, and looking out over the softly stirring lake, she then went more slowly ; and when Gunnar turned hastily toward her, as she already stood quite near to him, and as, with a gleam of joy on his sorrowful countenance, he opened his arms for her, she sank into them, and a long and sacred silence ensued, during which both Gun-nar and Elin prayed to God that they might die at this moment. But—*such* prayers are *never* heard, and Elin quickly made her-self free of Gunnar's embrace, saying—

" Oh ! this was not as thou promisedst !"

" I know it," answered Gunnar, " but yet *once more* in life to press thee to my heart, that can not be so great a sin that God can not forgive it *thee*.   That which concerns me—may be equally good !"

" Ah, no !   May he only pardon *thee*, and punish *me !*" an-swered Elin ; and perhaps these firmly-trusting ones could not give each other a greater proof of reciprocal affection, than precisely in this contention.

" And now, my dear and precious Elin," said Gunnar, " seat
thee beside me in all tranquillity.   I will never tempt thee, thou
innocent child, but I will speak with thee as the most honored
sister, and to thee—to thee alone in the world, confide all that
lies heavily on my poor bruised heart, and then of thee who
art as pure and good as a living angel of God, will seek to know
what I ought to do, or not to do ; for on that point I am not yet
become at unity with myself."

And now sate they by each other's side.   Gunnar took Elin's
hand in his, and confided to Elin for the very first time, how his
union with Lena had properly come about, how awfully Lena
had deceived him, and what dreadful hatred and vengeance
Gunnar from that hour swore—not exactly against Lena, whom
he had before the altar of God promised to love in weal and
woe—but against *him* who had been the occasion of Gunnar's
grand misfortune of being bound to a wife whom it was impossible, do what he would, endeavor as he might, that he could
ever bring himself to like.   Gunnar made it clear to Elin how
the hatred of the squire grew every day, till he saw Elin, and
discovered that it was she whom he could have loved in life and
in death, had he only been free—if the crime and villainy of
another had not hung a millstone about his neck.   He described
how this hatred, this burning thirst of revenge, acquired a vast
accession of strength, when he got it into his head that the
squire was endeavoring to lure Elin into his toils, and to ruin
her.   He portrayed faithfully all the martyrdom that he endured in this belief and through this cause, and thereby cleared
up much to Elin which before had been obscure, although she
had seen it.   And finally, without any circumlocution, without
any palliation, he related to Elin, how he—carried on to the
uttermost pitch of hate, desire of vengeance, and fear of Elin's
ruin, added to the madness of being looked upon as a thief—
had, at length, when accident brought them together, himself
taken this vengeance, and cooled his inflamed mind in——the
squire's blood.

" *I* and no other, was his murderer," said Gunnar, with a
steady voice ; " and to thee, Elin, I will not attempt to excuse
myself in that.   *In the instant itself*, I neither cared for life nor
death, for him nor myself, though in the one immediately preceding, as well as in that immediately following, I certainly
desired nothing more than to give him a sharp remembrance of
the person whom he had so pitifully injured.   I can therefore

P

say that I, both *with* and *against* my will, inflicted death upon him; but that he received it from me is certain, for Olle was just the man to belie and rob people, and very likely, when crimes dragged him down into the pit of perdition as deep as possible, to become a robber, a felon, an assassin; but that he should attack a great strong man in the middle of the day!— nay, that he never was equal to; but he has really this time, the first and the last time, perhaps, in his life, spoken the pure truth, when he said that he had merely *looked* at the squire, and, after he was dead, taken his pocket-book and also his money."

Here Gunnar ceased, and some moments of silence follow- ed. Elin had looked down, without once moving, during the whole of Gunnar's relation. But she now felt that he was look- ing at her, and she looked up, and their eyes met, and Elin ex- claimed—

"Oh, Gunnar! Gunnar! how hast thou bewitched me! Here I sit by the side of a murderer, and do not shudder, and do not abhor thee, nor draw my hand out of thine, but look upon thee as in the former innocent days, when neither thou nor I had guilt, but merely sorrow for our love. But I never *can* abhor thee! Thou hast, indeed, incurred this crime, to speak plain- ly, for love to me. Others, therefore, but not I, may condemn thee. Not I, for I *understand* thee; I read thy soul; I know what thy beating heart means; I know—Oh, I know *too well* what thou wishest to *say* to me, and what thou wishest to *ask* me."

Here Elin closed her eyes, her cheeks grew pale, her lips trembled, and her voice became merely the whispering of a spirit, but yet she added, clearly and distinctly—

"My Gunnar will confide to me, that he, *self-incited*, goes to atone for his crime, goes to surrender himself, and to set free the unjustly accused. My Gunnar will *voluntarily* go to death, that he may arise among the angels of God. My Gunnar *will* suffer all that our dear Redeemer suffered for us; all this wilt thou suffer for thy mother's sake and for mine, for thou wilt meet us in the kingdom of heaven, and I will endeavor to find out the way, through a long, painful life, *there* to meet thee. Say, my Gunnar, my dear friend, whether I have not under- stood thee aright. And ought I not to call thee *mine*, at this moment that I relinquish thee forever in this life: that I bid thee *die*; and that I yet sacredly promise to live myself; to live merely for thee, for that which is dear to thee—for thy aged mother, my poor faulty sister, and for that little innocent child, which came to occasion so great a crime, but which thou still didst wish so well."

"O Elin! Elin! now is my doom pronounced!" said Gunnar, and pressed his hands to his face. "*Now* I know perfectly what God the Father in heaven commands me to do. My conscience has indeed said it before; the pastor, to whom I opened my heart to-day, said the same; but out of *thy* mouth would I also hear it, for through *it* God speaks to me immediately, for I feel that within me. Yes, Elin," he continued, "I would ask thee whether I should die a shameful death, or should myself end a life which I have forfeited; but I felt persuaded that thou, God's pure creature, would call that letting innocent blood flow, however covered with crimes Olle may be; and therefore, see thou, I go as thou sayest; but, I tell thee, if thou hadst said, 'Come, we will go and confess every thing, and let them proceed as they will with Olle, and then bind a stone about our necks, and cast ourselves into the lake,' mark me, I believe that I could not have withstood that—withstood that—to die with thee. But thou say'st it not, and I will now leave thee at once, dear Elin."

At this last word, Elin burst forth in hot and agonized tears. Before, all had stood so solemn, so holy before her. She had contemplated the matter from a certain spiritual elevation, and with senses altogether in a state of exaltation. But, now!— now she was once more the weak, loving woman, here, down upon this earth, who sate by the side of the beloved one for the last time. She would in another moment see him depart —and for what purpose? To die a shameful death! She wept, she sobbed, she pressed his hands to her lips—she pressed these lips to his forehead, his cheeks, but not for a moment did she seek to retain him, or to shake his steadfastness, or cause his courage or his resolution to waver. If she could have ransomed his life by her own, she would have done it at that moment; but she could not save his life at the price of his own soul.

"No, my Gunnar," said she, weeping aloud, "thou *must* die —and thou wilt do it with calmness and resignation, as a true follower of Christ, and because both divine and human laws command it; but *then* shalt thou in heaven receive thy Elin, for *thou* will be there, and mother, and Lena, our kind, repentant sister."

And for the very first time did she give herself up to a lover's innocent blandishments. She put back his hair from his noble forehead, kissed the fine image of an almost spotless soul, and not a thought sullied her tears, or reminded her that it was a malefactor that she had before her. She saw his offense already atoned for, through the resolve on his voluntary death, and she loved him more warmly than ever in this painful but yet pure moment. But—it drew toward midnight. Gunnar *must* go, and Elin *must* tear herself away from him.

"Farewell! my Elin," said Gunnar; "I shall probably see thee once more in life; but *when, where,* and *how*—that God only knows, who knows all things. I must now hasten to the rector's. He has promised to accompany me to a judge named R—, and who is said to be the greatest and most able lawyer in the whole country round; and the pastor wishes me to ask him how I shall send my confession, so that Olle may be discharged, but that I may receive as mild and mitigated a death punishment as possible;—for, see thou!" added Gunnar with a feeble smile—"I am cowardly; I am just like others, and will suffer as little as I can help. The pastor spoke, indeed, of *mercy,*" added Gunnar with a melancholy and sorrowful indifference—"of royal *mercy ;* but how shall I get that when I never will petition for it ? And what should I do with it ? For a convict prisoner I am certainly *too good.*"

Great pride lay in these last words; and while this feeling yet somewhat mingled with the bitterness of parting, Gunnar tore himself away from Elin, to see her again—where ? We can not yet say that.

CHAPTER L.

ELIN writhed like a worm when Gunnar was gone. If she had *hitherto* been the strong woman, the enthusiastic martyr of her religious opinions, she was now a weak, loving girl, who for the last time has seen and embraced her lover. She called his name aloud; she added to it a thousand endearing epithets. She wept; she rocked to and fro; she cast herself down on the thin grass, with her face on the earth, and prayed in the most burning words, that the All-father at this moment would open the earth for her, that she might meet her Gunnar at the gate of heaven. But to all such prayers are the ears of the All-father perpetually closed.

Poor Elin was not so happy as the noble poet's amiable Viola.* No; Elin must live, return again to her little chamber, and there weep tears whose bitterness few have ever experienced. There now awaited her a terrible hour, the winding up of a dreadful business. She was appointed by Gunnar to announce all this woe to his mother and wife. Gunnar supposed truly, that the aged mother saw and understood far more than she had been willing to avow, and he also had imparted this belief to Elin, but Elin did not give credit to it; she could not believe that the mother's love could see more clearly than —her own love. Elin did not know the myth of Love's blindness.

We will now leave Gunnar and Elin—the one going to his certain death, the other suffering a death in every moment of her terrible solitude—and we will speak of something quite different, now a long time past. We think not on the young Gunnar, on old Mother Ingrid, on Lena, who yet continues, through all changes, to live in the world; on Elin, who now has her chief walk in heaven; on Abraham, faithful to the death as a dog; upon little Gustaf and Lotta. We say to all this a long if not an eternal, farewell.

———◆———

CHAPTER LI.

EXACTLY a year to-day had flown sadly away since the Sunday when all the inhabitants of Vika went to the Lord's table, and there laid down the confession of their sins, and their vows of amendment. A year was completed this evening since Gunnar took his last farewell of Elin by the lake shore, and for the *last* time cast a melancholy parting glance on the cottage, the lake, the wood, the whole neighborhood where he had lived through such eventful moments. A year had flown since Elin's heart broke—broke, and beat still! A year only had lapsed

* The wife of Zanoni.

into the flood of time; but—but how long had this year seemed
to those, who, in sorrow, in fear, and in continually defeated
hopes, partly of *death*, partly of *life*, had dragged on through
this time! All looked so like itself, and yet how *unlike* was
every thing! The May sun warmed and shone now, as then;
the trees grew green; the cherry-blossom flew on the summer
wind; the birds sang, and the flower-buds expanded; but ah!
the heart of man has but *one* spring, and when the deep snow
falls over it, then the heart grows icy cold, is pressed down, and
seldom raises itself again.

Mother Ingrid sat now alone in the house, but with eyes in
which the tears were dried up, and with the Sacred Writings,
open at the book of Job, on her knee. Lena worked and
bustled in her household, was ever in a hurry, but was extremely still—still, and yet not in the least degree angry; and
her features were sharper than ever, and her eyes deep-sunken
with tears and wakefulness. She was far from so nicely clean
and ornamental as formerly; and with a mood as dark as her
coal-black hair, her heart was somewhat improved by sorrow.

Little Gustaf played silently on the floor. Abraham had
much to do in the farm-yard; drove nails into Bläsa's shoes, and
by necessity and care was become conspicuously more knowing and experienced, and he worked always like an actual
beast of burden.

Lotta was a capital servant, of whom one might say, as the
Viking said of his stolen bride, "For three days she wept, but
then she became contented;" for she had quickly allowed herself to be consoled for all her griefs, including that of her giving evidence, which Elin had, indeed, so often protested to her
was quite right, and what she ought to have done, notwithstanding it occasioned such terrible events; and a young laborer
in the next village had found the best grounds of comfort for
her. She now stood by Lena with all kinds of necessary help,
ran in and out, and was in a great hurry.

But how is it with Elin? How is she? Shall we say it?
Yes; pale, not as a fresh lily, but as a faded rosebud, and thin
and transparent as though she were a spirit, she sits on the
shore of the lake, on the same stone that we know so well, and
sews! But what does she sew—and sew with a rapidity in
such contrast with her pale indifference? Ah! that looks to
us like a shroud, for it is snow-white, and there is not a spot
upon it, except of Elin's tears, which fall, but which are merely

seen while they are wet, for they are so pure, that when they are dried up they are seen no more.

She had long sate thus, sewing and weeping with equal diligence, when Lena came with hasty and irregular steps down the hill and said—

"Sittest thou here? I have been seeking thee. Thou wilt get a headache if thou sittest thus in the heat of the sun, and weepest. Wilt thou not take a crumb of food? Wilt thou not have a cup of coffee? Not that neither?——Shalt thou be ready soon? We must set off when the sun is down; the way is long, and we are many of us for one horse. Canst thou lend me a little black shawl to put on my head?"

Elin nodded yes—to all except the coffee, and Lena returned as hurriedly as she came; and when the evening came on, and the sun went down, there stood by the house-door three women, clad in black from head to foot, the youngest with a white bundle under her arm. The cart, the fine cart which Gunnar formerly bestowed much labor upon, and which once constituted his pride and joy, stood now cleaned and harnessed to Bläsa, and Abraham, downcast and awkward, held the reins. Clumsily did he endeavor to help Mother Ingrid up into the cart, but Elin and Lena came to his assistance, and thus it succeeded. Next he helped up Elin, but this seemed much better. Lena remained yet a moment standing, speaking partly to Abraham, who endeavored to think on and remember what she said, although his poor head and heart were at this moment so over full of other things; partly to Lotta, who stood with little Gustaf in her arms, and endeavored to quiet him, for he screamed,

"I will go with you to fallé! I will go to fallé! I will see fallé!"

"Silence, Gustaf, dear," said Lena, sighing with a dreadful heaviness, "silence, and be good, and thou shall have sugar-plums when I come home! Dear Lotta, look well to the boy. Don't be thinking about any young fellow, and don't spoil any thing if that Satan's Peter comes. Don't forget to take in the linen at evening, and whatever thou dost, go and look, ever and anon, at Valrosa that is near calving. Weave and be diligent; and be careful of fire, in Jesus' name."

To Abraham she said—

"Ay, as I told thee, don't go to-day to the squire's work, but go into the pasture ground and put down the hurdles, and do what thou canst ; for if we are not in order at the survey, I shall certainly not be allowed to keep the farm, and that would be worse for us all."

"I will do all that mistress says, and all that I am able too," answered Abraham, and meant all that he said. And now sprung Lena also up into the cart, and took the reins ; and Abraham's *stupid head* said, "A happy journey !" but his *good heart* whispered to Elin, on whose side he stood, "Greet him, and greet him for the last time from me ; and tell him that I shall slave for *his* till my *last* hour ;" and great white tears rolled out of his large light-colored eyes. Lotta also wiped her eyes, but whether they were tears, or thoughtlessness, or indifference that were in them, no one could tell, and no one thought further about it. Little Gustaf screamed frantically, and the cart set forward, and the night was already dark, and on the following day one might have quoted the words of Clärchen, in Goethe's Egmont :—"The sun ventures not forth ; it will not denote the hour in which he shall die ;" for it was dull and cloudy.

The day following was clear, and bright, and soft, as a May-day can be. The sun shone as joyously as if no sorrow were ever found in the world ; and when this golden sun, which sometimes seems with his rays to mock all the earthly pain that he shines upon ; when he became gentle, and drew near to evening, and finally sunk down behind the mountain where dwells the maiden Echo, then came the three black-clad women again to the cottage door. Abraham helped them out of the cart, but with sunken heart ; and little Gustaf shrieked with joy, and said, "Where is fallé ? How is fallé ? Won't fallé come home soon ?" And the women were exhausted with weeping ; they had scarcely a tear left ; but at little Gustaf's questions fresh ones started forth. They went silently in, and not a single word was spoken that evening.

Some months after this eventful day, or just as the hay-harvest was ended, and the reaping began, Elin sate again, one evening, on the lake shore, on the stone which we well remember ; but now she sung, in a low voice, one of Wallin's most beautiful hymns, and was sunk in this her song, when a man's rapid steps, in haste, but not running, approached her. She started, and looked quickly round, for, during her singing, she had had her face turned toward the open, clear, and calm lake. And who stood now before her tearful but astonished gaze, but the friend of her childhood, Erik! He came so joyously, so full of kindness and zeal, but he stopped short, quite startled and confounded at the change which had taken place in Elin. Beautiful was she, certainly, still, but the eyes which should discover that must be something more spiritual than those of the young, lively, and joyous farmer's son.

"Bless me! Elin dear!" said Erik, "hast thou been ill? Thou lookest so pale and wasted. That I did not know of, but now I can see it clearly. But thou wilt soon be as thou wert before, I fancy," continued he; for love, which, a moment paused in its course, now looked forth again; "thou wilt be brisk and lively enough soon, for I can believe that thou hast had an attack of this severe typhus fever which has spread and raged every where."

Elin neither assented to, nor dissented from, these suppositions of Erik's; but endeavored to collect a little interest for the past, and inquired kindly after Erik's home, and their native village.

"Yes, I thank you for the inquiries," answered he. "Now will I greet thee such a dreadful deal from our people. There is much that is good, but"—and here Erik assumed a sorrowful mien—"father is dead, as thou mayest very likely know. He died last midsummer, and was buried on midsummer-eve itself. That was something of a sorrowful midsummer's wake, thou mayest believe. Mother wept so dreadfully, and I too, like a dog, for father was very kind, though he was horribly cross, too, sometimes, and dreadfully strict was he always; and never would he hear with his ears that I should have thee, Eli', dear. But think only of his very last resolve, when he lay quite as if speechless in bed; then said I to him, that I never shall be happy if I don't have thee; and he answered nothing, but merely raised his head a little; and I believe for certain, and mother believes it too, that he meant that we might freely have one another, if we would. And if thou now *wilt*, dear Elin, so *will* I; and so we shall soon come together, that I feel persuaded; and mother prays thee a thousand times to be welcome to our home, as her son's wife."

"God bless you, my dear and kind old friend!" said Elin, and wiped an unseen tear from her eye; "and God reward you, that you think with so much kindness of a poor fatherless and motherless girl. But ill should I reward your kindness, if I accepted your flattering offer, dearest Erik. I am no longer

P*

what I was in earlier days.   Not sickness, but sorrow and suffering have made me so unrecognizable by thee, as thou hast
found me, my kind Erik: and never more can my lips smile, or
my eyes be free from tears, or my heart feel any joy in this life.
And I have sworn and promised to my————brother, in his last
awful hour of death, that to my latest day I would tend and
protect his aged mother, who can neither live nor die, but only
suffer the pains of both life and death ; and therefore, my dear,
good Erik—"

And again Elin ran over all the thousand effective reasons
which a girl has always in readiness when she will put off a
lover with " No," but will by no means speak the only powerful and all-effective words, namely—" I *will* not, for I do not *love*
you."

The poor Erik pulled and crumpled his new hat, made *his*
thousand excuses also, and proposed finally—" They would
take the poor old creature to them at the same time, if Eli'
could not trust her sister to take care of her ;" but Elin continued equally immovable ; and the young Erik, who came so
full of glad anticipations, returned the following day with a
heavy heart and a heavy basket ;* and his horse, the swift
Brunte, seemed to know that the load was heavier than usual,
for he was uncommonly dull; but perhaps this might come from
the fact that Erik drove extremely fast in the journey out, and
whipped more than ever in " sali-fars-ti," so that Brunte would
take out his recompense on the way home.

CHAPTER LII.

ONE of the most mighty reasons which Elin gave the young
Erik for her resolute refusal, was, however, very soon removed :
for when the first November snow came, it bedded down and
concealed as well the green and newly-laid turf on Mother
Ingrid's grave, as that of her son's by her side ; for the only
grace which Gunnar asked for, had been granted to him, and
that was, a quiet but decent burial, and to lie in the churchyard

* A Swedish as well as German expression for a refusal.

due north of the church. And there, north of the church, beneath the tall and dark elms, were soon found other sleeping guests ; for when the next month of May arrived, then swelled the narcissus and daffodil buds which formerly grew in Elin's little flower-garden before her chamber window at Vika, among thin, deep-green, spear-shaped, fresh leaves on Elin's grave, at Gunnar's right side. Abraham had planted them there on a Saturday in April, and that they flourished so finely was his only remaining joy in life.

Lena retained the farm, was, and always continued, a clever country woman, and with satisfaction can we also add, a tolerably discreet one, who brought up little Gustaf as well as she understood, till other hands took charge of him ; and little Gustaf wept long, if any one chanced to mention the name of father, grandmother, or Elin. Lotta continued an ordinary peasant-girl.

CHAPTER LIII.

As a little *pendant* to this story of peasant life, we may perhaps add a letter which the rector, already somewhat known to the reader, wrote to one of the friends of his childhood and youth, who, with light and winged feet, went on his way up the steps of honor, for he had already reached almost the highest wordly distinction that he could ever expect, and had not the care of *one* fold of sheep, but of many, for he assumed and worthily adorned a bishop's throne. To him wrote the rector, in May, 1843 :—

" DEAR FRIEND !

" Thus I called thee in our joyous boyish years, when I wrote small gossip to thee, and sent it by the cook, Kajsa, down to the cross street were thy parents lived, when the weather was so bad that we were forbidden to go out, and thus were unable to converse verbally. Thus did I write when thou, ever going before me, came to school a year earlier than I ; thus did I write when thou stretchedst thy strong wings for the Upsala flight, and I must still stay awhile at the gymnasium at Skara.

Thus did I write when our paths altogether diverged, and thou soaredst upward, and I followed the earth and its most unpretending children. And thus did I write also at that time that *she*, the only woman that was ever dear to me, told me candidly, fairly, and honestly that she loved *thee!* And *thus* do I also write *now*, when life has nearly outblossomed; at least can never offer me any change, except that into the region of thought, except that between life and death; *now*, when I probably do not stand on the brink of the grave, for so we are not wont to say in my vigorous years; but when I daily and hourly have before me the only remaining earthly goal which I can ever reach, namely, the churchyard, where my grave, one day, when I have finished and laid down my work, shall open for me.

"I sit just now, and from my desk in my chamber window, I contemplate its green grassy carpet, and the lofty trees which stand around and shelter this dwelling of the dead; and this view amalgamates strangely with thy last request, that I would give my opinion on this 'Almquist' question and answer.

"Thou say'st that thou *believest* and *knowest* that I *think* upon it, and thou believest and knowest truly; for *thought* upon it I have certainly, but *thought*, as I still *think*, that is to say, only in silence, without permitting a word of my thoughts to find its way to the point of my tongue, or the point of my pen.

"No, sealed up by me, let all these thoughts, *pro* and *con*, lie; and even to *thee* will I not utter them, fearing that they are not yet fully matured; fearing that with me they never will be; for as soon as a new idea reaches a certain height, there comes another and knocks it down; and I begin to believe that the *oldest*, the *simplest*, those which even a child can comprehend, are the only right ones.

"Every day, every occurrence seems to strengthen me in this belief, although the high-flying thoughts are, as it were, wroth that they cannot effect something, that they are always compelled to return whence they come; that is to say, to those simple precepts which were given us thousands of years ago, and which we have since endeavored to twist and turn to our advantage in such innumerable ways.

"Thou knowest that I also have grieved over all the *evil* which, for example, the irrevocable marriage-vow has so often occasioned; but time has certainly shown me that the *evil* never can be put in comparison with the *good*, which in all ages must

be a consequence of a sacred vow made before God, and which,
if not all, yet the greater number, regard as not to be broken,
but in the most determined opposition to their consciences.
The marriage-vow is almost the only *oath* that we swear; take
that away, and you will see not a happier, but a lukewarm and
reckless generation, crawling on just like beasts, each caring
only for himself, and no longer doing homage to any thing but
the most odious egotism. I have lately had striking proof of
the correctness of my view of this matter; and this striking
proof lies daily, in the form of three silent graves, under my
eyes, as they are directed to the churchyard.

"I have seen a young man deem himself so firmly bound by
his marriage-vow, that even the infidelity of his wife did not
free him from it. I have seen how this oath was his only shield
against another attachment, which was as powerful in this young
man as any love can be, and of which the examples ought only
to be sought among the least educated and lukewarm classes.
I have seen how the restraint of this his vow, and the fire of this
his love, and the smart of the sting which another sinner gave him,
in an unguarded moment lifted his arm in revenge, and made
him a murderer. I have seen how he, not exhorted thereto by
the law, nor any human counsel, but merely driven by his conscience, went forth and laid his head beneath the ax, liberating
him who was innocent of the murder, but laden with another
great crime, even against him who thus freed him, and against
whom he had always shown himself the most vindictive foe.

"I have seen how a mother, who possessed on earth nothing
of value except her son's life, could not bring herself to implore
mercy for this life, which she regarded as forfeited, and its
sacrifice as necessary for the salvation of the beloved soul.

"I have seen a young girl of twenty years of age only, who
loved this young man, entertain the same exalted views; and
heard her exhort, strengthen, and give courage to her lover, in
the very hour of an ignominious and dreadful death.

"I have seen a wretched, untruthful, fallen woman become
almost kind and pure-hearted from the atmosphere which surrounded her. I have seen remorse for a guilty love call forth
the exercise of the highest virtues, and among them, that of
dragging out of dark and deep crimes, two beings who would
otherwise have certainly been the pray of the evil powers,
which had already struck their talons into them, but shrunk
back before *faith*, *hope*, and *love*, in the form of a young

maiden. I have seen how the death-doomed has forgotten the impending pains of dissolution, and, as unlike Victor Hugo's 'last moments of the condemned prisoners' as Victor Hugo is unlike I well know *whom*, altogether forget himself, and only think, speak, pray,——— us who should live, 'to bring up, and bring up well, as a servant of the Lord,' the child of that man who had traitorously murdered his happiness, and whose murderer the death-doomed had thence become. I heard him, when the executioner stood ready, call to me, 'Pastor! remember what you have promised me for Gustaf!' And these were his last words; and I—I promised; and rather would I forfeit every joy of my whole life, yes, even life itself, than I would break this vow, which I shall endeavor to keep and fulfill to my utmost power, glad to have *an oath*, which also gives *me* a single tie to life; for, in my mind, *great and holy vows* are precisely the powerful wheels which draw forth *great and superhuman virtues*. The stronger the bands and the chains, the greater the powers which develop themselves.

"Is not the marriage-vow good, then? not necessary? O my friend! Let us pray that the day never may come when the earth shall be heaped on it, for that dirt should be cast on it signifies nothing; the pure and the holy ascend so much the clearer and lighter out of the dust and rubbish—and that as a consequence.

"Thou seest well enough from this, that this 'question and answer,' have not escaped my thoughts, but that they ever remain there, but———but what they effect there, I pray thee not to ask me yet, perhaps never; for Heaven knows best, whether the time be not yet far distant, when I can freely and openly answer thy questions, and lay my views in the broad day, even if they have acquired the maturity that I myself demand, before I will describe a single one of them. Love, but, therefore, question no farther, thine,

"Dear friend,

*   *   *   *

"P. S. I had so nearly forgotten to give force *by a luminous example*, to my perpetual vindication of the marriage-vow and its sacred inviolability. I saw myself, a few years ago, compelled to the terrible and revolting duty, first, to celebrate the marriage rite between two the most dissimilar beings in the world, and then, immediately after, to lay the hand of a young, blooming girl of twenty in that of an old worn-out chamberlain, dried up in soul and body. I was agonized, and wished to close my eyes on this abomination, against which I exerted myself to my utmost power, though this was rendered abortive by a father's hard and immovable will, and a daughter's boundless submission.

"But thou shouldest have seen the young wife, how she, with all the acquiescence in her hard fate which a woman can muster, fulfilled her duties and her vocation as the sick-nurse and cherisher of the peevish husband, whom I at length had the great satisfaction of flinging three shovelsful of earth upon, and whose widow has only some few weeks ago put off her mourning, and having lived out the customary period of respect, has, clad in *couleur de rose*, both in mind and body, given her hand to the friend and lover of her youth, and promised him all that fidelity which she had faithfully maintained, even when her marriage-vow had bound her to another. Oh the happiness to merely see such a felicity on this earth! And the marriage-vow, the marriage-oath, must it not be good!"

THE END.

STANDARD ILLUSTRATED WORKS

RECENTLY PUBLISHED BY

Messrs. Harper & Brothers, New York.

Arabian Nights' Entertainments.

A new Translation, arranged for Family Reading, with Explanatory Notes, by E. W. Lane, Esq.

Illustrated with 600 exquisite Engravings. In 12 Numbers at 25 cents each, to be completed in Two elegant Volumes.

Speaking of this edition, says a bibliographical writer, "We hail this splendid work as the richest gift in literary fiction that has ever appeared. It is worthy of particular remark, that this edition by Lane, which is *original*, and especially designed for *family reading*, possesses great advantages over its predecessors in this important respect. The surprising popularity of these tales is sufficiently evinced by the fact, that most European legendary traditions and romances owe their origin, in a greater or less degree, to the 'Arabian Nights.' It may also be stated, that it was this work which gave the first impetus to the mind of Dr. Adam Clarke, to his attachment to which we are primarily indebted for the most valuable Biblical commentary in existence."

Pictorial History of England.

Being a History of the People as well as the Kingdom to the Reign of George III.

Profusely Illustrated with 1200 Engravings. 4 vols. royal 8vo, half Calf extra, $16 00 ; Sheep, extra, $15 00 ; Muslin, $14 00.

One of the most entertaining works in the language. There is no single work on English history more valuable.—*New York News.*

We value the "Pictorial History" as a repertory of facts, but we estimate it still more because it suggests to the reader the true philosophy of history. The work will long continue without a rival, its cheapness and its merits defying competition.—*Athenæum.*

The very thing required by the popular taste of the present day.—*Edinburgh Review.*

For sustained and thrilling interest this work is equal to a romance, and a thousand-fold more instructive and valuable. It can not, as a book for the family collection, be too strongly praised.—*Albion.*

Harper's Illuminated Bible.

Superbly Embellished with 1600 Illustrations, exquisitely engraved by Adams after Designs by Chapman. Magnificently Bound in Morocco, super extra gilt. $22 50.

A more fitting gift from parent to child—a more appropriate souvenir from friend to friend —can not be imagined.—*Columbian.*

An edition of the Bible equal to this, in every particular, was never before issued in any age of the world.—*Maine Cultivator.*

Pictorial Book of Common Prayer.

Richly Embellished by several Hundred Engravings. Royal 8vo, Morocco, extra gilt. $6 00.

The high testimonials which have been bestowed upon this truly beautiful and national edition of the Common Prayer, render it superfluous to say more than that it is worthy to rank in companionship with the superb edition of the Holy Scriptures.—*Mirror.*

Harper's Illustrated Shakespeare.

With Notes, by Hon. G. C. Verplanck.

Embellished with over 1400 Engravings, after Designs by eminent Artists. 3 vols. royal 8vo, Morocco gilt, $25 00 ; half Calf extra, $20 00 ; Muslin, $18 00.

Unquestionably at the head of all the editions of Shakespeare ever published. With the editions of Payne Collier, Singer, and Knight, to select from, and the entire wealth of art which England has recently lavished on the illustrations of her great poet at the command of the engraver, it could not well have been otherwise.—*Standard.*

Thomson's Seasons, Illustrated

With 77 exquisite Designs by the Etching Club. 8vo, Morocco gilt, $4 00 ; Imitation Morocco gilt, $3 50 ; Silk gilt, $3 50 ; Muslin gilt, $2 75.

These splendid designs are in accordance with the spirit of the author ; exceedingly beautiful : the book richly deserves a place on the drawing-room table.—*Athenæum.*

This is a rare book : it is all beauty—poem, print, illustrations, and binding.—*Tribune.*

A most charming volume—the most popular of poems—the poem for peer and peasant. We shall read it with renewed pleasure in this most fascinating garb. The tasteful and refined will thank the publishers for such a contribution to their collection of beautiful books. Such volumes are indeed treasures.—*New World.*

Goldsmith's Poems, Illustrated

With numerous exquisite Designs by the Etching Club. 8vo, Morocco gilt, $3 75 ; Imitation Morocco gilt, $3 25 ; Muslin gilt, $2 50.

Beauty in design and refinement of the art of engraving conjoin, in these long-familiar and ever-welcome pages, to render them in so charming a garb that it would be the present we would choose, first of all competitors, for the one we most respected and loved.—*Ainsworth's Magazine.*

Immediately after the exquisite edition of Thomson comes Goldsmith, enriched in like fashion, and beautiful beyond any thing of the kind yet attempted. The pastoral character—the beautiful domestic tone of Goldsmith's poems give the utmost scope for a rich imagination in the artist. There is scarcely a page in his "Deserted Village" that does not give to the fancy some exquisite home scene, some rural nook which the pencil can best fill up. In this work, poetry and art are harmoniously blended. When Milton and Cowper take their place in the same set, the four great poets will make the pride of every boudoir where taste and intellect prevail.—*National Magazine.*

Milton's Poetical Works, Illustrated

With 120 exquisite Engravings. 2 vols. 8vo, Morocco gilt, $5 00 ; Imitation Morocco gilt, $4 25 ; Muslin gilt, $3 75.

Of the numerous embellishments in this splendid edition, it is sufficient to state that they are in unison with the genius of the great poet—very ideal and beautiful.—*Albion.*

We have need only to add that the Harpers have given to these two volumes all the embellishments which the typographical art can furnish, so that the great English poet is presented to the reader in a dress that is adapted to his exalted rank.—*Presbyterian.*

Cowper's Poetical Works, Illustrated

With a Biographical and Critical Introduction by the Rev. Thomas Dale.

With numerous splendid Engravings. 2 vols. (In press.)

One of the most delightful of poets, as he was the most affectionate and just-hearted of men. His feeling of social beauty and enjoyment is not surpassed, perhaps not equaled, by any poet in the language : his sense of natural imagery unerringly true ; his feeling of domestic comfort gave him a wonderful power of domestic pathos.—Mrs. S. C. HALL.

He was endowed with all the powers which a poet could want who was to be the moralist of the world—the reprover, but not the satirist, of men.—STEBBING.

His language has such a masculine idiomatic strength, and his manner, whether he rises into grace or falls into negligence, has so much plain and familiar freedom, that we read no poetry with a deeper conviction of its sentiments having come from the author's heart ; and of the enthusiasm, in whatever he describes, having been unfeigned.—CAMPBELL.

Life of Franklin, Illustrated

With numerous exquisite original Designs by J. G. Chapman, engraved in the best style. To be issued in the serial form at brief intervals.

This splendid pictorial edition of the life of Franklin will, it is hoped, be found in all respects worthy of the advanced state of art in this country, as well as of the fame of the distinguished patriot, printer, and philosopher.

Valuable and Attractive New Works

RECENTLY PUBLISHED BY

Messrs. Harper & Brothers, New York.

Ruxton's Adventures in Mexico and the Rocky Mountains.

12mo, Muslin, 62½ cents; Paper, 50 cents.

No book could be more certain of a public welcome: it gives a much more life-like and vivid picture of the country than any other book we have seen.—*Albion.*

The author's dashing, picturesque style reminds us of Captain Head's "*Rough Notes on the Pampas:*" it is rife with adventure and wild exploit. It is exactly the kind of book we require at the present moment.—*Mirror.*

A more racy delineator of incidents we have rarely met with: he never flags, but carries the reader with him, unwearied and delighted.—*Methodist Protestant.*

The best book of the kind we have seen for a long time.—*Courier and Enquirer.*

Warren's Now and Then.

12mo, Muslin, 62½ cents; Paper, 50 cents.

Mr. Warren's skill is of a peculiar kind; it is earnest and emphatic. This tale excites strong interest.—*Athenæum.*

"Now and Then" is a graceful and firm movement forward on the part of Mr. Warren. Few sermons inculcate the highest religious duties of faith and untiring love to man more effectually than this tale!—DOUGLAS JERROLD's *Newspaper.*

We scarcely remember a work in the whole range of modern fiction so thrilling in its character, and so beautifully natural and life-like in its details, as this new tale by the gifted author of "Diary of a Physician."—*Albion.*

Lamartine's History of the Girondists.

With Portraits. 3 vols. 12mo, Muslin, $2 10; Paper, $1 80.

A magnificent and oratorical style—spangled with gems, some of "purest ray serene," some dazzling and gaudy even to giddiness—abundant, yet not prolix—rythmical and measured, yet wanting occasionally in variety. The reader is sure to find in every chapter treasures many.—*London Athenæum.*

No work in our day seems to have created such a ferment in Paris. The tale of the victims of the Revolution is told with pathetic splendor by De Lamartine; he unites so many of the highest qualifications for a great historian.—*Edinburgh Review.*

No history, romance, or poem has for a long time appeared, that possesses more attractions, or that will have a wider popularity.—*Knickerbocker.*

Simms's Life of Chevalier Bayard.

"THE GOOD KNIGHT."—"SANS PEUR ET SANS REPROCHE."

With Engravings. 12mo, Muslin. $1 00.

Chevalier Bayard is one of the most romantic and attractive figures in history, and Mr Simms has made a hit in selecting him as his subject. For the public, it will have more attraction than a novel, and we predict for the book an extensive popularity. The style has an agreeable quaintness quite appropriate to the theme.—*Tribune.*

The Chevalier Bayard stands in history as a type of the noblest properties of the chivalry of the Middle Ages—pure in life, great in exploits, self-denying, courteous, and manly—a realization of the highest ideal of the gentleman, in the chivalric sense of the word. The romantic incidents of his life, as well as his generous and attractive personal characteristics, are delineated with unaffected admiration and with a happy tact. It is a picture of the age of chivalry which, as illustrating the peculiarities of a marked era of the history of civilization, is well worth the study of the literary man and the Christian. There are several well-conceived embellishments, which adorn the beautiful pages of the volume.—*New York Evangelist.*

Scenes at Washington.

12mo, Muslin, 50 cents; Paper, 37½ cents.

This is a graphic picture of scenes and persons, "sayings and doings," at the Capitol half a century ago: the incidents of the narrative, and the fluency of its style, will ensure the perusal of all to whom the work comes.—*Christian Intelligencer.*

The curiosity excited by the title of this volume is abundantly stimulated and satisfied in its perusal.—*Protestant Churchman.*

Melville's "Omoo;" or, Adventures in the Pacific.

12mo, Muslin, $1 25; Paper, $1 00.

As fascinating as Robinson Crusoe.—*London Times.*

The book is excellent, quite first rate.—BLACKWOOD.

Since the joyous moment when we first read Robinson Crusoe, we have not met with so bewitching a work as Melville's "Omoo."—*John Bull.*

Leigh Hunt's Men, Women, and Books.

With Portrait. 2 vols. 12mo, Muslin. $1 50.

Full of variety, beauty, and cheerfulness. It is a book to lie in the cherished corner of a pleasant room, and to be taken up when the spirits have need of sunshine.—*Examiner.*

Howitt's Homes and Haunts of the Poets.

With numerous Engravings. 2 vols. 12mo, Muslin. $3 00.

We have found the largest amount of enjoyment in these volumes.—*London Atlas.*

Full of beautiful descriptions, of lively and affecting anecdotes; full of the lessons of human experience, and the teachings of human weakness and griefs; and as full of inspirations to the young mind and heart.—*Golden Rule.*

Capt. Henry's Sketches of the Mexican War.

With Engravings. 12mo, Muslin, $1 00; Paper, 75 cents.

Apart from its authenticity, which is unquestionable, it is modest, spirited, graphic, and picturesque. The author's style is clear, concise, and lucid, his language perfectly correct, and his narrative rapid and well connected. The "Campaign Sketches" are evidently the work of a gentleman, a scholar, and a soldier—*Tria juncta in uno.*—*Spirit of the Times.*

Gleig's Story of the Battle of Waterloo.

12mo, Muslin, 90 cents; Paper, 75 cents.

This account is instinct with spirit, and many are the touching and striking anecdotes which add to its interest. It is likely to become one of the most popular productions of the day.—*Literary Gazette.*

Miss Pardoe's Court of Louis the Fourteenth.

With numerous Engravings. 2 vols. 12mo, Muslin, $3 50; Paper, $3 00.

The most romantic and dramatic portion of the history of France.—*Albany Atlas.*

We do not know of any book in the language which tells the same things so well nor so prettily.—*London Morning Herald.*

James's Life of Henry the Fourth, of France.

2 vols. 12mo, Muslin, $2 50; Paper, $2 00.

Mr. James is justly considered a very lucid and spirited writer of history; his descriptions are dramatic and interesting, and his portraitures of characters graphic in the extreme. The author has produced a deeply interesting and powerfully written work, which will be extensively read.—*Albion.*

Ik. Marvel's Fresh Gleanings.
12mo, Muslin, $1 25; Paper, $1 00.

This is decidedly the most agreeable book of the season. It reminds one by an occasional association of ideas, rather than resemblance or imitation, of Sterne's "Sentimental Journey." It abounds with acute observation, wit, and vivacity, and describes scenes of great interest rarely visited by continental travelers.—*Rochester Advertiser.*

Southey's Life of John Wesley.
2 vols. 12mo, Muslin. $2 00.

All will agree that Southey is the best biographer in our language: his life of Wesley is one of his most successful efforts.—*Britannia.*

As a library book, this edition is sure to make its way; we can hardly promise readers a more gratifying enjoyment than to go over the biography from beginning to end; we have found it a great treat.—*Literary Gazette.*

Smith's Consular Cities of China.
Illustrated with numerous Engravings. 12mo, Muslin, $1 25; Paper, $1 00.

A work as instructive as it is entertaining: we have met with none that has given us so full an insight into the individual character of the Chinese; that has made us so familiar with the thinkings and habits of an ordinary intelligent Chinese.—*Commercial Advertiser.*

This work is written in a graceful, flowing style, in an amiable spirit, and indicates an unusual facility in the matter of describing scenes and events. It reveals a large fund of interesting and valuable information.—*New York Recorder.*

D'Israeli's Amenities of Literature.
2 vols. 12mo, Muslin. $1 50.

In many respects this is the most valuable of all the literary productions of its erudite and curious author. It abounds in acute and learned criticisms upon authors and their works, and brings to light a vast deal of information respecting the early literature of the language, and shows the influence of authors and their views upon the age in which they lived. It is charmingly intermingled with anecdote and incident.—*Biblical Repository.*

Browne's Etchings of a Whaling Cruise.
With Engravings. 2 vols. 8vo, Muslin. $2 00.

Quite worthy to be the companion of Dana's "Two Years before the Mast."—*Edin. Review.*

This is a minute and apparently faithful account of the romantic and exciting, but dangerous adventures of a whaling cruise. The extreme hardships to which the common sailor is often subjected by the tyranny of the officers, are described with the truth and graphic power which personal experience alone could give.—*Christian Intelligencer.*

Prof. Upham's Memoirs of Madame Guyon.
With Portraits. 2 vols. 12mo, Muslin. $2 00.

The subject of this remarkable biography was a woman of rich endowments; her sufferings and her triumphs can not fail to endear her memory to the Christian world.—*Presbyterian.*

He writings and life constitute a bright page in the history of that period. Her life was active and useful, and her writings evince a vivid intellect.—*Albany Journal.*

Schlegel's Philosophy of Life and Language.
12mo, Muslin, 90 cents; Paper, 80 cents.

For a book to replenish wisdom and solidify the cast of your mind's habit, we scarce know a better one than this. It is sound, elaborate, and most instructive, and has already, by wise consent, passed into a sort of philosophic gospel.—*N. P. WILLIS.*

Parker's Outlines of General History.

12mo, Sheep. $1 00.

I have examined Mr. Parker's "Outlines of History" with sufficient care to enable me to form an opinion of its merits, particularly with reference to its plan. The great use of a manual for early instruction in history, is not so much in imparting historical knowledge as in creating an interest in the subject, and inducing the pupil to read and instruct himself. Mr. Parker's book can not fail to do this: by his course of judicious Questions he calls up those events in the history of every age and nation most likely to arrest the attention of young persons. and give them a taste for historical reading. It also contains as great an amount of historical information as could be given in the same number of pages. Its great excellence is its perfect adaptation to the purpose for which it is intended, showing, as all Mr. Parker's manuals do, that it is the work of an experienced and successful teacher.—Prof. J. G. Cogs-WELL.

Prof. Schmitz's History of Rome.

12mo, Muslin. 75 cents.

It will undoubtedly take the place of every other text-book of the kind in our schools and colleges.—*Bibliotheca Sacra.*

Indisputably the best school-book, on the subject it treats, existing in the English language. We trust that it will be immediately and universally adopted as a text-book in this country.—*Methodist Quarterly Review.*

It will be esteemed a real treasure by all whose time and means forbid access to the more elaborate and extended classical historians.—*Literary World.*

Abbott's Summer in Scotland.

With Engravings. 12mo, Muslin. $1 00.

This book has great freshness, and not a little novelty. It is, indeed, exceedingly interesting. and well worthy a careful perusal. The author, who is well known as a writer to the public. has the happy faculty of picturing the minute incidents and details which give character to every thing, and he thus gives an exact and definite representation where too many writers offer only vague outlines. without any precise character, and which make no vivid and definite impression. The history of a visit to the collieries, in this work, is very graphic and highly interesting, and the entire narrative is one which will be read with pleasure.—*Courier and Enquirer.*

Sismondi's Literature of the South of Europe.

2 vols. 12mo, Muslin. $2 00.

This is a thoroughly revised edition, including all the notes and additions incorporated into the late French edition; comprising, among other interesting novelties, some unpublished verses by Lord Byron, translated from the Italian of Casti. The translations of French, Portuguese, and Spanish verse, are by Wifflin, Cary, Roscoe, and others. An extended index is appended.

A work written in that flowing and graceful style which distinguishes the author, and succeeding in all that it seeks to give—a pleasing and popular, yet not superficial or unsatisfactory account of the best authors in the southern language.—HALLAM.

Webber's Old Hicks the Guide;

Or, Adventures in the Camanche Country in search of a Gold Mine.

12mo, Muslin, $1 00 ; Paper, 75 cents.

This book abounds with stirring details of most thrilling and startling adventure in various parts of the Indian country. It is the personal narrative of a Texan ranger in search of a gold mine. and includes a rapid succession of incidents of the wild and wonderful, rarely, if ever, surpassed. The volume forms a complete counterpart to Melville's "Omoo," presenting a series of new and surprising encounters in the western interior, as that work did in the isles of the Pacific.

Boyd's Eclectic Moral Philosophy.

12mo, Sheep, 87½ cents; Muslin, 75 cents.

As a selection of the best thoughts of other writers on the various topics usually comprised in a system of morals, claiming originality for its plan, it is eminently worthy of admission into our private libraries; and I have no doubt may be used with advantage in our literary institutions of every grade.—Prof. MANDEVILLE, *Hamilton College, New York.*

A careful examination of this work, we are satisfied, will not fail to produce the conviction that it possesses more substantial merit than any other work of the kind yet published.—Professor DODD.

The work has an additional advantage, which no other of the kind can possess, of suggesting to the pupil the works and authors where the various topics are more extensively treated It is, in fact, an excellent guide-book for an exploration of the wide and tangled field of moral science.—*Biblical Repository.*

Boyd's Rhetoric and Literary Criticism.

12mo, half Bound. 50 cents.

This is a valuable school-book. It contains, in a small compass, the cream of the more labored compilations of Blair and Watts, and has thus to the student saved labor in the acquisition of useful knowledge. This work is highly recommended by the Secretary of State.—*Albany Argus.*

Draper's Text-book on Chemistry.

With nearly 300 Illustrations. 12mo, Sheep. 75 cents.

For a concise, lucid, and complete analysis of this delightful science, this manual must take undoubted precedence. The recent improvements and discoveries of the German and English writers on chemistry have their appropriate notice in the present volume, and, as far as we have been able to ascertain, Dr. Draper has given in a succinct form the best arranged system of chemical lore yet offered to the student. The origin of the present work was the outline courses of the professor's lectures to his classes at the University.—*Methodist Quart. Review*

Draper's Text-book on Natural Philosophy.

With nearly 400 Illustrations. 12mo, Sheep. 75 cents.

This new work of Dr. Draper's is well deserving the grateful acknowledgment of teachers; never was there a book more wanted. We cheerfully recommend this volume to the various academies and institutions where natural science is professed to be taught.—GILBERT L. HUME, *Professor of Chemistry and Natural Philosophy.*

Harper's New York Class-book.

Arranged by William Russell.

12mo, half Sheep. $1 25.

This book ought certainly to be universally introduced to the youth of the state, whose history, biography, &c., it illustrates. It has long been regretted that the popular reading-books were not made to subserve some other purpose than mere instruction in the uses of language: and here we have a large and very carefully-prepared volume, which, while it is not deficient in point of style and language, will impress upon the youthful learner's mind that sort of knowledge which is most of all essential, as well as interesting, to the citizens of this great state.—*Methodist Quarterly Review.*

Russell's Juvenile Speaker.

12mo, half Bound, 70 cents; Muslin, 60 cents.

It gives excellent rules, which are so simple that all may understand them, and so strikingly necessary that all must respect them. In fact, the work is in keeping with the progress of the age, and is therefore a great improvement on all that have gone before it of the same class. The selections, by the way, are all gems.—*Farmer and Mechanic.*

Harper's New Catalogue.

A NEW DESCRIPTIVE CATALOGUE OF HARPER & BROTHERS' PUBLICA-
TIONS is now ready for distribution, and may be obtained gratuitously on
application to the Publishers personally, or by letter, post-paid.

The attention of gentlemen, in town or country, designing to form Libraries or enrich their literary collections, is respectfully invited to this
Catalogue, which will be found to comprise a large proportion of the standard and most esteemed works in English Literature—COMPREHENDING
ABOUT TWO THOUSAND VOLUMES—which are offered in most instances at
less than one half the cost of similar productions in England.

To Librarians and others connected with Colleges, Schools, etc., who
may not have access to a reliable guide in forming the true estimate of
literary productions, it is believed the present Catalogue will prove especially valuable as a manual of reference.

To prevent disappointment, it is suggested that, whenever books can
not be obtained through any bookseller or local agent, applications with
remittance should be addressed direct to the Publishers, which will be
promptly attended to.

82 Cliff Street, New York,

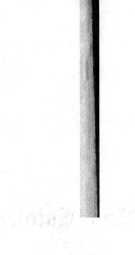

CPSIA information can be obtained
at www.ICGtesting.com
Printed in the USA
BVHW011149101121
621282BV00015B/126